# tantra for all

# Some Other Titles from Falcon Press

Denny Sargent
*Naga Magick: The Wisdom of the Serpent Lords*
Christopher S. Hyatt, Ph.D.
*Undoing Yourself with Energized Meditation and Other Devices*
*To Lie Is Human: Not Getting Caught Is Divine*
*Secrets of Western Tantra: The Sexuality of the Middle Path*
*Hard Zen, Soft Heart*
Christopher S. Hyatt, Ph.D. with contributions by Wm. S. Burroughs, Timothy Leary, Robert Anton Wilson et al.
*Rebels & Devils: The Psychology of Liberation*
Christopher S. Hyatt, Ph.D. & Antero Alli
*A Modern Shaman's Guide to a Pregnant Universe*
S. Jason Black and Christopher S. Hyatt, Ph.D.
*Pacts with the Devil: A Chronicle of Sex, Blasphemy & Liberation*
*Urban Voodoo: A Beginner's Guide to Afro-Caribbean Magic*
Antero Alli
*Angel Tech: A Modern Shaman's Guide to Reality Selection*
*Angel Tech Talk (audio)*
Peter J. Carroll
*The Chaos Magick Audios*
*PsyberMagick*
Phil Hine
*Condensed Chaos: An Introduction to Chaos Magic*
*Prime Chaos: Adventures in Chaos Magic*
*The Pseudonomicon*
Joseph Lisiewski, Ph.D.
*Ceremonial Magic and the Power of Evocation*
*Kabbalistic Cycles and the Mastery of Life*
*Kabbalistic Handbook for the Practicing Magician*
Israel Regardie
*The Complete Golden Dawn System of Magic*
*What You Should Know About the Golden Dawn*
*The Golden Dawn Audios*
*The World of Enochian Magic (audio)*
Steven Heller
*Monsters & Magical Sticks: There's No Such Thing As Hypnosis?*

**For up-to-the-minute information on prices and availability, please visit our website at**
http://originalfalcon.com

# tantra for all

## The Path of Nath Tantrika

by
Denny Sargent

Foreword by
John Power

THE *Original* FALCON PRESS
TEMPE, ARIZONA, U.S.A.

Copyright © 2021 C.E. by Denny Sargent

All rights reserved. No part of this book, in part or in whole, may be reproduced, transmitted, or utilized, in any form or by any means, electronic or mechanical, including photocopying, recording, or by any information storage and retrieval system, without permission in writing from the publisher, except for brief quotations in critical articles, books and reviews.

International Standard Book Number: 978-1-61869-985-5
ISBN: 978-1-61869-987-9 (mobi)
ISBN: 978-1-61869-988-6 (ePub)
Library of Congress Control Number: 2023933346

First Edition 2023
First eBook Edition 2023

Front Cover by Kat Lunoe
Original Graphics by Peter Carr

The paper used in this publication meets the minimum requirements of the American National Standard for Permanence of Paper for Printed Library Materials Z39.48-1984

Address all inquiries to:
The Original Falcon Press
1753 East Broadway Road #101-277
Tempe, AZ 85282 U.S.A.
(or)
PO Box 3540
Silver Springs NV 89429 U.S.A.

**website: http://www.originalfalcon.com**
email: info@originalfalcon.com

# TABLE OF CONTENTS

| | |
|---|---|
| DEDICATION | 9 |
| FOREWORD | 10 |
| PREFACE | 15 |
| IS TANTRA FOR ME? | 20 |
| THE HISTORY & ORIGIN OF NATH TANTRIKA & THIS WORK | 22 |

## PART ONE
## TAMAS—KNOWLEDGE:
## THE ETHOS OF TANTRA

| | |
|---|---|
| TOWARDS REAL HAPPINESS, PEACE & FREEDOM | 29 |
| TANTRA TODAY | 33 |
| APPROACHING TANTRIKA | 42 |
| WORKING WITH TANTRIKA GODS & GODDESSES | 45 |
| FOUR KEY TERMS | 48 |
|     1. Svecchacharya | 48 |
|     2. Samarasa | 49 |
|     3. Sama | 49 |
|     4. Sahaja | 50 |
| OM (AUM) | 52 |
| SHIVA & SHAKTI | 54 |
| ON TANTRIC GODS & SPIRITS | 59 |
| KEY TANTRIC CONCEPTS | 64 |

## PART TWO
## SATTVAS—WILL:
## CORE DISCIPLINES OF TANTRIKA

| | |
|---|---|
| YOGA (UNION) & MEDITATION | 71 |
| THE FIVE KLESHAS | 73 |
| ON KUNDALINI | 80 |
| TANTRIC TRIPLICITIES | 84 |

# PART THREE
# RAJAS—ACTION: DOING TANTRA

THE UMBRA ZONULE: YOUR SACRED TANTRIC
   SPACE .................................................................. 95
   CONSIDERATIONS FOR THE UMBRA ZONULE ............... 96
   PREPARING THE NEW UMBRA ZONULE ....................... 98
   SOME GENERAL REMINDERS ABOUT WORK IN THE
      UMBRA ZONULE ................................................ 102
   PREPARATIONS & DISCIPLINES WITHIN THE UMBRA
      ZONULE ............................................................ 105
   EMPOWERING THE ZONULE WITH THE ZONULE RITE .. 123
   UMBRA ZONULE MAINTENANCE & SUGGESTIONS ....... 131
   OFFERINGS ......................................................... 132
   REGULAR PRACTICE ISSUES ................................... 133
   PRACTICES & RITUALS IN THE ZONULE .................... 134
   PRACTICES TO ADD TO YOUR TANTRIC ZONULE WORK 145
      PRANAYAMA (CONSCIOUS ENERGY BREATHING) ......... 145
      MANTRA ........................................................... 149
      MALA WORK ...................................................... 153
      YANTRA WORK .................................................. 158
      CHAKRAS/BODY CENTERS .................................... 165
      NYASA ............................................................. 174
      MUDRAS .......................................................... 181
      KAVACHA (TANTRIC 'ARMOR') ............................. 192
      AND SO… .......................................................... 196
   YOUR TANTRA SADHANA OR REGULAR PRACTICE ....... 197
   THE 'ART' OF MAGICK .......................................... 198
   BASIC RULES OF TANTRIC MAGICK .......................... 199
   ASPECTS OF TANTRIC MAGICK ............................... 201
   OTHER TANTRIC MAGICK ...................................... 202
   PROTECTING YOUR ZONULE ................................... 205

**PUJAS** ............................................................. 208
   ABOUT PUJAS ................................................ 209
   PREPARING FOR A PUJA ................................. 212
   SEQUENCE FOR EACH NATH TANTRA PUJA .......... 214
   GANESH (GANAPATI) THE LORD OF OBSTACLES &
      CLASSIFICATIONS .......................................... 222
      GANESH NATH TANTRA PUJA ........................ 240
   SHIVA: THE KIND AND AUSPICIOUS ONE ............ 250
      SHIVA NATH TANTRA PUJA ........................... 272
   SHRI LALITA—TRIPURASUNDARI: THE RED GODDESS,
      THE BEAUTIFUL ONE, SHE WHO PLAYS ............. 285
      LALITA-TRIPURASUNDARI NATH TANTRIKA PUJA ......... 305
   THE GODDESS LAKSHMI ................................... 321
      MAHA LAKSHMI NATH TANTRA PUJA ............... 331
   THE GODDESS KALI: KALI MA—BLACK GODDESS OF
      TIME ............................................................ 344
      KALI NATH TANTRIKA PUJA ........................... 358

# APPENDICES

GLOSSARY ............................................................ 375
BIBLIOGRAPHY ...................................................... 392
ABOUT THE AUTHOR .............................................. 396

# DEDICATION

**OM**

I bow to Shri Gurudev Dadaji Mahendranath and the Nath Lineage of Adi Nath Gurus; and to Lord Shiva, the Adi Nath; and to OM the origin of all. Dadaji Mahendranath urged me to reopen the doors of Tantra to Western mystics looking for this deep, pagan path that was a part of Western occultism. May what was divided, be united.

I also honor Mike Magee, who went by the name of Gurudev Lokanath, and honor and thanks to Gurudev Vilasanath (John Power), without whose added wisdom and help with this work I would have been lost. I honor my direct initiators as well: Shyamanath and Sandhya Devi who offered me this gift four decades ago; and to Sahajanath (Mogg Morgan). Memoriam shout-out to the delightful Shambalanath, and to my very close brother Minanath, who passed away too soon, may they abide with Shiva and Shakti in Peace. I thank also all the lovely Tantrics I have met and worked with; sharing amongst our clan is *Amrita*! Also honors to the several wonderful and honorable Naths I have initiated, may Kali Ma embrace the rest!

Blessings and OM to all who have furthered the work with love and will and blessings to those have blessed my many Pujas.

I must offer much love and will and blessings to all but one of the members of the Forest Yurt Kula. Without our joyful and powerful circles and many years of practices, *Pujas,* deep conversations and wild Tantric parties, this book would not have been possible. You brought help, power, wisdom and creativity to our work! Namaste! Finally, love and gratitude to the blessed Tantric members of Emerald Shambala (Seattle, Washington) and Rose Shambala (Portland, Oregon)! Shanti and Svecchacharya!!!

May this work add to the growing Tantric Tree, and aid the attainment of happiness for all sentient beings. May the coming age of freedom, truth and happiness arise from the chaos as all awaken to the eternal stars they are. Svaha!

*The Will to Love is the Law to Live.*

# FOREWORD

I first got to know Denny when he was the major force behind the Horus Maat Lodge, and after Mandrake Books editor, Mogg Morgan suggested that I post some articles in their magazine. I did so. I was at that time enthralled by Hindu cosmology with which I had fallen in love in 1979. Denny and I, it turned out, both became tied in with the Nath lineage, offered by Gurudev Dadaji Mahendranath, a name you will see repeatedly in this book. It was his wisdom that Denny learnt from and from which he gained experience and deep practice. Gurudev Dadaji Mahendranath lived from 1911–1991 and succeeded in transferring the ancient Tantra wisdom of the Nath lineage to the West which is now offered to you through this book.

His teachings blossomed in the UK in the form of AMOOKOS (the Arcane Magical Order of the Knights of Shambala). AMOOKOS was established in 1978 by Dadaji and Mike Magee (then using the name Lokanath), a member of Kenneth Grant's Typhonian OTO, and editor of *Sothis Magazine*. The idea was to create a Westernized form of the Adi Nath Indian tradition, and expand the teachings and initiations that flowed from Gurudev Dadaji. Nath means 'Lord' and the historic cult became most popular due to the monastic developments of Goraksnath in Nepal and Northern India. The Adi Nath lineage originally stemmed from his *Kaula* (Tantric) guru, Matsyendranath, and this was the tradition into which Dadaji had initiated. Dadaji also brought to us an adapted form of the Uttarakaula lineage. He considered this northern Tantric lineage his other most important initiation, and one he asked me to help spread in the West. It is a potent Goddess-centered Tantric tradition, and informs this book because Denny is an initiate of this lineage as well.

An 'infamous' occultist that Dadaji met near the end of his life was Aleister Crowley. Dadaji regarded him as a Taoist scholar, who was then working on the Thelemite translation of the *I Ching* oracle. He also apparently advised Dadaji to travel to the Orient to extend his studies of this, which he did. In India, the two Tantric initiations came when he first set foot in Bombay (Mumbai) on the full Moon day of July in 1953, on Guru Purnima—the day when Hindus venerate their teachers. Here he mysteriously met Sri Lokanath, Digambar-Avadhut of Uttarakashi (of North India), who he held in great esteem until his death. This was the man who initiated Dadaji into the Adi Nath sect. Dadaji said that he was thus the last of the line of the Adi Nath tradition that originated with Matsyendranath, the *Kaula* Tantrik, as seen in the book ascribed to him, the *Kaula-Jnana Nirnaya,* written in the 12th century C.E. This branch of the Adi Nath lineage became scarce due to Mogul and British Raj Christians who, for many centuries, suppressed the joyous Tantric cosmology of native peoples.

The Uttara Kaula initiation that Dadaji was so proud of took place in the Kali Temple in the town of Ranchi, about 200 miles west of Kolkata, and was given to him by Pagalababa (the 'mad father') of the Uttarakaula Tantriks. He was an amazing 92 years old at the time, and died in 1967. Dadaji gave the date for the auspicious occasion of the initiation as 1963, and said that after his Nath initiation in 1953 he travelled around Bengal and Bihar before his Uttarakaula initiation took place. Afterwards, Dadaji considered a merger between Naths and Uttarakaulas, but not being fully aware of other native lines of initiation, was not in a position to make such a merger. A native Uttarakaula tradition continues today in India with the Guru Kulavadhut aware of his Westernised associates. Much of the information that Dadaji gave me for the 'Western' Uttarakaula was never published, but it has informed the structure of the Fellowship of Uttara Circles of Kaulas that I facilitate, and its wisdom informs parts of this book, some through my advice.

Gurudev Dadaji was handicapped by the mentally and physically degenerative cervical spondylosis when in his 70's. This severely impacted his life.

When Dadaji reached the age of 80, he suffered strokes which further impaired his mental functions. Under these circumstances, he decided that AMOOKOS was not in line with his goals. (More information on this can be found in the essay 'When Your Guru Goes Gaga' in Mogg Morgan's book *Tantra Sadhana.*)

Meanwhile I had told Dadaji that I was tired of the hassles and infighting and preferred to work with a smaller local group while continuing with my work in Art and Teaching. So, I just kept my head down and worked with a small East-West, Wiccan-Tantric circle, while I continued to research the cosmology of Dadaji's system for the Uttarakaulas in the West.

Dadaji had previously asked Mike Magee to form the Tantric group that became AMOOKOS, and which led him to leave the OTO. Kenneth Grant sought to use the Tantric Gnosis within his own 'Typhonian' magick. Grant also asked Mike Magee to initiate him into the Adi Nath tradition; Mike said no, but Grant did give Dadaji an honorary OTO 7th degree in 1976, which bemused him and he used it as a humorous title on the Uttarakaula charter!

As you will see, this book is a confluence of many of these streams. Denny Sargent was a member of Grant's OTO, is an Initiated Nath, and has initiation in the Uttara Kaula form of which I am the source. These two Tantric linages, and the long intense personal correspondence he had with Dadaji until his death, come together in this book. This requires a bit more information on these lineages.

Despite the Adi Nath tradition stemming from Matsyendranath which arose out of family (Kula), tribal origins centered on the Mother Goddess. Its direction under Goraksnath led to more of a Shaivite monastic and *Sadhu* phenomenon. The Uttarakaula side of his legacy is more obviously *Kaula,* where the first three levels of practice are for householder Tantrics. These rites do lead to *Siddhi* (magical powers), and can be utilized by householders as well. Sexual rites at any level are about mental Liberation from relative conceptual thought, and Union between Shakti's energy and Siva consciousness. They are not to be confused with Crowley's sex magic which is put to different ends. Kaula Tantra is about the here and now, and Liberation can occur during practice at any stage if conditions are right. There is no hierarchical route to be taken.

Despite all his health problems, Dadaji continued to produce scrolls to illuminate his followers, although the last, *Magick Path of Tantra,* revealed great memory discrepancies to events previously described. Denny, and others like him, were able to tell diamonds from dust, and mostly reference his early material as the basis for

## TANTRA FOR ALL

practice, along with his decades of Tantric work. This informs what Denny now shares with you.

Denny references the origins of Siva in the most ancient form: Pashupatinath, horned Lord of the Animals, whose image originates from 3000 BCE. This primal, horned god is almost identical to the ancient Keltic Cernunnos, as well as other horned fertility gods, this showing the interconnecting traditions of East to West. There is also the ancient deity Rudra, that invading Aryans—after their arrival in India 4,000 years ago—attached to their image of Siva for their pantheon. He was a God of storms and thunder that Dadaji regarded as a beneficial protector during war years: Da-Da, Boom-Boom is the sound of thunder, hence Dadaji and several of us got struck by that lightning! Denny was a lightning conductor who dealt with the storm!

Given the name Hermeticusnath by Dadaji in the early 1980's to cover the broad range of his activities, Denny set up a *Zonule* in the late 1990's to put into practice Dadaji's Nath teachings. *Zonule* was a name given by Dadaji to describe the cone of power that envelops a practitioner or group when performing rituals and meditation. It took on a secondary meaning for group practice gatherings. Denny's was called the Emerald Shambala Zonule. This intensive work, the evolving practices, and the ever-creative *Pujas* (devotional rituals) resulted in great expansion, and eventually, this book.

Denny will also take you on a trip through Indian terminology as he rolls out Nath practices characterized by the levels of energy known as the Gunas: Tamas, Sattvas and Rajas—dull, bright and commanding. You will employ these practices as you sharpen your Svecchacharya (Will) on the road to Self-discovery, with "real peace, real freedom, and real happiness." You will hear of the Alpha Ovule, the Union of the two great cosmic forces given form as the God Siva's consciousness and the power of the Goddess Shakti's energy, along with other Gods, Goddesses and spirits that respond to Nath Tantric practice which can transform itself into the brighter Sattvic world through the Yoga of union, meditation and *Mantra*. Part of this expansion is the control of the *Shakti* energy that has been called *Kundalini,* symbolized by a phallic snake as her aspect of the Goddess Kaulini. This wave of *Shakti* completes the magick circuit and helps you cast off the pain-bearing Kleshas: ignorance, ego, repulsion, attachment and clinging to life. In your Tantric or *Umbra Zonule* (shadow circle), you will build your power and meet your higher guardian spirit. Through cosmic experiments, journaling and art, you will evolve and become the *Raja* (king) and take control of your Self on every level. Equipoise, Equality and Spontaneity *(Sahaja)* are qualities you will develop.

For those interested in spirit contacts beyond your own Guardian Spirit, you will find many other spirits and beloved Tantric Gods and Goddesses, and those of special localities (genius loci) that will respond to your *Pujas*. There are also deities of this planet Earth, the Solar system and the Galaxy! All are aspects of our deep mind consciousness that we use to conjure and work with.

These gods and spirits have guarded the *Kaula* Tantric traditions since the Indus Valley Civilization at Mohenjo-Daro from 4,000 BCE. These first indigenous Tantrics met the invading Aryans in 2,000 BCE, absorbed what was useful from their Vedic religion, but in secret continued the older Pagan ways. This ancient wisdom passed on to myself and to Shri Lokanath, and then to Hermeticusnath (Denny), and to many others through our initiations. Now this wisdom is being passed on to you. Today in the West, Tantrics who follow these lineages live as householders rather than as wandering *Sadhus*. Why not become a part of this exceedingly ancient spiritual path rooted in the most ancient times? It's a path of Wisdom and Pleasure, and that can't be bad!

— John Power, aka Vilasanath

*John studied at Colchester Art School, England, and London University: MA in Jungian Psychology and Art Therapy, 1982. He taught Art in Junior High Schools and Adult Education in Prisons and Colleges, as well as working in Therapeutic Regimes until he retired. He continues to write and paint.*

*He received the Uttarakaula transmission to England from Dadaji Mahendranath in 1979 with instruction to transform the tradition into a suitable form for Westerners to practice.*

# PREFACE

Tantra means 'to weave.' Sometimes it means 'a special occult book.' Let's start with that.

The goal of Tantra is 'to live a free, open, natural Pagan life, devoid of restrictions, and the concepts of sin or shame about what is natural.' So says Shri Gurudev Dadaji Mahendranath, whose wisdom pervades this book.

**Note:** The terms *Tantra, Tantric* and *Tantrika* are often used when discussing 'Tantra' and it can get confusing. In this book I will use *Tantra* rather than the *Tantrika* to mean the ancient, esoteric, magical tradition as opposed to Hinduism, which is a religion. I will use *Tantric* to refer to those who practice *Tantra*. I will only use the term *Nath Tantrika* to refer to the branch of Nath Lineage that informs this book.

Tantra is not a sex cult. Nor is it a religion with dogma and belief systems as Hinduism is. Tantra is the ancient practice of Magick for real change and attainment of personal liberation. Hindus pray to the gods. *Tantrics talk with their gods.*

Unlike other Tantra books—some well done, many slipshod—this is not a survey book **about** Tantra, nor is it a book on sex magick (though sex is, of course, a part of the magical world). This is a book on how **to do** Tantra. In that sense it is unusual. This book takes you into the *Kula* (Tantric circle of initiates), and is about practicing effective and powerful Tantric Magick to help you attain real balance, prosperity and spiritual liberation. It provides mentoring and guidance to begin working directly with the gods, goddesses and spirits of Tantra to empower yourself and improve your life. If you follow the instructions and do the work—beginning with daily meditation—you will attain remarkable success, I am sure. Tantra is thousands of years old, as are many of the techniques and teachings. There is a reason it is still practiced.

Begin by asking yourself: "How can I 'weave' or manifest the kind of life I want to live?" This is the goal of all Tantric practices. In this book I seek to provide a balanced and empowering path for you to learn, understand and practice the ancient art of Tantra without interference or confusion. My goal is to show you the way to liberation and becoming your own Guru, in control of your own spiritual path.

I have been a practicing Tantra since I was initiated in the Nath Lineage in 1980. My Tantric name, Hermeticusnath, was given to me directly by Dadaji Mahendranath, the holder of that and other lineages. I have organized and worked with several different *Kula* circles of initiates, and performed hundreds of Tantric *Puja* rituals in a variety of places for a number of different purposes, including a wedding. The Tantric gods and goddesses have been a part of my daily life for forty years.

Before we go further, a note must be made concerning Tantric Buddhism. Though there exist many complex and fascinating traditions of Tantric Buddhism—including one I am connected with—this book is not about these paths. Instead, we'll focus on what has been called 'Hindu' or 'Indian' Tantra. Though there are many similarities between the two, they have different philosophies. Buddhism is a religion; Tantra is a path. However, they are 'sister' traditions which share techniques, methods, iconography and many ideals. It is not unusual for practitioners of one to be involved with the other, but in this book, the terms Tantra and Tantric will refer only to 'non-Buddhist Tantric practices.'

## A Short History of Nath Tantra

In the summer of 1953, a middle-aged English mystic and magickian who had studied the *I Ching* and other aspects of magick under the infamous Aleister Crowley, arrived in India penniless, and was immediately greeted by a Tantric Guru named Shri Lokanath who had somehow been expecting him. This British spiritual seeker took initiation from this Guru, becoming a follower of Tantra and a wandering holy man, a Sannyasin. As such, he vowed to renounce everything to follow spiritual truth. During the initiation in a small Kali temple or cave, he had his mind blown asunder and after this initiation was given the name Dadaji Mahendranath, possibly the first white Tantric *Sadhu* (holy man). His name means Dadaji (little brother), Mahendra (Mountain), and Nath (Lord).

Dadaji Mahendranath received a number of other initiations in his wanderings (Zen, Taoist, Lamaist, Buddhist, etc.), but he focused on the initiation that had profoundly affected him, the ancient Adinath stream of deep Pagan Tantric wisdom and magick. Adinath translates as the Primal Lord, meaning the most ancient form of Shiva. This transmission formed the core of his writings and teachings.

Some twenty years later, Gurudev Dadaji Mahendranath had become one of the most respected and venerated spiritual teachers in Ahmedabad, India. At that time, he sought to pass the vital current of the Adinath Sampradaya (lineage) on to the West, and so he initiated another British occultist who came to India; he was given the name Shri Lokanath. He then passed the initiation and empowerment he'd received to many others. Two of those who received initiation from Shri Lokanath, Shyamanath and Sandhya Devi, initiated me in 1980. I originally received the Tantric name 'Pandunath' by my initiators, but Dadaji Mahendranath disliked this name, and gave me the name Hermeticusnath which means 'Magick Making Lord'. This was the first 'Western' Nath name. When I asked him about this, he wrote and told me that he had a special plan: he charged me to offer Tantra to Western mystics and occultists in a way that would bridge Eastern and Western Magick, and I said I would try. This book is, in many ways, a result of this promise I made to Shri Dadaji Mahendranath.

When I traveled extensively in Nepal and India, I was fully accepted as a Tantric once I communicated my devotion, lineages and knowledge. I was always embraced, accepted and invited to worship and sit with fellow devotees everywhere I went. My purpose with this book is to offer a similar open acceptance and welcome. I am providing a path to the benefit and power of Tantra to all who are interested, something I was charged to do. Tantra accepts that where you are from, the color of your skin, the language you speak, or your work or lifestyle have nothing to do with your eternal Spirit, soul or what Tantrics call Atman. We are all divine; we are all seeking awakening and liberation. As long as you are sincere, the Tantric gods and practices will empower you and help you grow. OM.

The practices of Tantra were developed to help you to weave the life you Will through Love and spiritual practice so that you may attain the spiritual goal of real freedom. There are no restrictions, taboos, rules or restrictions in Tantra beyond the prohibition against causing needless harm to other living beings. Tantra tells us that we are free, natural beings—stars who exist on Earth. Only you can create your true unique path from birth to death by discovering your True Will. Tantra is a path of Magick, not faith; one of independence, not servility. Belief and faith are not necessary. All you need for spiritual attainment is engagement with your Spirit and with a set of proven practices that help you weave your body, heart and mind to awaken your own immense power and attain real joy.

A Sanskrit term sums up the practice of Tantra: *Svecchacharya*. In essence, it means 'doing your True Will'; that is, following the orbit of what you are meant to do in this life.

The truth is, you already are utterly free, but everything in your life has programmed you to forget this. You believe that everything you seem to experience is what makes up your life Thus, you have been taught that you are essentially a passive bystander in your own world. This programming comes from your culture, your religion, your family, and all the rules and taboos you are pressured to follow, from birth to death.

Tantra shows that this programming is a lie, the greatest lie of all. As long as you accept that lie, you will never discover why you are here and who you really truly are.

The truth is, you are an eternal star, one with the universe. You have the power to 'weave' and follow and decide your own unique reality and life. No one else can do that for you unless you let them.

Go online and do an image search for Tantric *Sadhus*. Look at these wild, hardcore, spiritual-punk Tantrics! Often naked and ash-covered, these Tantrics sit amidst burning bodies in a trance and let go of *everything,* including ego, pride, repulsion, attachment and death. This is a radical path, based on ancient teachings and Pagan rituals and magick which seek to free you from the delusions of this crazy world we exist in. Escaping from our programming, this seemingly crazy world is not for the faint of heart. Yet here in the West we cannot exist like the often-naked, wandering, wild Tantric Sadhus in India.

Our goal is to experience the radical, mind-opening path of Tantra in different ways, often within our own holy places of magick and wonder. The wild, naked Tantrics and I follow the same path; our practices and goals are similar, and they are effective everywhere. You don't need to go to India or Nepal to practice Tantra.

Start with this simple truth: you are not a product of your environment or family or religion; it is your ego that believes that. Your true Self is timeless. Your ego is not 'bad,' but it doesn't reveal the truth. Think of it as the car you drive in this life. It is a very important vehicle, but *it is not who you really are*. This is why your inner self is often dissatisfied and seeks a deeper life and spiritual truth. There is one clear message: the primary goals of Tantra are to attain the three stated goals of:

### *Real Peace, Real Freedom, and Real Happiness.*

Tantric practice will awaken you to the truth that *you* are the cosmos and contain all the gods and goddesses. You have complete freedom to do your Will as you will in this life, and thus be at peace, free and really happy. Limitations can be physical, but most often they are imposed by our culture, family, faith and worldview. Tantric practices will break open this cage, and you can have a lot of fun doing this and leading a natural life. Welcome to the joyous world of Tantra! Svecchacharya!!!

— Hermeticusnath (Denny Sargent)

# IS TANTRA FOR ME?

I have been a Tantric in a Western culture for forty years, so I have a few things to say. Most importantly, I have written this book for you, and I am making a few assumptions since you are reading this. I am guessing that you are open to a more spiritual life and are somewhat familiar with alternative spiritual practices such as Yoga and meditation. You may even have a statue of Ganesh in your home! In some way, the magick of Tantra calls to you. You have likely read or heard about Tantra, and may be confused by the often-contradictory information about it, so let me clarify a bit.

It needs to be said that Tantra does not translate as 'sex', but sex sells in the West. Though sex is a wonderful part of Tantra, the fact that the term 'sex' has become synonymous with Tantra, is confusing, and says more about our culture than the actual practice of Tantra.

Tantra is a deep and ancient wisdom tradition that stretches back into prehistory. Unlike the later evolving religion of Hinduism—which shares many of the gods and goddesses of Tantra—Tantra is not an organized religion. Tantra offers no dogma, popes, hierarchies, taboos or rule books. It is a path of eclectic personal and magickal growth that is unique for each person. Tantrics use Tantras ('books of magick' as opposed to 'holy books') full of stories and rules like the *Rig Veda*. Tantra is about personal freedom and spiritual growth, not books.

Tantra does not require fluency or deep knowledge of Sanskrit, one of the most ancient languages on Earth. However, the powerful vibrations of Sanskrit sounds are important to Tantric magick. Many rituals in this book use key words or phrases in Sanskrit because they are directly linked to our ancient gods and goddesses, and often encode their 'names' and thus their essences. Most Tantric ritual work can be done in English or another language as is a lot of the ritual work in this book. Devotion and sincerity open all gates. Don't let the unfamiliar Sanskrit here and there concern you! As you read, definitions of these unfamiliar terms will be constantly offered and there is an excellent glossary in the back of the book. These things are just tools; what is important is your inner Self, the Star that you are.

Tantra does not forbid eating meat, drinking alcohol, engaging in all kinds of sex, and so on. There are no set rituals, beliefs or taboos. Most Tantrics follow spiritual beliefs that are shared by others, but are also happy to work with other Tantrics who have different ideas; all is open.

Tantra does not discriminate. While Hinduism has a variety of cultural and religious restrictions, castes, taboos and codes, Tantra rejects all of these things. Tantrics do what they will and have no dogma.

Tantra and the practices of Tantrika do not accept intolerance or bigotry. We are all OM, pure divinity. We seek to directly realize our divinity, and believe that each person has his or her own unique path for doing so.

So: If you believe in your own individuality and True Will, if you seek to directly work with ancient powers that can help you, and if you seek to embrace your own Guardian Spirit and awaken to your own divinity, you are ready to practice Tantra.

This book removes the veils of secrecy and much of the complexity from Tantra, the ancient, Pagan-Pantheistic path of magick that also accepts the unified spiritual existence of the divine in all forms.

Tantric practices incorporate many forms of meditation, Yoga and magick. This includes sexual magick. Our work in this is to weave a life that helps us attain real freedom so that through meditation, experimentation and focus we can achieve the goal of Tantra: a purposeful, natural and happy life.

# THE HISTORY & ORIGIN OF NATH TANTRIKA & THIS WORK

Nath means 'Lord' (Natha means 'Lady'), and connotes the sovereignty of each Tantric. As individual STARS, it is the True Will (Svecchacharya) of every being that is paramount. The Will to Love is the Law to Live.

Tantric practices, done well, lead to unity with the divine via magical rites and activities referred to as Sadhana.

I use the term 'NathTantrika' for this Work because it is rooted in my experience and initiation into an ancient Nath Lineage via Dadaji Mahendranath.

This is only one of many Nath lineages, and several branches have evolved over the centuries. For clarity, I am in the process of trademarking the term *Nath Tantrika* to identify my view and teachings on Tantra so there will be no confusion.

## Let's Get the Introductions and Old Stuff Out of the Way...

OM.

I write these words in the light of the Full Moon in January, 2020, but the actual work began almost exactly 40 years ago when I received initiation in the Nath Lineage in 1980. At the time I was a Pagan, a Witch and was involved with occultism and Magick. Dadaji Mahendranath was far away at the time, but his presence during and after my initiation were and are overwhelming. From that time, Dadaji and I began an intensive correspondence that lasted until his death. From 1989 to 1991 I was living in Japan, and I planned to hop to India to see him; but at the last minute he told me to not come due to rioting, and then he passed away soon after. However, before he passed, he wrote me and told me to expect his 'direct initiations.' Exactly as he told me, I received direct empowerments in the most amazing 'true dreams' I've ever had. These direct transmissions happened twice when he was alive and once after he had passed on. He predicted these spiritual transmissions, and told me exactly when they would occur. Much to my shock, they did.

In the years before his death, the Nath Lineage manifested in the USA in several organizational forms that I was directly involved in until I moved to Japan in 1989. These groups included the Sacred Stone Nation, based in New York City, and the Western Nath Order, which I helped form in Seattle, Washington. I was also involved with, and learned much from the Nath organization, the 'Arcane and Magickal Order of the Knights of Shambhala' (AMOOKOS), the Nath lineage organization founded by Lokanath in the United Kingdom. Blessings to all!

While I was living in Japan, the Western Nath Lineage split up in a confusing and traumatic manner. The story is found in Mogg Morgan's book, *Tantric Sadhana*. There was a schism among the western Tantrics, and Dadaji Mahendranath made Kapilnath, my once good friend and associate, head of what became the International Nath Order, and gave him copyright of all of his written works. This was done rather harshly and with a lot of confusion. The original Naths in the UK and elsewhere did not accept or follow this political change. Deeply upset by this schism, I wrote to Dadaji Mahendranath asking what was going on. He urged me to stay out of this situation, and continue to do my own Tantric Nath work because, as he said, I had a different path ahead of me. I was upset, but I honored his advice and still do. When I returned to the USA, I founded a temple of an in-group of interested occultists who I initiated. Our Kula (clan or family) of Tantrics spent years practicing and evolving Nath Tantra in our own laboratory and in our own way, based on the works of Dadaji Mahendranath and others. This resulted in a new and unique branch of Nath Tantra which we named **Nath Tantrika**. Gurudev Dadaji foresaw and predicted that this would be my work, and so it came to pass, though it took a long time! OM!

**For the record, I honor, respect and support all the Naths, all branches of the Nath lineage, and their Great Work.**

It is my hope that all the Western Nath Tantrics respect, honor and contribute to the Great Work as Dadaji Mahendranath wanted. May all advance the work of Gurudev Dadaji Mahendranath and the Nath Lineages as well as the lineage of the Uttarakaula 'Westernized Wing of the North Indian Kaula' Tantra brought to us by Shri Vilasanath. I have also received initiation in this venerated Tantric lineage, and it infuses *Nath Tantrika.*

My personal practice has been focused on Tantra for more than 40 years, though I also work in other occult and Pagan traditions. With the help of my Tantric Kula and my own work, what has evolved in this book is a path of initiated Tantric practice for Westerners under the term *Nath Tantrika.* It has taken decades to bring this all together, but I believe it is important and unique. I hope you feel the same way.

Guru Dadaji Mahendranath has been whispering to me in dreams and meditations to move forward with this work, and here are the results. Guru Om!

I claim nothing other than these three things:

1. Nath Tantrika is based on valid initiation into the Nath Lineage as confirmed by Gurudev Dadaji Mahendranath directly. It is also based on my valid initiation into Uttarakaula 'Westernized Wing of the North Indian Kaulas Tantric Lineage' as confirmed by Gurudev Vilasanath.
2. It is based on my ability *to transfer both Lineages via initiation directly to others* as has been confirmed in writing to me by Gurudev Dadaji Mahendranath and by Gurudev Vilasanath. I have initiated many people in the last forty years, most with great joy.
3. Nath Tantrika is a new synthesis of my direct creative gnosis and experiences with Tantra including many Tantric and occult practices. It is simply another new branch of the Nath Sampradaya (lineage), one of many branches created over the thousands of years since the lineage was founded, it is said, by the Adi Nath: Shiva. Such branches are not uncommon and we honor the great Tree.

## What is Householder Tantra?

Tantrics in India and Nepal have traditionally been homeless ascetics (Sannyasins), free-wheeling holy men and women who have renounced society and all attachments. Yet some Sannyasins were married! When the rule is 'do your will,' as it is in Tantra, everything is flexible. There are fewer wandering Tantrics now, but some still follow this path. As Dadaji Mahendranath has pointed out, this model does not work well in the West, if only because the weather and laws preclude naked saints! The Adi Nath lineage as a strict Sannyasin sect had become untenable in India, so Dadaji Mahendranath transformed the Adi Nath lineage into a flexible tradition, more appropriate for life in the West.

A more suitable model for our pragmatic Tantra is one that exists in India and Nepal. It is referred to as the 'Tantric Householder' path. This form allows people to follow the Tantric path of illumination and spiritual advancement 'part time' while dealing with all the issues of a normal life—family, job, home, and so on. In this way, Tantric devotees an do their practices and magick in their home temples part-time, often with their Kula (in-group). The rest of the time they worked, attended to their families, and so on.

I am basically a householder Tantric, and this book is based on this path. I cannot avoid work, family, and so on, but I can balance these obligations with my spiritual work. I have been a householder with a family and a teaching career for decades, and I ran a small home temple with a delightful Kula of Tantrics who led similar lifestyles.

Together we revised Pujas, added new invocations and ideas, and together crafted Nath Tantrika. Our Kula created a unique Tantric worldview that has informed this book and Nath Tantrika. It is rooted in ancient Tantric practices as well as Western Occult sensibilities, exactly what Gurudev Dadaji had hoped for.

*The Will to Love is the Law to Live*

# PART ONE

## TAMAS—KNOWLEDGE: THE ETHOS OF TANTRA

# TOWARDS REAL HAPPINESS, PEACE & FREEDOM

## A COMMENTARY ON GURUDEV MAHENDRANATH'S *ORGANUM OF THE MAGNUM OPUS*

As Lao Tzu said, a careful observation of nature conveys all one really needs to know about how to live.

In Tantra we have many wonderful allies and a pattern of growth and spiritual attainment. Gurudev Dadaji Mahendranath crafted the *Organum of the Magnum Opus,* (The Instrument of the Great Work) to make this pattern clear.

Most people rely on their parents, friends and society to provide a template or model for living the 'correct' life. Early and constant conditioning from social customs, religion, caste, and so on forms a difficult shell to crack and escape from. As a rule, we need help to crack that shell.

We Tantrics (called Cosmic People in the text) certainly have our problems, but we strive to be conscious of them to achieve Real Happiness, Peace and Freedom.

## THE MAGICK WAY OF LIFE OF THE COSMIC PEOPLE

(The following passages in italics are from: internationalnathorder.org/the-organum-of-the-magnum-opus)

*To see the delusions of the material worlds, its involvements, and its bondage, but also to understand its relative reality as a matrix for development. The cosmic people have only one precept: 'not to cause harm, loss or suffering to any other living creature beyond that of dire necessity.*

Awakening to consciousness of the web of life and death that surrounds us is, at best, an arduous task. In deep meditation, the 'true' world that transcends illusion is glimpsed and directly experienced as periods of transcendence. In the true center we find stillness, and can look at all the worlds we function in dispassionately, and see that none are the Truth, or OM; that is, the Godhead.

In Nature we can begin to see an optimal way to live—a natural one where we flow, living in balance. We can use the fantastic, unlimited worlds of our imagination to further our own spiritual evolution. In this way we can influence and change reality around us. *This is Tantric Magick.*

*To develop the powers and wisdom of the supraconscious mind; to become awake and aware; to attain freedom on all levels. We came from god and to divinity we must return.*

In Tantra, the development of the supraconscious mind is symbolically shown as the union of the SUN and MOON in FIRE, representing the God and the Goddess (Shiva and Shakti), and their union in the Fire of awakening. By unifying opposites, we achieve the power and clarity of going beyond duality. These three also represent the three great Tantric personal powers: Knowledge, Will and Action. In Tantra we are given all the tools we need to achieve a more conscious, joyous and creative life by using these powers.

*To establish contact with our guardian spirit and to live in harmony with it. Thus, we attain divine grace and guidance.*

As we practice Tantra, we discover, explore and grow by connecting with our Guardian Spirit or inner Self. Through meditation and individuation, this 'inner voice' awakens more fully as a unique 'personal god' or spiritual ally. The Guardian Spirit is your link with the cosmos. When you tune in to it, you are connected to the spirit of the cosmos.

*To live in accord with the natural law of earth and cosmos. This is the way of life of cosmic people and is without frustrations and oppression. Let us never forget that in our true nature we are divine and immortal.*

We have become separated from our own ecosystem, the Earth Mother. We have polluted our environment, and continue to contribute to global warming which is killing us, all out of ignorance and blindness. Civilization offers wonderful advances, but has rejected Nature, the source of life. The Tantric Goddesses and Gods embody Nature and natural forces. Nature is the root of everything in Tantra. Honoring and spending time in nature, we become more conscious and can directly honor the divinity inherent in Mother Earth by being part of it, not separate. Our gods did not 'give us dominion of the earth'; they and we *are* Nature, which gives us all. We must fully awaken to this.

*To study the secret sciences, to gain esoteric knowledge and guidance. To do the experimental work to confirm our beliefs and make all this possible.*

Every culture has a magical or hidden 'occult' tradition within the mainstream dogmatic religions and restrictive culture. Tantra is the hidden occult tradition within the Asian subcontinent.

The esoteric world of Tantra means individual effort and experimentation based on ancient teachings and practices. This means real spiritual work and practice, but also great successes. Our Guardian Spirit will guide us. Tantra rests on the foundation of experimentation and confirmation. Faith and belief are not useful; our magick causes real results as do the deities we work with. No one can reveal to you your true path in Tantra. They can share theirs and give wisdom, but it is up to you to adapt and choose practices that work for you. In the end you are responsible for your own Master Pattern of Life.

*To be free, to live free, and maintain freedom; to live by our own will and enjoy real happiness on all levels.*

As consciousness expands, the Inner Self awakens, and we begin to become aware that we have been 'asleep' much of our lives. Tantra helps us reclaim our spiritual independence, awareness and our own divinity. Everything we need to awaken to this is within us. Through meditation and Tantric practices, we can push away all restrictions and find true happiness.

*To spread our wisdom and work so that all worthy people may be enlightened by it and live in harmony and enjoy peace, freedom and happiness.*

What is the purpose of the Great Work? In short, it is to protect, enlighten, empower, teach, mentor and bring happiness to ourselves and to all people as best we can. The goal of all Tantra is to help all beings attain real spiritual autonomy and liberation.

*This is the magnum opus of all magick and esoteric sciences. It should become our objective, aim, and way of life.*

So may it be. **The will to love is the law to live.**

With great indebtedness to the Guru Dadaji Mahendranath. OM.

# TANTRA TODAY

*"In its essential basis, Kaula (Tantrika) is real nature
Where men and women attain divine ecstasy
By throwing off their artificial personalities
And reverting to their original natural self.
Thus in periods of ritual, rite and enjoyment
Kaulas express their revolt against civilization.
In this way they remold life and living
And let the real nature shine forth
And enjoy magick, divine and sexual ecstasy
Where spiritual attainment is not impeded.
Lord Shiva is the patron god of all magick
And all joy is embodied in Lalita-Shakti.*

*We war with none and desire only peace
And in our new freedom attain happiness.
As it is above in the Cosmos—so be it here—
And microcosm is the experience of Microcosm,
Is not this the true essence of spirituality?"*

— Levogyrate Tantra,
Gurudev Dadaji Mahendranath,
*internationalnathorder.org/levogyrate-tantra*

The lovely and flowing lifestyle of Tantra is based on the traditions of prehistoric India, and many believe that the Dravidian people of southern India are modern descendants of those prehistoric Harappan peoples. Tantra today has changed in many ways, but we base all we do on ancient roots. Evidence shows that women had a lot of power in Harappan city-states thousands of years ago. It is no surprise that the same is true in Tantra today. All female Tantrics are worshipped as manifestations of the Goddess. The Harappan culture was a surprisingly peaceful culture, and no weapons or defenses were evident. The archeological remains show that it was a Goddess-centered culture as evidenced by the many goddess images found. The 'the lord of the beasts' were also found on clay seals. These are still same deity forms we Tantrics hold dear: Maha Devi and Maha Deva; Shakti and Shiva. Also, the same central image we use to show the unity of the God and Goddess are basically identical to the ancient stone images of Linga (phallus) and Yoni (vulva) found in Mohenjo-Daro. Such a long unbroken lineage is a powerful thing.

Somewhere around 2000 BCE, larger, lighter-skinned, nomadic 'Aryan' people began migrating into the northern Indus river valley and interpenetrating the Harappan and Mohenjo-Daro cultures. In marked contrast to the native peoples, their sky-gods-centered pantheon, patriarchal hierarchy, and strict caste system became part of the more ancient cultures they invaded. Over the centuries, the mixing of these two pantheons and cultures created a syncretic, widely varying religious tradition called Sanatana Dharma—what we call Hinduism. While Tantra and Hinduism share much because of history, Tantra today maintains its core primal magical system based on the Pagan traditions of the ancient cultures from which it came. Things like a caste system, a patriarchal culture, and the focus on holy rules and taboos are all part of Hinduism and ignored by Tantra. Some deities are shared by both Hinduism and Tantra, but many, like the Aryan Indra and Varuna, are fading from Hinduism, and have always been ignored by Tantra. The same goes for scripture. Tantra practice is generally rooted in the ancient Tantras, the ancient books of ritual magick. Tantrics in general do not focus much on the Hindu holy books like the *Rig Veda*. That is why Gurudev Mahendranath calls our path 'Avedic'—that is, not-Vedic, not rooted in what the Aryans brought or their taboos, casts, and so on.

There were said to be 64 'Tantras'. Many of these ancient books of magick are still in existence, though some still await translation. They are often in the form of conversations between the God (Deva) and the Goddess (Devi) in their various aspects. They offer pragmatic occult teachings and a lot of magical tools, spells and practices, and as you will see, our Tantric practices are still based on these ancient teachings. Tantras might be seen as 'grimoires,' or ritual 'books of shadows' to Western occultists.

Here is the beginning of one typical Tantra:

*"Devi said, God of Gods, Natha of all the Cosmos,
Cause of Creation, Maintenance and Destruction,
Without you there is no Father, just as without me there is no Mother."*
— from *Yoni Tantra,* translated by Lokanath (Mike Magee)

The Goddess then asks Shiva to explain some secrets. The rest of the Tantra is a back-and-forth conversation between both of them that is full of spiritual wisdom and practical magick. In these Tantras, we can see the roots of ancient Tantric systems that are still used today. The supreme divinity manifests as a primal Goddess and God who have many aspects and who are, together, all things; and from their union comes the infinite play of the cosmos as OM.

Much can be understood about the simple, yet rich, cosmology of Tantra from this history. Even in the ancient Tantras, the Goddess is the origin and essence of the whole universe. As the Goddess is the entire universe, Shiva is CenterPoint of the universe, and so focuses the swirling cosmos of Adi Shakti, the supreme Goddess of all.

Even today, the ancient idea that the God and Goddess, conjoined together, are OM, the One Divinity—God. So, the truth is that Shiva and Shakti are One. Like Yin and Yang, they are the two manifestations of the infinite divine Unity. As it was taught in the ancient Harappan cultures and in the Tantras, so we believe today.

## Tantrika: Yesterday & Today

Tantra quietly survives within the post post-Aryan Hindu culture and, often hidden, flows through many different lineages and forms. Indigenous pre-Aryan gods like Shiva and Kali were absorbed into the Hindu pantheon, and though somewhat tamed, remain important in that religion today. Some of the indigenous Tantric gods and goddesses became absorbed into other god-forms or remain quietly venerated as local deities, while many Aryan gods faded from importance over the centuries.

Keeping in mind that there were, and always have been, thousands of cults, sects and traditions in Pagan India, three main 'streams' of Tantra survived in a variety of secret lineages. All honor the God and Goddess, but have slightly different views.

Shaivite Tantra gives prominence to the God Shiva, while Shakti Tantra gives prominence to the Goddess in various forms. The third Tantric tradition gives equal status to both Shiva and Shakti. Some Tantras present Shiva as the Guru teaching the Goddess special magick rites or knowledge, but many Tantras have the Goddess as the Guru teaching Shiva. This tells you much about the historical culture of Tantra.

In India people say that 'there are a million gods and goddesses!' Having traveled about India, I can say that that is no exaggeration! Some, like Shiva, Hanuman, Lakshmi or Parvati can be found everywhere; others are small, obscure village deities. This reveals a layer of animism as some of these lesser deities are more like local spirits. The line blurs sometimes, and this is the norm here. Such helpful demigods—like the serpentine Nagas—can heal, and Yakshis—powerful tree spirits—are venerated and honored for good luck. Spirits and gods are all based deeply in the world of Nature.

No matter the lineage, Tantrics maintain and work with the older layers of pre-Hindu Paganism and Animism. However, as Aryan, Dravidian and other tribes and cultures mingled, what emerged as Hinduism became a religion with dogma, many rules, and strict taboos. There still exists a strict patriarchal caste system and a priesthood made up of upper-caste Brahmins, and women are not as venerated today as they likely were in Harappan cities.

Tantra is not a religion. It is a way of life, a magical tradition offering personal, natural, spiritual practices with no dogmas, taboos, restrictions or hierarchies. Priests are not necessary since every Tantric is a priest or priestess, and can perform rituals directly with the gods. Many Tantric Gurus are women, something rare in Hinduism. In general, doing your True Will and living a natural, happy life are most important to a Tantric, as is seeking spiritual growth and liberation. There are no taboos, nothing is forbidden except 'causing harm without dire necessity.' There is no holy scripture, just the Tantras, books of Magick! Tantrics work directly with Gods, Goddesses and spirits, and see them as friends and family, while Hindus pray and petition deities who are 'above them.' These practices are very different, even when working with the same deities!

Tantrics know they are divine and do rites and magick as they will, using their three personal Shaktis (powers): Knowledge, Will and Action. As a Tantric, you follow your unique path in life and do your True Will to gain real freedom and happiness.

The roots of the various Nath lineages, including Nath Tantrika, come originally from the Adi Nath lineage. This lineage existed from prehistoric times, but did not become a recorded historical lineage until about 400 C.E. It emerged from a period of great religious rebellion against what later became the orthodox Hindu religion. It is at this time that the 'hidden' Tantric sects rose up and came to the fore as reborn traditions, though they had existed in secret for ages.

The original founder of the Adi Nath sect is said to be *the* Adi Nath, the 'greatest lord,' Shiva himself! In our history we encounter many other fantastic Gurus who were said to have great Siddhi (magick powers). We know that Guru Siddhi Carpati gave initiation to Siddhi Kakkuti who passed the Adi Nath initiation down to Minanath, who then passed it down to Matsyendranath, who then passed it to the great Guru Gorakshanath. During my wanderings I was able to visit temples and hermitages of both of these Gurus in Nepal. They were very powerful and holy places, and both are venerated. It is with Gorakshanath that the Adi Nath sect really flowered, and then burst into several branches. Even today he is considered the greatest of the Naths. Around India and Nepal, several temples are dedicated to him as well as other Nath Gurus. It is he who wrote the book *Laya Yoga* and other texts on working with Kundalini—Tantric Yoga that is misunderstood today by many.

The Nath lineage continued down through the ages until Guru Lokanath initiated Dadaji Mahendranath when he arrived in India. He then passed it on to others in India and the West, and it was eventually passed on to me. The importance of this unbroken Nath lineage is why, before every Tantric rite, I honor the 'lineage of the crystal line of Gurus' that have brought this initiation and wisdom to me, in unbroken succession.

Initiates are called 'Nath' (for men, 'Lord'), or 'Natha' (for women, 'Lady'). (Women initiates are also often called 'Devi': 'Goddess'.) This literally means that each Nath Tantric *is recognized as a god or goddess*. Every initiated Nath can initiate others if given permission by his or her Guru or initiator. Thus, the current of the lineage is passed on. In Tantra we have *Tantras*—magick books—but no 'holy book' can take the place of real ritual experience, experimentation, magical work, meditation and awareness. As Gurudev Dadaji Mahendranath often said, "For further information, consult your pineal gland."

## THE TWO PATHS OF TANTRA

The Tantra I am expounding on is called 'left hand' (Vama Marg) because it about the autonomy of the individual, unconstrained by society or religion. However, there are other, more socially conservative, schools of Tantra which are religious—'right hand' devotional paths—and are often interconnected with Hinduism. All Tantrics do reference Hindu holy books and use them at times in devotions, so there isn't a strict line between the two. Still, rules, dogma, taboos and castes are all anathema to Tantrics.

The Tantric path you are reading about is the 'left turning' path and so the work in this book and tradition denotes a rejection of organized religion, taboos and imposed restrictions. Instead, it celebrates and encourages ecstasy, equipoise and equilibrium—doing your own True Will and passionately embracing the world and all its delights and challenges. By focusing on sensory joy, we seek happiness, liberation and spiritual attainment. This path can be challenging because it is tempting to simply forget the spiritual goal and enjoy pleasure for its own sake instead of as a way to grow spiritually. Tantra is a faster method of realization than religion and is more joyous and wilder, but it is easy to fall from it. This is why it is often called the 'radical' path, because it takes more personal dedication, focus and balance.

There are no set rules or restrictions for doing Tantric magick, but the practices revealed in this book fall into two generally different kinds of exercises as you'll see in the following chapters.

**Meditation:** The goal is to detach from mental chaos and thoughts, and go beyond the ego. There are many ways of meditating. It is important that Tantrics meditate daily, no matter how they do it. Dadaji Mahendranath taught that 'Intensity, Stability, Quiet, Determination and Expectancy are the qualities for meditation.' Many Tantric meditations are quite calm and traditional, but some are radical. Smashana Sadhana meditation—meaning meditation in a cremation ground full of burning corpses—is considered especially powerful for facing and releasing one's fear of death. It is said to offer great power and bliss. I have practiced this kind of meditation as my father, and then my mother, lay dying. I chanted and meditated to help them move forward, and then sat and meditated in silence with their corpses. Strong medicine indeed.

**Magick:** This is any sort of manipulation of reality through Knowledge, Will and Action, often with guidance from your Guardian Spirit and the Gods or Goddesses you have positive relationships with. Rituals (Pujas) can be of devotion or of a magickal intent, and are made up of techniques whose goal is to cause change to occur, mostly for the benefit of the Tantric or those who need aid. As a Tantric, your focus and magick causes willed change in line with your will to make things happen. Some examples: to attract, banish, heal, harm, gain wealth, remove obstacles, bless a person or place. A balanced and positive attitude is often crucial in this work. A quote from Gurudev Dadaji Mahendranath offers some clear ideas about this:

> *"These teachings are based on the Yogi or Natha sitting ...inside a circle. From the circle he creates or rearranges energy to form a cone. Mind projections sent outside of this cone are classified as EXPANSION while those drawn in are called ABSORPTION. Either a mixture of the two, or even independently, the Yogi-Natha can practice PROJECTION. This is identical to the Will projection...as well as being the vital factor on which magick much depends."*
> — Londonium Temple Strain,
> Gurudev Dadaji Mahendranath,
> *internationalnathorder.org/the-londinium-temple-strain*

The goal of these Tantric magick practices is to focus the five senses simultaneously. Hearing, taste, sight, touch and smell should all be excited and intensified. Gestures, dance, singing, chanting, love-making—all may be part of the energy that charges a Tantric rite. Sensory intoxication, ego-abandonment, joy and illumination can be the result. The following chapters explain how to do this.

## On Tantric Partners & the Energetic Body

Though you can certainly be a solo Tantric, it can further you to have a partner. Why? Because, according to Tantra, the universe is flowing and 'weaving' eternally in the form of Shiva-Shakti, and though each of us is spiritually both Shiva and Shakti, in birth we are generally incarnated in the energy-matter forms of men and women. Thus, when a couple (gay or straight) get together in psychic, spiritual and erotic Tantric work, they conjure and manifest as Shiva and Shakti: their play becomes the play of the universe, and their union becomes the Big Bang of creation. One's partner is intensely visualized as Shiva or Shakti, and should be worshipped as a God or Goddess. The alchemy of two empowered, deific people joining together as One—sexually or not—is powerful Magick. This is the magical path of Tantric pair work and Tantric sexuality. This work with another is a special spiritual 'weaving' that is, by the way, also fine to do by yourself! Self-love simply focuses on the internal union of Shiva-Shakti and all focused energy or sexuality and bliss is a powerful and useful magick practice accepted and embraced by Tantrics. All such work, with a partner or solo, is about the empowerment and focus of the energy body.

Your body—especially the energetic body—is the primary mode of transformation and 'union' (Yoga) with the divine. This is why Tantric temples are modeled on the human body. Tantrics are encouraged not to procreate, unless it be by Will, but instead to use the divine sexual energy of union to further liberation and bliss.

Tantra is a way of *weaving* the divine energy of your body and nature, enhanced with some proven techniques and the energy and blessing of some gods and goddesses, often with or without an intimate Tantric partner. The keys are always Love and Will. It is always up to you, and it demands daily practices and taking real control of your own life to the greatest extent possible. It is the path of remembering that you are, in truth, a Nath—a god or goddess!

> *"People have talked and written much about Tantra, yet still there is much confusion and blindness. This is because they have tried to make patterns of a science which is volatile.*

*They try to press into molds and speak of rules and customs and even to make a religion of that which is beyond all religions and because it is the fluid essence of a Spiritual Cosmos, it cannot know any fixed rule. It must vary, even as people vary, for what is Cosmic must be as versatile as the wind and have as many changing patterns as the clouds in the sky."*

— *Sinistroversus,* Gurudev Dadaji Mahendranath, *internationalnathorder.org/sinistroversus*

# APPROACHING TANTRIKA

## TRADITIONS, GODS & FLEXIBILITY

In Hinduism, traditions and holy texts like the *Puranas* and *Rig Vedas* offer rules, traditions and set ways for doing things. They speak to who can and cannot do certain things within both the religion and society. It is ingrained in the culture, and some taboos are enforced in certain areas. Of course, Tantra has none of this; each follows his or her own path with the blessing of the gods. Generally, vegetarianism is the rule in much of India, and animal sacrifice is not usually practiced, but in Bengal and Nepal meat is often eaten. I have seen goats being sacrificed to Kali Ma at temples.

Rules and norms that are strictly followed in many places are disregarded in other places. Every part of India and Nepal is different in many ways. If we begin with the idea that ALL is OM, and that all of the gods and goddesses are facets of this supreme divinity, then the gods or goddesses with whom you have a deep and powerful bond are indeed the supreme OM for you. In India, every god or goddess I mentioned working with elicited, "Oh! You believe in God!" After a few weeks I began to understand: each one IS God; such a wonderful, flexible and open pantheistic point of view. Do you believe in many gods and goddesses? Yes. Do you believe in one God? Yes. Is this a contradiction? In the West, yes. In the Pagan world and in Tantrika? Not so much. These sorts of seeming contradictions are accepted in many Pagan cultures. In Tantra this is called 'the Twilight World' where myth and materialism mix.

## ISHTA DEVAS OR PERSONAL GODS

It is understood that Tantrics gravitate to certain gods and goddesses. More commonly, the Gods and Goddesses that are attracted to you will show up in your life, meditations and dreams. A deity that you bond with is called an 'Ishta Deva', a personal god. You will likely attract several as you go further in Tantric practices and form more intimate relationship with your Ishta Devas. Here is a personal example of how Tantric gods can suddenly become your friends.

I had never worked much with the monkey-god Hanuman until I went to India decades after my Tantric initiation. I went to focus on devotion to Shiva and Kali, which I did, but Hanuman literally leaped on me the day I arrived and never stopped. The temple near the hotel? Hanuman temple. The huge, three-story-high statue across from the next hotel? Hanuman. My guide in Delhi? A Hanuman devotee. Most everywhere I sat, I'd find a Hanuman image near me to the point that it got hilarious. As my guides said, "Oh Hanuman likes you!" Then, one day I ended up at an obscure temple complex in the foothills in the forest and a Priest of Hanuman was literally waiting for me. With little fanfare, he guided me to his cave shrine and did a powerful Hanuman Puja with me, all unasked for. He gave me a Mantra and an empowerment of energy *and did not ask for any money. Why?* Because Hanuman had *told him to.* Now Hanuman is one of my Ishta Devas and, hilariously, none of my friends are surprised that the wild and playful monkey god would choose me.

So, the forms and manifestations of the divine in Tantra are much like human relationships—quite varied and personal. It is common that everyone honors each other's deity 'friends' as they do in India and Nepal. One unique aspect of this process is that some forms of deities come with Tantric traditions and initiations, and the forms of our deities, like Shiva, are often wilder and more primal than Hindu temples display. And Tantrics often have certain gods and goddesses associated with their initiations or lineages, meaning the protection and help of such deities comes with the initiation. For example, the Adi Nath lineage imbues the goddess Kali as our protector and guardian. However, in general, all are free to follow and work with the deities and spirits in line with their True Will.

## Those Who Honor the Gods and Goddesses are Kin

When I first went to Nepal and then to India, I was embraced almost immediately as a 'pilgrim' when both Hindu and Tantric folks saw that I honored a variety of gods and goddesses with correct Mantras. The fact that I knew Tantra as well, instantly made me a brother. As such, I had experiences tourists do not get to have. I was allowed into 'Hindu only' temples, blessed at large Pujas, invited to festivals, and on Bali, participated in a wedding.

Unfortunately, being a Householder Tantric in America does not give us that kind of spiritual support and embrace. For this reason, it can be difficult to remove ourselves from the overwhelming influences of the culture we live in. But once you call to the Tantric deities with sincerity and begin the Tantric work, they will come and support you in several ways.

In this process, the inner work of meditation and the outer active work of Pujas (including Magick) are the dual horses that will drive your spiritual chariot. Through such practices you will connect with your divine 'Ishta Deva' helpers with love and excitement.

# WORKING WITH TANTRIKA GODS & GODDESSES

How should you relate to 'your' Tantric Gods and Goddesses? Your Ishta Devas can be approached in a few ways that are appropriate and useful. Your special deities can be seen as distinct beings who operate autonomously, just as other living beings do, but at a higher spiritual level. They have their own likes, dislikes, personalities and drives.

You may also work with your deities from the viewpoint of what C.G. Jung called 'archetypes' which exist within the group unconscious mind as aspects or facets of your own psyche.

You may choose to see them as ancient and growing egregores—energy beings that emerged from the deepest strata of Indus-Valley culture 4,000 years ago, and expanded, grew and changed as human belief and worship created collective energy manifested as emerging deities. As you enter our Tantric 'Twilight World,' meditate deeply on ways of accepting and understanding the Gods and Goddesses you work with as real and personal helpers. In the end, what matters is that they exist and can help you, just as your Guardian Spirit does. However you end up interacting with them, your Ishta Devas offer you surprising powers and deep experiences. You will see.

## Tantric Gods and Goddesses: Building Relationships

Once you have felt a connection forming between yourself and one or more deities, ask each one to 'show you' the right image or statue to work with. Such deity images, called Murti, are important in your work, so seek the Murti of each deity that feels correct. Remember, there are hundreds of aspects of many of the deities.

Your deity friend will help the 'right' image come to you through luck or synchronicity, but make it easy by visiting import shops or looking online. I've often heard from people about how the right deity image or statue 'came to them' when they asked. Once you enter the 'Tantric Twilight World' and honor a deity, that deity will respond. Once you have an appropriate image of that deity, gently clean it or sprinkle it with salt water with focus; then offer a simple Mantra like OM as you honor that deity with love. Then set it up in your sacred space and meditate upon it.

Take time to speak to the deity from your heart. You might burn some incense, offer a flower, open up to that god or goddess, and listen with your heart. This is like a first date! Pay attention, and if the deity touches you, have a silent conversation with it. Write down everything in your Journal. As you do this practice, you will create a bond of love until you can readily visualize him or her, and you will deepen that relationship as you move further into Tantric magical work.

## Tantric Gods and Goddesses: Building Communion

As you get to know your gods and goddesses, you form deeper and more powerful relationships with them, and you will then be doing Bhakti Yoga, a loving, devotional union with that deity. This is a crucial part of Tantra. Continue learning more about your special gods and goddesses. When Hanuman and I fell in together, I began to studied his myths, legends, prayers, likes and dislikes, what offerings he preferred, and his various epithets or descriptive titles. I learned not to eat meat before honoring him; he is strictly vegetarian.

The most potent human-deity relationships are the ones you build with Bhakti (divine love). Such relationships with our deities and Guardian Spirit form a bedrock of Tantric work. How well you and your gods integrate and communicate is a primary indicator of your own personal integration and spiritual advancement.

As you work through the practices in this book, keep all of these things in mind. Focus on your instincts, intuition and insights, and on building loving relationships with your personal deities. You have caring guides and helpers as you enter the Twilight World of Tantra. As Dadaji Mahendranath often said:

> *The Will to Love is the Law to Live.*

# FOUR KEY TERMS

Gurudev Dadaji Mahendranath points to four key terms that sum up the philosophy behind Tantra. The Sanskrit terms are important because there are no English words to convey these concepts.

Meditating on these key concepts will help you focus on the goals of Tantric practice.

## 1. SVECCHACHARYA

> *"Svecca means one's own wish or free will. Svecchacharya means a way of life where one acts as one wishes and does what is right in one's own eyes. Doing one's own Will. The concluding Sanskrit expression in the Avadhoota Upanishad is 'Svecchacharya Paro.'"*
>
> — *The Magnum Opus of Twilight Yoga,*
> Gurudev Dadaji Mahendranath,
> *internationalnathorder.org/twilight-yoga-ii*

'Paro' means the mysterious matrix of the unfolding of one's own True Will. It is similar to the ancient Norse term 'Wyrd', which speaks of the mysterious complex forces at work in our lives and in Nature. The point is summed up in Dadaji Mahendranath's constant refrain: "The Will to Love is the Law to Live."

Only you know what is right for you, and doing your True Will is the most important thing you can do in life. This is the difference between the open, magickal lifestyle of Tantra, and all conventional religions, including Hinduism.

Your chief spiritual duty as a Tantric is to reach a state of liberated consciousness, and so let the divine flow through you. Letting go of restrictions and all the social programming you have absorbed in your life will open this gate.

## 2. Samarasa

The next key Tantric term is *Samarasa,* meaning to be free of all things so that the mind is at rest, clear, open, free of attachments and deeply calm. This is an ancient, term that is seen in Tantras, but not in Hindu literature or practices. Dadaji Mahendranath describes it as:

> *"...the equipoise of equanimity, the supreme bliss of harmony, that which is aesthetically balanced, undifferentiated unity, absolute assimilation, the most perfect unification, and the highest consummation of Oneness."*
> — *The Pathless Path to Immortality,*
> Gurudev Dadaji Mahendranath,
> *internationalnathorder.org/the-pathless-path-to-immortality*

In short, this means reaching a state of consciousness that the sorcerer A.O. Spare called 'the neither-neither'—a fugue state where you are detached from the hurricane of Samsara, the crazy illusionary world. In this way, you are not pulled this way or that emotionally, but remain calmly centered. You have had moments of Samarasa when you were feeling balanced, calm and at peace. Finding those moments and learning to extend and live in them is the goal.

## 3. Sama

The third term Dadaji Mahendranath focuses on in is *Sama.* This roughly means staying balanced and in a state of equilibrium. It refers to that state of consciousness which reflects neither attachment nor repulsion, being centered and free—but aware—of both. Attachment and repulsion are the two Kleshas (spiritual blockages) that confront us the most in our day-to-day life and in our spiritual work. When engaged in life, we tend to go back and forth between these two states. However, Sama means to remain focused and balanced in the center, not taking one view or another, but to see clearly both views or experiences at the same time. All choices between two things are problematic because both attraction and repulsion throw you off kilter, and you lose your inner balance of impartiality that is *Sama.* Tantra points to accepting several seemingly contradictory things as all true in their own light. With Sama we acknowledge differences between such things or emotions without being caught up in the differences. In this way we may be mentally at rest and avoid being ensnared by competing feelings or ideas. Sama is **detached perspective,** and leads to being more free and more liberated.

## 4. Sahaja

*Sahaja* means 'the Natural way' and feels very Taoist to me. The root of Tantra lies in prehistory, but as civilization expanded, more complexity and rules were placed on people and the simple, natural way of living was abandoned. Sahaja means a natural, open and unconditioned way of living within Nature. This important lifestyle goal still exists in Tantric sects as well as Kulas of Tantric 'in groups.' Dadaji Mahendranath has this to say about Sahaja:

> *"Man is born with an instinct for naturalness. He has never forgotten the days of his primordial perfection, except insomuch as the memory became buried under the artificial superstructure of civilization and its artificial concepts. Sahaja means natural. It not only implies natural on physical and spiritual levels, but on the mystic level of the miraculous. It means that easy or natural way of living without planning, designing, contriving, seeking, wanting, striving or intention."*
>
> — *The Pathless Path to Immortality,*
> Gurudev Dadaji Mahendranath,
> *internationalnathorder.org/the-pathless-path-to-immortality*

## In Summation

In summation, keeping it simple, how can you apply these ideals?

**Applying Svecchacharya**—Do your True Will within the flow of your life to the best of your ability. Follow your real purpose in life and love with the divine help of your Guardian Spirit and your Ishta Devas. Meditate on this daily.

**Applying Samarasa**—Work hard to attain a state of open and balanced joy in life that is unattached to any specific event or thing. Be grateful every day for this wonderful life and all you have, and remember that this is your true state. Maintaining this state of equipoise in our crazy world takes time, but it is our goal, and it's good for your blood pressure as well!

**Applying Sama**—Note how you allow yourself to be thrown off balance daily. To attain Sama consciously, work on not being jerked around by thoughts, events, emotions or conflicts. Work at pausing before getting upset, and learn to disengage from inner turmoil and so develop more control of your reactions. In this balanced state, you will default to being happier.

**Sahaja**—Strive to live a natural life, free of excessive restrictions and distractions. Meditate on your primal self; we are all animals, and are happiest in the natural world. Spend time in Nature and observe, absorb and feel the rhythms of the natural world that have been forgotten today. Hike, garden, cook fresh healthy food, simplify your life. Accept your natural body and keep it healthy; accept your natural feelings and urges. Tantra is 'a natural Pagan life,' as Dadaji Mahendranath often said. Living this path is harder in our crazy, modern world, but it is possible. Nature is the Great Mother, and all the gods, goddesses and spirits of Tantra are of Nature—as are we.

It is not easy to utilize these four key ideas, but they all help to manifest the Great Work of Tantra.

# OM (AUM)

*OM (AUM) The Prime Vibration of All*

In the beginning was OM, the divine vibration of All.
OM appeared as Shiva and Shakti, Yin and Yang.
All Gods and Goddesses and Spirits are facets of this Unity that some call God. In Tantra:

OM is All: there is nothing that is not OM. Call it God if you like.

> *"The realization of Thee and Me is called Alpha Omega*
> *When we know that there is only one Supreme Substance."*
> — *The Magnum Opus of Twilight Yoga,*
> Gurudev Dadaji Mahendranath,
> *internationalnathorder.org/twilight-yoga-ii*

The most used, widespread and often misunderstood Mantra in Hinduism, Tantra and Buddhism is **OM.** OM (often written as AUM) has been popularized in the West by Yoga and 'New Age' stores, but is not deeply understood. Often it is shown as the pre-Sanskrit glyph, a very simple form which was found in Mohenjo-Daro.

Gurudev Dadaji describes OM as the Alpha-Ovule (first seed) of all things. It is described as the **Prime Vibration,** and is often identified as the cosmos, supreme divinity or God, but this is only part of the truth. An important clue to really understanding OM is hidden in the term Alpha Ovule, a term that offers a new viewpoint.

> *"The Ovule of Alpha is the link between all the Universes; The smallest of the small, yet infinite in its expansions."*
> — *The Magnum Opus of Twilight Yoga*,
> Gurudev Dadaji Mahendranath,
> <u>internationalnathorder.org/twilight-yoga-ii</u>

Dadaji Mahendranath had a number of superlatives for OM, but a lot about it is communicated by the Greek term 'Alpha Ovule'.

Note that the term Ovule directly points to the female origin seed from which life arises, a nod to the Great Goddess or primal energy who embodies the universe.

OM can be seen as the single vibration that caused the whole universe to come into being—the Big Bang that created all things.

Many Hindu and Tantric traditions—especially Shaivite—honor OM as 'Shiva's Mantra.' This is because he is the center of all, the supreme Bindu and core vibration of the cosmos: OM.

> *"I bow to the supreme Lord who is the formless source of 'OM' The Self of All, transcending all conditions and states. Beyond speech, He understands the sense perception."*
> — from *Shree Rudraashtak Stotram*, a hymn to Shiva

Shiva is named Omkara, or 'embodiment of OM.' However, some Tantric sects worship Ganesh as the supreme deity and see Ganesh literally as OM. Other Tantric sects, however, believe Adi Shakti, the infinite Goddess, is the hidden reality of OM. In the end, all Hindus, Buddhists and Tantrics agree that OM is beyond classification, it being the infinite vibration and unity of ALL!

The reality is that all living beings and deities, regardless of gender, are OM, for there is nothing that is not OM. This is a multi-level meditation and will be a continual point of contemplation for you. It is the heart of mystery and the ultimate Truth.

# SHIVA & SHAKTI

*Om Shanti Shiva Shakti!*

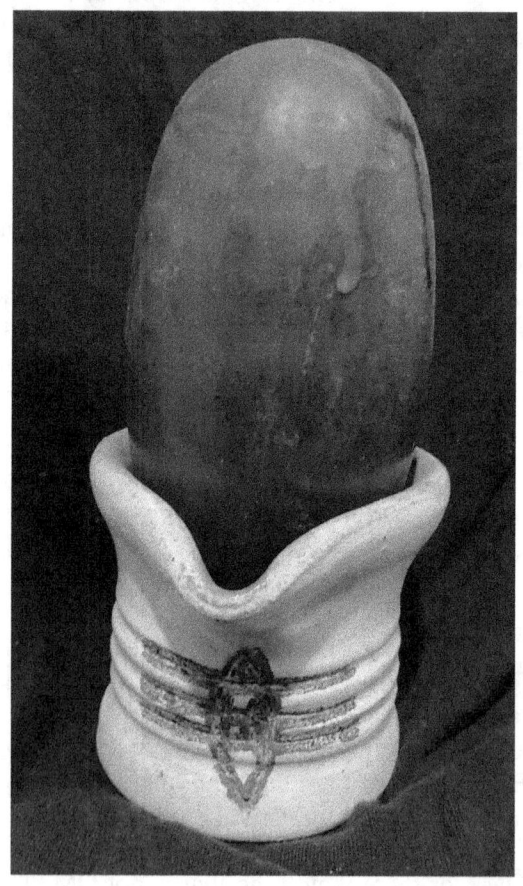

*Yoni-Lingam*
*(Photo by the Author)*

This Mantra of sacred words—*Om Shanti Shiva Shakti!*—is extremely popular in Tantra and means *'OM: the Union of Shiva and Shakti manifests peace.'* In our Tantric work we end every ritual with this Mantra because it states our basic cosmology: the union of the God and Goddess brings the peace of OM, the union of all.

Shiva and Shakti, the eternal masculine and feminine, emerge from OM (or God, if you like). The Tantric god, Ardhanarishvara, who is always shown as half God and half Goddess, reminds us that Shiva and Shakti, though manifesting as separate forms, are always one, always OM, and this reflects the truth that all of us contain male and female aspects.

The most common images that symbolize this axiom are the Yoni-Lingam stones that show the vulva and phallus joined as one. Found in prehistoric Mohenjo-Daro, this is the primal image of Deva and Devi united as one. It also affirms that natural sexuality is an important part of Tantric worship. It is a reminder that you *are* the union of god and goddess, and when uniting in sexual ecstasy, you become the eternal Union OM, the infinite divinity of the cosmos.

*"There is no Shiva without Shakti nor Shakti without Shiva."*
— *shivashakti.com/goddess.htm*, Shri Lokanath

*"...Tantrics continued the non-Aryan tradition of Shiva as the cosmic person and his Shakti personified as the mother goddess. ... Yet in spite of this there is something unique, wondrous, miraculous and most fascinating about the very concept of Shiva and his lovely Shakti."*
— Notes on Pagan India, Gurudev Dadaji Mahendranath, *internationalnathorder.org/notes-on-pagan-india*

## SHAKTI

*"The word Shakti means power. It is, according to the Tantrics, the Power by which the Absolute manifests itself. The worship of Shakti therefore implies the worship of God as the Mother. In symbolism, the universe is seen to issue from a womb, as in human birth and this implies Mother-*

*hood. ...Shakti or Shakti Devi is also a reference to the consort of Shiva. As Devi, she is the personification of God as the Divine Mother and represents the active, dynamic principle of feminine power."*
— *The Magnum Opus of Twilight Yoga,*
Gurudev Dadaji Mahendranath,
*internationalnathorder.org/twilight-yoga-ii*

Shakti is the pervasive energy that forms the entire universe. Also referred to as the creative, fiery whirlwind Prakriti, it is Shakti who empowers the cosmos and everything in it. Maya, the world of illusion which we perceive as reality, is formed of Shakti. Without Shakti nothing can manifest.

Shakti can be translated as 'energy' or 'power' in a cosmic and magical sense. 'That ritual raised a lot of Shakti' is often said by participants in a ritual, and someone might note that a very vibrant person 'has a lot of Shakti,' that is, magickal energy.

Shakti is also a manifestation of the Kundalini, the specific power or bio-energy that can be focused on and moved when working with this magick.

'A Shakti' is also a term traditionally used for a female Tantric in sacred ceremonies. As such, she is worshipped as a goddess (Adi Shakti), the primordial power, just as the male Tantric is worshipped as Maha Deva or Shiva.

Let's now look at Her other half, her other aspect, the great Maha Deva or Great God who sits in the center of the cosmos in silence.

## SHIVA

*"The embodied soul is supreme, whole, eternal, consisting of nothing, stainless. It is the ultimate atomic particle, the point of all It is supreme Shiva, all pervading...the soul of Shakti"*
— *Kaul-jnana-nirnaya,* ed. P.C. Bagchi, Calcutta, 1915

Shiva literally means 'The Auspicious One', or 'The Blessed One'. Yet, there are hundreds of epithets that describe Shiva, and just as many different aspects. Most of Shiva's aspects began as separate gods from various regions, and then, through syncretism, became seen as different forms or 'faces' of Shiva. Some of the more common are: Maheshwari, the great Lord; Mahadeva, the great God; Shambhu, Kind One; Mrityunjaya, conqueror of death; and the ancient, likely Harappan god, Hara, 'one's natural self.' He is, of course, the mate and 'other half' of the Goddess in all her many, many aspects, including Shakti! As the wild Rudra (the Howler), Shiva is identified with the star Sirius (Sothis), and is the supreme hunter. But many just call him Great God (Maha Deva).

It is important to note that Shiva is also identified as your Atman (soul) and thus your Guardian Spirit; as such he is also called Adi Guru or ultimate Guru, teacher or guide.

As every Yantra (a design used for Tantric worship) or Mandala can be seen as the whole universe—as Shakti—the centerpoint (Bindu) in the middle of each of these diagrams *always represents Shiva.*

Meditating on this will give you a deep and intuitive understanding about the nature of both Shiva and Shakti.

*Kali Yantra, with Bindu Center Point of Shiva*

Authors such as Alain Daniélou identify Shiva's most ancient origin as a primal god of Fire. Much could be said about this, but I just visualize a tribal circle of prehistoric animists with a single, all-important fire in the center. Fire has always been a liminal gateway, a mysterious energy that 'eats' things—including bodies—leaving nothing but ashes. In India, fiery cremation grounds are common and Shiva is identified as a deity of transition, eternity and transcendence, and thus is often shown with an 'ash covered body' and his followers likewise. It is common in Tantric rites to mark the forehead with ashes for this reason.

In images, Shiva is often depicted as a wandering, naked or near-naked holy man who owns nothing and cares for nothing, often shown sitting on or wearing a tiger skin, a shout-out to his mate Kali whose symbol is a tiger.

Shiva is the Lord and creator of Yoga (Union) in all its forms. On his matted locks he wears a crescent moon. He wears the serpent demi-god Nagaraj and Rudraksha-seed prayer beads about his neck. He is most often seen intoxicated with cannabis in deep meditation. This is one reason Shiva is often called the Lord of Ecstasy. Shiva also commands many strange and monstrous spirits and the undead, including Bhutas (elementals), Pretas (ghosts), Pishachas (flesh eaters), goblins, vampires, and so on. Collectively, these wild creatures are called the Ganas.

The chapter on Shiva in the **Pujas** section offers much more about this amazing god, but at this point three things are most important:

• Shiva is the centerpoint within every sphere or circle. He is the lynchpin that keeps the somewhat chaotic, universal, creative, fiery energy that is Shakti centered and focused.

• Shiva is both the Great God as well as the *spark* of God within you; that is, your soul or Atman and source of your Guardian Spirit. Just as OM is all, the Cosmos, so is OM the point of pure spirit within you.

• Unlike many other Hindu Gods, the far-older Shiva is a Wild God and is often shown as such. This primal Shiva is especially venerated by Tantrics. He smokes cannabis, sits around naked, fears nothing, is utterly chill and detached, and seeks nothing but liberation and ecstasy. He is far more 'Dionysian' than 'Apollonian,' and the use of psychoactive fungi—'Soma'—is ascribed to his followers. In his earliest image he is depicted with horns and surrounded by wild beasts. In this he is closer to the horned gods Pan or Cernunnos. He lives in the wilderness always—sometimes atop snow-covered mountains, at other times in the jungle. He is the ancient god of wildness!

# ON TANTRIC GODS & SPIRITS

Gurudev Dadaji Mahendranath succinctly laid out the spiritual world that manifests in Tantric ritual-spaces or temples. While the cosmos manifests as a swirling, pure, primal Shakti-energy centered about a CenterPoint of Shiva, this cosmos generates your Guardian Spirit and many different greater and lesser gods and goddesses, spirits, elemental beings, demons (Asuras), and other beings. This is like the Western occult view of a universe filled with supernatural forces.

The following list, offered by Dadaji Mahendranath, provides a general guide to the Tantric universe of magickal beings. According to Gurudev Mahendranath, these are the spiritual forces that are the 'manifold spirit values' of the Cosmos, listed from that which is closest to you and easiest to work with, to spiritual forces that are often far beyond our normal states of consciousness:

## 1. THE INDIVIDUAL GUARDIAN SPIRIT

This is your most important spiritual being; it is your core inner voice. Once you have attuned to your Guardian Spirit through receptiveness and meditation, your Guardian Spirit will guide you. In this way, all of Tantra and magick will be open to you. The closer you become with your Guardian Spirit through meditation and ritual work, the more your insight, intuition and instincts will grow. You will receive wisdom and knowledge from many sources, and important synchronicities will become commonplace. Your Guardian Spirit, Atman or Guru is the embodiment of your very essence, your True Will, and therefore that which guides you in all your Tantric work.

## 2. Household Family Spirits or Gods

In our universe, spiritual beings are everywhere, and as you move into the Twilight World of Tantra you will form relationships with an array of gods, goddesses, demi-gods, nature spirits, and honored ancestors. These are all part of the Tantric cosmology, some dark, others very light, most with human-like reactions depending on your attitude. Your Guardian Spirit can help you to understand and communicate with such spirits so they can help you. Once you become aware of them and enter into cordial relationships, they will come and help you in many ways, especially with your magickal work.

## 3. The Spirit of a Tribe or Community

Most people no longer have a tribe, but think in terms of family, circles of friends, co-workers and spiritual brothers and sisters. In life you bond with various groups, often around a calling of some kind. These are your tribes as well, those you feel close affinity with. All such circles of caring and friendship are part of your spiritual world, and such circles form collective energies that can be worked with as living beings. They may be connected to your ancestry; if you identify strongly as Irish be open to Irish spirits like the Sidhe. Your ancestors offer powerful help as well. You should honor those who have passed on and work with them. Our ancestors—our friends and loved ones who have passed on live within us. Consider creating a small 'ancestor and honored dead' shrine somewhere in your home or sacred space, and work with them as you are guided.

## 4. The Spirits of an Area

Think of where you live. The 'genius loci' or spirits of a place are potent spiritual helpers if you choose to bond with them. Such nature spirits should be honored before working in a specific place. All Earth-centered traditions speak to, honor and make offerings to the guiding spirit/intelligence of a place where they will do spiritual work. Honoring such entities is critical because you are honoring a power with immense history. Such spirits are, in part, conscious beings, and should be honored. Meditate on the native peoples who once lived and died where you are. Touching the earth, honoring the place, and coming to terms with this entity offers you a direct connection with the Great Earth Mother and potential support in your work.

## 5. The 'Evolved Spirits of this Planet'

This refers to wider-scope nature elementals in your area, and of course, Gaia, the awake and aware consciousness of our planet. In my biome there are powerful conscious spirits of the Cascade Mountains, the Hoh Rain Forest, and Puget Sound, for example. As you meditate, part of your work is to extend yourself deep into the ground and the waters, as well as to connect with the heavens above. The Great Nature Spirits that surround you may be called upon for aid, and should always be respected, since Bhu Devi (Mother Earth) is crucial to all our work. From her we access deep wisdom; when we are confused, we go into primal nature to find healing and answers. You should always honor Mother Earth and the greater Earth spirits at the end of every Tantric practice, no matter what it is.

## 6. Sun, Moon and Planetary Gods and Goddesses

From the atoms of our being to the great cosmos, all things reflect the master patterns of the Divine. As you sit within the center of this swirling, alive and playful cosmos, you become as Shiva and Shakti, sitting in bliss upon Mount Meru. The Sun provides all life; we are literally solar energy! The moon and its rhythms affect all water, including that within us. The archetypes of love (Venus), action (Mars), quickness and intellect (Mercury), and so on are embedded deep within our culture and our deep mind. In Hinduism and Tantra these planetary forces are deities called the *Navagraha* (9 planet deities), and they are honored and offer magical aid. Surya, the sun; Chandra, the moon; Mangala, Mars; Buda, Mercury; Brihaspati, Jupiter; Shukra, Venus; and Shani, Saturn. Those are the seven main planetary gods; Rahu (the north node of the moon), and Ketu (the south node of the moon) are added to make nine. They are all presented as very interesting images and worth looking up. Each one has an image, a special symbol, a magical square, a Mantra, and so on. In Hindu and Tantric temples, the planetary spirits have their own shrines. As with Western magickal systems, you can work with the planetary gods for real gains; for example, you can conjure Shukra (Venus) for love magick. Many people honor all of them. They all have Yantras, magick squares, and so on as you'll discover. If you like astrology, see what these gods are doing in your chart! As a Tantric, you will form your own relationships with them as with other divine forces.

## 7. The Supreme Spirit of the Solar System

In Hinduism, a complex hierarchy of spirits and gods is adhered to, but Tantra is more open and generally ignores hierarchies, realizing that your inclinations and experiences are unique. Just as there is a Holy Guardian Spirit for each person, and there is a god for each planet, and there is a greater 'god' who embodies each whole solar system. Our solar system behaves like you do, as a conscious and aware cosmic being. You may choose to meditate upon, contact and work with this being in your work. It is fascinating that other religions (e.g., Mormonism) ascribe gods to different Universes as well, possibly the only Mormon-Tantric connection I can think of!

## 8. The Supreme Ruler of the Galaxy

In Tantra, the galaxy we are part of is seen as the great cosmic being or 'great soul'—Ishvara. More traditionally, the Galaxy Spirit is seen as the entwined dancing Shiva-Shakti, a swirling stellar wheel about a central hub of light and power. This is a very abstract and overwhelming god to work with; there is only one aspect of the divine that is higher.

## 9. The Divine Cosmos or 'Absolute Ruler of the Universe'

The universe as a whole is OM (God), the purest form of divinity, the vibration that embodies the entire universe. In essence, we are back to where we began: here, now; all is God. The ultimate rule of Tantra, *Tat Tvam Asi* ('I am that') expresses the absolute truth that you are OM or God, the pure essence of divinity. In your most sublime states of deep meditation, you will experience this, for you, too, are pure divinity and one with OM—once you remember.

§ § §

We began with the Guardian Spirit, our innate divinity, and we have expanded our consciousness to embrace all the divine manifestations of ever more spiritual power and intensity until we arrive at God, the cosmos, OM: the absolute. Yet we are where we began! For the Guardian Spirit that is 'you' is the internal OM, and the external cosmos is OM and they are, in fact, one thing.

So where does this lead us?

Sitting in meditation, we work to evolve our consciousness and work with all the vast, endless variety of divine manifestations, from the smallest (the spark of divine within us) to the Absolute Godhead whose communion is Samadhi, the dissolving of Self into the OM, merging with the pure divine, for they were ever the same.

You are divine, you are infinite, you are beyond all things and have always been so, but you have forgotten. The physical world and its demands, your family, society, educational system, work, relationships, and on and on have all convinced you that you are something that you are not. Yes, the divinity that is you wears many masks—child, parent, worker, caregiver—but, ultimately, are you any of these? Of course not, and all such labels as well as your perceived reality is illusionary. It is named Samsara, the realm of appearances and delusion. Only when we open to all aspects of the divine can we awaken to the internal cosmos within us. Then, we can take a deep breath, relax, let go of everything, and open to the OM that is and pervades all things.

# KEY TANTRIC CONCEPTS

## Bhakti, Dharma, Karma, Siddhi & Sadhana

Tantra offers ancient and successful approaches to spiritual growth, a successful life, and liberation. Here are some of the key applied concepts that have been successful for centuries:

### On Bhakti

Loving devotion to the gods and goddesses is a cornerstone of Tantra. The term *Bhakti,* meaning intense personal love of the divine, is a key method of bonding with your gods. For it is love that binds the cosmos. The process of 'falling in love' with deities, not just praying to them, is key to much of magick, and dissolves the barriers among us. In Tantra, direct relationships with our gods empower the magick we do. True spirituality is about relationship-building, whether it is with people or with gods and goddesses. Only with sincere love can we directly experience the truth of the divine.

Tantra is based on mutual communication and love between you and your gods. Our gods do not lord over us; they are part of us, parts of our deep mind as well as personifications of Nature. As a Tantric, you do not need a priest to intercede between you and your gods. You will have your own personal relationships with your gods and goddesses. You'll bond with them, talk to and petition them, listen to them, and do magick directly with them. Tantrics go right to the source of divinity because we are part of that source. Bhakti, or real spiritual love, is therefore key and offers real personal interface with the divine.

We Tantrics think of the gods and goddesses as our beloved mentors and friends and, as you'll see, they come to feel this way about us as well.

Once we have reified our love, devotion and respect for our gods, and have established relationships, we can ask for divine help...and get it! Much of this book and my work comes from the gods and goddesses *communicating directly with me* in multiple ways. Tantra, like so much in life, relies on direct communication and loving relationships.

## On Karma

*Karma* is a difficult concept to grasp for Westerners who are programmed to always think about 'sin' and 'forgiveness.' Tantrics don't believe in set morals or sins, other than not harming others except when necessary. Karma is physics. It means your actions have reactions, and that is it. It is not about an angry God punishing you; you are responsible for your own actions. Karma means 'action, deed or work,' and in short, places responsibility on you for your actions and work in both your mundane and spiritual life. To me, Karma promotes Spiritual Evolution, working to be a better being. *It is not about reward or punishment!* If you overeat, you get fat; if you exercise, you get strong. If you are cruel, others shun you. You make choices that affect you and others around you. You are responsible for your path and your decisions—over many lifetimes, if you believe in reincarnation. Karma can be seen as the natural way things go depending on your actions. Raising our awareness and becoming *more conscious* of the vast web of causality that surrounds us helps us see and understand the patterns of action and reaction we create. 'Good' karma is 'right action,' but in Tantra there is no rulebook, no commandments. *It is up to you,* with advice from your Guardian Spirit.

*Svecchacharya,* or doing your True Will, is at the heart of 'right' Karma. Doing so brings you closer to both understanding and benefitting from divine forces while becoming more aware. Karma reveals the flow of your experiences and your work back to you as you dance through. Our actions and reactions and choices are our responsibility. What you do matters on every level. Your actions (or inactions) are part of a vast spiritual ecosystem you are both creating and experiencing. Meditating on this and making the most thoughtful decisions and choices as you do your True Will is the Tantric path. As Gandhi, who understood Karma well, said: *"Be the change in the world you want to see."*

## On Dharma

*Dharma* is often described as following divine and social rules that are beneficial to society and the world. Tantrics have a very different view of Dharma. To us, Dharma is not about following dogma, taboos or human laws. To Tantrics, *Svecchacharya* is not about societal rules; it is about liberation or 'following your bliss.' Dharma is the cosmic balance we keep as we dance through life doing our True Will, doing our best to help those who need it, and leaving things better than they were. This is quite relativistic and very different from scripture-driven taboos or commandments. Dadaji Mahendranath teaches Dharma as "The will to love is the law to live!" This works for us.

## On Siddha

Devotion to your True Will, your Guardian Spirit, and the gods and goddesses you love can offer you real help when you need it. Manifesting things with your willpower, or with the help of a god or goddess is a sign that you are developing *Siddha* (magical skills). All people are all born with such abilities sleeping within them, but most never learn how to use them. Tantrics do. Connecting and working with your Guardian Spirit and deities will help you develop your Siddhas. It is straightforward; making serious effort and focusing on your True Will brings results. When meditating, you are the center of the cosmos. Once you have experimented and built relationships with your Guardian Spirit and your deities and have mastered a number of Tantric practices, you will be able to easily and intuitively direct the forces in your circle, petition the gods you invoke, and manifest the Magical goals you will to accomplish. Real Siddha-Magick comes *from the cosmos through you,* just as a beautiful song *'comes from and through'* an inspired singer. Though it may involve help from our gods and goddesses, it is you, embodying your Guardian Spirit, who centers and weaves the magick. The gods are your backup band.

So: When should you involve the gods, goddesses or spirits, and when should you do your Magick alone with your Guardian Spirit? Think of it as fixing your car yourself, or hiring a mechanic to do it. If you do it, it will be a lot more effort, but you'll learn a lot. On the other hand, getting a good mechanic will cost you more, but it will likely be faster and a more professional job.

Say I need immediate protection from a bad work situation. As a Tantric I can proceed one of two ways:

1. I can invoke the kick-ass goddess Durga who is famous for intense protection. Even the other gods fear her. I will go to my Tantric temple space and do a ritual to Shri Durga. Using her divine chant with proper offerings—and knowing that we are pals—I'll invoke her with full intensity and all senses, and in a polite and grateful manner ask her to do what I need done. Then I let it go, leaving it in her hands; how it unfolds is then up to her until it is resolved. Or,

2. I can sit in my sacred space, meditate deeply on the situation, call upon my inner Guardian Spirit, and seek advice on the best magick to apply. Then I would raise power through any number of ways, with intensity and focus, and directly cast the right Magick spell utilizing proper empowering Tantric techniques and my own kick-ass Self. It is simple and forceful, and I retain more control than when I call upon other spirits or deities for help. However, to err is human, so things may go differently than expected because a deity has a more transcendent consciousness and a much wider view of things than I do.

Either path to magick can be appropriate and your Guardian Spirit should always be your guide. When in doubt, use your intuition, meditate, and maybe do some divination to check the best way to proceed.

## On Sadhana

The spiritual work we *do* with our gods—our rituals and our meditative practices—are called *Sadhana*. Sadhana translates as 'realization', but often means 'our spiritual work' or daily practices. Such practices are personal and vary widely from person to person. Much depends on your goals, intuitive feelings, and the spiritual guidance of your Guru-Teacher or your Guardian Spirit. Meditation, regular devotions to favorite deities, or Siddha Magick are the three most common elements of a Sadhana. Much of this book will discuss the many techniques and practices that may be part of your Sadhana, but once you know them well, it will be up to you. The short-term goals of a Sadhana may be spiritual or materialistic, but of course the long-term goal of any such spiritual and magickal work is to evolve, grow and attain spiritual liberation. So, onward and Svecchacharya!

# PART TWO

## SATTVAS—WILL: CORE DISCIPLINES OF TANTRIKA

# YOGA (UNION) & MEDITATION

Yoga is the transformation of the mind complex and its activity;
The Helix form Path of Magick leading to higher spiritual levels;
To vanquish the conditioning and habits inflamed by civilization,
Restoring our original nature and magick charisma of Divinity
By the union of individual spirit with the Supreme Atman.
Yoga presupposes that the Supraconscious mind retains the
    memory
Of its divine origin and vast potential of its magick power
But the conscious mind obstructs and causes it to forget.
And illusion dominates a life in which clarity should rule...
Yoga is the process, and the goal is to return to the One Absolute.
It is the spiritual Magick-Alchemy, independent of religions.
Its process and methods are based only on cosmic natural law.
It has its parallels with the findings of modern science;
So, patterns of our ancient past become science of the future.
Its motif is fluid, because Yoga has no fixed rules or dogmas;
Only a wisdom base is the matrix to guide and help the student
Thus, experiments and guidelines must be adapted and used
To assist one to find their own individual system of harmony.
Yoga is an integral part of the Pagan Magick Way of Life.
— *The Magnum Opus of Twilight Yoga,*
Gurudev Dadaji Mahendranath,
*internationalnathorder.org/twilight-yoga-ii*

*Yoga* means 'Union', and is essentially everything you do to unite with the divine—from meditation to Sex Magick to Pranayama breathing to the postures familiar to Hatha Yoga fans. A better definition may be 'union with the divine essence of the cosmos and your being.' The invention and teaching of Yoga is said to have originated with Shiva, and thus he is called Maha Yogi—the Greatest Yogi. The most important text of Yoga, *The Yoga Sutras of Patanjali,* is a holy text on what Yoga is, and how to practice it in a variety of ways. It was written around 500 BCE by the renowned sage Patanjali who crafted it from many existing ancient texts and teachings. It is powerful, well worth reading, and will change your mind about what Yoga is. It is interesting to note that only two sections of this book refer to what we in the West think of as physical Yoga. Almost all of the Tantric practices in this book can be considered varieties of Yoga. Siddha Yoga, for example, is the work of Magick.

The first step you take to a divine union is always regular meditation. Sit quietly and focus inward as the first step to clarity. The center of the Wheel is always calm—as is the eye of the storm of this existence. Gurudev Dadaji Mahendranath often referred to Yoga as the heart of Tantra in the widest sense because there are so many kinds of Yoga and it represents so many practices.

The origin of Yoga is ancient and even clay seals from Mohenjo-Daro show people and gods in Yoga postures (Asanas). In deep meditation, and after much practice, you will have moments and glimpses of real union with the absolute. As you progress, you will be guided down the path to attain spiritual freedom that is right for you. This book exists to start you on this path so you can acquire enough information and experience as you work. It is designed so your Guardian Spirit can guide you deeper into union with the absolute. If you are doing a form of Yoga now and it works for you, by all means, continue; it will lead you naturally into the practices of Tantra.

# THE FIVE KLESHAS

The 'Five Kleshas' in Tantra are called 'the five pain-bearing obstructions.' Kleshas is sometimes translated as 'blockages' or 'knots' that need to be 'pierced.' They are, as Guru Dadaji Mahendranath says, "The Root Cause of Trouble and Strife." These 'blockages' to spiritual liberation and happiness are: Ignorance, Ego, Repulsion, Attachment and Clinging to Life (sometimes called 'fear of death').

> *"They are the cause of all the miseries and afflictions of life.*
> *The vast mass of mankind lives and suffers through these defects,*
> *And they must be understood before real practice can begin,*
> *For nothing can be attained until the mind knows these obstacles.*
> *They are impediments to Yoga, happy life and cosmic harmony.*
> *Unless they are controlled, we will always be frustrated*
> *From entry to the Twilight Zone between two worlds."*
> — The Magnum Opus of Twilight Yoga,
> Gurudev Dadaji Mahendranath
> *internationalnathorder.org/twilight-yoga-ii*

There is tremendous suffering, subjectively and objectively, in Samsara, the world of illusions and difficulties in which we are immersed. Much of this suffering is caused by the Kleshas, our own blockages. Tantrics, Hindus and Buddhists all agree in general about these blockages and are focused on 'piercing' or eliminating the Kleshas as a way to attain liberation. Tantrics seek to actively work with all the Kleshas, and move through them as we can. Most Buddhists seek a mystical detachment from the world, while Tantrics seek a more enlightened, active embrace of the world. Abstaining from excitement, love, sex and ecstasy is not our general path;

embracing the joys of our troublesome world and side-stepping the negative effects of Samsara is a core part of Tantra.

All do agree on the importance of self-discipline and 'letting go' of the Kleshas—those painful and entrapping aspects of our world. The goal is to thoughtfully embrace our experiences without letting them control, delude or hinder us. This is why Tantra is a much trickier, and some say, a more dangerous path. Simply withdrawing into a Buddhist retreat and embracing celibacy and lengthy daily meditation is a powerful path, but the Tantric way is more active and embraces life more completely. We seek to remain fully engaged, a part of this wonderful, glorious world, while avoiding being trapped or restricted by the inherent illusions and snares it offers.

This requires a lot of practice and spiritual work. On this path we must remain ever-watchful, and work continuously to 'pierce the knots' of our Kleshas lest we be ensnared by them. Working on getting past the Kleshas is a huge part of attaining or preparing for Liberation.

## The Kleshas

Here is a description and explanation of the five Kleshas and what they represent:

**Ignorance:** Untrue things, unreality, being unenlightened; ignorance, delusion, being unaware of facts. The biggest issue here is believing you *do* know something when you don't; or being blind to knowledge you don't see or that you dismiss. This includes rejecting empirical facts and science, and embracing irrational hate, prejudice or superstitions. Think of all the unexamined prejudices, biases and assumptions filling your mind from family and culture! Gurudev Dadaji Mahendranath points out that this Klesha is the 'root' or soil from which all the rest of the Kleshas grow. Mistaking belief for fact, or social or religious indoctrination for truth, are insidious examples of ignorance. Two of the prime illusions that materialism has imprinted on us, and which lead to ignorance are: 'You are your physical body,' and 'Scientifically proven reality is the only reality there is.' Tantra sees both of these absolutist statements as ignorant. Ignorance is dissolved with real knowledge, not facts and figures, but through direct knowledge (gnosis). To know that you are, in fact, the cosmos is utterly liberating, but this leads to a 'who says so?!' conversation. Thus, to the next Klesha:

**Ego:** The Ego is the 'I' or 'ME', the person you think you are: your job, your family, your likes and dislikes, and so on. For 'ME' it is the illusion that the person typing this now is the consciousness and true self of this being. In ignorance, I (the author) am led to the belief that 'I' am the center and focus of this universe, and that when 'I' die 'I' will cease to exist! How frightening! Thus 'MY' point of view, opinions, thoughts and beliefs are all-important. 'MY' life revolves, of course, around 'ME.'

None of this is true. 'I' is an imagined creature; there is no way to verify the existence of this unique 'person.' I can verify my flesh and blood, but the conscious 'ME' that has a personality is simply a construct of my experiences and social and cultural programming. The Ego is a useful construct that aids survival. Ego is the mask we wear to make sense of our world, and to try to understand and control it. Yet much of the pain and suffering in our history comes from Ego-centered humans seeking self-gratification. A healthy relationship with your ego begins with meditation on 'Who am I'—a lifelong work. We can acknowledge and honor the usefulness of the ego and how it helps us function while remembering *that it is temporary,* that it will die when we do, but out Guardian Spirit or Atman never dies and is eternal. Truly knowing this helps pierce this Klesha.

**Attachment:** This Klesha means to have a sense of possessiveness, attraction, desire for, or actual ownership of things, people or even ideas. It is negative because it is like a fishhook that never lets go, and it can possess us, often in unhealthy ways. Ego incites attachment. When we focus on ownership, possession, fixation and desire, we no longer desire freedom and liberation. It is a trap. Nothing is permanent, nothing is real or eternal except OM and the spiritual cosmos. Things, people, feelings and ideas all come and go; all are transitory. Attachment causes pain, fixation and suffering. Hateful and wrong beliefs are hurtful, dangerous attachments. Even love and desire can lead to suffering. The issue of attachment can be solved with 'Contentment, Neutrality, Tranquility and Knowledge' according to Gurudev Dadaji Mahendranath. By accepting without attaching, we can love and appreciate things, ideas and people without possessing them. This is real truth and love. Mindfulness and meditation begin this work.

**Repulsion:** The opposite of attraction is repulsion. Both are equally harmful. Repulsion means a feeling of dislike, aversion or outright rejection of things, feelings, people, places, experiences or ideas. Yet, deep dislike can help us understand things about ourselves that we need to face. In many Tantric traditions, a visceral dislike or repulsion of something indicates that one should *confront and embrace what is repellent,* and work through that fear or revulsion until it is no longer upsetting or unbalancing. The goal is to become emotionally neutral to such things, and to respond with equipoise—with a neutral, objective view of something that could be upsetting. Confronting fearful or repulsive things (e.g., spiders), helps us come to terms with this fear, and neutralize the power it has over us. In India you will see Tantric Sadhus calmly wearing dangerous cobras for the same reason. Nothing is innately horrible; such things are only in our mind. Confronting repulsive things and neutralizing negative reactions brings calm emotional balance, clarity and acceptance. This leads us to the final Klesha, the hardest one to crack, facing our Death.

**Clinging to Life:** This Klesha is often called as 'Fear of Death.' If we think that 'ME' is real, then our Ego will do anything and everything to continue its own existence. We are always in fear of death because 'I' (Ego!) knows (Ignorance!) that death is truly the end of everything! We Tantrics know this is not true, but nonetheless it is natural to fear death. This is why this is a very, very difficult Klesha to 'pierce' and move past. All the other Kleshas reinforce this fear of death. It is connected to Attachment by the things you think show the life you have lived. It is connected to Ignorance of your true eternal and divine nature. And it is connected to the Repulsion of not 'you' not 'being' anymore. The solution is to experience the real truth of your spiritual immortality. To *experience* that your divine self is eternal, and that all the Kleshas are just phantasms—not real except in our mind. At the moment of death all of this is revealed, of course. Yet to attain that truth and understanding, and let go before we die, prepares us for a conscious spiritual awakening and liberation.

As you can see, the Five Kleshas are interwoven blockages that reinforce and empower each other. These blockages cause you and others a lot of suffering, and it is said, many unnecessary rebirths. If we remain caught in this web, then we will be unnecessarily unhappy. Through our practices, we can attain more freedom, peace and happiness as well as a productive rebirth!

## Releasing the Kleshas— A Simple Rite

This rite is to be done within your ritual space after a time of meditating on the Kleshas. This very simple rite works directly on 'piercing' the Kleshas as much as possible. It can be done as often as you like, for this work is never completely done.

Klesha work is an ongoing and important part of Tantra because no serious progress can be made without acknowledging and working towards eliminating the negative influences of Ego, Ignorance, Attraction, Repulsion and Fear of Death in your life.

The goal of this meditation-rite is to acknowledge the Kleshas, bring them to consciousness, and continue the work of releasing them. Intense visualization is encouraged. The long-term goal is to Cut Through the Kleshas towards Liberation.

**Note:** In the following, 'Neti Neti' translates as 'not this, not this!'

Review the section on setting up your Zonule (**Preparing the New Umbra Zonule,** below), and based on that, set up your sacred space. Banish as you wish, and create a protective sphere of magick. Meditate on what you will to accomplish in this rite. Then, begin by saying:

Om Gaang Ganapataye Namah
Lord Ganesh, Namaste!
O Wielder of divine AXE and NOOSE
Please Aid me here and now

in the Great Work of banishing the Kleshas
OM GAANG!!

**Face the East:** Open the right hand, and make a chopping motion while you visualize cleaving a knot of negativity:

OM GAANG!
I release and let go of all Attachment!
I am attached to nothing
Neti Neti! Svaha!

**Face the West:** Open the right hand, and make a chopping motion while you visualize cleaving a knot of negativity:

OM GAANG!
I release and let go of all Repulsion
I am Repulsed by nothing
Neti Neti! Svaha!

**Face the South:** Open the right hand, and make a chopping motion while you visualize cleaving a knot of negativity:

OM GAANG!
I release and let go of all Ignorance
I know Nothing.
Neti Neti! Svaha!

**Face the North:** Open the right hand, and make a chopping motion while you visualize cleaving a knot of negativity:

OM GAANG!
I release and let go of all Fear of Death
Nothing separates Death and Life
Neti Neti! Svaha!

**Center Yourself:** Close your eyes. Visualize Ganesh and the weapons he holds with his upraised hands. One is the noose, representing attraction. The other is the axe, representing removing obstacles. As you meditate, see the axe of Ganesh descending upon your crown, cleaving right through your body, through your Chakras, crown to earth. Then shout:

OM GAANG!
I release and let go of Ego
Cause of all unhappiness
'I' am No Thing. I am free.
Neti Neti! Svaha!

OM

Meditate on this for a time. Work through each Klesha, letting go of each with deep breaths. Feel your body relax as the weight of the Kleshas fades away. Then say:

All is One, One is None;
There is No Difference
Between my True Self and All Other things
There is Only OM.
I am Eternally Free, Ever and Always.
Svecchacharya!!
Svaha!

# ON KUNDALINI

*"The Manipulative energy of desire, wisdom and action
(Iccha-Shakti, Jnana-Shakti and Kriya-Shakti)
Is called the Supreme Yoga of the Psychic Centers,
Presided over by the power of the Goddess Kundalini.
(Meaning: She who is coiled as is a serpent in sleep)
For she is the Devi of this our most spiritual path
And the ever-ascending way which leads to attainment.
It is also called Guhya Yoga by Kaulas because it is Secret
As a cave may be hidden in the mountains and is unknown
Yet not too difficult to find by those who seek it.
This is the yoga of the enjoyment of objects and aspects,
For our secret twilight language is full of symbolism.
So, to the uninitiated the Devi remains but latent power,
As is a serpent when it is coiled and asleep.
Hence, She is called Kundalini and Kulini
Residing in the body and also the In-group,
For they represent spiritual unity to be attained."*

*— The Tantra of Blowing the Mind,*
*Gurudev Dadaji Mahendranath,*
*internationalnathorder.org/the-tantra-of-blowing-the-mind*

Kundalini is a term often mentioned in Tantra books and websites without clarity; thus, it is very misunderstood. Tantra is often conflated with the concept of 'raising Kundalini.'

The expanding mythos of Kundalini is over-hyped, confusing and mixes up factual discourse with the ancient Tantric 'twilight language' of aphorism, symbolism and poetic alliteration. This 'twilight language' offers hidden truths in symbolic form, and sometimes, intentionally misleading statements for the uninitiated. If you are familiar with alchemical texts, you will find a similar sort of twilight language, referring to everything with symbolic and colorful names to both hide and reveal chemical, sexual and spiritual processes.

It is not the goal of this book to teach Kundalini Yoga. That is impossible in any book. Kundalini requires a Guru, time and intense focus. However, as you move forward with your work in Tantra, you will expand your skills and perceptions, and will experience the wave of intense energy that flows upward through your body during various practices. As you have these experiences, you will see that you have been working with the fabled Kundalini energy all along.

Let's begin with the fact that there is no 'serpent' involved. It is only a symbol representing the energy that flows through your body, especially your nervous system. Some believe that there are many kinds of energy that manifest in your body, but in essence, they are all seen as Devi, the Supreme Goddess, identical with Adi Shakti. The energy that flows through your mind and body and keeps it functioning is the energy that manifests the whole cosmos. That is the Adi Shakti, also referred to as the 'cosmic fire' or Prakriti, the fire of all creation.

We see this primal Goddess as supreme because all things manifest as energy. It is in matter—or the physical manifestation of that cosmic power—that Shiva manifests as the earthing of that energy as the Bindu (the center or 'anchor') for that energy. The Kundalini 'serpent' is thus pictured as red, symbolizing vibrant life, and is identical with 'the red goddess' Tripurasundari, also known as Lalita Devi, she who plays, as you will see. This 'red serpent' reveals that the life energy of the cosmos is in constant swirling play as it is within our body, moving and shifting as different parts of the body are maintained by this flow of power.

Like electricity we use daily, Kundalini is bioelectric energy that pervades and regulates out body. Through willed practices and training, you can focus and direct the electricity coursing through your body which can be focused and channeled up your spine, the densest bundle of nerves, to activate and open your mind. That is Kundalini.

Tantric practices for this work often include special breathing, physical Asanas (postures), key Mantras (sounds), Mudras (hand gestures), meditations, visualizations, and so on. Tantrics seek to gently encourage the unity and upward focus of the collective energy and power to light up our higher brain centers. This should be done carefully, with meditative focus and physical and magickal exercises. Part of the process involves removing mental, physical and emotional energy blockages. The result is the ability to arouse power, focus it, and 'direct the arrow' of 'serpent' energy from the base Chakra to the crown, up the spinal column. In this way Samadhi (liberation) can be attained.

There are three 'energetic' paths of the central nervous system that the 'lightning' of Kundalini uses to arise. They are the two energetic meridians (Nadi) on either side of the spinal column—called Ida (lunar feminine) and Pingala (solar masculine)—and the crucial middle pillar or Sushumna which, not coincidentally, flows up through the spine and into and through the brain. In traditional Kundalini Yoga, the balance of Ida and Pingala, linked to right and left nostril breathing practices (Pranayama), are balanced, and in this way the Kundalini surge of power is made to flow directly up the Sushumna (spinal nerves) like a serpent arising through the ubiquitous seven Chakras emerging at the crown.

The 7-Chakra system is only one system, however. There are hundreds of Chakras in our body, each with a Bindu or eye to be opened. I have seen 4, 9, 12 and more Chakra systems, often varying with the deity you are working with. Everyone is familiar with the often misrepresented 7-Chakra system (minus the rainbow please!), and that is fine. However, we focus on three body-center Chakras, as you'll see.

There is no one 'true' path to working with Kundalini (though many sources claim there is). Some focus on the need for sexual union to 'get' Kundalini. I guess it's because sex sells, but doing so without knowing what you are doing could be dangerous. Buddhist and Taoist texts sometimes describe Kundalini Dhyana (illumination experiences) occurring spontaneously during deep meditation, without conscious cause, like a Zen Satori experience.

This is all I will say about Kundalini practice. I have addressed it in this book because it is part of Tantra. I personally have had Kundalini experiences, some intensely positive, some not so much, due to my ignorance at that time. Kundalini Yoga is not something that can be taught from a book. If you are intent on working with Kundalini, know that the Tantric practices in this book prepare you to do this, and you will experience the flowing currents of Kundalini at times as you do your work. If you wish to concentrate on Kundalini Yoga, I suggest that you research it carefully and find a legitimate Guru who takes the time to know you well and who can work with you directly. So, I leave it up to you, to explore the path of the Fire Serpent. Please see the **Bibliography** as well.

**A final note:** As you work in your Tantric temple-space, using the techniques and practices that will be introduced in the next section, you will get to know the feel of Kundalini Devi's energy. Keep in mind that this energy is pervasive, and 'raising the Kundalini' is but *one use* of this energy. Let all energy flow naturally as it will in your work. Don't seek to manipulate it, but simply become aware of it, and remember the patterns of such energy flows in connection with specific techniques.

Before every meditation session, do body stretches. Pretend it is a pre-workout at the gym. In this way you will 'unblock' your muscles and nervous system so this energy can flow smoothly through your whole system. As you monitor the energy flows, let your Guardian Spirit guide you. If the energy starts to feel too jittery or uncomfortable, stop that exercise and do rhythmic breathing (Pranayama) to calm things. Alternate nostril breathing helps to balance the different paths from the base to the crown of your body to keep the energy unblocked, balanced, focused and flowing gently as it needs to.

# TANTRIC TRIPLICITIES

## The Three Gunas, The Three Shaktis,
## The Three Bindus: Sun/Moon/Fire

*"Hindu tantras are discourses between Shiva and Shakti, the male and female aspects of divinity whose play creates the entire universe. The Jnanasankalini Tantra...outlines the dynamics of this interplay. Of particular importance...is the emphasis placed on the syllable Om, made up of the three Sanskrit letters A U M. These represent Shiva, Shakti and their union and can also be represented by the three Gunas or qualities well known as rajas, tamas and Sattvas."*

— *shivashakti.com/jnana.htm*

*"Shiva and Shakti are Fire and Moon bindus and the contact of both causes the Hardhakala to flow, which becomes the third bindu, Sun. ... She [the Great Goddess] is every kind of Shakti, including Iccha (will), Jnana (knowledge) and Kriya (action)."*

— *shivashakti.com/hridabst.htm*

The Three Gunas, the Three Shaktis, and the Three Spiritual Powers (representing the Sun, Moon & Fire) are often discussed together in Tantra. Balancing these three powers is crucial for spiritual and magickal success. Shiva's Trishul (trident), with its three points, represents the union of the Three Gunas (primal elements), the Three Bindus (forces), and the Three Shaktis (Will, Knowledge & Action). Some suggest that the Trishul of Shiva symbolizes other 'triplicities' such as the Three States of Consciousness—wakefulness, sleeping and deep unconscious sleep. All of these triplicities are distinct philosophical and magickal concepts, yet, as is so much in the 'Twilight World' of Tantra, they are interconnected.

For further clarity, research each of these 'threefold' divine aspects, keeping in mind that you will find many points of view! Remember, Tantra is primarily a magickal system of uniting with the divine, and embraces many unique, visionary viewpoints.

## THE GUNAS

'Gunas' means 'special qualities,' and is translated as 'threads or strands.' In Tantra, the Gunas are seen as primal elements or forces that are woven together to form the universe and everything within it. In the Tantric work you do, you will be weaving these forces. The Gunas are roughly analogous to the Three Alchemical Elements of Sulphur, Salt & Mercury (Rajas, Sattvas and Tamas respectively) presented in Western magick.

Each of the three Gunas has its own special attributes:
- Tamas (stability/darkness/calm)
- Rajas (activity/intensity/fierceness)
- Sattvas (consciousness/purity/spirituality)

All are aspects of the Great Goddess, Prakriti (the Creative Fire), the fiery Adi Shakti that manifests all creation. Thus, our world manifests as the three interacting Gunas in constant play. In combination, these three elements or qualities make up all things, and different Gunas tend to be more dominant than others at different times. In meditation and Tantric work, we seek to balance these three powers. After all, if Knowledge, Will and Action are not balanced, how can you succeed at anything?

## THREE POWERS OR SHAKTIS

We have introduced the three Shaktis; now let's dig a bit deeper so you can see how it fits with the work of Tantra. The three powers of the supreme goddess (Knowledge, Will, Action) are identified as the Three Shaktis or aspects of the Great Goddess who are conjoined with Shiva. Thus, the Great Goddess is called Adi Shakti, or great primal Shakti. Keep in mind that while Shakti is the name of the

Great Primal Goddess, it can also refer to 'the cosmic energy of the universe,' or refer to a female Tantric partner. As we discussed, all Tantric goddesses are different aspects of the One Goddess: Adi Shakti or Maha Devi; and all Tantric gods are One God: Great Shiva, the Adi Nath (Great Lord) or Maha Deva. Shakti and Shiva are two sides of the same Tantric coin, being really One truth: OM.

The Three Shaktis of Shiva are his triple goddess-mates, but also his emanations. These Three Shaktis are the core powers of Tantra, and everything in this book relies on the balancing and conscious work with these three because they are the manifestations of our consciousness, power and magickal effectiveness as Tantrics. In the end, they help us achieve Liberation. To reiterate, they are:

**JNANA (Knowledge):** Not in the sense of intellectual knowledge, but closer to the idea of *Gnosis*—direct knowledge of the divine and of human consciousness. Such True Knowledge encompasses deep Instinct, Intuition and Insight.

**ICCHA (Will):** Not what you want to do or wish to do, but rather True Will—that which you are *meant* to do, your true Path in this life. Your Iccha is influenced by Karma and Dharma, if you believe in reincarnation. Importantly, your True Will helps your Atman (Guardian Spirit) express who 'you' truly are, and accomplish what your Great Work is in this life. We discover and stay attuned to our True Will through our Guardian Spirit, our inner Guru, the spark of God that is within us. This is why creating a positive link and communication with your Guardian Spirit is the most important initial work in Tantra.

**KRIYA (Action!):** Represents the action of atoms, of cosmic events, of physical movements, and the actions of your life from birth through life, and even in death. All things move all the time; change is the great constant. Kriya is also the call to action to Tantrics to put things into practice and strive to get off our asses and get things done! Meditating is great, exercising is just as important. Kriya-Action means regular mundane and spiritual action in the world—making a living, working at building relationships, and moving our bodies and minds to keep them fit, as well as Yoga, ritual work, and so on. Kriya manifests as real effort, and this includes the drive and discipline of doing Tantric work.

Balancing these different forces in life is crucial to Tantra. Knowledge with no Action or Will leaves you a hidden intellectual who only contemplates life. Action with no Will or Knowledge leaves your uncontrolled energies and actions without clear thought or purpose. Will with no Action or Knowledge makes you overbearing with no plan of accomplishing something (Action) nor concrete information (Knowledge). You likely know people who are overly focused on one of these Shaktis to the detriment of the others; it is not uncommon. We focus on these three Shaktis to remind ourselves that when living our lives, we must monitor and balance what we are doing and manifesting so we achieve equipoise and happiness. All it takes is constant balancing, watchfulness and a lot of meditation!

*Sun, Moon, Fire: The Sun (Devi) and The Moon (Deva) Embrace, Manifesting Their Fiery Union—Aum!*

## THE THREE GREAT POWERS/BINDUS: SPIRITUAL SUN—MOON—FIRE

One of the most important symbols of Tantra (and Nath Tantrika especially) is the symbol of the sun and moon conjoined with a halo of fiery solar rays. Together the conjoining of sun, moon and fire form an image that is an ancient and powerful symbol of divine Unity. It encodes the union of goddess and god (sun & moon) in the fire of passionate union. As one image, it reveals the unity that is

OM, your Self or the integration of your Guardian Spirit. In this one icon we see the whole Tantric cosmos.

In the Tantric twilight language of symbol, metaphor, archetypes and mythic wonder, things often mean more than one thing at a time, and so images, ideas and aspects always remain fluid, visionary and somewhat intuitive.

Thus, there are many ways to translate this symbol. Shiva wears the crescent moon; the goddess Adi Shakti can be seen as the solar power that made everything; and the fire is the energy we call Kundalini. Tantric cosmology and symbolism are liminal and dreamlike. The great goddess embodies and is revealed as primal cosmic energy (Shakti) or cosmic fire, and is associated with the sun. In some of her other aspects the great goddess is sometimes connected with the moon. One such goddess, Lalita Devi, symbolizes and manifests the Kalas (emanations and powers) of the moon through female Tantrics. The union of Shiva and Shakti is thus the union of sun and moon, and results in the 'third' form, sometimes called Prakriti, the fire of their creative union that pervades and makes the cosmos. On these esoteric levels, intellectual analysis dissolves, for in truth Shiva *is* Shakti and Shakti *is* Shiva and their union is OM, everything.

I was offered this reduced Sun/Moon/Fire formula by a Tantric, stated in a more primal fashion as:

Moon/Silver/Sperm/Shiva/Deva (White) +
Sun/Gold/Female Blood-Emanations/Devi (Red)
→ Fire/Union/Orgasm-Kundalini/Union-Fire (Black)

The attribute of 'black' at first threw me until I learned that it refers to the charred ashes of the cremation ground. Another sage pointed out that the union of sun and moon in astronomy results in an eclipse umbra (black shadow) with a corona, the one time we can see the flame about the two. I offer all of this seemingly contradictory symbolism to take you into the 'Twilight World' of Tantric imagery. This free-flowing symbolism is part of the Tantric world rooted in the deep, unconscious mind.

§ § §

In the next section of this book—which focuses on *doing* Tantra—you will utilize the 'Three Body Chakra system' described in the chart below. This system integrates the three Gunas, the three Shaktis and the three Great Bindus of Sun-Moon-Fire. From crown to base, these three Chakra centers are seen as the Moon Center, Sun Center, and Fire Center. Using these energetic ideals and our Will, we may accomplish our magical and meditative work to attain awareness and liberation. By conjoining our alchemical Tantric work while focusing on the powerful aspects of the eternal triple aspects that show up so often, we can more deeply focus on balancing and integrating our spiritual and magical goals.

Keep in mind that in the lineages I follow, all such triplicities, in the end, represent the cosmic dance of the Goddess about the calm CenterPoint of Shiva; to her, from her, all things.

Note that each section of the chart below shows the three primal Goddesses with their 'seed vibration' (HREEM, etc.) also mated with an aspect of Shiva.

(This reminds me of a final moment in a conversation with a Western ceremonial magick friend on this topic:

**R:** So, Wait! Are Shiva and Shakti…deities of the sun, the moon, fire, everything, nothing, all things or…? Which is which?

**Me:** Yes.

**R:** WHAT?

**Me:** It depends. You can see it several ways. Remember first that Shiva and Shakti are the same—One thing, OM—and thus they are all things. There is no clear right answer. Shiva and Shakti have multiple aspects, both fiery and calm, solar and lunar. She is the fire of creation, but channels the lunar flows of magick. He is the fiery red form of Rudra, and the calm lunar-white god of ecstasy, Shankar.

**R:** Arrrgh! This is crazy! So, what is the answer for each deity?

**Me:** That is up to you to discover. No person is always sunny, cool, fiery or calm. Shiva and Shakti, like all mysteries, cannot be codified by aspect, planet or strict categorization! They contain multitudes. This is Tantra!

The following 'Chart of Triplicities' offers one interpretation of all the aspects and forms discussed above and may prove useful in your Work as long as you do not see it as being the definitive 'truth' or 'right way' to see these powerful ideals in conjunction.

| THREE SHAKTIS CHART (Aspects of Supreme Shiva Added to Goddess Forms) | | |
|---|---|---|
| MOON | SUN | FIRE |
| JNANA= KNOWLEDGE | ICCHA= WILL | KRIYA= ACTION |
| SHREENG | HREENG | KREENG |
| DREAM | WAKE | SLEEP/TRANCE |
| MAINTENANCE | DESTRUCTION | CREATION |
| TAMAS | SATTVAS | RAJAS** |
| SHAKTI* (w/Shiva) | LALITA (w/AdiNath) | KALI (w/Rudra) |
| WHITE | RED | BLACK |
| HEAD CENTER | BODY CENTER | BASE CENTER |

\* Jwalamuhki/Maha/Lakshmi/Shri
\*\* was Sattvas/Tamas/Raja

— Three Shaktis of Supreme Shiva,
*Yantra,* pg. 81, Mandrake Press

## The Three Tantric Gunas

*While the promise of the Orthodoxies is heaven*
*One never knows if those promises are kept.*
*The Tantric way offers surety*
*Bliss, not promises—for this is the gift of Shiva:*
*We are a cult of ecstasy!*
*To us real worship of the gods and goddesses is joy-in-action*
*The Love and Will of free spirits open to happiness*

## TANTRA FOR ALL

*Cultivating Ecstasy and awareness in the moment
Here and Now—not in some death-cult future heaven
For real bliss and the open heart of ecstasy
Is the Love of the Guru for all Beings
Is the love of the Parents for each other and their child
Is the love of friends and Tantric playmates
And Shiva with Shakti offers the paths to Ecstasy here and
   now—and they are 3:*

*The work of Rajas in Bliss-Work manifests as focused
   sexuality,
Sex and the erotic alchemy in every form leading to
   Samadhi
The Action Shakti!*

*The Bliss-work of Sattvas manifests as The Bacchic Trance
   Dance
Ecstatic Dance and Wild Heart Music, becoming the play
   of Lalita, the rhythm of the tides and winds and
   seasons, all leading to Samadhi.
The Will Shakti!*

*The Bliss-Work of Tamas, of opening the mind, the third
   eye, the crown center unfolding lotus of consciousness,
   this is the work of the sacred Entheogens of Bhola Nath
The trance-plants Earth Mother Bhu Devi gives us to reach
   Samadhi
Jai Soma! Bom Shankar! The Knowledge Shakti Ma!*

*Uniting these are the Bliss-work of Destroying the Three
   Cities, uniting the Fire, Sun and Moon, dancing with
   the three lovely Shaktis!
Embracing the cremation ground Smashan work of
   complete detachment—Life and Death and beyond—
Om Maha Shakti!!! Svaha!
OM*

*Thus: Moving past Ecstasy to Awakening—in joy and
   bliss—Svaha.*

# PART THREE

## RAJAS—ACTION: DOING TANTRA

# THE UMBRA ZONULE: YOUR SACRED TANTRIC SPACE

> *"The practical directions related to the Umbra Zonule could go on endlessly since the entire universe is based on the interplay of correspondences. The ritual substances are classified as the five elements of which our world is composed. These are Earth, Air, Fire, Water and Mind. When the four mundane elements are assembled, the fifth element attains to its fullest power. Here we mean power as expressing itself as Will."*
>
> — The Londinium Temple Strain,
> Gurudev Dadaji Mahendranath,
> *internationalnathorder.org/the-londinium-temple-strain*

The Tantric space where you will regularly meditate and do your work is called the 'Umbra Zonule,' which means a small, sacred temple-space (Zonule) where the Umbra (shadow) between light and dark reside. Your Umbra Zonule will be where you ritually manifest, through your meditations and other Tantric work, a divine 'Twilight World' of spiritual adventures. The word Umbra sometimes refers to an entity which 'shadows' a person, referring to one's 'daemon' or Guardian Spirit which helps protect, guard, empower and facilitate your work in the Zonule.

The first step is to decide where and how it will be set up, and how you will prepare and bless your new Umbra Zonule.

## Considerations for the Umbra Zonule

Dadaji Mahendranath outlined the basics of how to set up and do Tantric practices in an essay called *The Londinium Temple Strain*. I offer his instructions in my own words below.

The first step is to choose a place for your sacred space. A dedicated room is best, but using part of another room will work. Keep it as separate as possible from the rest of the house or apartment.

The Umbra Zonule is your 'magical laboratory' for Tantra. It will grow in power, and becomes the center of your spiritual universe, your *axis mundi* and holy place. It needs to be used consistently to build the power and intensity you'll want to access.

In the center of the Zonule will be placed the Dragon Seat where you will sit. This marks the centerpoint within the circle of the cosmos, like the centerpoint of every Yantra.

The Dragon Seat is represented by a natural blanket, a meditation pillow or a chair. It is where you will sit in meditation as the whole universe spins about you, so make it comfortable. The small blanket or pillow or other 'seat' should be 100% natural material; wool is traditional. White is common, but any color is appropriate—white and red are the colors of Shiva and Shakti respectively. Your Dragon Seat is very important, and can be taken anywhere you wish to do your practices or meditate. Constant use of your Dragon Seat and Zonule will make your temple quickly become a protecting, empowering and healing refuge.

Before the Dragon Seat is the sacred altar. Traditionally it faces North or East. However, much depends on where you are setting up your Zonule and what works for you. In the end, any direction is acceptable, especially if you have limited options.

The altar is the place where microcosm and macrocosm meet, the balancing between you and the universe. The altar is your 'laboratory table' and functions as the meeting place or nexus between you and your Guardian Spirit, as well as the Gods and Spirits. The altar is where your Work is done, and is the focus of concentration, visualization, devotion and magick. With frequent use, your Zonule space, Dragon Seat, and altar will grow in power and energy very quickly. The meditative and magical practices you do in your Umbra Zonule are what Tantra is all about. What you do and when you do it is wholly up to you and the guidance of your Guardian Spirit. It is best if you meditate daily and do other Tantric work as you will.

Dadaji Mahendranath described what should be on the altar, and they include simple symbols of the four elements—Air, Earth, Fire and Water—as well as the fifth 'element,' Spirit. These symbols can be as basic or complex as you wish. My altar has an incense burner for stick incense, a pantacle or disc of clay representing Earth, a ceramic cup for water or other liquids, and a candle in a nice holder representing fire.

Finally, I have a Lingam & Yoni (Yoni-Lingam) to represent Spirit and the union of the God and Goddess. This is traditional, but something simpler, like a crystal or special stone, would work as well to represent Spirit or OM. Of course, you can add more items to the altar. I often have images of deities, flowers, offerings of fruit, and more.

In correspondence, Dadaji Mahendranath wrote that the minimum items for Tantric ritual work would be a *flame* (representing the Yoni or vulva of the Goddess), and a *stick of incense* (representing the Lingam or phallus of Shiva). Intent and creativity illuminate our work. I have done powerful, impromptu Pujas on the beach by creating a simple Yoni-Lingam out of sand and using fresh water, a shell and a flower. Intent, focus, will and love are all you need.

Later in this third section of this book there are full Puja rituals where a god or goddesses is invited into the temple to be honored. Each deity has a different Yantra and prefers different colors, food, drinks, incense, symbols, and so on. A little research and meditative intuition will be your best guide. Your Guardian Spirit will offer guidance as well, but some planning and study will help!

In his writings, Gurudev Mahendranath also notes that "Nothing which has been written should be regarded as fixed or final as ideas. It is better that every experimenter adapts the fundamentals to suit their own fantasy and imagination." Tantra is a set of ancient, unbroken traditions and practices that have stood the test of time. Take advantage of that, and then get creative.

Over time, your Umbra Zonule functions as a psychic battery, a cauldron of energy and an alchemical lab. After a time, simply sitting in it will activate the spiritual and magickal energies you have been invoking. I often slide into an immediate meditative state when I sit upon my Dragon Seat.

If you allow other people to enter your Zonule, they must be in perfect harmonious relationship with you so as not to change the energies that will grow there. Think of a 'pristine' laboratory. If you decide to work with a partner or a Kula (a Tantric group), you may need a larger Zonule, of course—a separate room is best.

As Dadaji Mahendranath noted, "In all magick laboratory work and experiments, a new and higher level of thinking is essential for success."

Before you begin to set up your Zonule, consider every factor about that space. Are the windows, lights and other elements of the space conducive to your goals? What decorative items will you want in it? You will need items that are pleasing and conducive to your Tantric practices.

## Preparing the New Umbra Zonule

The first step for working within your Umbra Zonule is to thoroughly clean the area, and then consecrate it to the divine. Simple salt and water are powerful tools for removing all other psychic and physical influences. The area should be a *tabula rasa*—a completely renewed place—before beginning your work.

### Banishing/Cleansing

First, clean, vacuum and declutter the area where your Zonule will be. The space should then be banished psychically. What follows is a useful and traditional two-step banishing procedure.

1. Put some pure salt in a bowl of pure natural water while deeply chanting 'OM' several times and visualizing light filling the water. While still chanting OM, sprinkle the salt water about the area; use a clean, white cloth to wipe the area. Continue vibrating OM as you visualize intense light filling the area, and banishing all other energies. When you are done, take the dirty water outside and dump it away from trees or grass. Say SVAHA! (So Be It!) in a loud voice.

2. When you are done, stand in the middle of the space. Breathe and center yourself. Then hold up one hand with the index and point-

ing fingers extended up, and the other fingers folded together. This is called the Sword Mudra. In turn face East, South, West, North and Center, strike the open palm of your other hand with the two extended fingers and shout PHUT! As you do this, visualize a lightning strike that chases away all negativity.

## Sanctifying

The next step is to bless and empower your Zonule using 'Blessing Water'—pure water with a bit of lavender, sandalwood oil, or another oil of your choice in it. Rosewater, which is easy to find, is another powerful blessing liquid. As with the cleansing, the blessing water is charged by chanting 'OM.' It is then sprinkled clockwise about the area while again vibrating OM several times. Another Mantra I recommend for blessing is: SHANTI SHANTI SHANTI, meaning 'Peace, Peace, Peace.'

## Setting Up the Zonule

Things you will need to set up your Umbra Zonule include:

- Clean clothing to wear; red or white is best
- Your 'Dragon Seat' where you will sit in meditation and when doing practices. It can be a large pillow, a meditation pillow, a chair or another sort of comfortable place to sit for long periods
- An appropriate altar to place before the Dragon Seat
- A small vase of flowers for the altar, as you like
- Items representing the five elements:
  - An incense burner with stick or other incense (Air)
  - A candle in a nice holder (Fire)
  - An appropriate cup or bowl (Water)
  - A pantacle, flat stone or similar items (Earth)
  - And in the center, something to represent Spirit or OM (a small white stone, or best, a Yoni-Lingam)

Once the area is banished and blessed, the Umbra Zonule should be set up in this manner:

First, stand in the center of the space and clearly visualize a circle of positive, glowing energy about you. To empower your visualization and reinforce the glowing circle, remove your shoes and walk intently about the circle clockwise while visualizing a glowing circle and chanting OM. When you are done, stand with your arms up and eyes closed, and 'see' the circle glowing on the floor become a sphere of light filling the area with you in the center.

Then, place the Dragon Seat in the center with the chant of OM MANI PADME HUM (The Jewel is in the Center of the Lotus).

Now, visualize the circle/sphere and the Dragon Seat as the glowing centerpoint of light in the center.

Next, the altar should be set up in front of the Dragon Seat, facing the direction you have chosen (North or East being best). Place the elemental symbols you have chosen on the altar, and in the center of them place the small white stone or the Yoni-Lingam representing Spirit or OM, the union of the God and Goddess.

Other items may be added as you like. When the altar is set up, pause and chant OM SVAHA! (OM, It Is Done!), then clap your hands and see your completed Zonule as a full temple glowing with light and ready to be activated.

### Activating the Zonule

Sit in the center, breathe deeply, and close your eyes. Chant OM for a time while visualizing your Guardian Spirit as a glowing star in your heart. Breathe. Then visualize the star glowing in your heart expanding and filling the whole circle with light so that it becomes a sphere of light that encompasses your Zonule. As you do so, chant three times (3x):

OM MANI PADME HUM

Then see the sphere of light become brighter about you, reinforcing your physical and spiritual Zonule.

Now, sit upon your Dragon Seat in the center of the sphere. Chant 3x:

TAT TVAM ASI (I Am 'That'; i.e., the universe)
OM!

Light your candle and incense. Chant 3x:

OM SHANTI SHIVA SHAKTI (Om! The union of Shiva and Shanti. Peace)

Now, sit, relax and meditate in your new, sacred space.

Close your eyes as you like. See yourself as the center of the universe. You may meditate as you like or just sit, relax and open your mind.

The key is to feel the nurturing, protective, sacred space, and detach from your normal chaotic thinking. Calm your mind, breathe slowly, relax your whole body, and open your spirit. You are completely safe here, free of all the negative stresses of the outside world. You are between the worlds, in liminal space—Twilight. Let your aura expand and fill the sphere you have created.

When you are ready to 'come back' to the mundane world and finish your activation, bow three times. Each time take a drop of water from the cup and sprinkle it on the Yoni-Lingam or white spirit stone. With each bow say:

> HONOR TO MY GUARDIAN SPIRIT
> HONOR TO THE GODS AND GODDESSES
> HONOR TO THE CRYSTAL LINE OF TANTRIC GURUS
>    WHO INFORM THIS WORK!

Raise your hands, place your palms together before your heart, and visualize blessings flying out to all living beings and say:

> BALANCE, WEALTH, PLEASURE AND LIBERATION TO
>    ALL BEINGS—OM!

Finally, place your hands on the floor and bow deeply. Let all the excess energies you have conjured flow into Mother Earth (Bhu Devi) and whisper:

> BHU DEVI, TO YOU, FROM YOU ALL THINGS!

Gently pat the floor and say:

> SVAHA!

You are done and your Zonule is blessed, activated and glowing! Well done!

## Some General Reminders About Work in the Umbra Zonule

Before diving into the specific hands-on practices and techniques you will use in your Zonule, here are some general suggestions and a bit of review. As the circle of the Umbra Zonule is the cosmos—the expanding wonder of all creation—the Dragon Seat is the center of that circle and thus a doorway to a new, different and expansive world. The Zonule can be contracted or expanded. It grows more vital and more intense—energetically, psychologically and spiritually—the more often you use it. Always keep it clean and peaceful; avoid using it for other things.

### On Meditating

Sitting quietly in meditation is the best spiritual exercise possible, and should be done daily. Meditation is the opening of the deep mind that allows everything else to happen in Tantra. The chaos, confusion and negativity surrounding us in this chaotic world can blind us to the simple truth that all is divine and full of magical energies. Meditation shows us this truth. Shri Gurudev Dadaji Mahendranath says:

> *"Intensity, Stability, Quiet, Determination, and Expectancy are the qualities for meditation. It must be obvious that contact with another world or a different plane can only be done if and when the mind is in a condition to be receptive. Thus, the process of calming the mind and stopping the normal confused processes is an essential condition for all magickal operations and spiritual awareness, contact, and attainment on all levels."*
>
> — *Londinium Temple Strain,*
> Gurudev Dadaji Mahendranath,
> *internationalnathorder.org/the-londinium-temple-strain*

### On the Three Modes of Zonule Work

There are three modalities or kinds of work done in the Umbra Zonule. Think about their differences, and be clear on what you are going to do and how you will do it. The three modes are: **Expansion, Absorption** and **Stillness.**

**Expansion** means active magical work such as spellcasting or the projection of consciousness for energetic work—e.g., distance viewing or the healing of others. In this case you sit upon the Dragon Seat and ritually project your will outward to spiritually influence, communicate, observe or explore. Some traditionally call this Evoking.

**Absorption** means internally-directed, energetic and mystical work, such as calling protection, healing or wealth energy to yourself; or conjuring a spirit, god or a goddess into your Zonule to work or communicate with. Some call this Invoking.

**Stillness,** the final modality, is less a mode of work and more a deep inner peace or internal alchemy. Think of it as the fulcrum or still point between Projection and Absorption. It is the closed 'vessel of personal transformation,' and a calm center of silence and self-directed, internal contemplation.

**Note:** In larger rituals (Pujas), Expansion, Absorption and Stillness may all be used, but each in its own place. For example, you may banish, then send forth a spell, then call a deity into your Zonule for advice, and then meditate. The key is to be aware of what you are doing and why you are doing it in each part of the ritual.

Through these three modalities of magick you can manifest healing, growth and real changes in your life and in the lives of others. You can influence events and situations, and so improve your life. Through the power of imagination, power and intention, while focusing your will and love, you can begin the internal and external practice of Tantric magick in your Zonule. This includes getting to know the spiritual world of deities, spirits, elementals, powers, and so on. As you become more conscious, confident and educated on Tantra, this new 'twilight' world will unfold around you.

## On the Guardian Spirit

Your Guardian Spirit is a center and key to all your work. It is your True Self, your soul or Atman. Connecting with it and opening communication with it unlocks the rest of Tantric magick for you. The Guardian Spirit is your guide to all of the gods, spirits and powers. In sacred texts like the *Guru Gita,* the Guardian Spirit is actually the supreme teacher or Guru, and is referred to as the 'true Shiva.' In deep meditation, when you are 'one with your Guardian,' you *are* the center of the cosmos and thus one with the supreme Guru—and so one with OM. So, take time *every day* to build a strong relationship with your Guardian Spirit; it will become your Guru, which is why the term 'Guru' is translated as 'Light revealed from Darkness.'

A simple way to connect with your Guardian Spirit is to meditate on it as a shining star within your heart, as you have done. You may craft a simple heartfelt invocation of your Guardian Spirit and recite it to bring divine guidance, something like:

*OM! Guardian Spirit, be with me*
*Guide me, protect me, that I may see.*

The Mantra OM MANI PADME HUM is very powerful for this work, and an even simpler Mantra to connect with your inner Self is this potent Tantric Mantra:

*GURU OM*

As you and your Guardian Spirit forge a deeper bond, remember to write down all communications you receive. The more you focus on this, the deeper the connection will be, and soon you will begin to really hear the quiet 'inner guiding voice' of your Guardian Spirit. Dadaji Mahendranath noted that "many people practice meditation and think they have contacted a God or Goddess, but usually it is their own Guardian Spirit." Many religions say you are born with a Guardian Spirit (or Angel) to be your mentor and guide throughout this life and beyond. Animists and Pagans have held this same belief for aeons, and praise the idea of connecting with one's 'Daemon' or 'Genius.'

## Art & Journaling in the Umbra Zonule

Keep a Journal and suitable pens or drawing tools by the altar in your Zonule. During your Tantric work, your inner mind will open, and your Guardian Spirit and the gods will reveal many things from your imagination that will be forgotten if they are not written down or drawn. This is why the Journal is important. It can be used as a place to write poetry, invocations, art or information that will help you expand your power and your work. Once you leave the Twilight World of your Zonule, you will be happy to have drawn or written down what flowed out of you during your practices. When emerging from liminal states, we often forget the insights and images that come directly to us from our inner mind, much as dreams evaporate upon waking. These divinely inspired inspirations can be seen as the gold we are making in our alchemical laboratory, *but only if you write or draw it for later review!* As you venture deeper into your magical world, some of the artistic or poetic things you note down while in deep meditative states may form the basis for future rituals, spells or other work. This is the weaving of Tantra.

> *"When the mind awakens, we become aware*
> *That we have been brainwashed and conditioned*
> *From our very birth to accept society,*
> *Its morals, conventions, system and ideas,*
> *Its pattern of behavior and stupid nationalism,*
> *Its caste system of unfair social standards,*
> *The rule of right, privilege and preference,*
> *Of happiness as the exclusive right of a few*
> *And poverty, servitude and misery for most.*
> *None of these established patterns of society*
> *Can give expansion to any individual.*
> *They are worthless concepts for magickal life*
> *And those who seek the Cosmos must reject them."*
> — *The Magnum Opus of Twilight Yoga,*
> Gurudev Dadaji Mahendranath,
> *internationalnathorder.org/twilight-yoga-ii*

## PREPARATIONS & DISCIPLINES WITHIN THE UMBRA ZONULE

*"Hi! Ho! LET'S GO!"*
— The Ramones

This section of the book moves you to preparing your launching pad, and then to your first launch! You have learned about Tantra, and the stage is set. Now it is time to dive into full Tantric ritual work.

You have created your sacred space, the Umbra Zonule, and have had your first pleasant experience meditating there.

In the next section, you will expand your Tantric practices as you learn the full Zonule Rite, a daily Tantric ritual within which many new additional practices will be introduced and mastered by you. Your Zonule will become more powerful every day, and your work more amazing as you slowly explore and implement more practices. Once you get comfortable with the Zonule Rite, you will be further introduced to new practices and techniques step by step, as you master each in turn.

Each of these added techniques should be done for a time until you are successful and comfortable with it. Focusing on each new practice, one at a time, is important to master it. As each practice evolves, there will always be more to learn and experience.

The point is for you creatively integrate them once you are on your way into your daily ritual work. As you do so, your gods and Guardian Spirit will guide you further down the path as you do your True Will.

## Getting Comfortable in Your Zonule

Once you have set up your Umbra Zonule, cleared your altar space and blessed it, you can meditate while sitting on your Dragon Seat every day. Make sure there is clean water in the cup, some flowers and incense, and a candle to light. Spend a week or more getting used to your sacred space and the routine of being the 'jewel in the lotus' for a time every day. Initially, the only tool you need is your Journal as you note ideas, images, and so on that come to you. Don't worry about your meditation technique. Simply relax, center yourself, and be open to your inner voice.

## Tantra 'Tools'

To expand your practice, you will need a few things for your Zonule and ritual work. These sacred 'tools' are useful to focus and utilize your energy and will. Some are physical, some are conceptual, but all are 'tools' for achieving success in Tantra. You have already been briefly introduced to several. The purpose of these tools is to help focus and activate parts of your unconscious and superconscious mind in ways that let your power flow and manifest according to your Will. These items are ancient, often thousands of years old, and are common to many different Tantric sects and traditions. Be open to divine synchronicities that will become more common as you progress; this is your Guardian Spirit helping you along.

There is a short ritual at the end of this section for consecrating your tools. During your work in the Zonule, if you ask the gods for the tools and other items you need, the right items will often 'show up' in your daily life as you seek them. This has frequently happened to me.

### *More on Some Items You Already Know*

**The Dragon Seat:** You set up your Dragon Seat when you created and blessed your Umbra Zonule. It is recommended that only *you* sit upon your personal Dragon Seat to build up its power as often as you can. Once you start doing regular Tantric work, you may decide to choose a better, more appropriate, or more comfortable Dragon Seat. Explore options like a zafu, zabuton, a special chair, or even a carpet. It is important that you be comfortable and able to sit for hours.

**Elemental Symbols:** On the altar you have placed representations of the five elements. More possibilities about them will be open to you as you move forward.

> **Air.** Incense is almost always burned for Tantric work. In India and Nepal, three sticks are usually burned at one time as offerings during intense Tantric work, but I often use one stick when meditating; it is up to you. A nice, appropriate incense burner is a useful addition. Stick incense is most commonly used, but herbal or powder incense burned on charcoal is great too, and may offer more creativity. Don't use incense that is overpowering or distracting!
>
> **Fire.** A candle or a small oil lamp is used. Choose a holder or lamp that is appropriate for Tantra. If using candles (as I do), the color of the candles should be appropriate for the work you are doing. Begin with a white candle, and then adjust

depending on the deity or focus of the magick. Only burn the purest beeswax candles if you can; ghee or pure oil is fine if you use a lamp.

**Water.** A nice and appropriate Tantric cup should be chosen within which is new pure water every time the Zonule us used. If doing a special ritual or other magick, you may use another, more appropriate liquid.

**Earth.** Earth can be represented by a pantacle, a flat or sacred stone, or even by a small vase of flowers (though flowers should always be on the altar in some form).

**Spirit.** The Yoni-Lingam, as an image of the union of the God (Shiva) and Goddess (Shakti) is a key Tantric symbol for Spirit. Alternatively, a small white stone to represent the alpha ovule OM can represent Spirit. The choice is up to you. I use a Yoni-Lingam because it has multiple layers of meaning.

These five elements can also be seen as real magical 'tools' used during ritual. Several of the Tantric tools presented in this chapter have elemental attributes:

**Air.** Is represented by the trident (Trishul) or wand or staff used by Tantrics.

**Fire.** Is represented by a knife or sword.

**Water.** The sacred cup, bowl or appropriate ritual vessel is a powerful Goddess symbol and tool.

**Earth.** A Yantra can double as an elemental symbol of Earth and an active tool.

**Spirit.** A small white stone, or crystal, can represent Spirit, but the Yoni-Lingam is most useful for serious Tantric Magick.

**The Yoni-Lingam:** Fertility symbols may be the earliest symbols used in the ancient world. The most common are the Lingam (phallus) and the Yoni (vulva). Together they form a 'Yoni-Lingam'. Yoni-Lingams are often honored during Tantric rituals. Offerings are placed on the top of the Lingam which is set within the Yoni. Liquids are empowered in serious rituals by pouring them over a Yoni-Lingam, and then collected and drunk. The conjoined Yoni-

Lingam is the most ancient image of the God and Goddess, and are thousands of years old, thus revealing the primal nature of Tantra.

However, the Yoni-Lingam is more complex and sublime, and more than a symbol of sex; it reveals the cosmic union of the divine male and female (Shiva and Shakti) as the spiritual essence of the cosmos *embodied* in the union which creates new life. Like the venerated Yin/Yang image, this union reveals the non-dualism of Tantra: neither can exist without the other because they are one, OM.

It is only through spiritual attainment that we directly experience the understanding of this truth or gnosis.

The Yoni-Lingam in the center of the shrine on your altar reminds you of the unified cosmic truth of Shiva-Shakti, but also epitomizes the Nexus Mundi, the axis of the universe. In Tantra, this axis of the cosmos is also venerated as the holy mountain Kailash (aka Meru) upon whose peak reside Shiva and Shakti in peaceful, often erotic, union. On my altar, it is the symbol that represents all these things and the 'Divine Spirit' of Shiva and Shakti's as unity— OM. This is why all offerings are touched to, or placed on, the Yoni-Lingam.

### *Murti (A Statue or Image of a God or Goddess)*

A Murti is an image of a god, goddess or sacred spirit that you are working with. The Yoni-Lingam is a powerful Murti, possibly the most ancient image representing the powers of Shiva and Shakti in union. The Murti is often key to your work, and can be abstract, like a Yoni-Lingam, or it can show the god or goddess in human form. It can be printed or drawn on paper, engraved on metal, or made of wood, ceramic, stone, and so on. Once blessed, empowered and 'awakened' by Tantric ritual, the Murti becomes the vessel of the actual deity and is considered sacred.

Each god and goddess has many aspects, and thus, many images. When seeking out a Murti, you must know which aspect of the god or goddess that you are focusing on. As I do Sadhana (magickal practice) to the god Ganesh, I focus on a specific 'aspect' or form of Ganesh called Vinayaka, 'the god who removes obstacles.' There are dozens of forms of Ganesh, each with a slightly different aspect, purpose and power. Traditionally he is shown with a mouse. Some Tantric forms show him riding a lion or a tiger. Since all of our gods and goddesses have various forms, it might be best to start with simple Murtis that are very popular and easy to relate to.

If you are seeking to work on wealth magick with a deity like Lakshmi Devi, first do some research, and study Her various aspects and symbols. Take time to meditate on Her. Why are you seeking to get to know and work with Her? In meditation, think of her various images, and let yourself be drawn to that aspect of Her that feels right. Ask Her to guide you to the Murti that will help in your relationship. Afterwards, go online or peruse a shop that sells such things until you find the right one for you. She will let you know. As you search for images, be careful to choose reliable sources.

Murtis have a lot to teach us. For instance, they often show a god or goddess with their Vahana (symbolic animal 'vehicle'). (Every Tantric deity you will work with has a Vahana associated with it. The mouse, for example, is the Vahana of Ganesh; Lakshmi's is the owl; Shiva's is the Bull.) Murtis can also show you what offerings each deity likes. Like people, the gods all have preferences, and Murtis offer much information on a variety of things. Once you have formed a relationship with a deity, he or she will communicate who they are and what they wish. Sincerity, devotion and awareness are the keys to success in such work.

### *The Mala (Prayer Beads and a Talisman)*

A Mala is a string of beads that is a holy symbol of the Tantric, Buddhist and Hindu. A Mala is worn or carried as a talisman to protect and empower the wearer. It is also used to count Mantras (sacred words) and sounds when chanting. It is also empowering, and signifies your status as a Tantric practitioner (Sadhaka). Like the Dragon Seat, constant use will make it a powerful talisman and tool in your work.

There are 108 beads on most Tantric and Buddhist Malas. These represent the full circle of the starry sky, and specifically, the circle of 108 sacred stars that encircle our world. As you explore the Tantric universe, you'll often run into the number 108, a sacred number. Aside from the Mala, 108 epithets are often chanted to invoke various gods or goddesses. For example, *'108 Names of Shiva'* is one such invocation.

Why 108? As with many esoteric practices, there are several possible answers, but as a Tantric I have been told that there are three reasons:

First, the Mala represents the sacred stars about us, represented by the twelve constellations which are divided into nine arc segments called *Chandrakalas* (moon emanations) and 9 × 12 = 108.

The second reason we use the Mala is to distract our chattering ego ('monkey mind'). It gives our hand and autonomic nervous system something to do rather than interfere with our meditation. It is easier to focus on a Mantra to keep your chattering mind busy and so free your spirit. For this reason, we most often use a Mala to keep track of how many Mantras we are doing without having to mentally count; it avoids distractions. It is traditional to 'do' or 'chant one Mala' (a full circle of 108 repetitions) of a Mantra. Often, we do '3 Malas' of a chant, sometimes more. Every night, for example, I do '3 Malas' to honor the god because it is ritually called for, and three is an auspicious number in Tantra.

The third reason we use a Mala is to focus our body, heart and mind on *that* specific Mantra which is often the vibration of a specific deity. As we hold each bead and chant, that bead is the center of consciousness, and often of a specific deity. In this way we focus, imprint, empower and use divine energy.

As your Mala is used more frequently, it grows in power and intensity as an amulet. Wearing it protects and empowers you; hanging your Mala up in a place protects that area. You may have just one Mala or, like myself and most Tantrics I know, you may end up with several. I have a variety of Malas that I use for different gods, goddesses or purposes. Here are a few Malas I recommend that you begin with:

**Rudraksha Mala**—sacred to Shiva
**Sandalwood Mala**—sacred to many goddesses
**Crystal Mala**—sacred to OM and all the gods

You may also find Malas made of Tulsi (a sacred basil bush), bone, special seeds, and various gems, stones and other woods. Malas should never be made of plastic or artificial beads.

Almost always there is a final bead that sticks up, denoting the end of 108. It is often different from the other beads, and is called the 'Guru bead.' Guru indicates a teacher but *The* Guru is your Guardian Spirit, the spark of the divine within you.

### *Mantra*

'Mantra' is an ephemeral 'tool,' and translates as 'a sacred message, spell or advice.' While many Tantra tools are physical, it is Mantra and sound/vibration that makes all of them come alive in ritual practice. The primal, first Mantra is, of course, OM, the vibration/sound of all the cosmos. Vibration is the essence and origin of all things, and thus an important part of magick and of Tantra 'weaving.' All Mantras create a web of vibrational causality that embody all aspects of the universe and the gods and goddesses that fill the cosmos.

The Mantra keys have been handed to us by the ancient shamanic holy men and women of prehistory who developed, crafted, tested, encoded and practiced Tantric 'vibration weaving,' as well as Yoga and other practices. Such ancient wisdom, through millennia of invasions and political, social and religious changes, evolved into two systems: the older strata of spiritual thought—Tantra—and the more modern religion called Sanatana Dharma ('the eternal way') which is called Hinduism by those in the West. Both share many aspects, like Mantras, and many 'esoteric' magickal practices which originated in Tantra were adopted by Hinduism, while many are hidden and not for the masses. Mantra and vibration are seen as a primary tool of spiritual practice, advancement and liberation. Always remember, Tantra is not a religion like Hinduism; it is a system of magick.

This ancient wisdom, manifesting in the form of ancient Mantras in what is now Nepal and India, reveal the vibrations of spirits, gods and goddesses. Some of these are thousands of years old and we continue to use them today.

### *Bija Mantras*

The ancient Sanskrit 'Alphabet' (a series of glyphs and sounds) is considered in Tantra as a means of encoding the vibrations of the cosmos. It is interesting to note that all such sacred 'alphabets' are said to be the same in this way. Words have always been seen as powerful, but it is the vibrations that they are made of that convey the deeper magick.

Bija (a seed Mantra) means 'deed'. The primal 'seed' Bija is OM, for it is the seed vibration of all things. OM is ascribed to Shiva in his most transcendent, non-dualistic form. Most gods and goddesses have a seed Bija, a key vibration which is literally the essence of that deity.

Ganesh, the elephant-headed god who removes all obstacles, is called by the Bija Mantra vibration GAANG. Lakshmi, the ancient Earth mother who is mostly worshipped now as a goddess of wealth and prosperity, is the Bija Mantra vibration SHREENG, and so on. Mantras can encode one or more Bija Mantras, like *Om GAANG Ganapataye Namah* for Ganesh.

If all things are made of vibration, then it makes sense that vibration is the most crucial part of working with divine forces. Tantra, being more consciously accepting of embracing the 'real world' (Samsara) and all it brings, sees vibrational magick as a way of working with the forces of that world so we may enjoy and grow within such a useful and pragmatic reality. Thus, Mantra—the use of divine vibration—is an important key of Tantric Magick.

### On Complex Mantras

Bija Mantras are often embedded in longer Mantras to create spells. As an example, let's look at the Mantra *OM Gaang Ganapataye Namah,* a 'spell' to invoke the elephant-headed god. Let me break it down:

This Mantra-spell tells a story: OM (the infinite, the cosmos, the origin of all vibration) manifests as the sacred deity Ganesh = GAM (pronounced GAANG[1]), his Bija. Ganesh is here called by a specific aspect-name—Ganpati—meaning 'Lord of the Ganas' (wild spirits). This 'spell' ends with Namah, a term communicating humility, and honoring something greater. Consciously knowing that this Mantra is a spell to invoke the divine essences of Ganesh in the specific form of Ganapati is important. Encoded into such ancient Mantras are potent invocations and each invokes a power, force, spirit or deity.

---

[1] You can find a pronunciation guide for several useful Mantras at *youtube.com/playlist?list=PL0fh2D6QB2jmQk_P8VqGOcfZaMF7dIAGN*

There are many thousands of such spell-Mantras, some quite long and complex, some very simple and succinct. It is important to note that you don't need to know Sanskrit for the vibration magick to work, and you can't possibly know all the Mantras out there. Like any good Tantra you do need to know a selection of important Mantras that you often use. Unpacking a Sanskrit Mantra can become a fruitful meditation in itself.

## On Mantra Practice

The best way to unpack the deep wisdom and ancient power of these vibrations is to first understand them, and then sit with them. Chant them with deep focus and understanding in meditation. Wait for the power to manifest and be open to the teaching it gives you. I have seen Mantras glibly uttered with no conscious thought. People uttering them haphazardly in this way do not really understand, hear or vibrate with that Mantra. They are then blind to the mystery of that Mantra, and cannot unlock the hidden wealth within it. Each Mantra, whether simple or complex, must be felt, engaged with, vibrated correctly, and embraced in the core of your being.

This is why Tantra initiations and empowerments are always given with a personal Mantra transmission from the initiator Guru to a Chela (student). This book is not a vehicle for initiation, but it is a form of empowerment. You do not have to be initiated to do Tantra; if you are sincere and devoted the gods will love you and respond to you, as will the cosmos. You will achieve results and your deities will gather, support, love and help you. After practice, if you and your Guardian Spirit feel the need for a Tantric initiation from a lineage and Tantra teacher, it will manifest for you. If you weave the divine vibrations of the cosmos, your True Will conjures miracles.

Let me end with this: Mantra vibrations are the most potent threads we weave as Tantrics, for the whole divine tapestry of our spiritual work is OM, the source of all cosmic vibrations. Tantrics delight in a variety of colors, scents, tastes, feelings, sounds and all things that intoxicate and enliven the mind, body and spirit! We weave all the vibrations, and thus invite into our lives the varied gods and goddesses we love. This is the sonic rainbow path of Tantra, of Knowing and directly experiencing the heart of the divine in all its forms so we may joyfully wear the wondrous fabric we have woven within our world.

### *Yantra*

The Sanskrit term *Yantra* is translated as a 'machine' or 'device' that does magickal things and helps them occur. A Yantra is a visual representation—a complex symbol—that encodes the vibrational essence of a god, goddess or power in visual form. As a Mantra offers the vibratory form of a deity or power, Yantras offer a symbolic form. Yantras are extremely ancient. They are composed of several design elements, and are often envisioned as a palace or temple where the deity symbolically resides.

Every Yantra has some basic forms. The square base with four 'gates' represents the Earth and the Earth Mother. Set inside is most often a circle, within which is a geometric design or image that represents a deity or power. Some Yantras are simple, while some are intensely complex, like the Shri Yantra (Divine Yantra).

Mandalas and Yantras differ in that Mandalas are placed on a wall to meditate upon, while Yantras are laid flat and operate as the center of a sacred space. One analogy is that Yantras function somewhat as the 'pantacles' used in Pagan and Witchcraft rituals that are used to 'empower' or bless items by ritually placing them upon it. Most every Tantric god or goddess—and other powers as well—have specific Yantras, or symbols that function as Yantras. Even specific deity *aspects* have different Yantras.

All Yantras have a centerpoint called the Bija which indicates the center of the cosmos and connotes Shiva. Think of Shiva sitting in the center of the cosmos upon his holy mountain. Many Yantras can be seen as three-dimensional forms that unfold in any number of ways as a lotus, which is often shown on the Yantra inside the circle.

Aside from the never-changing Bindu CenterPoint, everything in a Yantra can be seen of Shakti, the Great Goddess, in her many different forms and aspects. Thus, every Mantra embodies both Shiva and the Great Goddess (Maha Devi) that manifests all things about this centerpoint. When you use a Yantra (and Mantra), you magically create a sacred Zonule space with a specific center and sphere of power unique to the deity or power being called upon. Think of Mantras and Yantras as manifesting a deity or power through cosmic sound vibration (Mantra-chants) and a visual cosmic diagram (Yantra-matter).

When you invoke a god or goddess (Kali, for example), you will choose the appropriate Mantra, place the appropriate Yantra on the altar before her Murti (image), and then do your rite. During the rite, you'll place offerings and things to be empowered upon the Yantra as the Mantra is intoned, and the Murti is honored. This powerful interaction between the energies being invoked, the intense focus of your energy, and the conjuring of magickal forces is the key to the magick of Tantra. Yet, just sitting with a Yantra in meditation or hanging it like a Mandala and contemplating it, can create a sublime trance as well. Once charged, Yantras can act as powerful amulets, hung over a doorway or worn as jewelry, for example. If you have some drawing skill, creating a Yantra while chanting the appropriate Mantra is a powerful ritual, and results in a very powerful Yantra.

Mangala (ritual patterns drawn on the floor with various colored powders), are temporary but similar in potency to Yantras which are sometimes 'drawn' as Mangala. Why are Yantras so potent? They are often ancient symbols which have continuously been used by billions of people. That is a lot of energy to tap into.

When you ritually use the Mantra, Yantra and Murti of Kali all together, they may synergistically *manifest* Kali. This is ancient magick. Together, these tools and techniques make an open 'magical gateway' through which Kali can manifest and directly interact with you. This magick works for any of our deities, and is key to Tantra. Think of the Yantra as a divine 'landing' or 'launching pad,' depending on your objective.

### *The Trident (Trishul)/Magick Wand (Siddharasadanda)*

The trident is not only a key symbol of Shiva—often representing the presence of the god—but it also has layers of meaning and symbolism attached to it. It is a powerful tool, and is used for casting circles, centering power and energy, protecting your Zonule, as well as for active magical defense or forceful projection. In Puja (ritual) work, a small trident is generally used, and as I have discovered, can be easily purchased online! (Smaller tridents can be found easily, but larger ones are not easy to get in Western countries where they are apparently seen as weapons.) In Tantra and Hinduism there are multiple symbolic meanings ascribed to the three tines of the trident, and all are well worth researching. In the **Tantric Triplicities** chapter, the 'Chart of Triplicities' ('Three Shaktis Chart') offers attributes of the Moon, Sun and Fire as representing the crown, center and base of the human body.

The Trident has been used since prehistory, representing the primordial Shiva, and much more. Wherever a trident that has been blessed to Shiva is placed, that place is blessed and protected. Simply placing a trident in your Zonule calls upon this ancient, archetypal power, and is recognized by every Tantric and Hindu.

The magick wand is called Siddharasadanda, meaning 'magic staff.' In my ritual work I often use a Vajra (double Dorje), a metal wand that resembles a lightning bolt to cast circles or throw spells. So, either a small trident or wand of your choice is useful for banishing, sending power, or directing energy.

### *Knife (Kartari) or Sword (Khanga)*

In Tantra, the sword or knife is both a useful magickal tool for protection and doing magick, and a divine symbol of spiritual power. Intense Tantric gods like Bhairav or Rudra, and powerful goddesses like Kali or Durga usually carry swords or knives to denote their ferocity. The rituals of such hardcore deities can involve animal sacrifice using such swords, and the meat is always eaten. This is why a sacred sword or knife is often present for Kali Pujas as you'll see later in this book. As the trident creates the centering union of the three aspects of the universe, the knife manifests the unified force of action, self-sacrifice, protection and the banishing of negative forces.

### *Damaru (Small Tantric Drum of Shiva)*

It is traditional to have a simple ritual drum to tap out rhythms when chanting and entering a trance state. The traditional Damaru 'hourglass' drum is a symbol of Shiva, and is often seen in images in his hand or hanging on his trident. Other Tantric deities, such as Ganesha, are often shown playing such drums in divine ecstasy while singing, dancing or chanting. A Damaru can be bought online, but any small drum is useful. Even if you are not very musical, the simple playing of a drum helps bring together the Mantra, the breath, and your mental rhythms.

### The Ghanta (Ritual Bell)

Most every Hindu or Tantric ritual uses a ritual bell (Ghanta). The choice of bell is up to you, but it should feel suitably sacred and appropriate for Tantric work. It is easy to find a ritual bell made in India or Nepal, often decorated with deities. One that falls into your hands or is given as a gift is especially propitious.

The bell is rung whenever you begin to pray, or petition the god or goddess. It is also used as magickal emphasis at different parts of rituals. It is traditional to ring such a temple bell to announce yourself when you enter a holy place, and spells projected with a rung bell are enhanced by the conjoined vibrations. In Tantra, everything is seen as vibration, and shifting vibrations cause changes in consciousness if done with focused will. Used in this way, the ritual bell banishes negativity and unwanted thoughts as it blesses and empowers your Zonule. In ritual, it is common to ring the bell three times, three being a sacred number in Tantra. The best bell to get for your work is called a 'seven-metal-bell,' which creates a long-lasting tone, and can be made to 'sing' by rotating a stick or other item slowly about the rim, creating an amazing meditative vibration.

### The Puja Tray for Ritual Offerings

Whether you are doing a small ritual or a more 'serious' Puja (i.e., a full ritual to a god or goddess), you'll need some sort of tray, plate or shallow bowl to arrange offerings in. It is traditional to 'wave' the offerings in three or more circles before the Murti (image) of the deity being honored.

Traditional Hindi Puja trays are often quite ornate, with many small sections for items that need to be there depending on the deity and tradition. Nath Tantrika calls for a much simpler and more ancient attitude about this. In my work, I use a simple hand-thrown shallow pot where I place offerings that are local and natural, inspired by the deity, and assembled out of love and devotion rather than prescribed tradition. The gods have never seemed to care as long as I am mindful and sincere. Your Puja tray (or shallow bowl or plate) should be meaningful to you, be made from natural materials, and used only for offerings.

There should be enough room in this vessel for a small candle, a small cup of liquid, a stick of incense, a flower, and food items for the deity. After the ritual Puja, the food and drink are eaten by you and others who are present. This is called Prasad, holy food. When full, with the candle and incense lit, the tray should be easy to lift with two hands when honoring the gods.

## *Choosing Specific Offerings*

Rather than relying on ancient texts, ask for guidance from your Guardian Spirit and the god or goddess you are working with. Some advice is offered in the **Pujas** section later, but what is available to you and what feels right is most important.

**Incense:** When in doubt, sandalwood stick incense is traditional, but you may want to use different kinds depending on what is appropriate for each deity or situation.

**Amrita (liquid offering):** Pure water is always good, but the gods seem to like fancier drinks for Pujas. Who wouldn't? A traditional mixture to offer is milk, yoghurt, sugar, honey and ghee blended together, but anything you feel is pleasing to the deity you are working with is fine. I often use coconut water or fresh juices. For a Tantric, alcoholic drinks, such as wine, are appropriate for certain deities; Kali, Ugra Tara, and Rudra like such drinks. Others, like Lakshmi and Hanuman don't, so consult the deities and your Guardian Spirit.

**Food offerings:** Fruit, vegetables, candy, sweets of all kinds, nuts and other pleasing, natural vegetarian foods are appropriate. As usual, research, consult your knowledge of what is appropriate to that god or goddess, consider what seems appropriate, and meditate on it. Indian sweets shops have specific sweets for the various gods. Just ask.

**Flowers:** Flowers are always appropriate to have on the altar. Use your knowledge of that god or goddess or your intuition to choose the right color and kind of flower. Not having access to hibiscus or jasmine as per the Tantras, I've always felt that roses were appropriate for Kali and Durga and daisies for Shiva—the goddess is often associated with red, and the god with white. However, I have a garden and most often use flowers that are then in bloom; so, as I write this, lilac and foxglove flowers decorate my altar. If you are doing magical work, choose the flowers that fit the spell you are doing.

### *Divination Tools*

When you sit in meditation and seek divine guidance or advice, it is a good time to consult an oracle. This is not so different in any occult practice, and is normal in Tantra. There are many divination tools that can be used to access the spiritual realm and give voice to your Guardian Spirit or a deity you are working with.

Oracles give advice or show the will of the divine through the chance throw of cards, sticks, coins or other items. These patterns are interpreted through prior knowledge or through intuition and guidance from your Guardian Spirit. This is very different from fortune-telling, and is not about the future; it is about getting clear guidance in your work. Oracles offer specific advice and personal communication from a deity or from your Higher Self. Immersed in Samsara as we are, it is often hard to see what we should do; oracles help. When invited, your Guardian Spirit will use an oracle to communicate and mentor you. Oracles are a useful tool in the Umbra Zonule, and will often help guide decisions or explain experiences in your work. The more comfortable you are with the oracle of your choice, the better it will be for your Work.

Within your Zonule, oracular communications are enhanced because of the sacred space you have made. Extraneous thoughts and influences are kept out, and divine guidance is clearer. Some, like the Nordic Runes, may simply not jive with Tantra for you, so be open to inner suggestions and you will likely find one that your Guardian Spirit prefers.

Oddly enough, I found using Tarot cards to be successful, and still do. Each to his or her own! Dadaji Mahendranath always felt that the *I Ching* was the oracle best suited to Tantra, and had studied it deeply—part of the time with Crowley—even before going to India. It is a sublime oracle, fits well in our Tantric world, and is over 4000 years old, thus making the *I Ching* worthy of respect. It operates on the idea that everything is a combination of Yin and Yang, which we see as Shakti and Shiva. For decades I have been using the *I Ching* to do work in my Umbra Zonule and communicate with my Guardian Spirit. It has been a powerful source of clear answers and good advice. The hexagrams can also be used as powerful symbols to meditate upon or use in spells and rituals, something Gurudev Dadaji Mahendranath points out, specifically noting hexagram #50 ('The Cauldron') as crucial for understanding Tantra in deep meditation.

For our purposes we will regard the *I Ching* as an appropriate oracle as well as an excellent medium for spiritual communication, especially with the Guardian Spirit. There are many translations of the *I Ching*, the most authoritative current edition is the version by Rudolf Ritsema and Stephen Karcher, but for straightforward and clear readings, I like the pithy edition by R.L. Wing. Do a little research, and find what version works for you.

No matter what oracles you use, remember that the guidance of your Guardian Spirit through oracles will lead you to success.

### *Tantric Wear*

#### *Talismanic Jewelry*

Many Tantrics have their own ritual talismanic jewelry. The most obvious magick item to wear in our ritual work is the Mala. If you accumulate several kinds of Malas, then it is appropriate to use the one that fits the deity being called upon or the specific work you will do. The more you wear a Mala, the more energy it accrues.

I have several Malas that I use often. I also have metal bracelets with Mantras upon them (OM NAMAH SHIVAYA, OM MANI PADME HUM), and a variety of occult Tantric rings. In Tantric rites, I often 'wear' three horizontal lines of ritual ash on my forehead, often with a Tika (red dot) of Kumkum (red paste) on my third eye. This is a potent charm and symbol of Shiva. There are many Tantric talismans and amulets, including specific images, Yantras, magickal squares, arcane glyphs, rings, amulets, and so on. It is great fun to search out such occult talismans online. In India, these 'magical' things are *automatically* called Tantric. There are no hard and fast rules to any of this. Think of the deity you are working with, and use what you feel is appropriate for your ritual work.

## Ritual Clothing

It is important that you wear relaxed, natural, comfortable clothing for Tantric work—if you wear anything at all. I say this because most Tantric Sadhus in India wander about naked or wear a simple loincloth! Like other items, your comfortable ritual clothing will accrue power the more you wear it, and will get you into the right headspace quickly. Cleaning yourself before all ritual work is also important. Here are your three 'Tantric clothing' choices:

**Digambara:** 'Being naked' is best in Tantra. Initiation is always taken naked, and Dadaji Mahendranath often said that all Tantric work, even in Kulas (groups) should be done naked, if possible. (He also noted that in colder climes that can be uncomfortable.) Being naked is best because your body and your aura are completely free, and so can be utilized for magical work.

**Robe:** A simple, one-piece robe to wear over your naked body is an excellent solution for Tantric work. The robe should be comfortable, made of all-natural fabric, and set aside for this work alone. It will physically and mentally relax you, and prepare you for the work you are going to do. Dadaji Mahendranath said that the colors red and black are most appropriate for the Nath tradition, but it is up to you. A simple handmade robe is best.

**Loose clothing:** I do Sadhana three times a day now, so often I do not wear my robe or go naked, but instead wear lose, natural clothing or other similarly relaxed clothing. I enjoy doing Tantric rituals at the ocean or in the woods as well, and where I live this often calls for clothing, so wearing loose, relaxed clothing works!

## FINALLY...

Other magical tools and symbolic items can be brought into your Umbra Zonule to help facilitate your Work. They don't have to 'look' Tantric, but it is nice if they do. As you deepen your relationship with your Guardian Spirit and your deities, you may be gently 'told' by them what other things to bring into your Zonule. They may even subtly help you in finding or acquiring such items if you ask. When asking your Guardian Spirit for the right item, sometimes such things suddenly just show up! Many times, the right book, incense or image has simply 'appeared' before me in a store, often with gentle spirit nudges. When these sorts of things happen to you on a regular basis, it means you has entered the numinous Tantric Twilight World.

## EMPOWERING THE ZONULE WITH THE ZONULE RITE

In this section, you will 'turn on' your Zonule by performing the Zonule Rite. You have already set up your Umbra Zonule, amassed items necessary for your Tantric work, installed the Dragon Seat and the altar, learned basic banishing, and begun regularly meditating there. At this point, you have centered, focused and begun to empower your Tantric ritual sphere. Now you will truly begin your Tantric work. You are now ready to greatly expand your practices and begin regular Sadhana—specific, ongoing, Tantric work and Tantric rituals.

Before doing the Zonule Rite, you may want to take a moment to adjust aspects of your Zonule for comfort and ease, and to make sure you have everything you need. Review the ritual carefully. Make changes as needed to optimize its effectiveness and comfort.

Is your Umbra Zonule relaxing and pleasant? Is it lit with natural light? Is it a place where you can be alone, quiet and undisturbed? Do you wish to add anything before you move forward? Plants? Art? More pleasing furniture? Keep in mind that you will be sitting in your sacred Zonule for hours, so make sure it evokes calm, quiet and comfort, and is pleasant to abide in. When all is as it should be, perform the Zonule Rite slowly and with intent.

### THE ZONULE RITE

You have set up your Zonule, banished it, blessed it, and meditated in it. You are now ready to commit to advancing on the path of Tantra with this rite. This simple ritual announces your honoring of and dedication to the Tantric universe, the gods, and your Guardian Spirit. When you commit to them, they will commit to you. It is such in any important relationship, and this rite begins that relationship.

For this ritual you will need:

- All of the elemental symbols like so:
  - A small, natural incense burner and some sandalwood incense.
  - A small lamp or candle holder with a white candle in it.
  - A small, simple, natural cup of pure water.
  - One or more red flowers in a vase.
  - If possible: A Yoni-Lingam in the middle with a red flower upon it. A stone may substitute for the Yoni-Lingam.
- A sacred wand, or small trident you have cleaned and blessed to direct your energy and will.
- Your Mala (prayer beads), and any other Tantric jewelry.
- Loose, relaxed clothing.
- Your Journal and a pen.

All of these items have been described previously. Now add three new items:

- A simple red or white altar cloth.
- A bell of any sort (although a '7-metal-bell' is best).
- A small image of the elephant-god Ganesh.

Finally, while in meditation, compose a short invocation for your Guardian Spirit—a dedication to your higher self. You may use it to call on your inner guide at any time, and you will be reading it before a short quote by Gurudev Dadaji Mahendranath.

### *Preparation*

- Cleanse yourself. Put on your clean Tantric clothing, your Mala and any other items you have chosen to wear.
- Set up the Zonule and altar as you like. For example, you might do it in this way: Incense to East, Candle to South, Water to West, Flowers to North, Yoni-Lingam (or stone) in the center.
- Sit in the center, relax and think about what you are about to do.

When you are ready, do the following:

### *Rite of the Umbra Zonule*

Sit upon your Dragon seat. Have your Journal near you, and have your wand or trident on or before the Altar. Relax.

### Phat! Banishing

Now, stand before the altar. Raise your hand while extending only the pointing and middle fingers and closing the rest. Visualize it as a sword of power; this is the 'Sword Mudra.'

Extend your other palm out flat and face up.

Strike the palm sharply with the 'sword' fingers, and shout PHUT! (P-Uh-T!), first to the East, and then, in turn, to the South, West, North and finally in the center, over the altar. With each strike and loud PHUT!, visualize lightning bolts striking at each direction, banishing all negative energy and entities.

Then, sit and center yourself.

### Honoring Ganesh,
### The God Who Removes Obstacles and Opens the Way

The elephant-headed god, Ganesh, is called upon before any Tantric work is done. He removes obstacles and opens the way as he is, in many ways, the embodiment of OM.

Place the Murti (image) of Ganesh on the altar where you can see him. Close your eyes and hold the image of Ganesh glowing in your mind.

Open your eyes and sprinkle some pure water about you clockwise and chant:

OM SHRI GANESHAYA NAMAH! [3x]

Then, ring the bell three times and say:

OM GAANG! OM SHRI GANESHA! PLEASE, REMOVE ALL OBSTACLES TO THE GREAT WORK, NOW AND ALWAYS! SVAHA! [So Be It!]

Now, light the incense and candle, chant OM three times, and visualize divine light filling your Zonule.

### Casting the Circle

With your wand or trident, 'draw' a circle clockwise around your whole Zonule. Visualize divine light creating a sphere of love and protection about you. Chant:

OM MANI PADME HUM [The Jewel in the Center of the Lotus] [3x]

Hold the wand or trident at your heart. See yourself as the jewel in the center of the glowing lotus-sphere of your Zonule. You are the glowing star-center of the cosmos.

### Honoring the Gurus/Ancestors

Think about all the important teachers in your life, and the many Tantric Gurus who manifested this wisdom you are entering. Honor your own Guru, your Guardian Spirit, your soul-Self. Meditate on all of these luminous beings with gratitude. Sprinkle water upon the altar and the Yoni-Lingam or stone, saying:

GURU OM [3x]

Meditate, listen, be open. You may have things to note in your Journal. Do so as they arise.

### Honoring the Four Guardians and the Three Shaktis

Now, point your wand or trident to the four directions, one by one, beginning with the direction you are facing. Strongly visualize a glowing trident as you point and trace a trident at each direction in turn, then a fifth time over the altar, saying each time:

OM TRISHULA SVAHA! [Om, I invoke the Trident of Shiva! So Be It!]

Then sit quietly, and visualize the protective tridents of Shiva glowing about you.

Place the wand or trident down or lean it upright against the altar. With a little water, touch your head and say:

Knowledge Shakti, Bless and Empower Me

Touch your heart and say:

True Will Shakti, Bless and Empower Me

Touch your sex/lower body and say:

Action Shakti, Bless and Empower Me

Now sit in quiet meditation with your eyes closed, and visualize your whole body shining with three glowing symbols:

- Your head has a glowing crescent moon, pure silver-white.
- Your heart has a blazing sun, pure yellow-gold.

- Your lower body has a triangular flame, pure red-orange.

Meditate on these and feel the power of these three Shaktis, body centers, and the other triplicities you've read about.

See all three symbols merge into the moon/sun/fire symbol at your heart, shining like a diamond.

Open your eyes and ring the bell three times, saying:

> May the light of Tantra weave and manifest the powers I embody:
> True Knowledge, True Will and True Action—
> SVECCHACHARYA! OM!

### *Dedications/Offerings*

With your hand, wave the sweet smoke of the incense toward your head, heart and lower body, saying:

> OM—I honor the spirit of the air and every breath I take!

Then touch your head, heart and lower body, feeling and visualizing the fire of life within and swirling about you, saying:

> OM—I honor the flame of vital life that burns within and around me that helps me see!

Take the cup and use a finger to sprinkle a few drops of water on the Yoni-Lingam (or stone), then touch your head, heart and lower body with water, saying:

> OM—I honor the great waters of the earth and within me, filling me with feeling and life!

Take up a flower, smell it and touch it to your head, heart and lower body. Honor your physical body as the cosmos, saying:

> OM—I honor my physical body, my earthly Temple and vehicle, with joy and gratitude for the ability to physically manifest love and will for others and myself.

Place your hands together at your heart and visualize a great bright star glowing there and filling your entire being. Then say:

> I Honor all the elements and manifestations which are One Manifestation: The vibration of the cosmos. By the One Spirit may I attain Liberation: OM! SVAHA!

### *Honoring Shiva and Shakti*

Take up a red flower, hold it up, and in your mind visualize the primal Mother Goddess before you, she who is all power, light and joy. Place the flower upon the Yoni-Lingam or stone, and say:

> I Honor the Great Goddess Adi Shakti, Maha Devi, She who is the swirling, fiery, eternal light, life and laughter of the cosmos at play, by all her many names and aspects!! HREENG!

Sprinkle the flower and Yoni-Lingam with water and visualize Shiva, the water you sprinkle being the cascade of water from heaven that flows though him as he sits in deepest meditation, smiling. Say:

> I Honor the center and seed of the cosmos that is the Great God Shiva, he who manifests all that is wild and liminal, the one beyond life and death, by all his many names and aspects! OM!

Close your eyes and meditate. See yourself as *both* Shakti and Shiva, being wholly unified as one being who embodies One Divine Being. Then say:

> TAT TVAM ASI [I Am That]
> I am Whirling Cosmos Shakti and Shiva, Center of All,
> For we are always and eternally One.
> I am Shiva-Shakti and there is no difference between any one thing and any other thing soever: All is OM!
> He is the Inner Light of Truth, Holy Secret Self: Peace and Liberation!

Then chant:

> OM SHANTI SHIVA SHAKTI [3x]

Ring the bell three times.
Sit and meditate on this for as long as you like.

(Here is where you may add invocations to specific deities or even a Puja, if you choose to do so.)

After you 'return,' write in your Journal as your Guardian Spirit and the gods begin to speak to you and show you things. This is also a good time to draw or do divination.

When you are done, place your pointing finger to your lips and inhale with a **HAaaa** sound as the powers you have called fill and energize your body. Pause, press your lips together with an almost silent '**Mmm**,' then exhale with a gentle hissing **SAaaaa** sound. Do these three times, letting unwanted thoughts or energy locked within your body, heart and mind flow out of your body and down into the earth. Let go. Be still and calm for a time.

*Final Honoring of the Gods, Spirits, Ancestors, Gurus and All Living Beings*

Now, sprinkle water clockwise about the whole circle and on the altar saying:

> Honor to the Tantric Goddesses, Gods, Spirits, Ancestors, Gurus, Elementals and to all beings who are wild and free! By their grace may I attain Real Happiness, Real Freedom, and Real Liberation through the weaving of my Love and Will.
> SVECCHACHARYA! SVAHA! The Will to Love is the Law to Live!

Ring the bell three times. Stand, raise your arms, and offer all the energy and blessings you have created to all living beings, saying:

> Balance, Wealth, Pleasure and Liberation to All Beings! OM!

Now, blow out the candle, then place both hands upon the ground and see all the leftover energy from your rite flow into Mother Earth (Bhu Devi) and whisper to her:

> Bhu Devi, To You, From You, All Things!

End the rite by placing your hands together at your heart, saying:

> OM SHANTI SHIVA SHAKTI [OM—The Union of Shiva-Shakti brings Peace] [3x]

**Optional**: If you feel energy 'left over' and want to make sure that all energies and entities are gone, Do the **Phat! Banishing** again (see the beginning of the rite).

## Afterwards

You and your Umbra Zonule are now blessed, charged and firmly within the Tantra power zone! Sit and write or draw as you like; then you may simply leave the glowing Zonule. You should eat and drink something to earth yourself as well.

## Notes on the Zonule Rite

I trust you can see that this solid Tantric rite is a useful 'general ritual' within which many other Tantric practices and invocations can be done.

As you'll see, you will do this rite often, if not daily, with an eye to slowly adding other Tantric practices and techniques as they are introduced in the coming sections. However, before adding new practices, do this simple Zonule Rite several times to get used to it and to become 'in sync' with it until it flows easily. Once you are confident and successful with this rite, you'll be ready to add all the new practices and techniques coming up, and will be confident in changing and adding to the basic Zonule Rite as prompted by your Guardian Spirit.

**Note:** The basic Zonule Rite is a simple meditation empowerment, so the *Phat! Banishing* at the end is optional. However, if you still feel excess energy, or want it completely clear, **or** have done a more complex ritual invoking gods or other practices, then do the *Phat! Banishing*.

(The PHAT! Banishing is a very easy, powerful and useful technique that can be used anytime, anywhere. I've used it in a few sketchy situations for safety, within a nightmare to banish something scary, and to clear a room that was full of evil energy, always with great effectiveness.)

You have now entered real Tantric work. Keep in mind that the crucial ongoing practice is to *bond with and open communication with your Guardian Spirit, your 'inner Guru.'* Once your regular Tantric work gets rolling, everything else will unfold in a cosmic manner, and amazing things—ideas, poetry, art, books, friendships and more—will simply come to you as you learn to *let go* of your narrow view of this crazy world and let your Guardian Spirit, your inner Divine Star, take the wheel and push your whiney Ego—with its narrow worldview—to the back seat!

Christians often say "Let Go, Let God," but we Tantrics say "Let Go, BE God!"

OM!

## Umbra Zonule Maintenance & Suggestions

I hope that you will do this rite daily, so it is important that you regularly clean the Umbra Zonule area, the altar, the Dragon Seat, and so on. I clean my Zonule thoroughly every new or full moon. I also ritually clean the Yoni-Lingam since I leave offerings on it regularly. For cleaning, simple salt and pure water works well, and pure oil of lavender or sandalwood can be added. While cleaning you should vibrate a simple Mantra such as OM or—especially for cleaning the Yoni-Lingam—OM SHANTI SHIVA SHAKTI. When done, dispose of the water outside on the earth. If there is a carpet, regularly vacuum it. To increase the pleasant vibe, sprinkle or spray the Zonule with some pure water with a bit of natural oil in it. If the Zonule is part of another room, it is important to keep the rest of the room separate from the sacred space, and clean it as well. Messes attract negative energy.

Keep all the Tantric items you will be using under or near the altar—items like incense, candles, Yantras, Murtis, your Journal, special oils, and so on. Keep this book and other sacred texts within arm's reach, as well as items used for divination. I keep my *I Ching* coins and book nearby; they come in handy.

As you increase your practice, your Tantric work will become more spontaneous. Consider what you might want to use and have it there. My Guardian Spirit often directs me to do certain chants or practices, or to write or draw something, so I keep such useful items nearby. Finally, always have a small clean cloth there; things can get messy at times!

It is important that you always have a container of fresh drinking water with you. Tantra is thirsty work! Chanting, meditating and doing ritual work generates what Tantrics call *Tapas* (energetic heat) caused by intense magick and devotion. Stay hydrated!

Plan for breaks, if necessary. Before you begin any work in the Zonule, take care of things; you want to avoid interruptions as you may be immersed for long periods of time. I do work in my Zonule for many hours at times, and I sometimes need to use the restroom. Leaving the Zonule for a short time like this is not an issue; just visualize 'opening a doorway' with your hands thrust before you, and opening them like you would a curtain, then 'closing it' behind you as you would close a curtain. When you reenter the Zonule, repeat these gestures and visualize the 'door' being opened and closed behind you in the same manner. Another, simpler option, is to wear your Mala before leaving the Zonule, and visualize it as a symbol of your magickal circle. Then visualize the circle of your Zonule *as the Mala,* and see this circle about you when you leave the Zonule and come back. When you return, sit and visualize your Mala-circle becoming one with the Zonule-circle by touching your Mala and 'seeing' it expand into one.

## Offerings

Once you begin working with the gods, it makes sense to accompany your offerings with words of thanks. Such offerings can be simple, like a flower, a stick of incense, a few drops of water, or some candy. They may be placed on the Yoni-Lingam or in a small vessel with a few sincere words or Mantras honoring the deity. Simple Tantric rituals often are spontaneous and heartfelt; the gods love it and respond. After a time, dispose of the items on the earth if appropriate. If you are bonding with a specific deity, it is wise to begin each day with a simple heartfelt offering.

If you are doing a full Puja ritual dedicated to a god or goddess, you will place more complex offerings in a Puja bowl or tray for the deity being honored. It is fine to keep all the offerings in this vessel, including fruit, sweets, flowers, a small candle, incense and a small cup of liquid, but it can get a bit messy at times so some clean up after Puja is always recommended.

## Regular Practice Issues

It is best if you sit, meditate and begin your Tantric work at a set time every day. Think of it as being as important for your wellness as your regular exercise. Before you decide on a regular time to meditate and work in your Zonule, sit in it for a few days to see about the rhythms of the external world around you. You may want to avoid times when school busses or rush hour traffic is loud, for example. If you have children, it may be best to do your work when they are at school or asleep. When do deliveries come? When do you get the most phone calls? When are you preoccupied by work or parenting or other things? These all are detrimental to a calm, relaxed state of meditation and visualization. It's useful to think of the rhythms of your modern lives in this way, and choose a regular 'Tantra time' that is calm and peaceful.

### Others You Live With

It is important that you communicate with loved ones or roommates about your regular meditation and ritual time, and your needs in this regard. Discuss this, and together create a clear agreement, preferably in writing. Except for emergencies, your Tantra-time should be undisturbed. You will soon value this quiet island of bliss, believe me. With forethought, flexibility and regular communication, it will work out well. Your spiritual evolution is as important as any other part of your life, and should be honored.

### Moving Forward

You have prepared, consecrated and become familiar with your Zonule and its rhythms, and are now ready to expand your meditations and simple rites into full, complex Tantric work with more powerful practices and techniques. As you move forward in this process, other techniques and practices will be added to your daily Zonule Rite and, when you have mastered them, you will be ready to do full Pujas and other more complex rituals. Svaha! So may it be!

## Practices & Rituals in the Zonule
### Empowering & Expanding Your Zonule

Now that your Zonule is all 'lit up' by the Zonule Rite, you are ready to move forward and expand your knowledge and practice of Tantra. Your Zonule is your laboratory, launching-pad, sacred space, shrine and temple. It is a good idea to just sit there at times, with little or no ritual, getting the feel of your sacred space, and centering yourself. Soon you will slip into liminal space with just that simple act.

Avoid your Zonule if you are angry or agitated, very intoxicated, or not ready for magickal work. Your Zonule will act as a kind of psychic battery, absorbing the energies you manifest.

However, it is fine to use your Zonule if you feel down or confused, or need to unpack and sort out issues through meditation and divine help. That pretty much describes about 20% of my Zonule time! Sometimes simple tasks feel like ordeals; loneliness, separation and depression are endemic. This has been the most important time for me to set a schedule to sit and meditate in my Zonule. Meditation helps on every level.

The more you sit, meditate, chant and work in your Zonule, the stronger and more powerful it becomes. Every time you banish, cast a circle, center yourself, and invoke your Guardian Spirit, gods, spirits and ancestors to help your work, it becomes more powerful.

Focusing on this pushes the howling storm of the illusory world away, and you will suddenly feel immense calm. The Zonule is the eye of the hurricane of the world around us (Samsara), a place of calm balance where you get perspective and can breathe. All worry, stress and demands fade from your mind as you pull back to the Center and return to your natural, centered calm. When you reach this calm and clear mental and spiritual place, you have access to, and can communicate with, your Guardian Spirit to receive advice and blessings.

All of this happens here and now, where you are, for you are the glowing center of your Zonule, the Star, and the totality of all. My mom used to say, when things calmed down, "I can finally hear myself think!" This feeling of peace, refuge and clarity grows the more you meditate and do work in your Zonule.

Regarding such work, Gurudev Mahendranath often talks about the extreme importance of imagination. Your active, visionary mind is the crucial instrument in all Tantric work, and conjures your Knowledge, Will and Action. If you have the will to meditate just 15 minutes a day, and stick to it, it will become easier and more enticing until you discover that when you skip a day, you miss it.

Of course, building your relationship with your Guardian Spirit is the most important work of meditation and magick, and allows for all the rest. Dadaji Mahendranath was very clear: we are not here just to 'learn more stuff,' but to peel away the layers and REMEMBER. Everything important is within us, and the Guardian Spirit is the key to accessing lifetimes of wisdom.

Here's a quick review:

You have created a safe magickal 'laboratory,' your Zonule, which is now filled with real power. I suggest that every time you use it you:

- Banish and then cast a circle to define and keep out the chaos of the external world. This sphere you make is where microcosm and macrocosm meet; it is the cosmos.
- Honor the gods and your Guardian Spirit which exist to aid you. Then visualize yourself as the Center of All: OM.
- Empower yourself and expand your consciousness.
- Focus your mind and find the still, balanced center of your being.
- Let go of 'external reality' and breathe deeply with this centered focus and exist NOW.
- Still your chattering mind *and really listen* to the voice of the divine within you and *remember*.
- When you are done, center and then focus and honor your Guardian Spirit, Gods, Spirits and Ancestors with gratitude.
- Offer the energy you have generated to the benefit of all living beings.
- Banish extraneous energies and so put your sphere of power into 'sleep mode.'

In essence, this is the basic pattern of work in your Zonule where you will do the work of 'weaving' all that is your mundane and spiritual life and Self, the heart of Tantra.

It is all very simple! Yet, all the most important things are.

Of course, many kinds of work can be done in your Zonule. As this section unfolds, several practices and disciplines will be introduced for you to use within the basic Zonule Rite. The practices form the core of the most important practices you need to know to understand Tantra, but there are more techniques that build on this. However, remember this:

*The goal of Tantra is simple: To be happy. In this manner we can move towards liberation by awakening to the realization that we have always been one with the divine, but have forgotten.*

Your mind, imagination, will and love are the most important powers you'll ever need. The rest are useful, but it is the divine Self within you that manifests all things, not the other way around. A super Mantra is not the cause of great magick. You are. Any technique is just the focus and manifestation of your will and love.

## Working in the Zonule—Basic Tantric Practices

### *Cleansing/Banishing Review*

Before entering your Zonule, clean yourself mentally, physically, emotionally and psychically as you will. If you have techniques from your own traditions, use them.

Salt and salt with water is always useful for banishing; or you can use sacred smoke from special herbs like sage, bay leaf, or rosemary, or just sandalwood incense. An old 'spell' I use is to chant: "Out, out, throughout and about, all good come in, all evil go out!" Or I'll mentally repeat a simple Mantra such as "OM" or "Shanti, Shanti, Shanti" (Peace, Peace, Peace). A walk in nature provides a powerful cleansing, and spending time against a tree with some deep breathing is remarkably potent for removing all negativity.

Try one or more of these methods, or seek a simple cleansing blessing that works for you. I wrote a book on banishing called *Clean Sweep* (see the **Bibliography**) that offers many more ideas.

## Getting Mentally Prepared for Success

After cleansing, take a moment to shift out of your mundane headspace and into the sacred. Dressing in your relaxed Tantric clothes (or going naked), anointing yourself with special scents, and wearing your other symbolic Tantric items (such as your Mala and other jewelry), signals your deep mind and the cosmos that you are about to enter the twilight Tantric world of magick.

Why do all of this? You are preparing yourself and triggering sight, smell, sound, touch and taste with the message that you are 'stepping out' of the chaos of Samsara and entering the eternal liminal realm of the gods, spirits and magick with the guidance of your Guardian Spirit or Higher Self. You are announcing to the cosmos, "I am Shiva-Shakti, I am OM! I am a divine being and I seek to remember and embrace the eternal star that I am!" Time to rock the Tantra!

## Preparing for the Zonule Rite

Make sure your Zonule is clean and uncluttered, and has all you will need including water to drink, heat (if necessary), and so on. Make sure that the five elements are present and prepared. Make sure that other items you'll need are present: a lighter for incense and candle, your Journal, a sketch pad, and so on. Have a copy of the Zonule Rite with you! Trust me, it is easy to forget items.

Do the Zonule Rite (see the previous Chapter); then:

## The Meditation

Meditation is the key part of the Rite. It is where much of your work will be manifested, and where you'll receive most divine 'downloads.' The Zonule Rite meditation is left open so you can make your meditation time complex or simple as you learn more techniques and practices. Try many variations and use what works for you—remembering that as you move forward this may change.

There are many ways to meditate, from austere Zazen to long, silent practices like Vipassana, to Mantra-focused meditations, and so on. All of these and many more are fine; several meditation techniques will be offered here, but Tantra is not about strict rules or

remaking who you are. It is about remembering and rediscovering your true self and true nature. Here is the basic meditation practice:
- Sit quietly on your Dragon Seat and let your mind go free.
- Breathe deeply and slowly, in and out. Relax your body.
- Let thoughts and images arise and float away; as best you can, do not follow or attach to any. Let thoughts, feelings, internal dialogs, issues and so on arise and fade.
- Your ego will continue to distract you with work issues, annoyances, daydreams and so on. Gently dismiss them with your will. It is sometimes helpful to visualize 'a separate little ego beast' next to you! I visualize a little crazy monkey beside me. As mental yattering happens, I remember and 'see' that it is not my Guardian Spirit-Self, but my ego-monkey-mind. This trick helps.
- Eventually much of the chaos settles down. Continue to breathe deeply in and out.

That is all you need to do. Practice simple meditation and note in your Journal all your insights and experiences.

### *Calling to and Connecting with Your Guardian Spirit in Meditation*

As connecting with your Guardian Spirit is so important, you can begin the process within your meditation if you wish. Try this or something like it:

Meditate for a time. Once you are in a deep, relaxed, meditative state, center yourself with your eyes closed. Breathe deeply. Then, amidst the darkness, visualize a distant point of light—a star, a spark of divine light. Focus on it until it is clear and real. Cease all thought, focus only on that, brush aside all distractions and ego-chattering. Focus on this point of light. Nothing else exists. Let go. Be open. The point of light is the beginning and end of all. It is your Guardian Spirit, your Star-Self, the spark of OM within you. Maintain focus as long as you can. It may be brief and fade, or it may come closer and reveal much. Don't be discouraged, and don't force it. If the point of light won't hold steady, let it go. There is no hurry. Relax!

Do this practice in meditation as often as you like until you are able to 'communicate' with your Guardian Spirit. It may happen quickly, or it may take time. Persevere. Once you have a communicative relationship, you will have your own private Guru who will always help and guide you.

When you are done with this visualization, let it fade. Relax and enjoy the feeling of deep meditation. The world is far away, all is peaceful and calm.

Slowly come out of your meditation. With every breath in, you come back to your body; with every breath out, you let go of the twilight internal world until you are sitting in your Zonule.

Take out your Journal and write your experiences, insights and ideas. You may also want to sketch any images or symbols that came to you. All are gifts from your Guardian Spirit, and are breadcrumbs leading you through the forest of Maya to more wisdom!

### *Expansion of Practices and Techniques*

After you have done the Zonule Rite for a few weeks, you'll want to add more 'Tantric tools,' strategies and practices to your repertoire. Many of the following techniques and practices can be done during or after meditation, as you will, and you will adjust your regular Tantric work as you are guided to do so. In this way, do your will and experiment with where, when and how each practice fits into the overall work you are doing—with the help of your Guardian Spirit.

Mastery and expansion of the following techniques and skills, as with much else, depends on your enthusiasm, motivation and practice, as well as your focus and creativity. What follows are many of the most important Tantric techniques and practices, presented with examples so that you can easily use them and then expand on each one as you like. There are many other Tantric practices you can discover on your own, and they range from the *outré* and dangerous to the calm and peaceful.

### *Expanding Your Tantric Sadhana*

Do the Zonule Rite regularly until it's second nature. You may be happy with doing *only* this for a while. If so, great! You'll still want to learn more about Mantras, Yantras, and so on, but relax into these things. After you have done a few weeks of regular Zonule Rite work, you will likely want to add more practices and techniques.

We will start with simple practices. Once you are successful, we will add more complex practices to further enhance your abilities and offer more tools for your work as you expand your desires and goal.

Before we begin, review the Zonule Rite and notice that it is itself a set of interconnected practices. When you become comfortable with it, you can begin to see how and where to add or subtract other practices within the traditional basic structure of this Rite. Take note of the organization and sequence of the rite; it offers a useful traditional structure for Tantric ritual work that can be applied to other rites you create.

Now that you are practicing Tantra using the Zonule Rite, you are one who does Sadhana; that is, a regular practice such as we have described, often for a specific magical or spiritual purpose. Ongoing Tantric Sadhana can be seen as an alchemical working: you have created your laboratory (Zonule), and are placing yourself in the alchemical 'Cauldron.' The goal is to transmute your current being and consciousness (lead) into magickal gold (enlightenment)—a more fully aware and happy being sparkling with vital energy, power and success.

The following ancient practices are worth researching on your own, but here we are focusing on immediate practice and success.

Before we add more specific practices, you should master and expand three important techniques that help you expand your overall Tantric powers and skills.

### *Focused Visualization*

As you do your daily Zonule Rite meditation, you may simply relax, breathe deeply and let your mind become still. Taoists refer to this as 'letting the mud settle until the water becomes clear.' Simply doing so for a time allows all the chaos of your monkey-mind fade until your mind is clear and open to the light of awareness.

After a few times of just letting this process naturally proceed and easing into an alpha state of calm, you should begin to practice and improve your visualization technique.

Visualization and focused, controlled imagination are the keys of most Tantric magick. If you can't clearly visualize an end result, how can you manifest it? Most Tantric and other magickal groups put strong emphasis on visualization training for a good reason. To be able to clearly visualize a deity or symbol in your mind—and hold it—is critical for any success, and this is especially true in Tantra.

'Householder Tantrics' deal with work, play, socializing, relationships, travel and other distractions. This is different from Sadhus (holy Tantrics) who chant and meditate all the time. Thus, it is crucial that we who have so many distractions, work on meditation and visualization daily. The more you do so, the better and more focused your magick and deity work—indeed all Sadhana practices—will be.

### Some Steps to Improve Visualization

Begin with a very simple item to visualize. I suggest a simple point of light or 'star' representing your Guardian Spirit or OM—the Alpha Ovule.

Once you can hold in your mind that simple 'point of light' for five minutes, practice with simple symbols that are slightly more complex. The traditional Tattva symbols commonly used by Hindus, Tantrics and members of occult groups like the Golden Dawn, train to build up visualization skills and focus these skills on the five elements:

**Spirit:** A black egg
**Air:** A blue circle
**Fire:** A red upward-pointing triangle
**Water:** A silver crescent moon, 'horns' up
**Earth:** A yellow square

Note that in the classic 7-Chakra system, these are the lower 5 Chakras. The full list would be: Crown, Third Eye, Spirit, Air, Fire, Water, Earth.

Other important Tantric symbols worth visualizing intently are three classic ones already mentioned: simple images of the sun, the crescent moon and a fire, as well as the image that combines the three.

As you master being able to see and hold such images in your inner mind, you will become more proficient at this crucial practice. Move to more complex images. The goal is to be able to visualize and hold the images of Yantras (complex Tantric designs), and more importantly, various deities. This will become very important when doing more complex Tantric Pujas to deities like Shiva and Kali.

To work on this skill, begin with a simple image of Ganesh. Focus on it intensely within your Zonule Rite. In meditation, hold that image in your mind: open your eyes a few times to 'recalibrate,' then close them again until you can hold the image for a time. It may take several tries, but once you have a solid image of Ganesh in your mind's eye, call to him with a silent Mantra like OM GAANG GANAPATAYE NAMAH and watch him come alive! *This is how you bring the actual power and energy of the god into your temple.* This is one of the powerful secrets of deity Pujas! Once Ganesh is present in this way, then everything shifts. Once you get good at invoking, visualizing and honoring Ganesh, you can begin to internally converse with the god directly. This is the key to Tantra; no middleman! Intense visualization opens the door to the deities, and creates a liminal space to meet. You and the gods can then work together, and thus you will receive gnosis—direct wisdom. What could be more powerful and important?

### *Focusing on Inflaming the Senses*

Tantra practice is all about ritualistic inflaming and weaving the senses to incite ecstasy and intensity.

Tantra is about weaving reality—that is, what the senses and the mind thinks it perceives and knows. We have been brainwashed into believing that reality is 'external,' and that everyone senses the same things—though science has repeatedly pointed out the falsehood of this assumption. When different people experience the same thing or event, each of them perceives it differently. All such perceptions are filtered through our mind, including our knowledge base, our culture, our biases, and our programming.

Ancient Tantrics knew this millennia ago. By mastering and using our focus and concentration, we can enhance, shift or in other ways influence our senses to increase various feelings and emotions, and so change our states of consciousness. We can take the sensory experience of smelling a rose or having an orgasm to extreme heights of spiritual ecstasy.

Not only have we given away or forgotten how to control our senses and the emotions they trigger, we have surrendered our emotional autonomy! Seeing a skull on a shrine fills most Tantrics with a Shiva-filled religious awe; most Americans think only of horror movies. The strident sounds of ancient Japanese Shinto music freaks out most foreigners, as does the taste of the oddly garlic-vanilla durian fruit. Yet, over time I have come to love and appreciate and enjoy them both by the conscious shifting of my reaction to my focused senses. We have the power to control our mind and, therefore, reality. This is the key to 'weaving.'

Much of our magick 'weaving' focuses on the five senses and the emotional responses they engender. They, too, are linked to the five elements:

**Spirit:** Sound
**Air:** Smell
**Fire:** Sight
**Water:** Taste
**Earth:** Touch

Sound is ascribed to Spirit because all is vibration, remember? Sound is the subtle perception of the vibrations of the universe, of Mantras and of the 'hidden' sounds of the Nadis and Kundalini, of energy moving through the body. Of OM.

What all this means is that as you sit in your Zonule, everything you experience is crucial to the work you are doing, and all you are doing or thinking triggers the invocation of an emotional, energetic and spiritual reaction. You have the choice of having control over most all of those things with will and practice. Think of these things and how they could affect your mental state, emotions and magick:

• The comfortable feeling of your Dragon Seat and your soft clothing—Touch
• The scent of your incense and the smell of your flowers—Smell
• The items on your altar and in the room, the gentle candle light—Sight
• The lovely, pure water you are sipping—Taste
• The sound of your heartbeat, of your chants, of the hum of your mind—Sound

So, Tantra is about focusing on your senses, disciplining your mind, and controlling your emotional responses. This is how you strip away old programming and reprogram yourself! Remember the Kleshas (the five 'blockages')? You can now see that control of mind, perceptions and emotions is crucial to confronting and 'cutting through' ego, ignorance, attraction, compulsion and fear of death. Stripping away the conditioning from your environment and culture, and rewiring your mind towards spiritual enlightenment, is the key to Tantra. If you control your mind, you control your mental and emotional reactions, and thus your reality. If you can control your reality, you can use that to attain enlightenment. This is the weaving of Tantra.

### *On Asanas (Physical Body Postures)*

Every 'Tantric' resource includes a variety of Yoga Asanas that one needs to master to become enlightened. I find this amusing. Yes, positioning the body in such postures is powerful and opens the flow of energy in different ways, as any student of Hatha Yoga knows. However, you only need to focus on a few in your Zonule work at first; add more as you like.

If you are physically able, begin with what is called the 'half-lotus,' that is, sitting cross-legged on your Dragon Seat. But if you have back issues, as I do now, sit on a raised Zafu or a simple, straight-backed chair with your 'Dragon Seat' cloth or pillow upon it. The 'seated cow' Asana, alternating with the 'arching cat' Asana, is helpful during long meditation sessions. During Zonule work, several Asanas are useful for shifting the energetic flow through your nervous system, whether it is to calm your body, enhance meditation, or extend an orgasm. Your body is the primary tool of Tantra, so keep it comfortable and happy when doing ritual work. Avoid distractions to keep your body, heart and mind all focused, trained and programmed towards spiritual success and enlightenment, so carefully consider which Asanas are appropriate. You want to be comfortable, yet focused in your Zonule.

# Practices to Add to Your Tantric Zonule Work

## Pranayama
## (Conscious Energy Breathing)

*"Expansion of individual energy into cosmic energy is called pranayama (prana meaning energy + aya meaning, expansion)."*
— Rama Murti Mishra

The first important practice to add to your Zonule Rite is called Pranayama, and involves a focus on breath. In Tantra, breath is energy and power, and every breath is seen as a holy Mantra. This Mantra is called HAMSA (the Swan), which is vibrated as HA (in breath), M (silent pause), and SA (out breath). Every breath you take is a holy Mantra that denotes the beginning and end of all things. It reminds us that we have only so many breaths before we leave this life; thus 'breath is spirit,' or holy, cosmic energy. The wisdom of Pranayama reveals the tremendous power of focusing on and controlling your breathing. For example, by slowing, deepening and regulating the breath, you can regulate physical, mental and spiritual processes and experiences. You can calm agitated feelings, lower your heart rate, and improve your health and brain functions. Working with conscious breathing in conjunction with visualization, sensory awareness and control, as well as Yoga Asana postures, can help you consciously cause change on every level and achieve spiritual goals. As some *Sutras* say, "Breath control is spiritual control." This is why I suggest you add basic Pranayama practices to your Zonule Rite first. Once you have enjoyed and noted the power of Pranayama, expand your work as you like!

Pranayama is about three basic modes: inhaling, holding and exhaling. Shifting such breathing rhythms in various ways causes the body, heart and mind to shift as well. There are many variables, but those who are Hindu, Jain, Buddhist and Tantric all use Pranayama as crucial to the work of union (Yoga), liberation (Moksha) and magick (Siddha). Pranayama helps the brain, body and emotions activate and align with your True Will by making you more conscious and focused—key to all Tantric work. Pranayama also helps balance the energies coursing through our body as was mentioned in the chapter, **On Kundalini**.

Nothing will improve your meditative practice and state of consciousness faster than adding Pranayama practices to your Zonule work. The relaxed breathing you have already been doing is the first, basic step of Pranayama. Here are important practices to improve your entire being.

### *First Pranayama Practice*

Do the usual Zonule Rite. As you begin deep breathing in meditation, do the following:

- Breathe in slowly, filling your lungs completely as you mentally count to 7.[2]
- Hold that breath, and mentally count to 7 slowly.
- Slowly exhale, while you mentally count to 7.
- Hold that finished breath while mentally counting to 7 slowly.
- Repeat.

Do this for five minutes the first time. Build up to ten, then fifteen, then twenty minutes.

If you ever feel faint or light-headed, slowly relax back into regular, calm breathing. This can happen because most of us breathe shallowly much of the day, especially under stress, so when we start opening up and breathing with full lungs, we are suddenly oxygenating ourselves more than we are used to.

Tantrics believe that breath = energy: life. Since Pranayama suddenly fills your body and mind with new energy and power, you may not be prepared for it, so go slowly.

Think of weight training where you start slowly and build up. Same idea. Do it until you feel that energy flow into and clarify your meditation, but don't push it. Relax into it. You have plenty of time, especially since Pranayama is said to extend your life!

---

[2] That is, about 7 seconds. However, if 7 is too much, count to five.

## Second Pranayama Practice

Do the exercise above with one simple change:

- As you breathe in and count to 7, visualize light[3] filling your lungs.
- Hold for a count of 7; feel and 'see' the light filling and energizing your body.
- Exhale for 7 silent counts, and 'see' greyish 'smoky' negative energy expelled from your lungs and body.
- Hold for a count of 7, and see this 'negative energy' dissipate into the air, gone forever.
- Continue this process until all that negative energy and stale air is gone from you, and your whole body, heart and mind are glowing with positive, healing and helpful energy.

## Third Pranayama Practice

This is a simple 'alternate nostril breathing' Pranayama practice. It does three things:

First, it balances the flow of energy through your body. In the chapter, **On Kundalini,** you read about the three 'meridians' (energy pathways) that flow through the body and, in the case of Kundalini energy, up the spinal column. The two that flow on either side of your body are called Ida and Pingala, and the central spinal column is Sushumna. They all begin at the base of your spine and rise to the crown. The energy flowing through Ida and Pingala ideally should be in balance with the flow of energy up the central nervous system, but in reality, your physical, emotional and mental states shift around during a stressful day, and so does the balance of your body's energy flow. In Tantra, the open or closed flow of air through your nostrils mirrors imbalance. Most always one nostril is clearer than the other. Alternate nostril Pranayama balances the flow up the channels of

---

[3] You can visualize specific colors of light for specific purposes. For example, you might use blue for calm, red for more energy, and so on. I sometimes visualize green light if I am ill. You can also mentally direct the positive light energy to a part of your body that needs healing, like a sore back or arthritic knee.

energy on either side of your spine, helps them align, and so balances the flow of Prana (energy) up through your body. This can help your meditation practice and your magickal work.

One way to do this alternate-nostril, balancing Pranayama is as follows:

- Sit straight and relax. Having already mastered the ***First*** and ***Second Pranayama Practices,*** you are prepared.
- Place a finger or thumb next to your nose.
- Do a few regular Pranayama breaths *(**First Pranayama Practice**)* to relax and get into a rhythm.
- After a final exhale do this:
- Close off your left nostril by gently pushing on the side of your nose with your finger, and slowly inhale through the right nostril to a count of 7.
- Hold for a count of 7.
- Now, in the same way and using the same finger, close off your right nostril.
- Exhale slowly through your left nostril to the count of 7.
- Hold for a count of 7.
- Now, inhale slowly to a count of 7 through your left nostril.
- Hold for a count of 7.
- Close off your left nostril with your finger.
- Exhale slowly through your right nostril to the count of 7.
- Hold for a count of 7.
- Now slowly inhale through your right nostril to the count of 7.
- Hold for a count of 7.
- Exhale slowly through your left nostril to the count of 7.
- Repeat.

This might seem complex, but it isn't and you'll get it quickly. To review, the pattern is: close a nostril, inhale, hold, switch, exhale, hold, inhale (same nostril), hold, switch, exhale hold, inhale (same nostril), hold and switch, etc.

You will experience many things once you have the slow, relaxed rhythm down. You will likely feel the energy of your body balancing, and often the breathing in both nostrils soon opens up. You may begin to hear a strange, high-pitched sound or ringing. You are hearing the Nadis, the sound of the flow up through your Ida, Pingala and

Sushumna. Relax, let it go. If you feel some energy blockages start to open, stop, stretch your body and your spine, help your body adjust, and then continue. Go easy; don't push it.

If you feel lightheaded or have any negative feelings like muscle cramps or dizziness, stop the alternate nostril breathing, and relax into simple slow, calm, deep breathing. When you are done, let all that energy flow back down your spine, through your tailbone and into the earth. Start with five minutes of alternate nostril breathing, and slowly increase the time each Zonule Rite.

As usual, write all results in your Journal!

## Mantra

*OM MANI PADME HUM*
*('The Jewel in the Center of the Lotus' Mantra)*

Most people know what a Mantra is, and we have already been using a few such as *Om Mani Padme Hum* and *OM*. A Mantra is a sacred word or sequence of sounds that manifests a special divine vibration. Mantras are used as an aid to meditation and for magick work. They make things happen.

The word Mantra comes from *Manas* (mind) and *Tra* (tool). So, Mantras are tools of the mind which are used to focus the power of vibration to control your mind and Will for inward or outward 'weaving' of magick. Remember, vibration is everything in Tantra, the cosmos, and our world. The purest vibrations are the simplest primal vibrations, and are called Bija (seed) Mantras. They are usually one simple sound like OM, and are the manifestation of divine powers of gods and spirits.

## Bija Mantras

Bija Mantras consist of solitary 'seed' sound-vibrations, usually written as a single Sanskrit glyph. OM (AUM) is the most famous Bija Mantra and the most important, being the vibration of God. There are a set number of Sanskrit glyphs, and when spoken each creates a potent energetic vibration. Most of these glyphs are also Bija Mantras. These glyphs, called the 'garland of letters,' are some of the most ancient written symbols in the world. They are considered sacred by Hindus, Tantrics and Buddhists, and are at the root of many languages in Asia. Many Bija Mantra glyphs are revered as being literally *the essence of a specific god or goddess.* For example, the Bija Mantra GAM is literally the manifesting vibration of the god Ganesh.

Here are some of the most important Bija Mantras that manifest the Tantric gods or goddesses introduced in this book. These are only a few of the many divine Bija Mantras, and is a good place to begin. *Here I am showing how each Bija is written in English, and how each one is actually pronounced. The one exception is OM and AUM which have identical pronunciations:*

| BIJA (written as:) | DEITY | PRONUNCIATION |
| --- | --- | --- |
| OM | Shiva | AUM |
| GAM | Ganesh | GAANG |
| HRIM | Tripurasundari/Lalita | HREENG |
| SRIM | Lakshmi | SHREENG |
| KRIM | Kali | KREENG |

Often Mantras contain a Bija Mantra in longer strings of sounds. They include common Mantras like OM GAANG GANESHAYA NAMAH. (Roughly this means: *OM (godhead) GAANG (Essence of Ganesh) Lord Ganesh, I honor you!)*

Most common Mantras are used for doing ritual work, or simply for focusing the mind in meditation, and include other terms like the name of a deity and honorifics along with the 'core' Bija of the deity. Getting used to seeing the widely-varied, but focused Tantric cosmology through Mantras will help you see how Tantra works with the varied aspects of different gods and goddesses.

So, when I vibrate OM, (vibrated as *Aum)* I manifest Shiva as the supreme godhead.

When I vibrate GAM (vibrated as *Gaang),* I manifest the Elephant Lord Ganesh.

When I vibrate KRIM (vibrated as *Kreeng),* I manifest Kali.

This is because OM *is* literally the Supreme Shiva (Adi Nath, Great Lord), and GAANG literally *is* Ganesh; and so on.

This is why they are called 'seed' Mantras.

Thus, simply vibrating 'GAANG' will bring Ganesh to you, and infuse whatever you are doing with 'Ganesh energy.' Full Mantras, like the Ganesh Mantra (OM GAANG GANAPATAYE NAMAH) are often a string of terms that wrap around the key seed Bija, here being GAANG. In this way a Mantra can manifest a whole invocation in one string of vibrations. Mantras, when done well, *are* full invocations. This one can be translated as: "Om! Deity Ganesh be here (GAANG)! Lord of the Ganas (GANA-PATI)! Honor to you! (NAMAH)

Keep in mind that Mantras are pronounced slightly differently in different parts of India, Nepal and other places, so you will see varied forms of pronunciation and spellings.

There are a limited number of Bijas, but thousands of Mantras. The ones I introduce in this text are often-used ones that my Gurus have given to me.

### *Mantra Practice*

Take a few minutes to look at the Mantras within the Zonule Rite, and think about how they function to empower you. You are casting your circle with the Mantra OM MANI PADME HUM which means, "By the Ultimate Divine Force (OM), I am a Jewel (eternal Spirit) in the Center of the Lotus (the cosmos)." This is a very ancient, very powerful Mantra that has many powers to convey.

There are many different forms and kinds of Mantra, and different ways they are chanted. There are traditional set 'metres' or intonation patterns for specific Mantras that change a Mantra's power. One form of these is called Gayatri, based on the 3000-year-old Gayatri Mantra for purification found in the *Rig Veda*. Many gods and goddesses have 'Gayatri stanzas' dedicated to them. There are several odd Mantras (like PHUT!) that are not god-forms; and some are pre-Sanskrit—like BOM, which is used in Mantras like BOM SHANKAR which honors the cannabis-smoking Shankar, a laid-back aspect of Shiva. Once you have done the practices to the point of familiarity and success, research and see what Mantras are out there, what they mean, and so on. Especially once you have beloved Ishta Devas—the gods you are bonding with—look up their Mantras. Often gods and goddesses have several Mantras with nuanced meanings. Some will feel right, and of course, each god or goddess can be asked directly about which Mantras are appropriate for you.

There are several things a Mantra can do as part of our Tantra work:

• It can focus the mind. As you meditate, distracting thoughts and feelings arise; chanting a Mantra gives your monkey-mind something to do. This allows your Guardian Spirit to arise and expand in your mind.

• It can encode specific powers or even spells. Gurudev Mahendranath says that a Mantra can "blow your mind and pubes asunder!" Intoning a Mantra can invoke and call forth the power or deity ascribed to it to do things.

• A Mantra can call a deity into your Zonule! Then it can be used to consecrate a prepared image (Murti) of that deity so it can be present during rites. From then on, that image is a ready place for the deity to indwell, so when the deity is present in that Murti, you can directly deal with the deity. This 'magick tech' was common in the ancient world and still works. All of this happens through Mantra.

### *Mantras for Consecrating Murtis*

Honor to Guruji Vilasanath who has provided me these powerful Mantras that can be used to consecrate and empower Murtis—to bless and prepare them as vessels of gods and goddesses.

I reprint here his information from personal correspondence:

> *"These, below are Mantras to bring deities to indwell in statues, or perhaps, icons:*

*[For Murtis of] Siva:*
- Om Am Hreeng Kraam Yaam Raam Laam
- Vam Saam Saam Saam Haam Ksaam

- Hamsa-Soham
- Sivaji Jiva Iha Sthitt

*[For Murtis of] Devi:*
- Aim Hreeng Krom Yaam Raam Laam Vaam
- Saam Saam Saam Haam Ksaam
- Hamsa-Soham
- Devyah Jiva Iha Sthitah

*[For Murtis of] Ganesh:*
- Om Am Krim Krom Yaam Raam Laam Vaam
- Sam Sam Ham Kasim
- Hamsa-Soham
- Ganapati Jiva Iha Sthitah

*Repeat the Mantra you are using 7 times for yourself blessing your Chakras, and then 7 times for the image's Chakras, anointing both your Chakras and the Chakras on the Murti with sandalwood or other oil, ash and saltwater mixed."*

## MALA WORK

*Mala of Alternating
Rudraksha Beads (Shiva) and Crystal Beads (Shakti)
(Photo by the Author)*

In Tantra, Malas are crucial tools for chanting Mantras, usually by counting the 108 beads one at a time while chanting. At first, it is best to get either a Rudraksha Mala or one made of sandalwood beads. The Rudraksha Mala is made from seeds of the Indian Rudraksha tree, named for the God Rudra, an aspect of Shiva. These Malas are powerful, protective and blessed by Shiva. Sandalwood Malas are healing, focusing, protective and powerful, and are most often associated with the Goddess in many of her aspects. Neither is very expensive, and both are good to have. As you progress in your work, you may feel or be guided to get different Malas, as each has its own power. Bone and crystal Malas are powerful, and there are many others. Malas are also fairly easy to make; remember to have 108 beads plus a 'Guru' or counting-bead that sticks up to mark the end of the Mala.

When you get a new Mala, wash it gently in salt water (sea water is best), and 'banish' or cleanse it as you did your Zonule space. Anoint it with a sacred oil; sandalwood oil is a great choice. As you do so, chant OM or another blessing Mantra you are drawn to. Then chant the Mantra indicated on the Zonule Rite 108 times while counting each bead with one hand. As you do so, focus on filling the Mala with glowing energy. Wear it to bed for several days to bind the Mala to you. From then on, you should always wear a charged Mala in the Zonule. The more you wear it, especially next to your skin, the stronger it will become. The more work you do with it, the more potent and protective it is. It is both a tool and a protective amulet. When traveling in India, Nepal and Bali, I always wore my Rudraksha Mala, and I was often identified and honored as a serious devotee of the gods.

When you are chanting, hold the Mala in one hand while holding one bead at a time with the fingers of that same hand as you utter the Mantra. Do this each time until you have finished 108 Mantras and counted 108 beads. This is referred to as 'finishing one Mala.' I recently did a Sadhana where I chanted 'three Malas' of the Ganesh Mantra each time, thus $108 \times 3$ or 324 repetition of this Mantra. In serious chanting sessions with other Tantrics, we often do 1008

Mantras rather than the usual 108[4]. It takes a long time, but it is very deep work, and induces a lovely trance state!

Malas can be used as potent magickal tools in other ways. You can hang them over a doorway or other place to protect and empower that place. A Mala can be wrapped about something to charge it with energy, including parts of your body. I've seen some Tantrics use it for simple 'knot' magick spells.

As you introduce a new Mala and new Mantras into your Zonule Rite, note your experiences in your Journal.

**Note:** Do the following exercises, one at a time, but wait to do ***Exercise 3: Mala Mantras and Pranayama*** (below) until you are very comfortable with Mantra work. In this way, you will get the clearest feedback when combining these practices.

### *Exercise 1: Mala Chanting*

During meditation, after you have sat, breathed for a time, and relaxed your body, begin to intone the Mantra *Om Mani Padme Hum*.[5] As you chant, hold the Mala in one hand. Hold each bead in turn as you chant the Mantra.

Do so slowly and carefully in a rhythmic manner.

Project the chant outward. Fill your Zonule with the energy.

Concentrate on the inbreath as you touch a bead, then chant the Mantra exhaling; then move to the next bead and repeat.

Using the beads eliminates the need to count. Once you are at the end of your string—at the 'Guru bead' (the extended bead)—you have done 108!

After you finish one round on your Mala, sit in quiet meditation and be open to what arises. How did it shift or change you? How did the Mantra 'vibrate' within you? Note all of this in your Journal. Next time, try three cycles of this chant with your Mala (108 × 3), and see how it affects you and the Zonule.

---

[4] For more on the significance of the number 1008, see:
   *theyogicjournal.com/pdf/2018/vol3issue1/PartO/3-1-160-636.pdf*

[5] This is one of the most powerful and beneficial Mantras we know. It centers you, and helps to build up your higher spiritual eternal Self. The Dalai Lama says it is the most important Mantra of all.

### Exercise 2: Japa Chanting with the Mala

Japa literally means 'muttering', that is, chanting very quietly and often quickly, even subliminally. You have been intoning or chanting the Mantra in a vibratory 'outward' voice; now try muttering or whispering and internally focusing on the Mantra while doing it a bit faster with more of a rhythm. This means you won't be loudly chanting like: *Om-ma-ni-pad-me-hum,* but rather muttering it quietly and quickly in one exhalation like: *ommanipadmehum.* The first practice was a slow drum beat; now it is fast and flows together. It will take you less than half the time to do one string of 108. Focus on the Mantra, and as you mutter/whisper it, quietly bring it into your body, into your heart. Sink into the rhythmic, continuous wave of sound—almost a drone. Once done, wear the Mala and slide into quiet meditation. Be open to what arises. Again, how do you feel and what was different this time? What did the Mantra conjure within you?

Do this a few times, and then extend your chanting to 3 cycles or 108 × 3 chants.

Ask yourself: How were these two ways of chanting different? Think about when you would use each mode of chanting for different kinds of Tantric work.

### Exercise 3: Mala Mantras and Pranayama

Do the Zonule Rite, and when you have begun meditation, begin simple Pranayama, but with a slight difference. Instead of 'counting 7 in, 7 hold, 7 out, 7 hold' as you have been doing, you will use a silent internal Mantra to replace the 'count 7' part. Do this:

- Inhale and *slowly and silently* 'chant' in your mind: *Om Mani Padme Hum.*
- Hold and silently 'chant' in your mind: *Om Mani Padme Hum.*
- Exhale and silently 'chant' in your mind: *Om Mani Padme Hum.*
- Hold and silently 'chant' in your mind: *Om Mani Padme Hum.*
- Repeat.

You are simply replacing the distraction of counting to 7 with a slow, 7-count Mantra.

Once you get the hang of it, you can also use your Mala at the same time to count the Mantras. (You only need one hand for your Mala; the other hand can be used for alternate nostril breathing.)

All of this takes a bit of practice and coordinating, but soon it will seem natural, and the internal rhythms of the breathing and Mantra will sync-up.

The now-silent, internalized Mantra will fill you and flow in and out with each breath cycle.

When you are done, wear the Mala and meditate. Focus on the point of light—the Jewel in the Lotus—within you, as the internalized Mantra fades. I suspect you will find this a powerful experience. Be open to what arises. How do you feel? How did this experience differ from simple Pranayama and simple Mantra repetition? This synergistic practice of combining two (or more) powerful practices to make everything more powerful is a key to Tantric practices. As you add more practices and combine them, you will see how Tantric weaves them together to create powerful sublime experiences and potent magick. Note any experiences like these in your Journal.

### *Finally*

Of course, this is just the beginning of Mantra work. There are many books on this subject! Mantras can be chanted, muttered or even shouted (JAI GANESH!!!), and can be projected externally or absorbed internally, depending on what you wish to do. Mantras can 'supercharge' your ritual work, especially when combined with Pranayama and other practices like as Yoga Asanas and Mudras (sacred hand gestures)—among other practices. I've guided you to use the Mantra OM MANI PADME HUM because it brings many spiritual benefits. It also empowers and symbolizes your Zonule sphere (lotus) and the central Dragon Seat/you (jewel).

Once you have worked with this Mantra with these different modalities, experiment with other Mantras! Here are a few potent and useful Mantras, many of which you have been using:

OM GAANG GANAPATAYE NAMAH [Praise and honor to
   the god Ganesh.]
OM NAMAH SHIVAYA [Praise and honor to the god Shiva.]

HREENG SHREENG KREENG PARAMESHVARI SVAHA
[Goddess Shakti, Goddess Lakshmi, Goddess Kali—
Greatest Goddess of all, bless me!]

OM SHANTI SHIVA SHAKTI [Om, the union of Shiva & Shakti is Peace!]

As a devotee of the Tibetan-Buddhist Goddess Tara, I use and recommend this Mantra for healing:

OM TARE TUTTARE TURE SOHA [I bow to the Liberator Tara, Mother of all the Victorious Ones]

There are many thousands of Mantras, and more will be revealed as you explore our Twilight World. Some will blow your mind.

As you practice and master Tantric magick, your Guardian Spirit will point out Mantras and practice combinations that will help you find your own path. Follow that inner voice. The right Mantras for your Great Work will come to you.

## Yantra Work

*A Yantra of Ganesh*

Yantras are simple, often ancient, geometric symbols that come directly from Tantra, not Hinduism. They are increasingly popular images nowadays. As Bija Mantras are the vibrations that embody a deity's energy, Yantras are the key symbol or sigil that manifests the Tantric deity on a visual and magickal level. They are magick diagrams, and are often used in our work to create a place for a deity to 'land' after being invoked in Puja. *Yantra* comes from the Sanskrit root word *Yam* (a thing that supports the essence of an object); and *Tra* which comes from *Trana* (liberation from bondage). Therefore, a Yantra means 'a supporting tool for attaining liberation.' Yantra is sometimes translated into English as 'magick device' or 'machine' which seems a bit odd to me, so I prefer 'magick construct that manifests a sacred power.' With the right Mantra, Yantra and Murti, you can invoke and honor a Tantric god or goddess, and do magick with them. Most Tantric deities have one or more Yantras.

Nothing illustrates the commercialization of Tantra like the proliferation of Yantra stickers, bedspreads and t-shirts with little understanding of what they are, or how they are used. Yantras are not posted on a wall or used as decorations when doing Tantric rites. However, a Yantra can be set upright on the altar as a Mandala (an object of meditation), something many Tantric Buddhists do, and it is a good practice if you seek to deeply know the mystery of a particular Yantra. However, this is not how Yantras are usually used in Tantra; most often they are laid flat.

Yantras are first created, and then empowered before ritual use. Such Yantras, once empowered by a deity, can then be carried or worn as protective or empowering amulets. However, the normal ritual use of a Yantra in Tantra is quite different.

In Tantric rites and spells, Yantras—after being created and empowered ritually—are laid flat on your altar, often with a Murti of the deity behind it. The spiritual power of that deity is visualized arising from the center of the Yantra when it is invoked. Another use of a Yantra: items can be placed upon it during rites to bless and empower these items with the energy of that god or goddess. I always place a cup of water upon a Yantra during Pujas, and after the ritual I drink it to absorb the energy of that deity. This is also a common Tantric technique with food. If you are familiar with Craft, Magick or Pagan practices, it is akin to placing items to be blessed on a pantacle.

Yantras predate the Sanatana Dharma (Hinduism). Most contain several basic traditional shapes and forms in various combinations. Some of the most common design elements, from the center out, are:

**The Bindu:** the CenterPoint of pure spirit or beingness. It is always considered OM and/or Shiva.

**The Trikona:** A Trikona (sacred triangle form) is often part of Yantras, often the center. In general, a downward pointing triangle is the Yoni of the Goddess, and a simple upward pointing triangle may represent Shiva. A simple downward pointing triangle Yantra represents Kali.

**The Shatkona:** When the upward and downward triangles interpenetrate, a six-pointed star (or more complex image) is formed, representing the conjoining of Shiva and Shakti.

**The Padma:** This represents a circle of Lotus petals, and the unfolding of the cosmos. It encircles the main image of the Yantra.

**The Bhupura:** The Bhupura is a square image with four 'gates,' and is the outermost 'base' of the whole Yantra. Bhu means 'earth', and Bhu Devi is the Earth Mother; thus, she is, in many ways, the foundation of all Yantras.

Yantras are magick, and each one embodies a specific power or energy matrix. The construction of a Yantra opens like a flower, expanding outward from the Bindu centerpoint. Next are often one or more geometric forms, sometimes simple, sometimes complex. For example, in the Ganesh Yantra (above), the Bindu centerpoint opens up to a 6-pointed star, and then a triangle, then a circle, next an opening lotus and a circle, and finally, the deity energy is enshrined within the square 'wall 'of the Bhupura with its 'four gates.' This shows that this is both the essence of the deity as well as a temple to that deity. It will come as no surprise that Tantric temples are constructed in this manner.

As you have seen, our multifaceted Tantric world has many possibilities, some of which can seem contradictory. You will find that many Tantric goddesses and gods have a variety of both Mantras and Yantras for various aspects. A god like Ganesh, for example, has several different Yantras ascribed to him. Some, like the famous Shri Yantra, are ascribed to more than one Goddess. For example, both Lakshmi and Lalita Tripurasundari are represented by the most famous Yantra, the Shri Yantra, but in slightly different forms. Part of your Tantric work as a Westerner is to accept variations and variety in such things as part of our Twilight World, and work with what feels right to you when choices are offered. This multiplicity is the norm in Pantheistic, Pagan and Animist cultures. The **Pujas** section of this book offers the most commonly used Yantras for each deity. In your Zonule, the right Yantra to use is the one that the deity or your Guardian Spirit indicates. What works for you is most critical.

### Exercise 4: 'Entering,' Exploring, and Imprinting a Yantra

It is useful to meditate on a Yantra before you use this magick device. In this way you will be able to absorb and resonate with the ancient, complex power within it. Concentration and visualization will help you mentally enter the temple of the Yantra, and allow access to Yantra 'gateways' in dreams.

*Another Common Yantra of Ganesh*

• Begin with the Ganesh Yantra (above). It is helpful to have an image of Ganesh on the altar as well. The Yantra of Ganesh is simple, uses familiar imagery, and since we always begin every ritual with Ganesh, it is a good place to begin. He is, after all, the 'Lord who removes obstacles.'

• If you can, draw this Yantra when doing your Zonule Rite rather than just printing it. It doesn't have to be perfect, but using a ruler and compass helps. As you draw it, repeatedly vibrate Ganesh's Bija Mantra (GAANG) and visualize the elephant-headed God. When you are done, vibrate GAANG and bless your Yantra with incense smoke (Air), a quick brush through the candle flame (Fire), a drop of Water, and touch it to the stone or Yoni-Lingam (Earth). Then place your hands over it and visualize light flowing into it, thus charging it with Spirit. Visualize it glowing with the power of Ganesh. End by saying three times JAI GANESH! (Hail Ganesh!)

- Now, display the new Yantra so you can see it clearly, either flat on the altar or propped up.
- Meditate on it for a time, focusing on the center Bindu. Then, do Pranayama as you focus intently on the centerpoint. Let your consciousness flow into the Yantra through that point. With every breath cycle, enter the Yantra more deeply. Let it expand so it fills your world.
- When it fills your whole mind, vibrate OM GAANG three times, and see it come alive with energy and light. End the Pranayama, clear your mind, sit within the energy sphere of the Yantra, and open yourself to it.
- Be silent, open and clear. Let the Yantra speak to you. Watch how the energies of this ancient image flow and sparkle through the circuitry of the form. Open yourself to it.
- When you feel this experience coming to a natural end, return to doing Pranayama and inhale the energy of the Yantra and Ganesh into your body. Close your eyes and 'see' the Yantra glowing in your heart. Place your finger to your lips, and inhale slowly until it is only a point of light. Vibrate OM.
- Open your eyes and finish the Zonule ritual. You will keep this Yantra for future work, so color, improve and frame as you like. The next time you call on Ganesh, lay the Yantra flat on the altar, place his Murti behind it, and place offerings to Ganesh on it before doing Mantras to Ganesh or other work.
- As you work in your Zonule, any Yantra you place on the altar becomes the centerpoint of the magick there, and will continue to absorb and hold energy. Simply laying out the Ganesh Yantra immediately invokes Ganesh, for example. As you make and use more Yantras and collect Murtis of associated deities, it is best to put away the ones not being used, under the altar if possible. Leaving a Kali Yantra on the altar when calling on Ganesh, for example, will cause some energetic dissonance, so be consistent in your focus.

### *Exercise 5: Using the Yantra to Empower*

You will use the Ganesh Yantra for these next two exercises. You have created and empowered a Ganesh Yantra, so each practice with it will show you how to use any Yantra.

- Place the Ganesh Yantra on your altar with the Murti of Ganesh. Place a cup of pure water on the Yantra, and begin the Zonule Rite. As you do the Rite, meditate on Ganesh, but do not do Pranayama.
- Now, close your eyes and visualize the Ganesh Yantra as you meditate. You may look at the Yantra a few times as you do so until you can hold the image in your mind's-eye.
- When you can 'see' and hold the image, vibrate OM GAANG three times and 'enter it' as you did before. Then, slowly open your eyes and see the actual Yantra, now glowing with power.
- Take up the cup of water. Take a sip and pay attention to what it tastes like. Remember this.
- Now, place the cup back on the center of the Yantra, putting your open hands together at your heart. Imagine the image of the God Ganesh. Bow and honor the god by chanting OM SHRI GANESHAYA NAMAH! (Honor to Divine Ganesh!), and feel the energy of Ganesh flowing into you.
- Now, briskly rub your hands together, and feel them become energized with the energy of Ganesh. Hold both hands over the cup of water on the Yantra. Chant the Mantra OM GAANG eleven times. As you do this, visualize the energy flowing through your hands and into the water. See the Yantra and the water glow with the energy of Ganesh as you concentrate. Now, touch your finger to your lips, end the flow of power, and center yourself in your heart. Visualize the water still glowing, filled with the power of Ganesh.
- Silently thank Ganesh for this blessing. How has the water changed? Close your eyes and taste the difference. Meditate on this. You have changed the water into something divine. As you drink it, feel the energy of Ganesh flow into you and fill you. Meditate on this. How did it change you? What visions or thoughts did you have? Write it all down in your Journal for later contemplation.
- Finally, with your hands together, bow and thank Ganesh as you wish and finish the Zonule Rite.

This is a simple example of how a Yantra 'machine' can be used to conjure, focus and empower the divine energy of a deity into an object. You can do this with almost anything. Keep in mind the nature and proclivities of Ganesh and what he embodies: he removes all obstacles and brings good luck and blessings!

### Exercise 6: Enthroning the Deity in the Yantra

Before you do this exercise, consider getting to know Ganesh a bit more by reading the Ganesh chapter in this book, or by doing some research. Spend time memorizing what your favorite image of Ganesh is like so you can easily call forth the image in your mind.

• For this version of the Zonule Rite, the Ganesh Yantra is laid flat in the center of the altar, and your Murti of Ganesh is placed upon the center of the Yantra. A small cup of coconut water or another juice is placed on the Yantra before the Murti. The vase has special flowers for Ganesh, and a sweet or candy is in a small cup or bowl before the Yantra. Everything else is the same.

• Do the Zonule Rite as usual. When it is time to meditate, do so for a time on Ganesh. Use Pranayama as you like as you concentrate on your Ganesh Murti with your eyes open. After a time, close your eyes, clearly visualize an image of Ganesh, and use the energy from the Pranayama to expand and clarify this mental image. Now, silently call to Ganesh to manifest in the Murti by silently and internally vibrating OM GAANG SVAHA and inviting him to sit upon and reside in his Yantra—his throne.

• When you are done, visualize the image of the now-enthroned Ganesh glowing with a new power. Now, with open eyes, take one flower from the vase and hold it to your 'third eye.' Quietly intone JAI GANESHA! and 'see' it glow. Hold the flower to your heart. Again, intone JAI GANESHA! and 'see' it glow. Hold the flower to your loins/base center, and again intone JAI GANESHA! With your eyes half open, hold the flower before you and 'see' it glow.

• Chant OM GAANG! and place the flower directly on the centerpoint of the Yantra while intensely visualizing Ganesh glowing and enthroned on his Yantra, looking at you kindly.

• With your hands together at your heart, bow to the god and intone JAI GANESHA, NAMASTE! ('Yea Ganesh, Welcome!') three times.

• Now, take out your Mala. Sit and quietly chant OM GAANG GANESHAYA NAMAH! 108 times while communing with the god Ganesh who is now sitting right in front of you within his Yantra.

This combination of techniques comes together in a synergistic way to accomplish great magick in Tantra. The merging of Yantra,

Mantra, Visualization, Pranayama and other practices is key to many Tantric rituals, especially Pujas.

- Now you are in communion with the god Ganesh. What do you want from him? What questions will you ask? It is up to you, but listen! Ganesh is *now present,* enthroned within his Yantra shrine, pleased with the offerings and energy you have given him. What communication do you wish? You may ask for favors or wisdom. This is how we access direct gnosis or power from a Tantric deity.
- Sit with Ganesh as long as you wish. When you are done, bow three times and say JAI GANESHA! each time along with whatever heartfelt thanks you want to offer. 'See' the flame-energy of Ganesh die down, sinking into the Yantra as he leaves, returning to his abode on top of the Holy Mountain. Finish the Zonule Rite as usual.

**Final Notes:** You can use this simple exercise for any deity and his or her Yantra. In this way, you energize and bless the Murti, the Yantra, all the offerings, and invoke the deity into your very being for healing, help, protection—whatever you desire. Some deities come more easily than others, and with different powers! Some gods, like people, are easier to get to know than others, but building up one-on-one relationships with deities and our Tantric tools is crucial to success in this magick.

The food and drink offered to Ganesh is now Prasad (god-blessed), and should be consumed so you can receive its power. Or, you may share it with a friend who needs the blessing. Keep in mind that it is the charged Yantra that is acting as the portal, shrine or 'throne' of Ganesh since that Yantra is the *abstract* embodiment of Ganesh as his blessed Murti is his *visual* embodiment. Ganesh is well-known as an easygoing, caring and open god whom anyone can call upon for help and removal of obstacles. I have found that around the full or near full-moon is best for working with him.

## Chakras/Body Centers

Ah, Chakras. There is so much fluffy New Age stuff out there on Chakras—some good, a lot silly. For the record, Chakras do not exist as a rainbow in traditional Tantra or Hinduism, only in New Age shops. Let me now discuss Chakras as they are described in Tantra, and as I know and understand them.

Chakra is the Sanskrit word for 'wheel,' and describes energy-centers on the human body that can be felt, or even seen, by mystics. Much like acupuncture points, Chakras are generally places where bundles of nerves or specific glands are located. In other words, Chakras are about physical centers on the body based on real physiological and bioelectric qualities. There is nothing supernatural about Chakras. Such energy centers were mapped thousands of years ago in India, China and elsewhere so people could work with them for healing and balancing the energies running through our bodies. Bio-energy flows through our nerves and collects where they bundle, and so energize functions of key parts of our body. Those with paranormal abilities (Siddhis) can perceive these centers as 'spinning wheels,' or swirls of exceptional energy.

Are there seven Chakras? Though it has become a fixed, New Age belief in the West as a kind of Chakra trope, it is not accurate. There are many Chakra systems with different numbers of Chakras. The 7-Chakra system works fine—I've used it for years—but there are many different Chakra systems in India, and especially in Tantra.

I have seen depictions of Chakra systems with 3, 4, 6, 9, 12 or more Chakras. Most line up on the body from base to crown along the spinal column, but several include the important and often ignored Chakras on the palms and feet. Keep these hand Chakras in mind when we discuss Mudras and the Tantric magical work of charging items or sending spells! It is from *these* potent Chakras that we often project power.

If you do some research, you'll see that *different Chakra systems are often used when working with different deities.* Someone doing a Tantric Shiva-working will often use a very different Chakra system than someone focusing on the Goddess Lalita Tripurasundari. Also, some Tantric sects teach different, secret Chakra systems. There is not one universal Chakra system, and as you'll see, we use a very old 3-Chakra system in this book. Many Tantrics, including Dadaji Mahendranath, focus on the 7-Chakra system at times, but also reference others Chakra patterns like the 9-Chakra system used in the Shri Vidya System. As in all Paganism, there is flexibility and variety, and different magick tools for different purposes.

Tantrics firmly believe that the human body is the supreme tool for all our spiritual and magickal work. It is through our body and brain that we attain magical powers and enlightenment, and work with our ancient, archetypal gods. Here is what you need to know:

The most important energy pathways are the Ida, Pingala and Sushumna meridians that run from the base of the spine to the crown of your head. The Sushumna is the middle pillar bundle of nerves running up the spine—the path of the Kundalini power. Ida and Pingala are parallel bundles of nerves that run up the left and right side of the body, parallel to the spine/Sushumna. The goals of Pranayama, meditation, Yoga and other Tantric Techniques are to balance and open these pathways for healing and magick. The key power-points along them are the Chakras. Energy can get blocked, and thus cause mental, physical, emotional and spiritual issues. This is what Tantric techniques can help unblock—as can acupuncture. Free-flowing energy, when channeled, focused and activated, can cause bursts of healing, magick, ecstasy, and at times, enlightened states of consciousness. This work with natural bioelectric energy flows through the esoteric science behind Tantra.

As mentioned, there is no 'correct' number of Chakras. If are familiar with and like the 7-Chakra system, use it in your Tantric work. I'll be focusing on a more primal 3-Chakra system, but both are fine. (If you meditate on them both you'll see they are interwoven.) I urge you to avoid much of the 'New Age' take on Chakras because it is not Tantric and the hype is often used just to sell stuff. In my opinion, holding a colored stone will not activate a particular Chakra. Mantra, Pranayama and other focused Tantric practices will.

## The Three Body-Center Chakras

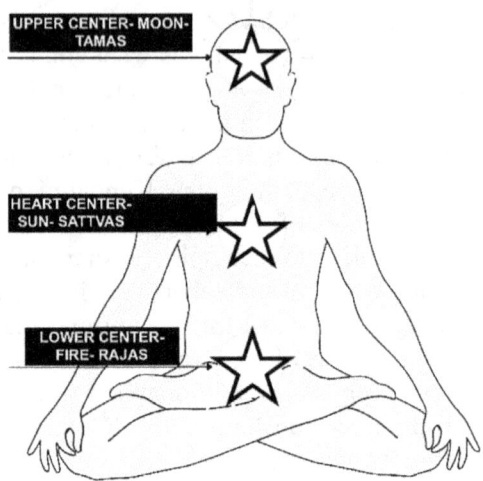

Nath Tantrika, the basis of this book, focuses on a more primal '3-body Chakra' system that lines up with many of the triplicities we have already looked at (e.g., the three Gunas, the three Shaktis and Shiva's Trishul. (For other examples, please review the 'Chart of Triplicities' in the **Tantric Triplicities** chapter.)

The three body-center Chakras are larger and more general centers of power on the body. They are:

The upper-body Chakra—Moon Center—Knowledge Shakti
The center-heart Chakra—Sun Center—Will Shakti
The lower-body Chakra—Fire Center—Action Shakti

If you are used to the 7-Chakra system, you can see that the three body-center Chakras include the seven Chakras like so:

The upper-body Chakra: Crown Chakra, Third Eye, Throat Chakra
The center-heart Chakra: Heart Chakra
The lower-body Chakra: Belly Chakra, Genital Chakra, Base Chakra

The three body-center Chakra model is useful in our Tantric Magick in several ways, and is an effective way to align the three-fold Tantric energies with the key fundamental symbols, purposes and powers that embody Tantra.

Here are three exercises for utilizing the three Chakra-centers in your practices, all within the Zonule Rite:

### Exercise 7: Activating the Three Chakra Body-Centers

Begin the Zonule Ritual, and when you begin meditating, use the basic Pranayama practice. Pay careful attention to the energy flowing through your whole body; then close your eyes and feel how it increases your energy flow and reinvigorates your body.

Next, with each breath, visualize an upward-pointing, triangular-shaped 'bonfire' igniting at the base of your body and rising up, incorporating your base, your sex center, and your gut fire-center. Feel and 'see' the warmth and power. You are gently accessing the collective body-energy called Kundalini, but that is not the main goal now. Visualize and feel the ever-moving vitality in your body, your sexuality, and especially the fiery 'action center' near your solar plexus. All of this collective bioelectric energy augments this powerful fire energy. Now awaken it as the Shakti that empowers, maintains and inflames your physical body.

Keep doing Pranayama as the tip of this rising energy reaches your heart-chest body center. Visualize this fire becoming a small sun glowing in your heart as it grows in brightness, size and power. Feel this sun expanding. Soon, beaming rays of golden light fill your whole chest, the great divine sun now filling you. Like the sun, your heart-center-sun is the center, the source of will, of life. Take time to feel this radiant sun warm your heart and soul and elicit emotions of peace, truth and True Will.

As you continue Pranayama, 'see' the light of the heart-sun shine upward, activating your upper-body center. As it flows through your throat and into your head, 'see' your 'third eye' as the center of this new expansion of pure light. As it slowly blooms, so too does the power of your mind expand. At the same time, see a silvery white glow begin to expand about your head and upper-body-center, a pale lunar halo fed by the rays of the heart-center that illuminate this now bright, moon-like glow that fills your head and shoulders. Visualize this increasingly calming and soothing moonglow increase in luminosity as the rising energy empowers this expanding, silvery, lunar body-center. The heat of the base-center fire has been focused by the sun, and is now a cool glow of reflection and mental expansion of consciousness. Continue Pranayama and focus on this visualization. Now, visualize your three body-centers as a triangle of fire arising from the base of your spine, with a sun balancing upon its point, filling your heart and chest, crowned by a silvery white halo about your head and shoulders within which faintly glows a lunar crescent, horns pointing up. Finally, a ray of light rises from the base of your spine, flows through all three power centers, and shoots up through the crown of your head into the infinite: OM. Continue Pranayama and meditate upon it in silence for a time.

Visualize the fire, sun and moon images amidst the intense light that now fills your whole body. When you can clearly hold this image in your mind, let it dissolve into pure light filling your whole body, and being absorbed, dissolving into your heart.

Stop Pranayama and just breathe deeply and naturally; then put your hands together at your heart. Feel the energy empower your whole body as you absorb the combined powers of the three body-Chakras. Then chant:

OM SHANTI SHIVA SHAKTI [3x]

Finish the Zonule Rite; record your experiences in your Journal.

After you have done this exercise a few times, you will have absorbed the symbolism and the powers associated with the three body-Chakras. Take time to review the 'Three Shaktis Chart' in the **Tantric Triplicities** chapter. You may find it has new meaning now.

### *Exercise 8: Focusing and Utilizing the Three Chakra Body-Centers*

After you have practiced *Exercise 7* a few times, it will be easy for you to activate your Three Chakra Body-Centers in this way. During this work, keep in mind the triplicities symbolized as fire/sun/moon. In meditation, let these things unfold naturally in your deep mind. The bio-energy you manifest and learn to enhance and channel is your energy source, and can accomplish anything with your will and imagination through the three powers of Knowledge, Will and Action.

The purpose of this exercise is to charge an item with this power for spiritual work—whether it is an amulet, a tool, or even a simple stone. For this practice, choose an item that you will use as a charm for protection or good luck. Find something new that feels right, then clear and cleanse it with salt water and a chant of OM, and put it on the altar. Now, do the Zonule Rite as usual. When you are meditating and in a deep state of calm, do Pranayama and visualize the Body-Center Chakras as you did before. Once you can feel and clearly visualize the three body-center Chakras glowing, then with your eyes closed, pick up the item you have chosen to 'charge' with one hand.

Hold the item against your lower-body-center, and see it immersed in the center of the fierce fire of that active power. With your will, have the fire-energy flow into the item until it flames and glows like a ruddy coal in a furnace. Do Pranayama as you are doing this, while in your mind you vibrate OM. Hold it there, relax the energy, and let it rise in your body as before.

Now, with your eyes still closed, and still doing Pranayama, raise the item up to your heart with one hand. Visualize the solar power of the Heart-Body Center flow into the item. 'See' the red glow and golden solar power mingle and swirl within the item as more and more solar energy is directed into it until it shines like the sun. Continue Pranayama and focus your will as you are doing this, while in your mind, silently vibrate OM. Hold it there and then relax. Pull your solar glow back a bit. The item is now glowing with the writhing power of the golden sun and a tinge of red fire. Now, while still doing Pranayama and with your eyes closed, raise the item to your third eye, the heart of the peaceful, potent moon-power of your upper body-center. Hold the item up to your head with one hand; use your will and visualize the silvery power of the whitish halo-light filling the item with intense, but calm power. Visualize the lunar energy swirling about the item, mixing with the fiery and solar energies. See them swirl together in a powerful alchemical bonding as they combine and glow with a pure, bright light. Keep doing Pranayama as you visualize this, while silently vibrating OM. Hold it there and relax.

Touch the item to your crown, slowly finish your Pranayama, and chant OM. Then place the item on the Yoni-Lingam or another place on the altar.

To end: Do simple, deep-breathing Pranayama for a time until all the energies settle down. Visualize your body absorbing them as before. Now, place your hands together at your heart and 'see' the final remnants of all that energy finish being absorbed. Let any energies left over sink down into the base of your body, and visualize that energy flowing down deep into the earth.

Finally, place your hands flat on the ground and let all the excess energy and tension in your body sink into the earth while offering it silently to the Earth Mother. You are now back to earth! Finally, wrap the item in the small cloth, finish your Zonule Rite, and later, hold the item and feel the power locked in it! This simple technique can be used to charge any item you wish; intent is crucial.

### Exercise 9: Empowering Your Bond with Your Guardian Spirit with the Three Chakra Body-Centers

In the *Guru Gita,* it is explained that there are two places that your Atman or Guardian Spirit manifests: the heart and the crown. This is similar to Western Ceremonial Magic where the 'Guardian Angel' is said to reside in the sun-sphere at the center of the Tree of Life *and* at 'the Crown,' the top of the Tree. I find this synchronicity fascinating.

The goal of this exercise is to use your Three Chakra Body-Centers to forge a more intense connection with your Guardian Spirit; this will help all of your work. Begin the Zonule Rite, and then do Pranayama just like in *Exercise 7*.

When you have visualized, empowered and manifested the lower fiery center, the solar heart center, and the upper lunar center while doing Pranayama, merge the three energies into a massive, bright light in your heart center.

Focus and visualize this heart-light clearly, and do Pranayama for a time. As you do so, silently ask your Guardian Spirit to reveal to you an image or symbol. Focus on this intensely, and silently chant **OM MANI PADME HUM** in sync with your Pranayama until an image or symbol appears. Honor this image or symbol as a personal icon of your Guardian Spirit, your Atman.

As you silently chant in your mind and continue doing Pranayama, see this icon shining with infinite rays from your heart, filling your whole body and then the universe with rays of love, healing and light.

Sit with this. Slow, then stop the Pranayama, and silence the internal Mantra. Breathe and relax into this vision. Be silent for a time, and be open to communication from your Guardian Spirit as you continue to visualize the icon given to you, glowing like the sun. Let the presence, power and love of your Guardian Spirit fill and inform you. This is a time of deep communication. Write down everything that comes to you.

You are forging an extremely important connection, one crucial to Tantric work and success in life. Listen to the 'silent voice' that will guide you.

When this intense 'gnosis' starts to fade, begin breathing deeply in a relaxed manner, and visualize the icon becoming a single point of intense light. See it rising from your heart, through your throat, then through your third eye, until finally the glowing star is hovering just above your crown.

As you do this, feel your whole body becoming a conduit of divine power from the cosmos, to coalesce in this crown-star, the true form of your Guardian Spirit. Chant OM. Be still. Accept the pure light of OM, the cosmos: God.

Then, with a great, full-body **OM!**, release the sacred energy up and out, and see the glowing light that is your Guardian Spirit, your Soul, merge with the cosmos. Place your finger to your lips and bring your body down to the earth. Feel the light of the cosmos gently come down through your crown, your heart, and finally, into your lower body and then the earth as you 'land.'

To end, place your hands together at your heart. Visualize the point of light that is your Guardian Spirit at your heart, for it is always with you.

As you let the light of your Guardian Spirit dissolve into your body, chant GURU OM three times. Touch the earth. Thank Her.

Sit in peace and let this settle for a time. Write or draw in your Journal everything important that you experienced. When you are ready, finish your Zonule Rite.

You can do this 'conversation with the Guardian Spirit' exercise whenever you want to, especially when you need guidance from your Atman, your personal Guru.

## NYASA

The purpose of *Nyasa* is simply to energize and empower you. If you have any physical problems, this can be used for healing as well. Nyasa (meaning 'setting down') is a powerful, hands-on technique that is Tantric in origin, but has spread to Hinduism. It is purely magickal in nature. Keep in mind that the palms of your hands have Chakras on them, and thus the hands are important in transferring energy. In the West this is called hands-on energy healing, or transferring energy onto a person for healing, empowerment or protection. This empowerment is usually done in Nyasa while uttering a Mantra. The Nyasa can be done simply, like the exercise that follows, but sometimes a Nyasa utilizes multiple Mantras. Nyasa work, if done well, can 'light up' a person's energetic body. Depending on the purpose, Nyasa can be a direct transfer of energy, or can be used to help a person by channeling the power of a particularly useful god or goddess. A well-known Nyasa that calls upon the goddess Tripurasundari is a complex, lengthy ritual that includes all the planetary powers and many aspects of the Goddess. It can take hours!

Traditionally a Nyasa is supposed to be done by a holy man (Rishi) who 'lays hands' on various parts of a person's body in a specific order, often while vibrating specific Mantras. However, self-blessing with Nyasa is acceptable, and I have worked with Nyasa in this way for decades. Once you are centered in your Tantric work, you can empower yourself or others with Nyasa. It is an amazing magickal technique.

The Nyasa offered here is simple and safe. The goal is to help you become familiar with this practice, gain some facility with it, and then leave you to explore and expand your skill. Once you get the hang of it, you can do research a variety of Nyasa practices, or create your own—with the guidance of your Guardian Spirit.

Before we begin: Safety first!

With Nyasa you will be generating, channeling and working with a lot of energy. If at any point you experience discomfort or feel overloaded, remember that you are in control and can slow the energy flow at will, or simply stop. A simple technique for doing this is like so:

Place both hands on the ground. Visualize all the energy you are working with flowing down into the loving, supportive Mother Earth. Then do Pranayama until the energy settles down and all is calm and settled.

In general, do not do Nyasa if you are sick or having any sort of physical, emotional or mental issues. If you are planning to practice Nyasa on yourself or another, make sure that you are calm and have showered with a bit of salt before you begin the Zonule Rite.

### Exercise 10: Nyasa Empowering with OM

Begin your Zonule Rite as usual. When you begin meditating, do the simple Pranayama practice, just breathing in, holding, breathing out, holding, and so on. As you do so, visualize your body filling with bright energy with every inhalation. When you feel calm, energized and centered, place your open hands palms up on your knees. Relax, continue to do this simple Pranayama, and focus on your hands. With every in-breath, visualize the energy flowing down from your crown and up from the earth, and flowing to your heart center. With every exhalation, see this collected light-energy flow down your arms into your hands.

Visualize your palms glowing with increasingly brighter light. Continue to do this as you begin to silently chant OM with every exhalation. Meditate on this: The bright energy pooling in your palms is OM.

Continue this process for a short time until your hands are fully energized. Now, slow the Pranayama until you are just breathing naturally and deeply. As you do so, feel the silent OM vibration flowing into your incandescent hands. It is no longer coming from your mind; the OM vibration is in your hands! Feel them vibrate with the essence of the cosmos.

Now, open your eyes slightly. Hold your hands up, with your palms facing each other about a foot apart, and feel the energy from each hand. Slowly move the palms closer together. What do you experience? Gently touch them together until you feel the intensity of the power growing. Feel your whole being filled with echoes of this energy. Take time to experience this new power.

Place your palms together, and chant aloud one long OM, and honor the divine power.

In the steps below, you will place either your left or right hand upon different parts of your body as directed, depending on which hand is closest to that body part. As you do so, you will slowly vibrate OM aloud, quietly and deeply, and visualize the glowing power of OM moving through your hands and into your body. You will 'see' the light fill that area of your body, and feel the humming energy of OM as it is pleasantly absorbed into your flesh, bones and muscle. Do this slowly and calmly, step by step like so:

- Place a hand on each foot, one at a time. Chant OM! Visualize the energy flowing in.
- Place a hand on each leg, one at a time. Chant OM! Visualize the energy flowing in.
- Place a hand on each thigh, one at a time. Chant OM! Visualize the energy flowing in.
- Place both hands on your genitals. Chant OM! Visualize the energy flowing in.
- Place both hands on your belly. Chant OM! Visualize the energy flowing in and empowering your belly and organs.
- Place both hands on your breasts. Chant OM! Visualize the energy flowing into your heart and lungs with positive energy.
- Cross your arms, and place your hands, one on each shoulder. Chant OM! Let the energy flow into your shoulders and back.
- Cross your arms, and place your hands, one on each arm. Chant OM! Let the energy flow in!
- Place both hands on your throat and empower it. Chant OM! Let the energy flow in!
- Place both hands on either side of your head. Chant OM! Let the energy flow into your skull and brain!
- Place both hands over your face. Chant OM! Let the energy flow into your entire brain and the third eye!
- Reach back as far as you can over each of your shoulders with both hands. Chant OM! Let the energy flow in and down your whole back!
- Place both hands, right over left, palms down, on the crown of your head. Chant OM! Let the energy flow down, infusing

your body, flowing down your spine, and pooling in the base of your body where it meets the earth, OM!
- Place your hands together at your heart. Visualize and feel your whole body glowing with the divine light you have placed there. You are one with the cosmos. All negativity, pain, worry, and so on is dissolving in this pure, warm, reviving divine light. Chant OM three times, and sit with this in meditation for as long as you wish. At a certain point, you will feel the power being absorbed into your body and you'll feel a calmness settle.
- Finish balancing this energy with several minutes of Pranayama. See the energy circulating and balancing throughout your body. When you are calm and balanced, slowly end Pranayama and finish your Zonule Rite.
- Write your experiences in your Journal, especially visions you may have had, and how areas of your body reacted and was benefited by OM, the energy flow.

**Note:** While it is traditional for another, more experienced Tantra to be doing Nyasa upon you, placing power upon yourself is both safer and easier to control in that you are experiencing it directly. In the future you may wish to explore other options.

### *Exercise 11: Placing Deity on Your Body Using Nyasa*

*Exercise 10* was a simple Nyasa, but it gives you an idea of how this practice works. When you are comfortable with *Exercise 10,* do this exercise.

You will be working with the energies of the kind, elephant-headed god, Ganesh. You already have a good relationship with Ganesh, and this will serve you well. This god can remove obstacles and sorrows from your body, and bring clarity and wisdom.

You already have a small image of Ganesh on your Zonule altar. Now place a small bowl with some sweets in it and a flower on top before his image, and put some cream or coconut water in your altar cup. These are offerings to honor Ganesh before you do Nyasa with his power.

Begin the Zonule Rite, but with a few small differences.

When you chant the Ganesh Mantra at the beginning, use your Mala and do it 108x. As you do so, focus on the image of Ganesh for a time and honor him. Then, close your eyes and visualize Ganesh as his energy fills the Zonule.

Bow to him three times, and silently ask for his energetic help with Nyasa, and silently ask him to remove any issues you have—whether mental or physical. When done, bow and silently say:

NAMASTE SHRI VINAYAKA! [Honor to you Remover of Obstacles!]

Continue the Zonule Rite as usual. Continue wearing the Mala.

Meditate as usual with simple Pranayama, and conjure the image of Ganesh into your mind's eye. You have called him and made offerings to him, so it will be easy to do so. Continue doing Pranayama, and begin silently, internally chanting his Mantra OM GAANG for every in/hold/out/hold cycle, and increase the intensity and clarity of the image of Ganesh in your mind. Continue simple Pranayama.

When you feel the presence and power of Ganesh arise, slow the Pranayama into natural breathing and relax. Place your hands together, bow and silently honor and welcome him. As you do this, silently ask for help from Ganesh. For example, you may wish for improved health, or more focus, or the elimination of obstacles in your life.

Now, with your eyes closed, hold out both hands with the fingers pointing up and the palms facing the image of Ganesh. (The upright, open palm is the Mudra for removing negativity and fears.) Visualize him doing the same.

As you do so, vibrate the Mantra GAANG aloud nine times, and as you do so, 'see' and feel the light of Ganesh's energy in your body flowing into your hands. Soon they will feel warm and glow with a lovely, healing light that feels wonderful.

When you have finished your chants, place your hands together and bow. 'See' your hands glowing with his brilliant power, and silently thank him.

With tingling hands, and your eyes mostly closed, repeat *Exercise 10* with three differences:

- Replace chanting OM with GAANG each time you place energy on your body.
- Instead of the white light of OM, visualize the warm, healing, calming light of Ganesh-energy suffusing your body.
- As you do this, close your eyes, and as you place the power on parts of your body, *visualize Ganesh himself placing the power on you.* 'See' and feel the energy and presence of the god flow through your hands into your body.

When you finish the Nyasa, place your hands on your crown, fill your whole body with orange light, and *visualize yourself as the god Ganesh*—trunk, big ears, and all! Now, filled with the power and aspect of Ganesh, use your will to remove any obstacles, blockages or imbalances you wish. Let your body release anger or toxic memories or a backache—whatever is hindering you. You are one with the energy of Ganesh now. When you are done with your Nyasa work, you may want to ask Ganesh for any wisdom and knowledge you'd like—if the bond is strong.

Finish the Nyasa as before. Then do Pranayama again and honor and say goodbye to Ganesh as his energy is absorbed by your body and dissipates. Finish your Zonule Rite as usual, and remember to thank Ganesh at the end and leave the offerings for a time.

### *Exercise 12: Nyasa for Healing*

Simple Nyasa is often about placing energy with a Mantra and visualization, but it can also be used to gently *move* the energy around in the body to where it is most needed. This exercise is a bit different than the others, and will be useful if you are feeling unbalanced or want to open up an area to healing. I use this for arthritis, headaches and muscle pain. Once you get the hang of doing this on yourself, you can do it to help others if you are focused and careful.

Begin your Zonule Rite. During meditation, begin basic Pranayama. After a time, close your eyes and become aware of where you have discomfort; i.e., where your energy is weak or blocked. *Place one hand on that place.* Focus your inner eye there, and continue Pranayama; but this time *begin alternate-nostril Pranayama* with your free hand and with your eyes closed. Visualize glowing energy flowing through your body and focusing on the issue; use the Pranayama energy and the power of your will to gently open up where energy is needed. Visualize that area filled with light that brings calm. You soon will feel a flow of healing energy filling you. Take your time; relax into it.

Continue Pranayama. Focus on the hand being used to direct the healing Nyasa, and with every in-breath, visualize the energy flowing to the place being healed. With every exhalation, see this collected light-energy flow down your arm into your healing hand.

Visualize the palm of that hand glowing with increasingly brighter light. Continue doing this while silently and internally chanting SHANTI (peace) with every Pranayama cycle. Continue for a time until you feel the healing is working.

When you are done with the Nyasa work, change your alternate nostril Pranayama to simple Pranayama while continuing the internal SHANTI Mantra. As you do so, feel your body become calm and relaxed. Take your time.

When you are done, you will have hopefully eliminated issues and redistributed positive energy with the pure light of your energy. When done, place your hands on the floor and see all excess or negative energy sink into the earth. Then, out loud, chant SHANTI OM!

Finish the Zonule Rite as usual, and then take a shower or bath with some salt to help banish the cause of the blockage or issue. If the issue continues, try this several times, and of course, see a doctor if it continues. For me, it has been very effective to deal with chronic arthritis, headaches and muscle pain as well as stress and anxiety.

Nyasa is a powerful and flexible technique, and a useful practice depending on what you are doing and what your goal is. Different Mantras can be used, of course. After you become proficient with the techniques, you can also (carefully) do this practice for other people.

## Mudras

*Abhaya Mudra*

A *Mudra* (meaning a 'special gesture') is usually a sacred, magical hand-gesture used during rituals. In Tantra, Mudras are potent signifiers and keys to manipulating energy and aiding magick. Some are well-known in the West, mostly due to Hatha Yoga and other exercises. There are literally thousands of Mudras; most originated in ancient India and China, and are still used in a variety of Taoist, Buddhist, Hindu and Tantric spiritual practices. Some Mudras are used for redirecting serious energy—like helping with Kundalini work—but in this section I will only discuss the more common hand Mudras we use in Nath Tantra.

According to some Tantric systems, the five fingers on each hand represent the five elements. Thus, touching or gesturing with different fingers adds to the potency and meaning of a Mudra. As you saw with Nyasa, your hands contain powerful Chakras. They are potent centers of manipulating and projecting power in our work. Every gesture and touch channels and conveys power and energy if you are focused and will it so. Think of the common obscene 'middle finger' gesture; we could call it the 'really angry Mudra'! It is, indeed, a projecting of angry energy, and thus is a real, potential curse! As a Tantric you will soon realize that your body is a conduit and 'battery' of immense energy and power. For this reason, you should become more aware of the ramifications and effects your movements and actions have on your environment when you direct energy consciously or unconsciously. This is one critical way we influence and weave our reality every moment of every day, whether we are aware of it or not. *Awareness is everything.*

§ § §

Since this is not a book on Mudras—and there are many—only a few of the most useful Mudras will be introduced. Mudras act as conduits of energy, and add the ability to use certain hand configurations to shape and direct the power you are working with. Nyasa *places* energy; Mudras *focus and shape* energy in different ways.

Take time to look at pictures of a variety of Tantric or Buddhist gods and goddesses. Look at their hands and you will see that most all are displaying special Mudras. Each gesture is meaningful and important. Each tells you a lot about that deity, their powers, and so on. Mudras tell us much about which specific deity form it is, what powers they are manifesting as that form, and how those Mudras can be useful in our magick. Many benevolent Tantric deities display a hand raised, palm out. This is the Mudra of removing fear and banishing negativity. They are popular deities for this reason!

What follows are several Mudras that increase potency and power in your magick along with suggestions on where and how use them in your Zonule work. Keep your Mudra practices simple and focused at first; eventually you'll feel comfortable combining them with your spells or other rites. As you learn and become comfortable with Mudras, be open to the idea of intuitively using them in your rituals when you are inspired. As always, consult your Guardian Spirit! Try out new Mudras in meditation, and be receptive to what you feel, think and 'see.' Your Inner Voice often knows what may work best for you, and can reveal hidden wisdom.

A few Mudras have already been presented in the work you've already done. Think about how they felt and how they helped manifest and channel energy in specific ritualistic and magickal ways.

You already know the *Sword Mudra* that you use for the PHAT! Banishing. When it is used with a visualized lightning bolt, it creates very potent banishing magick. Yet the Sword Mudra can also be used to defend yourself magically by focusing protective energy or casting a circle of defensive energy. Consider other creative, protective or energy-directing uses for this Mudra. Now you see that a Mudra can be a potent magical tool in many ways.

The common Mudra of hands pressed together at the heart in a prayerful pose is called the *Anjali Mudra*. Uniting the two hand-power centers, which you did for Nyasa, creates a powerful 'closed circuit' of your whole energy-being. Focusing energy on healing or to honor a deity projects a clear energy of blessing and honoring. It is also a gesture of respect between people, and of prayer in many cultures. In India and Nepal, it is often combined with saying NAMASTE ('I honor you').

Here are some of the most common and immediately useful Mudras to use in your Zonule Rite.

### *Exercise 13: Abhaya Mudra: Removing Fears and Negativity*

Find a picture of Shiva where he is seated in meditation, eyes half-closed, with one hand raised with an open palm facing outward. This is the *Abhaya Mudra,* and when used consciously and with real intent, it has the power to release one from fears and negativity. Shiva is often shown with this Mudra because he is the God of bliss and grants release from fear, anxiety and attachments. By using this Mudra consciously, you can remove fears you have or give this blessing to others. It is now time for you to get to know and practice a variety of Mudras to augment the other powerful practices you've learned.

First do your Zonule Rite. Take some time to meditate on dying and your future death. This may sound grim, but we all must die, and meditating on coming to terms with this is an ongoing spiritual practice. During the meditation, let the sadness and fear of your death fill you; then raise your right hand in the Mudra of Abhaya. Do simple Pranayama, and as you do so, breathe deeply, releasing your stress and fear. Take your time doing so.

Now, visualize yourself as calm, serene, eternal Shiva—for, in fact, you are all these things. Relax your upraised hand and relax your body. Begin alternate-nostril Pranayama with the other hand, and with each exhalation let the fear flow through you into the earth until you are calm and the fear is gone. Relax. Let go of everything, for all things fade away. Remember that this world of Samsara is an illusion, and that *you are eternal pure spirit.* Softly vibrate OM several times and visualize your body age, die and turn to dust; and see your eternal Self—which never dies—expand and fill the cosmos, for you are OM. Begin to breathe normally, lower your raised hand, and then press your palms together at your heart in silent gratitude for this moment. In the future, if you are ever full of intense anxiety or fear or any negative feelings, find a calm place to center yourself, breathe deeply, and do this practice. Once you able to create such calm with this Mudra, you can use it to help others. Shiva shows us that all things are transitory, yet all is eternal and there is nothing to fear. Such is the power of a Mudra.

### *Exercise 14: Varada Mudra: Granting Boons*

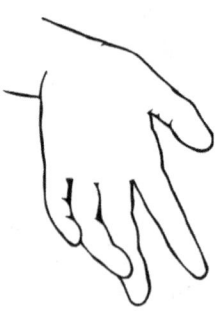

Another Mudra you commonly see in images of deities—often coupled with the Abhaya Mudra—is the *Varada Mudra,* the Mudra of Granting Boons. Find an image of Lakshmi where she is shown holding out her left hand pointing down, palm facing out. You will see many other deities like Lakshmi doing both Abhaya and Varada Mudras at the same time, since removing fears and granting boons or blessings are the two most common things devotees ask for! Now you will be like Lakshmi, and utilize the magick of the Varada Mudra.

Begin your Zonule Rite. When you begin meditating, visualize a friend or loved one who needs something badly. Maybe they need a job, money, an apartment, or just some good luck. As you enter deeper meditation, do simple Pranayama, relax and visualize yourself as the loving, generous Lakshmi, the Goddess of prosperity. (It doesn't matter what sex you are!) In your imagination, take on the aspect of this loving and nurturing goddess who only wants to help others. Think about some kind, generous things you have done for others and that others have done for you. Focus on feelings of generosity, gratitude and love opening your heart as you let your right hand gently extend into the Varada Mudra.

Now, continue Pranayama, and enter a deeper meditative state. Clearly see the glowing energy of caring and love flow into your Mudra hand as golden light. Visualize the energy flowing through the center of light in the palm of your hand. Using the Mudra, focus intensely on the person you are 'sending' boons to while softly vibrating Lakshmi's Bija Mantra, SHREENG, several times. At the same time, visualize a cascade of bright, golden light (or gold coins, if the boon is for money) flowing from your palm to the person in need. Let the SHREENG chant fade, release this boon, and visualize your happy loved-one getting what he or she desires. Relax your hand, and let it go.

Now, place your hands together at your heart, bow and thank the Goddess Lakshmi for working through you to help someone. Finish your meditation and Zonule Rite.

This exercise can also be done for yourself. Just visualize an image of Lakshmi while placing some simple offerings for her on your altar (like candy, which she loves). Then call to her and visualize her presence as you mirror her Mudra. Then ask away!

## Exercise 15: One-Hand Gyan Mudra, For Receiving and Generating Wisdom

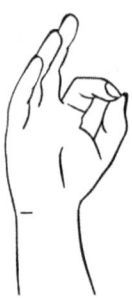

Tantric deities, Buddhas, Bodhisattvas and Taoist Gods and Goddesses are often shown doing this Mudra to generate or receive wisdom and enlightenment by using all power to focus their Mind on a single point of concentration—what we call OM.

In Tantra, the one-hand *Gyan Mudra* is exceptionally useful for focusing the mind, spirit and will on a single, spiritual goal. It is very helpful for calling forth and bonding with your Guardian Spirit or Atman—your spiritual center, focus and source of wisdom.

Do the Zonule Rite, and enter deep meditation with simple Pranayama. Focus your mind and spirit as you call forth your Guardian Spirit, the spark of OM that is your eternal Self-Star. Meditate on this point of infinite light, deepen your trance state, and slow your Pranayama. Let all fade away except the glowing vision of your Guardian Spirit as a point of light in the darkness before you. Use all your will and love to call it closer to you. When you have this bright star focused in your mind, raise your right hand and do the Gyana Mudra (thumb touching index finger, palm facing your heart). See the glowing star of your Guardian Spirit held between your thumb and index finger, filling your heart and body with brilliant light. Quietly vibrate the Mantra HA as the light fills your body, heart and mind. Then let the Mantra fade, but continue holding its energy. As you do so, open your heart and silently ask your Guardian Spirit to communicate with you directly. (It will do so, but it may be otherworldly.) Breathe deeply. Relax, take your time, and accept this wisdom with gratitude. When the experience begins to fade, open your hand, place it on your heart, and see the light enter and sit in your heart as a glowing jewel—a point of light.

Then quietly chant OM MANI PADME HUM once. Continue doing Pranayama, but now with HA (in breath), M (pause), SA (out breath), as you have previously learned to do. See the light of your Guardian Spirit now expand and fill every part of your body. Place your hands together at your chest, and bow in silent gratitude to this amazing power that is your core, eternal Self. Chant GURU OM. Then finish your Zonule Rite.

*Exercise 16: The Ganesh Mudra:*
*Removing Obstacles and Sorrows*

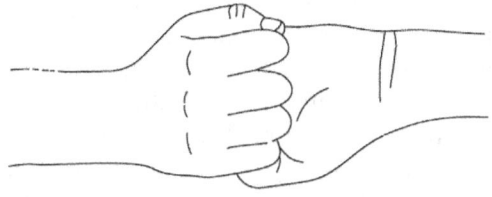

Like all people, you confront frustrating obstacles in your life, and when doing Tantric work, you will hit walls and have problems as well. This is life. When you are in this state of frustration or impatience, the *Ganesh Mudra* is very useful for removing such issues. It doesn't have to be done within the Zonule, though it would be more powerful if it were.

You can do the Ganesh Mudra anytime you like, wherever you have some privacy and time to relax and focus. It invokes the power of Ganesh, the remover of obstacles, to remove hindrances, blockages and problems.

Wherever you are, in the Zonule or not, first do the simple PHAT! Banishing either out loud or silently to clear the psychic space. Visualize a circle of light about you. Now, let the frustration, obstacle or issue arise in your mind with all the negative feelings attached. Then, raise your right arm to chest level with the palm facing your chest, and raise your left arm with the palm facing out. Then move your hands toward each other, and grasp them together so the hands are gripped together at heart level. Now, intensely visualize the obstacle, and begin to pull your arms, elbows out, in opposite directions. Feel the muscles in your arms tense. Quietly vibrate the Bija Mantra, GAANG, while silently asking Ganesh for help to remove the obstacle.

Shift your shoulders back, and pull your arms in different directions more intensely. Strain (but not uncomfortably), focus on the obstacle you want gone, then inhale deeply, and with a growled OM GAANG! SVAHA!, pull your gripped hands apart with a burst of energy while visualizing the obstacle breaking apart or dissolving.

You may do this procedure more than once if you like. Three times always works for me. When you feel that you have 'smashed through' your obstacle, relax your whole body completely, do some simple Pranayama to let go of the obstacle, and center yourself. Then, take a moment to visualize Ganesh before you. Slightly bow with your palms together at your heart, and thank Ganesh with a silent prayer of gratitude. Finally, touch the earth or floor with both hands and 'see' all excess energy flow into the ground. Then stand, stretch, relax and let go. Then either finish your Zonule Rite, or if you are doing this elsewhere, quietly do the PHAT! Banishing and go forth.

This is a simple, yet powerful Mudra practice for removing all sorts of obstacles—even tension, negative feelings, anger, frustration or other more concrete obstacles or issues. This Mudra is simple but powerful magick. Samsara is ours to weave, but Ganesh can help us break through some of the knots!

### *Useful Meditation Mudras*

When you are sitting in meditation, where are your hands? What are they doing? Whatever your hands are doing is a hand gesture of some kind, a Mudra, and Mudras are powerful. This is why consciously using Mudras should be part of your Tantric work.

Probably the most natural and relaxed pose for your hands when meditating is in your lap or on your knees, and it is natural that there are several simple but powerful traditional Mudras for this. Here are three that are easy to remember and can be used any time you are meditating to enhance and focus your magical work.

### The Bhairava Mudra

When you begin meditation during your Zonule Rite, place your relaxed, open hands palms up, on top of each other in your lap. Usually, the right hand lies atop the left, but in the ancient animist Bon Po tradition, it is reversed: left hand on top of right. I use either version depending on how I feel, the Tantric work I am doing, and whether I wish to balance my energy flow one way or the other. I do tend to use the Bon posture because Tantra, like Bon, is considered Vama Marg (left hand), meaning focused on magick and direct communication with the gods. If you are curious, Bhairava ('frightful') is an intense and wild aspect of Shiva. He is quite ancient, and so is his Mudra.

### The Dhyana Mudra

When you begin meditation in your Zonule Rite, focus on the Dhyana Mudra. This Mudra is similar to the Bhairava Mudra, except the thumbs are raised and touching. In this way they form an upward pointing triangle. This is a powerful Mudra for focusing and concentrating on a 'one point' meditation. It is said that the Buddha attained Nirvana while using this Mudra, and images showing this abound. Dhyana is a crucial concept. It is a transcendent state of bliss or being that is a step towards illumination—a 'small' Samadhi.

> *"Meditation is the pathway to a state of dhyana. Through the mantras and one-pointed attention, you can break through to total awareness. Dhyana is the state of pure Atman, which is consciousness and self-awareness."*
> — chopra.com/articles/dhyana-the-seventh-limb-of-yoga

Try this Mudra when you wish to work on deep, spiritual concentration and focus on one particular magickal or devotional practice. This is what we call 'active meditation,' a magickal, meditative state with a clear focus and goal.

*The Two-Hand Gyan Mudra*

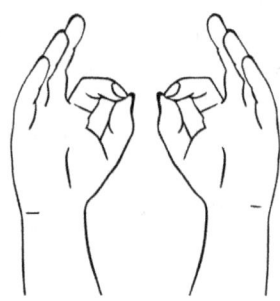

When you begin meditation in your Zonule Rite, focus on the Two-Hand Gyan Mudra, another potent meditative-magickal Mudra. You've likely seen it in several images, and you may have done it yourself in meditation or Yoga classes. With this Mudra, the hands gently rest, one on each knee, palms up. The thumb and pointing finger of each hand touch, forming a circle.

Gyan means 'wisdom'. This Mudra balances and enhances your overall ability to meditate, and creates a spiritual equilibrium that helps you receive and absorb deep wisdom. It is said that it also balances the left brain-right brain interface, and creates a unified aura which adds protection and stability to your meditation. In this way it enhances your overall equipoise. It is useful when you are feeling scattered, unbalanced or unmotivated; it is a great meditative 'reset.'

### The Padma (Lotus) Mudra

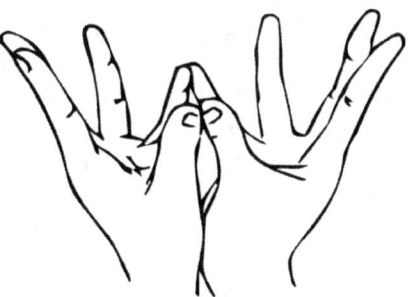

This Mudra is very powerful for centering, calming and receiving blessings. Using it activates heart-energy, and tends to fill you with feelings of love, peacefulness, compassion and gratitude. It helps purify your body and mind, and brings renewal. Think of a lotus bud opening into a full flower.

To make this Mudra during meditation or ritual, place your palms together, fingers up. Keep the pinkies, thumbs and bottom of both palms connected, then spread your fingers out, thus forming a blooming lotus. This Mudra can be held to the heart to focus on expanding your Heart center; it can also be placed on top of your head to open the Crown power center to receive divine energy from OM, the cosmos. I find it useful to center myself at the heart, especially when things are crazy, or if I feel unbalanced or upset. It can shift you into a more open, grateful and loving state of being when things are challenging. When in deep meditation, placing the Lotus on your Crown is intense and trance inducing—a way to directly receive gnosis. The lotus is particularly sacred to Lakshmi, who is also called Padma Devi (Lotus Goddess); it is also an archetypal symbol in Tantra of the Yoni and of all Goddesses.

### *Final Words on Mudras*

There are thousands of Mudras, and while this introduction barely touches the subject, it gives you several that will aid you in your Zonule Rite and other work. Know that there are many more out there. Working with Mudras in conjunction with Mantras is very potent. Some esoteric rituals contain sequences that combine a series of Mantras, Mudras and other ritual gestures, something you may build up to doing as your practices grow.

Begin with the simple Mudra exercises I have presented. Then do some research and master more Mudras as you expand your Tantric practices and repertoire. Each Mudra can do much more than I have explained, depending on other aspects of your ritual. As with much of this work, I urge you to practice daily, and then note down in your Journal your experiences and results. Keep trying new combinations; use reliable resources and experiment. Your personal experiences and reactions, with help from your Guardian Spirit, are the most important things in Tantric work. This idea is encoded in the term Svecchacharya—the goal is to do your own unique True Will. As a practicing Tantric, no one else will do what you do and be who you are and have the experiences you have. Use the knowledge and tools of past Tantrics and Tantras to aid your path to liberation. As Gurudev Dadaji Mahendranath says, "The Will to Love is the Law to Live."

## Kavacha (Tantric 'Armor')

> *"Each of the Tantric deities has her or his own Kavacha or armor, which protects devotees from the many dangers which may afflict a human being. These could either be recited in a ritual context, or written down on birch bark or other substances and worn on the body to give protection."*
>
> — *shivashakti.com/kavacha.htm*

Though other Tantric practices can be added to and combined with your basic Zonule Rite, I will end by explaining *Kavacha* (protective magical 'armor'). This is not a practice you would do often in your Tantric work, certainly not daily, but it is a powerful and useful technique if you need spiritual or psychic protection.

This practice can be added to your regular Zonule work or within any other Tantric ritual when there is a desire to be physically and magickly protected from something, or empowered and prepared for a serious undertaking. Like many of the other Tantric techniques, it can be done alone or within the Zonule Rite or another Tantric rite. It is not something you will do often.

Kavacha literally means 'armor'. It is a bit like Nyasa in that it involves a 'laying on of hands' and empowering parts of the body with energy, but with several crucial differences.

A Kavacha places protective, empowered energy of a deity on your body as visualized plates of armor conjured by magick and Mantra. Chants, Mantras, Pranayama, psychic power, and clear visualization are used to build a psychic suit of armor about your physical and energetic body; piece by piece each 'plate' of this armor is placed upon parts of your body. Think of a knight putting on his armor before battle, piece by piece. When this is finished, your energetic, spiritual and physical body will then be protected from mental, magical, emotional or even physical attacks. Your body may also be energized or even healed, depending on your goal. It is an amazing, ancient and clever piece of Tantric magick tech!

Kavachas can be defensive—for isolating and healing—or can be used to prepare for or respond to psychic attacks. It is a powerful psychic armor you can wear before entering magical, emotional or even physical fights. As a Tantric, you are free of purely pacifist views and actions if you choose to be. Even if you hold to non-violence, you are still allowed to protect yourself and go on the attack against evil forces, entities, illnesses and malignant people, as you will.

A Kavacha can also help you seal off and protect your aura and energy. So, if are recuperating from a trauma, it helps to keep your energy and power contained so you can heal—a psychic body-cast, if you will. I have successfully used a Kavacha as a protective practice and tool when I was under emotional and magical attack, and I have used it offensively to magickly fight a great wrong. Even the anger and hate being thrown at you by someone can damage you—protection is useful. You may have entered toxic situations where you have had to face terrible situations. Using a Kavacha before such events is useful, just like a Kevlar vest deflects a bullet.

In the Kavachas found in Tantric texts, there are usually a series of Mantras, and sometimes an actual spell, to 'cast away' or 'destroy' the power or being which is attacking you. Kavachas often invoke the power of a *specific* deity for a purpose. The *Kali Kavacha,* for example, is aggressively protective when you are under attack because the Goddess Kali is a frightening, sword-wielding goddess of aggressive protection and battle. Keep in mind that Kavacha is serious business, and is not something you'd normally incorporate into your regular rituals, but life is full of struggles and confrontations that call for protection. Tantrics are not Buddhists, nor do we 'turn the other cheek' when threatened or assaulted. Instead, we dispassionately, and without anger, confront evil directly with Tantric magick and Kavacha. Here is an example of a Kavacha you may want to try.

### *General Kavacha Instructions*

Try this within your Zonule Rite. Do it after your meditation, and after contemplating the need for the Kavacha. If you wish to do this Kavacha separately from the Zonule Rite, begin by doing the PHAT! Banishing and circle-casting from the Zonule Rite, and do the same Banishing after the Kavacha.

This Kavacha invokes the power of Shri Ganesh to help you remove specific obstacles from your life. It is essentially defensive, not aggressive as some are. Follow the simple instructions by doing the following for each step. You may wish to practice these steps first:

1. Hold up a hand, and visualize all your energy flowing into it, much like the Nyasa practice, by doing simple in/hold/out/hold Pranayama and visualizing.

2. Place your hand on the part of your body where you will 'place a plate of armor,' and slowly chant the relevant line of the rite as indicated. Visualize a plate of glowing armor covering that place on your body. When you can 'see' and feel it, move to the next part of your body and do the same. When you are done and your body is fully protected, place your pointing finger to your lips and intensely visualize yourself covered in the full armor—protected, safe and energized. You are now like Iron Man! Without ritual renewal, your Kavacha 'armor plating' will fade after a while; or you can remove it deliberately with a shower and some salt while you visualize it dissolving and chanting to the deity who has empowered this work.

## Vinayaka Kavacha—A Protective Kavacha
## A Protective Armor of Sri Ganesh

Here then is a Kavacha for you to try. Follow the steps as you chant each line, noting where you are placing the armor.

(The translations of the names of Ganesh used in this spell are in the *Notes* which follow. *Vinayaka* means the 'Remover of Obstacles,' and is an aspect of Ganesh.)

> GAANG May Vinayaka protect my crown
> GAANG May Vinayaka protect my head
> GAANG May Vinayaka protect my forehead
> GAANG May Mahodhara Ganesh protect my brows
> GAANG May Balachandra Vinayaka protect my eyes
> GAANG May Gajavakra Ganesha protect my mouth
> GAANG May Ganakreeda Vinayaka protect my tongue
> GAANG May Vinayaka protect my speech
> GAANG May Vinayaka protect my ears
> GAANG Vinayaka protect my nose
> GAANG Gunesa Vinayaka protect my face
> GAANG Vinayaka protect my neck/throat
> GAANG Skanda Porvaja Vinayaka protect my shoulders
> GAANG Vignaraja Vinayaka protect my breast
> GAANG Gananatha Ganesha protect my heart
> GAANG Heramba Vinayaka protect my middle
> GAANG Vinayaka protect my sides
> GAANG Vinayaka protect my posterior
> GAANG Vinayaka protect my genitals
> GAANG Vinayaka protect my hips
> GAANG Mangala Murtha Vinayaka protect my thighs
> GAANG Mahabodhi Vinayaka protect my knees and legs
> GAANG Ekadanta Vinayaka protect my feet
> GAANG Vinayaka protect my arms
> GAANG Vinayaka protect my fingers

Now, visualize Ganesh at all the quarters, facing outwards and protecting you:

> GAANG Vinayaka protect me in the South
> GAANG Vinayaka protect me in the West

GAANG Vinayaka protect me in the North
GAANG Vinayaka protect me in the East
GAANG Ekadanta Vinayaka protect me all day

Place your hands together at the heart, bow and say:

GAANG Kapila Vinayaka protect my life/existence
GAANG Gajanan Vinayaka protect me in all ways!

SVAHA!

### Notes

Vinayaka = Remover of Obstacles (the name by which Ganesh is usually called)
Mahodhara = Ganas—Ganesh as the ruler of the Ganas or spirits
Balachandra = Moon crowned
Gajavakra = One with an elephant mouth
Ganakreeda = Ganesh who gives empowerment
Gunesa = Lord of virtues
Skanda Porvaja = Elder Brother of the god Skanda[6]
Vignaraja = Lord of Obstacles
Ganapati = Lord of the Ganas (Shiva's spirits)
Heramba = A 5-headed Tantric form of Ganesh
Mangala Murtha = Auspicious Deity
Mahabodhi = Great Essence/Power
Ekadanta = One with the single tusk
Kapila = Here means grey
Gajanan = With an elephant's face

*Svaha!* (So Be It!)

This Kavacha was inspired by Agasthiar.Org

## AND SO...

This ends the introduction to several Tantric practices that you can use and combine creatively in your Zonule. It is best to add each new practice one at a time and use it until you have mastered it. By experimenting *with different combinations of these practices,* you

---

[6] Shanda is Ganesh's brother.

will become more flexible, creative and successful in your ever-expanding Tantric work. Constant practice is crucial to build your skills, powers and abilities. The more you practice, the more this universe will open to you, and the more meaningful your spiritual, physical and emotional life will become. It is important to expand and integrate your Knowledge (new practices), Will (meditative focus), and Action (daily Tantric work) in your Zonule, and thus in your life. When you can flow through the Zonule Rite, and deftly weave several different interlocking Tantric techniques and practices, then you will be ready for more active, creative and intense Magick.

## Your Tantra Sadhana or Regular Practice

I hope that you have spent a lot of time in your Zonule, doing the Zonule Rite, and trying out the practices that you added slowly but surely. Your regular practice we call *Sadhana*—that is, spiritual and magical practices with deities. This makes you a *Sadhaka,* a Tantric practitioner. As such you have most likely:

- Deeply imprinted the basic Zonule Rite.
- Deepened your practice and success in meditation.
- Added and been successful with several other practices, including:
  - Different kinds of Pranayama.
  - Many kinds and uses of Mantra.
  - Understanding and using Yantras.
  - Becoming familiar with and using the Three Body-Center Chakras.
  - Becoming familiar with and using many Mudras.
  - Understanding and doing some Nyasa practices.
  - Becoming close to and regularly communicating with your Guardian Spirit.
  - Getting to know a variety of Tantric Gods and Goddesses and forming bonds with several of them.
  - Understanding and being able to use Kavacha.

Congratulations! This is a lot to accomplish, something that took me years to do. Most of these practices will become regular additions to your Sadhana. Some will instantly feel right and familiar, others will take longer to fit into your work in ways that are spiritually and personally pleasing and important. You are now prepared to handle most aspects of Tantric practice. This is a good time to think about Tantric spellcasting, and doing what Tantrics do best: *making things happen with Magick.*

## THE 'ART' OF MAGICK

In the various occult traditions, 'real Magick' is referred to as an 'art', because there is not one correct way to do it; and knowledge, will, action and creativity are the keys to success. Knowing a bit about Western magick can be useful. Though the techniques and practices differ, the objectives are similar. Aleister Crowley defined Magick as *"The Science and Art of causing Change to occur in conformity with Will."*

Another, more sublime view of magick was stated by the amazing artist-magician, Austin Osman Spare: *"Magick is the art of attracting without asking."* In many ways this definition is closer to Tantra, and how Tantrics manifest Siddhas (magical powers). Those Tantrics who attain a degree of spiritual liberation generally cease doing rituals to ask for things, trusting to their gods and their powers to attract what they need.

This brings us to how to cultivate and understand the Tantric dynamics and use of *Siddha,* what we call *Magick.*

Your Zonule is your 'magick circle-sphere'—the cosmic launch-pad of Siddha work. There are three modalities for accomplishing this Magick:

**Projection**—The sending out of your conjured energy, power and intent to cause manifestation. This is active magick, implemented by your Tantric Knowledge, strong Will, and focused Action through the weaving of the practices you now know, focused in meditation, and guided by your Guardian Spirit.

**Absorption**—The attracting or bringing in to yourself and your reality energy or manifestations through Knowledge, Will and Action and the practices you now know.

**Stillness**—This 'silent' modality is less a mode of work and more a deep letting go of all desires so what you truly need manifests. This is a sort of internal alchemy, focused mostly on deep meditation and letting the cosmos come to you with complete detachment—without influence from the Kleshas.

*Projection* involves sending your Will and energy out from your Zonule into the external world to do something.

*Absorption* involves attracting and bringing into your Zonule something or some force you truly want or need.

*Projection* is a kind of evocation, sending forth magick from your circle, while *Absorption* can be seen as a kind of invocation which pulls magical energy into your circle and yourself.

Through Magick, Samsara can be consciously and intentionally embraced without attachment, and 'woven' to fit your Will. It is through the magick of Projection and Absorption where you manipulate aspects of Samsara (reality) to gain what you will, whether by projecting your power or using it to attract. Tantra is a magickal path as well as spiritual one. Tantrics don't seek to avoid or battle with Samsara; instead, we seek a degree of sublime artistic control through Tantric Magick. Until we attain real liberation, our goal is to be mostly happy, and live in Ecstasy, Equipoise and Equilibrium as Dadaji Mahendranath used to say. Tantra is a dance of weaving our own reality with all the joy and bliss that we are capable of weaving in our lives so that we may do our True Will and be free.

## Basic Rules of Tantric Magick

1. Don't be a jerk. Seriously. Dadaji Mahendranath notes that Tantrics should never harm others except in dire necessity. Don't ask for more than you need. Accept the world as the wonder it is, pierce your Kleshas, and *think deeply* before tossing a magick 'spell.'

2. Meditate a few days before you do magick. Meditate on all of the possible ramifications and unintended consequences.

3. Consult your Guardian Spirit as well as omens like the *I Ching*, Tarot, etc.) before doing active magick. It is always good to get a second opinion.

4. Clearly write down in very specific terms what you want to absorb or project, and why. Think about it, and reexamine your written words. You should consider thinking over and rewriting the words clarifying your magickal objective several times to make sure it is exactly what you will.

5. Before doing magick in the Zonule, you should be proficient and comfortable with the Zonule Rite and the various practices, such as Pranayama, Mantra, and so on. Active magick is your projection of that mastery.

6. Avoid magick if there is an easier, more direct, or more honest way to achieve your goal! Tantra magick is not an 'easy way' to get anything. Keep in mind that every magical action causes a reaction. Think twice about the effects of what you are doing with your magick; there often is a simpler way.

7. When doing Tantric magick be humble, fearless, egoless and unaffected by attraction or repulsion. This is why regular meditation is crucial: it cultivates that state of being. Be centered first.

8. Be kind. Tantrics can be fierce, terrifying, and at times, ruthless, but never arbitrarily abusive or without cause. Remember Karma? It is better to defend yourself rather than attack; it is better to redirect energy thrown at you. You are here to do your Great Work and help others. If you must push back or defend, be dispassionate and clear-headed.

9. Always honor the cosmic forces and the divine flow of the universe. They tend to indicate the 'natural way things should go.' Tantric Magick may go awry or not work if it goes against the flow of the universe, often for reasons you may not be aware of. The best magick flows through you without effort, and shifts things in a way that flows *with* the universe.

10. Finally, do you really need to 'do' Magick? Of course not. Even today, holy Tantric men and women wander without attachments. They own nothing, have renounced all things, and wander in the bliss of liberation. They receive what they need without asking, and give as they will, and so have little need of conscious magick. You can be very happy without casting spells.

## Aspects of Tantric Magick

With focus and utilization of Knowledge (you know *what* you are doing), your Will (you know *why* you are doing it), and Action *(doing it* daily), you are ready to use Tantric magick.

All of the following are done in your Zonule or another safe, sacred place. In general, the best time to do magick is just after meditation in the Zonule Rite.

### Tantra Magick

**Projection Magick:** Focus on your external goal with wholehearted intensity. Decide what tools, images, sigils, and so on you will use, and what gods, if any, you will invoke to aid you. Then, use energy-creating activities or practices to amass power; then send it with your mind like a laser beam towards your clear goal. Imagination is the key. In your mind, intensely visualize your goal succeeding while completely letting go of attachment; then release your 'spell.' When you release this magick, place your index finger on your lips, and let it go. Banish when you are done. It is traditional to end with a loud SVAHA! [So Be It!]

**Absorption Magick:** Meditate on and visualize what energy, item or action you will to attract. As before, the needed energetic power can be conjured in different ways, depending on your desires and the 'spell.' Use wholehearted focus and intense imagination. Relax your mind, go into deep meditation, and become completely receptive—a magnet for your objective. Gently, but intensely, pull it toward you like an empty cup attracts tea being poured into it. Avoid desire or greed! Open your hands in the *Lotus Mudra* and clearly 'see' your desire flow into the Lotus. Place your palms together at your heart, and visualize the receiving with gratitude. Then let go. Place your index finger on your lips and forget your spell.

**Stillness/Non-Action Magick:** Simply being in the Zonule and 'sitting with' your Will can be enough if you are in tune with your True Will and your needs. Meditate deeply without desire on what you Will to occur, open to your Guardian Spirit, and in your deep-mind imagination, follow your intuition and the gentle guidance of your Spirit. No stress, force or action; just let it unfold without 'you.'

If you are immersed and egoless in the flow, you'll know when the work is done, like when a song ends.

## Other Tantric Magick

### Guardian Spirit Magick

You are more likely to attain your goal with no karmic backlash if you call on and listen to your Guardian Spirit which allows 'a wiser head' to prevail and guide you. Your Guardian Spirit exists to protect you. Listen to that loving voice when planning and doing Tantric Magick.

When doing Guardian Spirit Magick during your Zonule Rite, focus on connecting with your Guardian Spirit by using Pranayama and the Gyana Mudra.

Then do *Exercise 9: Activating Your Guardian Spirit with the Three Chakra Body-Centers* as explained in the earlier **Chakra** section. Be receptive to advice—including advice you might not like—and sit with your Guardian Spirit until you have received the advice and knowledge you need.

Before releasing the 'spell,' visualize your Guardian Spirit as a glowing, white star just above your crown, and let its light flow into you. Let it be absorbed into your heart; then finish *Exercise 9.*

### Through Various Tantric Spirits or Other Entities

We have not spent much time speaking of the various Tantric spirits that you can work magick with. Most are nature spirits, demi-gods or Asuras (daemons), which are more 'wild' than 'bad.' These include:

- Yakshas or Yakshis which are powerful tree spirits.
- Asuras like Kubera, who is friendly and brings wealth.
- Tribes of spirits that entertain the gods, like the Apsaras (river spirits) who are singers.
- I have worked for years with the Nagas—serpent spirits who can appear as half-serpent and half-human, or as all serpent, or even as a powerful and beautiful human. See my book, *Naga Magick: The Wisdom of the Serpent Lords,* Falcon Press, for more on Nagas.

There are hundreds of spirits or demi-gods that you can work with. Many of them are ancient and originate from prehistoric animism. Many wild demi-gods and spirits, including gnomes and some ghosts, are part of the Ganas, the retinue of Shiva led by Ganesh.

Be aware that these spirits can range from helpful to dangerous, depending on what they are and how you approach them. *Do your research.* Keep in mind that their perceptions and agendas are not human, and many are furious at the way nature is being destroyed by humans. Approach them carefully with a lot of respect, appropriate gifts, and clear focus. It is best to work with such spirits out in nature. For example, Nagas are serpent spirits who live in springs or lakes, so I often set up my Zonule near a lake to do Naga spell work.

**Note:** Do *not* work with these spirits until you have finished doing all the work in this book, and have worked with and become close with at least a few of the Tantric Gods and Goddesses, especially Ganesh. It takes time to get to know the spirits. Research them, meditate on them, slowly get to know them, and give offerings before asking for their help. It's like earning the trust of wild animals.

## MAGICK WITH SPIRITS

When working with the Ganas and other spirits, first develop a positive relationship with them. On your altar, possibly out in nature, set up an appropriate Yantra, Mantra and Murti of the spirit you seek. Then, after meditating on them, call out to them, giving appropriate offerings including incense, drink, flowers and food. Intensely visualize them, and when they appear, clearly and simply ask them to go forth and accomplish what you wish them to do.

## PRACTICAL DEITY MAGICK

If your work is focused on long-term magical goals, you are wise to defer to the gods and goddesses for help. Deities have a broad, long-term view of life and the complexities of manifestation. Thus, working with gods and goddesses in this way is safer, though results are often subtler and take longer to manifest.

As a human stuck in time and space, it is difficult to see the long-term physical, spiritual and karmic ramifications of your magick. Hindsight is golden. Many times I've done magick and later looked back with regret because I didn't know all the variables involved in a spell I'd done.

Deities have a much broader consciousness and understanding of the cosmos. The gods are far-seeing, far-knowing and not limited by time and space, but it is through humans that they can most clearly function and act.

Gods and goddesses have likes, dislikes and often, many aspects and personalities.

So, working Magick through the gods you are close with and who care for you is the safest and best-informed way to do Tantric magick. Keep in mind that your desired results are not assured if the deity you call on is inappropriate for what you wish to do; for example, calling on Kali in a love spell is not wise, but invoking Lalita Tripurasundari is. A deity may know, or see reasons why it is unwise for you to do what you seek to do. This may be frustrating, but it is likely out of love. Think of a parent stopping a child from playing with matches.

There are two ways you can elicit magickal help, or politely call upon a god or goddess to do magical work for you. The first is by doing a powerful and intense Puja—that is, a devotional ritual to that deity—in your Zonule. This involves giving offerings, invoking that god or goddess, and intently petitioning for the success of a specific magickal spell or empowerment. See the **Pujas** chapter (below) for examples. Most importantly for Magick, the Puja must generate a lot of power. The more energy raised and offered to the deity equals a happier deity and stronger magick.

A slower and more relaxed way to do such deity Magick, is through a Sadhana—that is, long-term, daily devotions to that deity. For a magical objective, I recently finished a year-long Sadhana invoking Ganesh three times a day.

I do Magick in this way because I know generally what I want, but I have no way of knowing exactly how it should manifest in the best way. I cannot see all the possible vectors of this desire, but being a long-term god-friend, Ganesh has a wider view of things than I do. My magick was successful, but not in a way I expected. This is not uncommon when doing Magick with deities; that is what divine pals are for. Having personal relationships with the Tantric gods offers many benefits.

## Tantra Protection Magick

Tantra is about direct working with powers—our own and those of our Guardian Spirit, Gods and nature spirits. Taboos, laws, social norms and restrictions are not important to Tantra. As a Tantric, you are inherently divine, an awakening god, and therefore do what divine gnosis tells you to do.

That said, a Brahman temple priest has a lot of innate protection and support from his religion, dogma, caste and worshippers. What is lost in such a religious structure is the complete autonomy and freedom that Tantra offers—freedom from social and religious dogma, and all restrictions on True Will.

Tantra is about doing Magick and becoming a god while receiving Gnosis directly from divine powers of all kinds. However, this path, like sailing a boat across the Pacific alone, offers both more rewards and more peril. This is why Tantrics often work in small Kulas (clans or in-groups) of fellow Tantrics—for support, joy, shared ecstatic rituals, and added magick power, without restrictions or religion.

Now that you are practicing Tantric Magick, possibly alone, let's look at how you can magickly protect yourself and your Zonule from negative forces, situations and people.

## Protecting Your Zonule

Always keep your Zonule clean and organized. Negative energies and spirits are attracted to clutter and filth. All items should be neatly stored in an appropriate place that is easy to reach. Periodically purify the Zonule with salt and water—maybe once a month. Make sure all the tools and other items you use are also cleaned in this way, especially the Yoni-Lingam. Flowers, water and incense should be renewed often. The Zonule should always feel clean, well-tended, safe and well aired-out, ready for you to sit in and do Tantric work at any time.

If you do ritual work in your Zonule and things don't go well, end your Zonule Rite, and after Banishing, get a simple glass or ceramic bowl full of pure water and put some salt in it along with some lavender or another natural, scented oil. Then place it on the altar and leave it overnight. Afterwards, throw the water outside on the earth. This will remove and transform any negativity.

## Using Protective Tantric Amulets as 'Wards'

A number of things can be placed in your home or Zonule to protect your space. Such protective items are called 'wards,' and can take many forms: deity images, symbols like OM, Yantras you make and charge, or jewelry that is sacred to your work. It is up to you, but whatever you use should be cleansed, blessed and empowered in the Zonule Rite, and charged with power to protect. It is most powerful to create such wards, but you can buy them, often online. Some that are useful include: small deity images (I have images of Ganesh in several places), appropriate Yantras, engraved Mantras, and other auspicious symbols which can be used after being imbued with protective Magick. Even Tantric tools—such as well-used Malas, tridents and more—can be hung up or displayed as protective Tantric wards or amulets on the door of your Zonule, or elsewhere in your home. I even have a Ganesh image in my car, and a small one on my keychain! Such positively charged, Tantric wards protect and empower your home and yourself, and bring good luck and prosperity.

## Charging & Empowering the Ward or Amulet

The easiest method is to cleanse the item with salt and water, place it on the Yoni-Lingam or the center of your altar, and do the Zonule Rite. In meditation, hold the ward or amulet, and do Pranayama while visualizing the ward glowing with your channeled power to bring protection and prosperity. If it is dedicated to a deity, like an image or Yantra of Ganesh, then take your Mala and do the appropriate Mantra 108 times while placing that energy into the item. Then finish the Zonule Rite.

A more potent way to do this is within a Puja for the appropriate deity. This should be done when the offerings are blessed, and you are asking for boons. Of course, it is best to do this after you have bonded with the deity that is appropriate for your goal. For protection or aggressive Magick, Kali is recommended. For calm, peace and solid protection from occult things, call on Shiva. For removing obstacles or interference or for general luck, Ganesh is best. For money or prosperity, invoke Lakshmi, and for love or sexual objectives, Shri Tripurasundari (Lalita) should be reverently called upon.

Anything you have been using can likely be utilized as an amulet, charm or ward. This is an area where you should be creative and listen to your Guardian Spirit in meditation. In Tantra, Magick pervades all that we do, so a well-used Mala that glows with power can be hung over a bed when you are traveling; or placed under your pillow when you seek healing, or if you wish to invoke specific dreams. Use your imagination and instinct as well as guidance from your Guardian Spirit and your personal deities. Yantras, tridents, swords, Malas and items from a ritual such as ashes, flowers or blessed water are all potent items that can be used to protect, empower or bless. Practices like Mantra work, Pranayama, Nyasa, and so on, can be combined at will and used to charge an amulet or a ward or other useful, sacred items. These empowered items are alive in a sense, and are directed in their function by your will and intent. They also make cool, and possibly profound, gifts to those in need of protection, healing and prosperity.

The more you learn to use Tantric Magick, the more you will become as Shiva, the Lord of Magick, and so the wiser and more powerful you will become in the way of Tantra. Svaha!

# PUJAS

*Puja Altar*
*(Photo by the Author)*

## About Pujas

*Puja* means 'magick'. Pujas are devotional rituals which can be very simple or deeply complex. Having mastered the basic Zonule Rite, various practices, and Tantric Magick, you are now ready to perform and master the escalating power of a full devotional ritual—a Puja.

Though burning incense, chanting a bit, and placing a flower on a Yoni-Lingam while praying to Shiva is a simple Puja, traditional Pujas are complex, have many stages, and take anywhere from an hour or two to several days. The Nath Pujas that follow can be done in an hour or two, but can easily last longer, especially if you have others involved. Some of the more formal Pujas I've attended were exceedingly complex! They often included many different sections, the recitation of holy texts, a lot of chanting, deity invocations, music, singing, complex diagrams on the floor (Mangala), and many of the Tantric practices you now are familiar with. Having been to public and private Hindu Pujas at many temples in the USA, Nepal, Singapore and India, I attest that they vary greatly in many ways; different temples, sects and lineages have their own set ritual practices based on their unique mythos and traditions. On the other hand, Tantric Pujas I have been to are often less religious and much more open, spontaneous and magical. We Tantrics literally invite the gods to come, and then let these gods inform our practices, and even speak through us at times. Such Pujas rarely follow a set dogma of liturgy. Welcome to Tantric Pujas!

### On the Following Nath Tantrika Pujas

After initiation, I worked with simple Pujas as I mastered the basics, but with helpful advice from Gurudev Dadaji Mahendranath and other Tantrics, I began to assemble and do more complex and multifaceted Pujas of my own. The Nath Tantrika Pujas that follow reflect over 25 years of this process. With the help of my Kula, these Pujas have all been performed and revised many times. These rituals are powerful, and include much more English and far less Sanskrit than traditional Tantric Pujas. They were drawn from a number of different traditional and modern Tantric sources, including the works of Dadaji Mahendranath and other Nath Gurus.

I've worked with and communicated directly with each deity being honored, revising each Puja after each was performed several times. I began to do them in my Zonule, and later, often with my Kula, a core group of serious Tantrics who were initiated into the Nath lineage. So, our *Forest Yurt Kula* met as often as we could, doing Pujas to a variety of deities, and discussing Tantra, all while having a great time.

The members of the Kula also did practices in their own Zonules, and their views and creativity have added a lot to these Pujas, including ideas for improving rites, and so on. New things were added or changed by consensus in accord with the free-flowing, egalitarian nature of a Tantric Kula. The Pujas evolved through practice and improvements over several years, and what follows are the core Nath Tantrika Pujas. (There are others we crafted for different deities and spirits that I hope to see published in the future.)

Each Puja we did together became more potent, powerful and ecstatic—and so much fun. Unlike formal Hindu Pujas, we played music, danced wildly, laughed a lot, told jokes, and generally had a fantastic time. Most of our Pujas—including those that follow—lasted 3 or four hours. However, we added a lot of things like deep meditation, a lot of rhythmic music, laughter and joking, deep discussions on Tantra and Magick, and after the offerings, there was feasting and partying. Our Pujas got kind of wild, joyful, and at times, hilarious; that is the point of Tantric Pujas.

As members gained experience, they began to bring their own Pujas to the temple, and the roles of priest or priestess soon rotated. This is natural because Tantra is not hierarchical, but collective and egalitarian. As the honored Guru Mogg Morgan said about the nature of Tantra today, *"The Kula is the Guru."* Collective wisdom, sharing and cooperative creativity have replaced the old-aeon hierarchical structures of magick. I always learned as much from the Kula members as they learned from me.

What we did was quite new and based on the directions Shri Gurudev Mahendranath had given to me in letters: that is, to adapt and evolve Tantra and Tantric practices for the modern world, and specifically for people in the West, to make it new, adaptable and relevant. All of the Nath Tantra Pujas thus resulted from a mixture of the ancient, the new, the traditional, and the freshly created. The goal was to revive, renew and revitalize Tantra to make it accessible for *all* people. From my experience, the Tantric gods and goddesses are quite enthused about all of this!

## Your Pujas

I mention our Kula because working with a small, intimate group is likely something you may wish to do after a time. When you do, I recommend that you always do the Puja to Ganesh first to 'open the way,' and remove all obstacles.

In the Twilight World of your Puja, you will bring deities into your space, and honor and communicate directly with them. Once you are in communion with the gods and goddesses in this way, they will communicate with and teach you. As you all work together, everything you learned in your Zonule will have prepared you for success.

### *Some General Advice*

Plan carefully so that everything is understood and you have everything you need for the Puja. Go shopping for items you need days before the Puja; prepare the temple space a day beforehand as well. I speak from experience! Make sure the following is ready:

The Murti (image) of the deity has been purified and ritually empowered during your Zonule work *before* the Puja. You will treat the Puja like a party for a famous guest who appreciates nice things, so prepare appropriate offerings. Be creative and open. Tantrics in India use what is natively available—like fresh papayas—but finding exotic offerings can be an issue. Before all this, contemplate the god or goddess being honored in the Puja. Use this book and other research to decide what items and offerings are appropriate. These do not have to be from India! I use appropriate, locally-grown fruits, foods and drinks that the gods seem happy with. I think they like the variety.

Finally, write everything down as you plan the Puja. Of course, after the Puja, record your results. Everyone in my Kula always had their Journals, and during our post-feasting we all took time to write down the visions, poems, symbols and ideas that the gods had given us, and we'd share what we'd scribbled down. It was shocking at how similar our experiences often were! This is great magick.

## Coda

I think of each Puja as a work of performance-art, dedicated with loving devotion to a deity and to our own joy. The gods of Tantra are potent, ancient, powerful and very adaptable, and love this free-flowing interaction. Every Puja is a weaving of the participants with the deity and the divine world that surrounds us. The 'Twilight World' of every Puja offers trance-states or joy as well as equipoise, ecstasy, freedom, creativity and a place to open your soul to the cosmos and receive its blessings. The Tantric gods and goddesses want to play and party with us! They love to be honored, to teach, and to help us. They are deep, archetypal parts of us and of the universe. If you invoke them with focus, joy, will and love, they will manifest as divine light and intensely empower you through every Puja you do.

## Preparing for a Puja

### Items Needed & Preparations

In general:

- The Zonule should be very clean, banished and at a comfortable temperature.
- Set up the altar and the items you will use ahead of time.
- If the Puja is just for one or two people, the preparations will be easier. A larger group, of course, takes more time and attention.
- The Puja should be scheduled at a time when there will be no interruptions. Never stop a Puja except for dire necessity. The negative pull of chaos—of Samsara—will attempt to interfere whenever a powerful ritual is being done. Take precautions; you must be left alone to do this work.

You can certainly be naked during your Pujas, but it is also fine to wear loose, relaxed, natural clothing or robes. Black or red clothing is traditional in our Tantra, but is not necessary.

What follows are the basics for Puja set up. Feel free to make adjustments as you see fit. Many of the following items mimic your Zonule Altar, but will be more festive and ornate than usual. On the altar should be:

- An altar cloth, preferably of a color sacred to that deity.
- A 'charged' Murti (image) of the deity.
- Some appropriate stick incense and a simple incense burner.
- A ritual cupful of a liquid offering appropriate to that deity. I often offer coconut water, but have used juices, and even wine.
- At least one vase of lovely flowers.
- Two candles of the appropriate color for that deity on either side of the Murti.
- The Yoni-Lingam is placed before the Murti, and the Yantra of that deity is placed flat in front of the Yoni-Lingam.
- A lighter and a ritual pipe filled with Kusa (cannabis) for honoring Shiva, if it is legal and appropriate where you are.
- A small trident or wand to create the sacred circle/sphere.
- A special offering tray or plate, called an Arti Tray. It is usually placed on top of the Yantra in front of the deity before offerings are made; some Pujas vary in this a bit. The Arti Tray contains smaller amounts of food offerings for that deity, a small cup of appropriate liquid, a small candle, a flower, an upright incense stick which can be stuck in the food offering, and a small, charged image or symbol of the deity being honored. (Note: Fire, Air, Earth, Water and Spirit!) The entire tray or plate should be easy to pick up and pass around. Some of these things are duplicative, but this tray will be offered directly to the deity, charged with magick, and then eaten by the Kula as Prasad (blessed food).

**Note:** If the Puja makes direct use of the Yantra in the ritual, the Arti is placed to the side until it can be placed on the Yantra later.

**Note:** For Pujas, food offerings are mostly vegetarian, and liquid offerings are mostly non-alcoholic, but know your deities and what they like. When unsure, keep it vegetarian. The goal, as with any good host, is to not offend the guest! After finishing our Puja and closing the Temple, our Kula would often drink wine, and sometimes eat meat as we hung out; it never seemed to be an issue.

If other items are needed for a particular Puja, be sure to include them. The Kali Puja calls for a sword or knife, for example. There is a lot to keep track of! This is why all should consult and go over the Puja script a day before, and again just before it is performed.

Near the altar should be:

- Extra food and drink, if you wish.
- Lots of natural, fresh water. You will need to hydrate after chanting, invoking, playing music, and laughing!
- Your Journal.

You may want to have other optional items present, depending on the Puja and how many people are involved. These are the sorts of things I always keep in my temple:

- Drums, rhythm sticks, rattles, flutes and other musical instruments to use at will.
- Large pillows or Zafu (meditation pillows) to sit upon; or mats or carpets or low chairs. Make sitting comfortable!
- Enough candles or subtle lighting so you can read the Puja script without glare or discomfort. I have a shaded light and many candles.
- Notebooks, art supplies, and any other creative items for artwork.
- You may think of other things. Consider what the deity being invited might like.

## Sequence for Each Nath Tantra Puja

*This is the template for each Puja that follows. For clarity the headings are included in each Puja.*

### Honoring Ganesh

At the beginning of every Puja, Ganesh is honored because he is the Lord Who Removes Obstacles. For obvious reasons, most Tantrics are all about removing obstacles before doing a big ritual.

## Banishing

'Salt' and vacuum the area before every Puja.

For all of the Pujas, you will be using the same PHAT! Banishing rite with Sword Mudra from the Zonule Rite, but this time we stand tall and shout it loudly to empower it! Clearly visualize lightning bolts and all negativity fleeing.

## Creating the Sacred Sphere

Next, we 'cast the circle' and visualize it as a sphere, our sacred space. This is done with a wand or a simple, small trident. This conjures the liminal 'Twilight World' where gods and people may mingle. This is also why dawn and twilight are the best times to do a Puja. The circle-sphere protects us from negative forces, and ensures that only the deity we call into the Zonule may enter. Visualizing the powerful, glowing tridents of Shiva at the four quarters protects us and centers the temple, thus further preparing it for the deity. There are many spiritual forces and beings which are drawn to the power of a Puja like moths to a flame, and though we never fear them, a tight, protected space assures more powerful, well-focused magick.

## Honoring the Powers

In the next stage of the Puja, we honor the most important Tantric spiritual guides, mentors, helpers and forces of nature who assist us in our work. This is one section that has changed and evolved over the years as I worked with a Kula, and could easily be modified.

## 'Mea Culpa'

I refer to this as the 'Get Out of Jail Free Card.' Buddhist, Hindu and Tantra rites often have a statement that asks forgiveness of deities for potential screw-ups and mistakes in the ritual. We are human, we err. I don't think I've *ever* run a Puja where something didn't mess up! Missing pages, miscues, cups knocked over, wax on the carpet, you name it. But we relax; we know intent is everything. Our gods and goddesses love us—are part of us—and if we offer the wrong thing or mispronounce a Mantra or…well, you name it, all is forgiven because we mean well and are polite and honor the deities in this way. We are coming from a place of love and devotion.

## Purification (By Devi)

We use this Mantra and blessing on our body to invoke the blessing of the Goddess in all her forms. Placing this purification blessing on our three Body Centers (head, heart, lower center), empowers us with the vibrations of the three Tantric goddesses as well as the triplicities/powers associated with each body center. Each goddess brings a key vibration and manifests the core goddesses in the Nath lineage: Lalita Tripurasundari (Hreeng), Lakshmi (Shreeng), and Kali (Kreeng); thus, this blessing is in every Puja. Our very bodies are the manifestation of Her, for we are born of great Devi and return to her when we pass. Sandalwood oil is appropriate to use for Devi, but there are many other lovely oils that can used, like rose, jasmine or lavender. Be sure that the oil you use is completely natural.

## Centering & Kusa/Sacrament (Blessing of Deva)

After you have invoked the triple forms of Devi to bless yourself with her power, you need to center and focus those divine energies—which is what Shiva does. He is the Tantric CenterPoint of the cosmos, the Bindu of every Yantra and every Tantric temple. We thus center our selves and our divine space by calling upon Shiva. This is done by the invoking of Shiva, and the offering and sharing of his sacrament—Kusa (cannabis). However, it is not necessary to incorporate cannabis into your Tantric rituals, especially if it is illegal or uncomfortable to use where you live. If so, simply ignore that as an offering, and burn another sacred herb (such as rosemary), and share the scent while chanting to Shiva. Others can drum or clap as the cannabis or herb is passed around, and those who do not smoke cannabis can hold the smoking pipe and offer it to Shiva without inhaling. Those who do partake should use the same gesture after inhaling. It is an ancient and powerful sacrament of Maha Deva or Lord Shiva, and as such it centers us and opens our mind.

## Preliminary Invocation

This is an initial prayer, invocation or chant to the deity being invoked. It is done while ringing the prayer bell to 'alert' and 'wake up' that deity as an invitation to the Puja. It can be adapted from a traditional text, or can be original and from the heart. The following Pujas all have somewhat traditional preliminary invocations. Try them as is, and then change them as your Guardian Spirit or the deity informs you.

## Visualization Meditation

This is a time to meditate on the deity. We begin by meditating deeply on the image of the deity on the altar. Then we close our eyes and hold that Murti in our mind until it 'comes alive' within our imagination. This is a powerful and important moment, and it takes practice. Once you have a clear image of the deity, you have moved into the visualized invocation of the deity. This will help you to form a deep connection. You are forming an astral relationship that is both spiritual and archetypal. This forms the foundation for future work with this deity.

## Empowerment of the Deity

Here we call the Prana or energy and essence of the deity *into the charged and prepared Murti,* and thus it 'comes alive' as the Murti is inhabited by the deity. This is done by chanting a key Mantra of the deity, and offering a loving invocation with intense visualization of the glowing deity descending into the Murti. When this is done, the deity is *manifest and present* at the Puja, and can then directly communicate with us and we with him or her. *In this way the inhabited Murti becomes the portal between the worlds in our twilight space.* Until this moment the deity has been meditated upon, honored, invoked and visualized. All these steps have been in preparation for 'installing' the deity, and thus we have given our deity a 'throne' to sit upon as the honored guest of this Puja. *After this, the deity is seen as actually present, and the image is treated as the actual god or goddess.* The Murti can then be praised, anointed with oil, have a Tikka (forehead mark) placed on it with Kumkum (red sandalwood powder), dressed with cloth or jewels, decorated with flowers, and so on. Later, he or she will be offered food, incense and candlelight, and in general will be treated as a royal guest. Through the Murti, the deity can enjoy all such things and becomes joyful at the love and attention you are offering! You will feel it, and when closing your eyes, see the happy deity as well. Later, the deity will directly interact with you, and can be communicated with. The deity can grant boons and give advice. From this time on, the deity should be treated as an honored guest.

## Magick Work

Now that the deity is present, if we choose we can do spells or other magical work with help from the deity. Tantra is rooted in magick, not faith. We offer love and devotion to our deities, but we also expect them to communicate with us and help us, like parents help their child. It is a relationship based on love, but also on practical desires and needs on both sides.

Such serious Tantric Magick is not always necessary or appropriate in a Puja. A Tantric Puja is often like a party as well as a serious rite, but doing Magick is always an option *if* that 'magical work' is aligned with that deity and all take that time to be serious and focused. For example, in a Ganesh Puja, we may do Magick for the removal of specific obstacles in our life. However, that is not appropriate for a Puja for a festival, like Diwali (the festival of lights), because it is a time to celebrate and receive the general blessings of the goddess Lakshmi without casting spells! Appropriacy counts.

If Magick is done in the Puja, all 'spells' should include the following:

• The operation must be appropriate and well-planned. If you are doing it with others, review it carefully with everyone beforehand, and do a 'walk through.'

• If there is a question of the attitude of the deity about this spell, a short meditation and maybe some divination with the now-present deity should be done to check.

Some typical magickal operations done within a Puja include:

- Creating or blessing an amulet or talisman.
- Blessing and empowering a Tantric tool such as a Murti, amulet, Yantra, or knife.
- Candle or cord magick to heal another, or to banish evil from one who needs help.
- Conjuring a much-needed job, home, money, prosperity or luck with a specific Mantra or Magick charm or image.

Do some research. There are tons of magickal charms, sigils, spell chants, etc. in the vast wealth of Tantric lore and history.

Generating a lot of energy is important in making spells effective. This energy can be raised in many ways. Loud chanting, drumming, dancing, singing, intensely intoning invocation, intense visualizations, Mudras, and so on can be used to empower and project the spell. Enthusiasm and focus are the key.

When done, shout SVAHA! (So Be It!)

Be creative and focused and meditate on clear goals, possibilities and techniques for your Magick before doing it.

### Offering to & Feeding the Deity

Food is charged or blessed with Mantra and Mudra as indicated in the Puja, but that too may be changed. The Arti tray with food, liquid, incense, candle and an icon of the deity is prepared and blessed at this time as the candle and incense are lit with the appropriate Mantra and Mudra.

### Communing with the Deity

The Arti tray is then picked up and 'waved' before the deity in clockwise circles in the air before the altar. If there are several people, this is first done by the priest or priestess, then passed clockwise about the circle to each person. As each person does this, they silently pray to, and commune with the deity. You should clearly visualize and feel its presence. Take a moment, and with focus and intensity, ask for blessings and boons either aloud or silently. At this point you will have entered a trance communion with the deity if all is going as it should.

Then eat and drink some of the offerings (Prasad) that have been empowered by the deity, and feel the energy of that deity enter you.

Finally, when all are done—and this may take some time; there is no rush—the Arti tray is returned to the priest/ess who communes with the deity, eats some Prasad, and places the Arti tray back on the Yantra while Mantras or short prayers are continually offered.

Then all bow to the deity, commune in silence for a time, and end this 'sharing time' with a short prayer or Mantra as all visualize the delighted deity 'eating' the energy of the food and items.

This is a good time to relax and chat. Maybe even do divination and ask for advice from the now-present deity.

This is also a time to play a drum or other instrument, to deepen your trance state and bond with the deity with simple, rhythmic music; and, if others are present, for camaraderie and power. It honors and pleases the god or goddess when laughter and joy fill the space with more Magick and swirling energy. Sing some appropriate chants or short songs, or get up and dance 'with the god' if you wish! These are all ancient and common Tantric Puja practices that enhance the trance state and visions.

Entertaining the honored, divine guest should be lively and enjoyable for all. After any wild 'energized Puja enthusiasm,' we relax in this chill, positive energy, and relax with the deity as we prepare to end the Puja. If done with a group, this is a great time for casual teaching and mentoring, discussions on Tantra, or just socializing and partying.

## Farewell to the Deity

All good things must come to an end, and that includes every party. A final prayer or chant of love, devotion and gratitude is offered to the deity to bring things back to a more focused state; the energy begins to coalesce as the rite wraps up. We thank the deity for coming, bow, accept the love and power that the deity is giving us, and offer gratitude and love, with hands together at the heart, a bow and maybe other final Mantras, or a phrase, depending on the Puja.

A final thanks is given to the deity. He or she is bid goodbye as the way is opened for the deity's departure from our Twilight World.

With our hands together at our heart, all make a final bow and chant words that unite the supreme Goddess and God into OM:

OM SHANTI SHIVA SHAKTI

## Ending & Dedications

Finally, all the leftover energy of the Puja is offered to the benefit and enlightenment of all beings. There are many ways to do this, but we offer the traditional offering of the 'four Purusarthas' (blessings of life) namely, Dharma (ethical way), Artha (prosperity), Kama (desires), and Moksha (liberation or freedom) with the chant:

*Balance, Wealth, Pleasure and Liberation to All Beings!*

In our mind, we see all beings in the universe receiving those blessings. Then the bell is rung three times to send the blessings.

The PHAT! banishing is repeated, and all lurking energies fly away as the glowing tridents at the four directions dissolve. Finally, we touch the earth, and visualize any lingering energy sinking deep into Mother Earth to honor and aid Nature. We say:

BHU DEVI [Earth Mother]: To You, From You; All Things! OM!

Svaha! All are now free to whoop, howl, dance and laugh. Leftover offerings can be shared, given to others, or left outside in a wooded area for wild animals; liquids should be poured out at the base of a tree. The deity's Murti may remain on the altar for a time after clean-up to absorb the vibes; it may then be put away with honor.

It is time to reenter the mundane sphere. Go forth and have more fun if you like. If you are doing this with others, move the party to another room, crank up some Bollywood dance music, and have more fun! That is how Tantrics roll.

# Ganesh (Ganapati)
# The Lord of Obstacles & Classifications

*Lord Ganesh (Ganapati)*
*(Photo by the Author)*

OM Praise be to thee O Ganapati
Thou art the ultimate reality, the one truth...
The Universe is born from thee
The elements—earth, water, fire, air, Spirit—are manifest in thee
We meditate on thy countenance, enlighten therefore our powers
 of understanding
Thou art the Eternal...OM!
 — Traditional hymn from *Ganesha,* Jagannathan

## On the Deity

One of the most popular deities on the planet is the Elephant-Headed lord, Ganesh. He is commonly known to devotees as Ganapati (Lord of the Ganas), or Vinayaka (the Remover of Obstacles). He is venerated in most Hindu, Jain and Tantric households, temples and businesses. Several other religions also venerate the Elephant-

Headed God. He can also be found in Sikh, Buddhist, Shinto and other temples and shrines. I have even seen his image in Taoist and Confucian temples in China! Ganesh generates energy, and is one of the most popular gods in the world. This offers a massive psychic pool from which any Tantric can draw on in his or her Work.

'Ganapati' is formed from **Gana** (a group of wild supernatural beings), and **Pati** (Master). Thus, his name means 'Master of the Hordes of Wild Spirits'.

Vinayaka means 'he who removes obstacles, hindrances or sorrows,' and in many ways, this is the most common way he is invoked, for obvious reasons.

Ganesh, the first son of Shiva and Parvati, was given the role of the GanaPati by his dad, Shiva, because these wild spirits were followers of Shiva. As such, the Elephant-Headed God is often depicted as their parade marshal, leading the wild and rambunctious host about Mt. Kailash where his mom, Parvati, and his dad Shiva reside—it being the center of the universe. Maybe because of his being the first child of the holy couple, or because of his control of the Ganas, Ganesh is always invoked first for any ritual in Tantra. His veneration is so widespread that his image is often displayed in massive temples as well as in folk-spirit shrines, like those of the Naga (serpent demigods).

Ganesh is far more than Shiva's 'manager' or kid. In some sacred texts, he is also said to *predate* the primal Shiva. Some sects profess that he, not Shiva, is supreme—that he created the universe, and thus *is* the cosmos. Indeed, the *Uchchhishta Ganapatya* sect of Tantra honors him as the supreme divinity, OM.

Some scholars translate his name as the 'Lord of Classifications', meaning he knows what and where everything in the cosmos is, what its purpose is, and where its place in the order of things is. Thus, amongst his worshippers, he is revered as the god of knowledge, writing, science, organizing principles, and intelligence. On a more practical level, he helps guide every worshiper in the correct manner. As the lord of animist and occult nature spirits, he helps those who call on him to work with occult powers, remove obstacles, understand and communicates arcane concepts, and protect those who are traveling, whether physically or spiritually. He embodies the Map of the Cosmos, so he knows where all the cool stuff is, and on top of that, he brings wealth and prosperity! He is a very handy god.

## History

The earliest known images of Ganesh are about 3,500 years old, but it is clear from older images (Pre-Aryan, Mohenjo-Daro, ceramic seals) that the elephant was sacred and venerated widely, and was often shown with primal 'Shiva' images. As usual, when focusing on Tantra, we can find some mythic clues amidst the ancient indigenous religious traditions in the Harappan culture that venerated a wide array of animal/animist spirits and god-forms. In fact, quite a bit of Ganesh's history relates to the primal Shiva-Shakti cult complexes. However, he is possibly even older than this as he is one of the very few Tantric or Hindu gods who still retains his animal form. The *Tantras* and the earlier *Puranas* manage to retain some of the earliest myths, and it is here that we can find the roots of Ganesh in early history. Long ago, a prehistoric elephant-headed deity called Dantin existed, and may have been absorbed into the cult of Ganesh. Dantin is shown holding what looks like a Neolithic club, which tells us much, and is called *Pellu* (teeth) in Dravidian and *Pillaka* ('one with tusks') in Pali. These are some ancient possible sources for this god, and Dantin was linked to the Ganas as well:

> *"soon [Dantin was] identified with the countless spirits that roamed the nether world, spirits whose non-Vedic origins cannot be in doubt...as a rotund, elephant-headed figure, Dantin became their lord and master and thus became Ganapati."*
>
> — *Ganesha,* Jagannathan

We know from archeological digs and other historical information that huge elephants and other tusked elephant-precursors have roamed India for thousands of years. The sheer size of these monstrous beasts ensured that a nature-based, religious tradition would honor such creatures. Countless prehistoric ivory charms from these beasts have been used in animist and Tantric traditions as powerful and numinous charms. It thus seems, from prehistoric and modern ivory cult items, that the power and strength of the elephant deity emerged as a core deity in what became Tantra long ago.

In short, Ganesh embodied the greatest, most powerful animal the ancient Dravidians interacted with, and so became an ancient and powerful god-form. He survived and emerged, like Shiva and Devi, through the later Aryan invasion. This is how the gods of Tantra survived from the earlier Harappan cultures—going underground only to emerge in hidden Magick Tantric cults and folk traditions. As this complex interweaving between top-down and bottom-up mythological foci progressed, Ganesh emerged with a key role in what became the Hindu religious pantheon while maintaining his role in the more hidden Tantric sects. Even today his lingering attributes and functions point to the ancient, even primal, source of his being.

As Sanatana Dharma (Hinduism) emerged from this grand synchronous synthesis, Buddhism also was spreading; and of all the gods, Buddhists adopted Ganesh as a key deity that would help spread Buddhism! As Shaivite Tantra spread throughout Southeast Asia, followed by Buddhism, Ganesh was carried everywhere. Today in both Mahayana and Hinayana (Theravada) Buddhism, across all of Asia, Ganesh is still venerated in temples as a guardian. I have seen such images in a dozen countries, from China to Tibet to Indonesia to Thailand to Japan and beyond. No Hindu/Tantric god is so widely venerated or more honored today than Ganesh!

Ganesh is a marvelously accessible god, open to all with little trace of mystery or forbidden teachings. Unlike other gods and goddesses, he is truly ecumenical. It is often said that anyone, regardless of cast or initiation, can access Ganesh and his spiritual and magical energies for blessings, for removing obstacles, and to bring prosperity of all kinds. Amidst all the in-fighting among sects in Hinduism, all venerate and bow to Ganesh. This is why Ganesh became a key unifying symbol when political liberation movements began to organize against the British occupation of India. Everyone could agree on Ganesh as an icon of removing obstacles! In India, Nepal and many other places, it is common to find Ganesh images and shrines on corners, above gates, and in doorways. He is truly a folk god—a god for everyone—and cheerfully helps everyone gain prosperity. This is why he often sits next to cash registers and other places where wealth changes hands!

### *Myths*

Let's start with the creation of the universe. According to Hindu mythology, the universe came into being 432 million years ago when a beautiful vibration began, and it was OM, the supreme God-Energy Big Bang. The Ganapati cult in India, which is wholly dedicated to Ganesh as the godhead, believes that this first manifested vibratory origin of creation was also the embodiment of Ganesh, and they point out that his physical form actually forms the OM symbol. The Tamil OM (AUM) is explicit, with trunk and all, like so:

*Ganesh as OM (AUM)*

So, in the Beginning, according to this sect, Ganesh is said to have blown a conch shell making the OM sound vibrate outward, creating ALL. He was in the form of *Nritya Ganapati* (the Dancing Ganesh), and so he danced and created and organized the universe. From this moment, so says this myth, the Hindu trinity of Brahma (creator), Vishnu (preserver), and Shiva (destroyer) were manifested, but they did not know what to do or how to manage all of creation. Ganesh instructed them on their responsibilities, set them all straight, and the world as we know it began. The Tantric scholar Daniélou declares Ganesh to be 'the lord of classifications'—the God who organizes all aspects of existence, all that makes up and orders the universe, and who keeps track of all things. In this way he knows the right roles of all the spirits, the gods and the goddesses.

As is the case in the shifting mythic landscape of Tantra and Hinduism, there are many versions of such myths. In one written Tantra, the cosmic creation of the universe was the manifestation of *Shiva* as OM, and thus were created the gods and goddesses; but they were at a loss as to who was who, what was what, and how things should be organized. It fell to Ganesh to sort it all out, which he did. In the end, the point of both creation myths is the same: Ganesh informs the classification, categorization, and thus, the manifestation of all beings, things and ideas. Therefore, he is the lord of understanding of all the patterns and functions of creation. Keeping this in mind will help explain all the various things Ganesh is said to do in the cosmos, as well as what he can do for those who petition him.

This is a main reason why Ganesh is invoked before every Puja, and before beginning any sort of new venture or project, including building a home or temple. Not only does he remove obstacles, he knows the overall pattern of all things.

There is a myth that Ganesh's four arms reach out to the four directions, and he is thus always at the center of the manifest and unmanifest worlds. Being the 'leader of all of Shiva's spirits and demigods' who fill the world, it makes sense that he has a high position, and is called on before all things are done. You cannot begin any task, ritual, or meditation without first centering your mind, and then organizing thoughts on how to go about it. Thus, without the organization and conceptual frameworks of Ganesh, nothing would be possible.

Even Shiva...

There is a myth that Shiva, being the Absolute and Liberated godhead, set out to slay a powerful demon, but he was unable to do so. Vexed, he meditated on why he, the Supreme deity, was unable to do this. He realized that he had not obeyed his own divine order to the gods that Ganesh be honored before any undertaking. So, he honored and bowed to his 'son' Ganesh, and was able to think logically, figure it out, and win the day by handily defeating the demon!

### *Birth of Ganesh*

How Ganesh was born is a varied, but amazing tale. There are many different versions in the Puranas, Tantras and other holy books. One thing is sure, he was the son of Shiva and Parvati

(Shakti), the supreme God and Goddess who reside upon the top of Mt. Kailash, the center of the created universe. Many call Ganesh the 'mind born' of Shiva, meaning he emerged from the primordial OM or non-differentiated divine presence of Shiva. Still others tell the story of a more natural divine birth from the union of the divine pair. And, as mentioned, some myths declare Ganesh the primordial first godhead who created the universe and all the gods! Such is the varied mythic universe of Tantra and Hinduism.

How he got his elephant head is also told in several ways. One version has him secretly created by Parvati from her dead skin during a bath, because she wanted a child and Shiva had been too busy meditating for ages! After divinely creating Ganesh through her own power, Parvati continued her bath and told her new son to guard the door to protect her privacy. Shiva came out of his bliss-state at that time, and wanted to see his wife. When he went to the bath, he was stopped by his then-unknown son who barred the door. Heated words were exchanged, a fight ensued, and Shiva cut Ganesh's head off with his trident! Parvati, attracted by the ruckus, came out and was horrified, as was Shiva when he discovered that he'd beheaded his new son! So, Shiva went in search of a new head for his son. He had no luck until a sacred elephant bowed before him and offered his head for the divine kid. Shiva, with a little magical surgery, then created and revived the now elephant-headed Ganesh, and all was forgiven. I suspect that what we see here may be the survival of a prehistoric cult of elephants or mammoths that existed at the same time as the Harappan culture did (4000 BCE). It is my theory that the even older god Dantin became part of the pervasive indigenous cult of Shiva-Shakti, and thus merged with and became Ganesh over the ages.

## *The Stolen Conch*

As the Vedic culture, brought by the Aryan penetration of India, entered and combined with the existing Harappan mythologies and gods, there emerged a rivalry between the cults of the indigenous Shiva and the new god, Vishnu. This may be reflected in a myth involving Vishnu's Conch Shell, one of his important symbols.

One day, young Ganesh was playing with the Ganas at the foot of Mt. Kailash, and for fun he found and stole the sacred Conch Shell.

Vishnu then complained bitterly to Shiva that some thief had taken his conch! I'm sure Shiva chuckled, and (feigning seriousness) told Vishnu that to catch the thief he should worship Ganesh who removes problems! Vishnu reluctantly did so, and Ganesh suddenly appeared and returned his conch. From then on, Vishnu also worshipped Ganesh! One wonders if Vishnu ever caught on. Today Ganesh is often shown with the sacred conch shell, so in the end he never really let it go.

## The Missing Tusk

Looking at images of Ganesh, you may notice that he has lost much of his left tusk. One version of how this happened has him losing it in a fight with a hot-headed devotee of Shiva, Parasuraman, who was challenged by Ganesh when he was guarding Mt. Kailash. Another has Ganesh breaking off and throwing *his own tusk* at a demon who could not be slain, causing the demon to turn into a rat or mouse, which Ganesh then adopted as his 'vehicle' (Vahana), and on which he still rides around. Even today, Ganesh is worshipped as the one who controls or restrains crop-eating rats, an important job in rural India.

However, the most interesting myth—one that explains Ganesh's reputation as the lord of wisdom, writing and learning—is that of Vyasa. In this story, it was Ganesh who wrote the *Mahabharata,* the famous, sacred Hindu text, as it was dictated to him by the sage Vyasa. The story goes that his pen (stylus) broke, and rather than stop and awaken Vyasa from his trance, Ganesh broke off a tusk and used it as a pen to complete the sacred text.

Another version, one that may be older, is this: once Ganesh had a huge meal of honey-drenched Modakas—sweets that he loves— which helped him gain a huge, distended belly. Lurching home at night, riding on his rat, there was a snake lying in the road; the rat tripped on it and Ganesh fell. His belly burst open, losing all the sweets! Chandra, the moon god, saw this and laughed. Ganesh, furious, grabbed the snake and tied it around his belly to close himself up. After that he cursed the moon to never again shine, broke off his tusk and threw it at the moon, thus putting the moon out! All the gods and humans were upset at this and all prayed to Ganesh and begged him to relent and let the moon shine! Being a nice god, he did so, but dictated that the moon would no longer be full every night, but must wax and wane. Today it is still unlucky to look at the full moon on Ganesh's holy day, Ganesh Chaturthi, because of this.

Some historians have indicated that this myth refers to a time when Ganesh was venerated *as the moon god,* long before the later Vedic god Chandra came and took over that role.

In images of Ganesh, you will find him holding his broken tusk in his lower right hand in some of his aspects. In these and other images, it may represent a writing tool or a club used as a weapon. Archeologists have found that curved tusks were used as weapons as well as ritual 'wands' or tools of magick in prehistoric India. Today, elephant ivory is still seen throughout India and all of Asia as having divine magickal properties, and this has made Indian elephants endangered. Today Ganesh is invoked and his image is used to stop this illegal slaughter. Jai Ganesha!

## *Around the World*

Ganesh is not an only child. He is the brother of the god, Murugan (aka Kartikeya), the human-looking warrior-god who rides upon a peacock, also a child of Shiva and Parvati. Once, when the brothers were competing for their parents' attention, they quarreled. So, mom Parvati and dad Shiva offered them a challenge: Who could circle the world fastest? Murugan—all martial—jetted off to circle the globe, but Ganesh won by simply walking around his parents, declaring that the whole world was, in fact, Shiva-Shakti. Poor Kartikeya returned exhausted, likely in a peevish mood, when he found himself bested in this way.

§ § §

There are many other myths about Ganesh; every village has one it seems. He helped establish rivers and temples, put demons like Ravana in their place, ate the wealth god Kubera out of house and home until Shiva intervened, and was a wild child. In most of these myths, Shiva is involved, but we must remember that as ancient as Shiva is, it is possible that the elephant-headed god, by whatever name, may be just as old.

## Iconography

There are a seemingly infinite number of forms and images of Ganesh (including one I have of him using a laptop computer!), but he has several traditional forms. He is most often shown as a jovial, tubby, sweets-loving, elephant-headed god with a human body who removes obstacles, offers good luck, and brings prosperity. The most common form has him seated cross-legged on a throne with bowls of sweets, and holding up an axe and goad with his mouse or rat helper at his feet. There are many variations of this.

In his upper left hand, he holds the looped noose, which represents attraction, or attracting what you need.

In his upper right hand, he holds an axe or a combination axe-goad, which represents cutting through or driving off obstacles, hindrances and problems.

In his lower left hand, he often holds a bowl of sweets (Modaka), which represents wealth in the form of food, but sometimes his left hand is held palm up, thus making the Varada Mudra (the boon-giving, blessing hand-gesture).

His lower right hand is raised up, elbow bent, palm face-out in the Abhaya Mudra (fear-dispelling hand-gesture).

Depending on the image and aspect, he may hold a number of other things, each with a different esoteric meaning. Sometimes, he is holding his father's trident or a conch to blow.

He is most commonly depicted with the grey skin of an elephant, but sometimes he is human-flesh colored. In more esoteric Tantra forms, often found in Nepal, his skin may be white, orange, red or even purple, and he may hold a variety of tools. In popular festival floats, there are no limitations! His image can be any color and any form, sometimes quite humorous. He is often shown with a variety of deities. He can appear with two, four or many arms, and different aspects often hold different symbolic items. The simpler forms of Ganesh are widely worshipped, but in Tantra there are older, secret forms that are used for more esoteric kinds of magick.

### *The 32 Forms of Ganesh*

Some of the oldest Tantric forms of Ganesh seem to come from Nepal, and some of the older forms show him riding upon a lion, not a rat. This implies that he was a more powerful and awe-inspiring deity in the distant past, as opposed to the kindly, plump god of the good life he is often shown as today.

One text reveals 32 'Tantric forms' of Ganesh. It is interesting to note the symbols, colors and titles, and how they change; it is also wonderful to see the varied patterns. These forms are likely much older than the Ganesh seen everywhere in India today. Unlike most Hindu gods, Ganesh is rarely shown with a Shakti (wife), but the Tantric forms often show him in erotic union with various female Tantric partners. I have occasionally seen him in India with symbolic female personifications of his spiritual power: Siddhi (Magical Power) and Buddhi (Wisdom).

However, the 32 Tantric forms of Ganesh reveal a god with a wide range of powers. Among other things, he helps with agriculture, and is identified as the god of the moon, the god of removing obstacles, and the god of wealth, war, learning and protection. Some forms of Ganesh emphasize his sexual nature as well. Truly, Ganesh has always had a multitude of aspects and powers. Note that some of the items mentioned are only found in India and Nepal, yet all these aspects can be used in ritual with some adjustments. He won't mind, I'm sure.

## The 32 Forms of Ganesha
### (Derived from the Dhyana Slokas)

1. **Bala Ganapati**—Beloved Child.
   Color of the rising sun, his 4 arms hold a banana, sugarcane, jackfruit, and mango; he has a Modaka sweet in his trunk.

2. **Taruna Ganapati**—Youthful Ganesha.
   Red color, 8 arms, he holds a noose, goad, Modaka, wood apple, rose apple, broken tusk, herb & sugarcane.

3. **Bhakti Ganapati**—God of Devotees.
   Full moon color, he holds a coconut, mango, banana and a cup of sweet milk.

4. **Veera Ganapati**—Valiant Warrior.
   Red, 16 arms, he holds a demon, spear, bow, arrow, discus, sword and a shield, as well as a hammer, mace, goad, noose, axe, pickaxe, trident, serpent and banner.

5. **Shakti Ganapati**—Powerful One.
   Four arms, sunset-colored, having a green-colored Shakti (goddess) with him. Ganesh holds a garland of flowers while offering Mudra of blessings.
6. **Dwija Ganapati**—Twice-Born.
   Four-headed, color of the moon, he holds a book, a Mala, a Puja vessel, and a sacred Guru staff.
7. **Siddhi Ganapati**—God of Achievement.
   Yellow color, he holds a mango, sugarcane, flowers, an axe, and a sesame-ball sweet in his trunk.
8. **Chishti Ganapati**—Tantric.
   He holds a goddess/Shakti in one arm, blue in color; in other hands he holds a blue lotus, a pomegranate, an herb, a Veena (musical instrument), and a Mala.
9. **Vighna Ganapati**—Creator of Obstacles Against Evil.
   Golden color, his 8 arms hold a conch shell, a discus, a handful of flowers, sugarcane, an arrow, a noose, and a garland of flowers.
10. **Kshipra Ganapati**—Quick-Acting Intense God.
    Red color, beautiful, he holds his broken tusk, a noose, a goad, a branch of the Wish-Fulfilling (World) Tree; a pot of gems is held in his trunk.
11. **Heramba Ganapati**—Protector of the Weak.
    Five faces, dark green, he is riding a lion. Two hands are in protecting and giving Mudras, the others hold a noose, his tusk, Mala, flower garland, axe, hammer, Modaka and fruit.
12. **Lakshmi Ganapati**—Giver of Success.
    This form is pure white. On either side he has his two 'personified powers' or wives: *Siddhi* (Magical Power) and *Buddhi* (Wisdom or Gnosis), both holding blue lotuses. Two of his hands are in giving and protecting Mudras; other hands hold a noose, a goad, a parrot, a sprig of the sacred tree of life, a ritual vessel, a sword, and a pomegranate.

13. **Maha Ganapati**—The Great One.
    Green in color, he holds his Shakti/wife who has a lotus. He has 3 eyes, wears a crescent moon, holds a pomegranate, a mace, sugarcane, a discus, a lotus, a noose, a blue lily, an herb, a tusk, and a pot of gems.

14. **Vijaya Ganapati**—Giver of Success.
    Red-skinned, he is riding his rat. He holds a goad, a noose, a tusk, and a mango in different hands.

15. **Nritya Ganapati**—Happy Dancer.
    Gold color, dancing under the Wish-Fulfilling (World) Tree, he wears many rings, and holds a noose, a goad, an axe, his broken tusk, and a sweet cake in various hands.

16. **Urdhva Ganapati**—An Erotic Tantric Form.
    With gold-colored skin and many arms, he holds a green Shakti/wife, a blue flower, a sprig of herb, a lotus, a sugarcane bow, an arrow, and his broken tusk (possibly as a phallic image.)

17. **Ekaakshara Ganapati**—Being the Bija Syllable GAANG.
    Red skin, clad in red, he wears a garland of red flowers, a crescent moon crown, is three-eyed, and carries a pomegranate, a noose and a goad, and holds his hand in the boon-granting Mudra. He sits in meditation riding his rat.

18. **Vara Ganapati**—Giver of Boons.
    This form of Ganesh is red-skinned with three eyes. He wears a crescent moon crown, and holds a noose, a goad, and a dish of honey; he has a pot of jewels in his trunk.

19. **Tryakshara Ganapati**—Of the Seed Syllable AUM (OM).
    Golden-skinned, he has fly whisks in his flapping ears and holds a noose, a goad, a tusk, and a mango; he has a Modaka sweet in his trunk.

20. **Kshipra-Prasada Ganapati**—Who Rewards Promptly.
    Adorned with much jewelry and with a big belly, he sits on a throne of Kusa (sacred grass); he holds a noose, a goad, a pomegranate, a lotus, a tusk, and a sprig of the sacred tree.

21. **Haridra Ganapati**—Golden One.
Golden in color with yellow clothing, he holds a noose, a goad, his broken tusk, and a Modaka sweet.

22. **Ekadanta Ganapati**—Of the Single Tusk.
He is blue-skinned with a big belly; he holds an axe, a Mala, a sweet, and his broken tusk.

23. **Shrishti Ganapati**—The Creator.
Red-skinned and riding his rat, he holds a noose, a goad, his broken tusk, and a mango.

24. **Uddanda Ganapati**—Punisher of Evil.
He has a green Shakti/wife in his lap, and holds a lotus; in his ten hands he has: a pot of gems, a lotus, a blue water-lily, a mace, sugarcane, a sprig of herb, a noose, a garland of flowers, a pomegranate, and his broken tusk.

25. **Runamochana Ganapati**—Who Releases Mankind from Bondage.
He looks like white crystal, is dressed in red, and holds a goad, a noose, a rose apple, and his broken tusk.

26. **Dhundhi Ganapati**—Of Kashi.
Red in color, he holds a Mala, a tusk, a pot of gems, and an axe.

27. **Dwimukha Ganapati**—God of Two Faces.
This form of Ganesh has two faces, and is blue-green in color; he wears red clothes, and a gem-covered crown; he holds a noose, a goad, a tusk, and a pot of gems.

28. **Trimukha Ganapati**—The Three-Faced Deity.
This form of Ganesh has three faces, is red-skinned, and is sitting in the center of a large, golden lotus; his left hand in protection Mudra, his right hand in granting boons Mudra; he also holds a noose, a goad, a Mala, and a pot of sacred nectar.

29. **Simha Ganapati**—Riding on a Lion (Simha means lion).
White in color, riding a lion as his vehicle; he also holds a lion, a sprig of the World Tree, a Veena (musical instrument), a lotus, a bunch of flowers, and a pot of gems.

30. **Yogi Ganapati**—Master of Yoga (Union).
    He is the color of the rising sun and is sitting in Yoga Asana with a yogic band about his crossed legs; he wears blue clothes, and holds a Mala, a Yogi staff, a noose, and sugarcane.

31. **Durga Ganapati**—The Savior (Durga is an ancient, powerful, warrior-like goddess, much like Kali).
    This Ganesh has a huge body, and burnt-gold skin; he has 8 arms and holds a Mala, an arrow, a goad, a tusk, a noose, a bow, a flag, and a rose apple. He wears red clothing.

32. **Sankatahara Ganapati**—Remover of Sorrow.
    Seated on a red lotus and wearing blue clothing, he has skin like the rising sun; he has a green Shakti/wife in his lap who is holding a blue lotus.

## Symbols

Many symbols of Ganapati have already been discussed, and each symbol is seen as magick code for an aspect of the god that has a particular meaning in the 'twilight language' of Tantra.

The goad means pushing away something. The axe means removing obstacles. The bowl of Modaka sweets means prosperity and wealth. And so on. All of these and more are deep symbols of the elephant-headed Deva, and all the Tantric gods have similarly encoded meanings in their Mudras and tools.

In his many ornate Tantric forms, Ganesh is shown with a variety of other symbols like pomegranates, mangos, sugarcane, and other tools and items, each having a different esoteric meaning. For example, a red fruit indicates an erotic aspect, and the mango may denote a more nurturing form.

Many believe that Ganesh was primarily an agricultural god, and the broken tusk is often compared to 'a simple plow,' another sublime symbol. Another icon attached to Ganesh is his Vahana (vehicle), which is a rat or mouse named Mooshak. The common wisdom seems to be that Ganesh, as a god of the earth and of agriculture, helps with pest control for farmers.

Other myths say that his rat represents the small intrusive 'chattering' thoughts that Ganesh can crush in meditation. What an image! Yet another explanation points to the fact that rats easily break into most any place, and gnaw through most obstacles, something this god is renowned for. Keep this 'twilight language' of images in mind as we explore other Tantric deities.

Ganesh shrines are everywhere he is worshipped. He is very much a 'folk god,' and it is interesting to see 'Ganapati Stones' or stele images everywhere you go. They are often set up under sacred trees at the entrance to villages, sometimes with images of spirits like Naga (serpent demigods) and other folk deities, to protect and bring prosperity to the area.

Sometimes, Ganesh is shown with his two philosophical wives: Riddhi (prosperity) and Siddhi (spiritual power). They are less wives and more allegorical images of powers that Ganesh manifests: money and magick.

The Sankha (conch shell) is often shown being held by Ganesh, and as such is often on his altar. This conch is blown at the beginning of many Pujas; you can hear them being blown constantly in India, especially at dawn and twilight. The conch has multiple meanings, and is held by a variety of gods like Vishnu; but the divine sound vibration of a blown conch also imitates an elephant trumpeting in the jungle. I can attest that this is true! The intensity and force of this vibration is said to dispel all evil. This makes it particularly appropriate for the god who always starts every Puja by removing obstacles.

Another of Ganesh's symbols, though often connected with his dad Shiva, is the Kamandalu (water vessel). It symbolizes fullness, giving and purification, and is often used in Pujas and rituals. Sometimes Ganesh is shown with Shiva's Trishul (trident); often the mark on his forehead is a Trishul, sometimes with three horizontal lines added, indicating the power of his dad.

Ganesh is connected with scholarship, writing, spiritual rituals, and teaching; thus, some of his symbols include the Mala, sacred texts, pens, scrolls, and today, computers! I have not touched upon all of his symbols so, if you are planning a Sadhana or a serious study of Ganesh, you would do well to explore all of his aspects, symbols and tools. Once you have connected with Ganesh and built a good relationship with him, he will be quite happy to offer you information concerning many of these things in meditation. OM GAANG!

## Offerings

**Colors:** Often he is visualized as 'smoky' grey, like an elephant, though other colors are seen depending on the aspects of this god. Lunar white, purple, saffron, red and especially orange are often used with Ganesh.

**Incense** (both are sacred to Ganesh):
Sandalwood (yellow)
Frankincense Dhoop. Dhoop is a kind of soft, malleable, Indian incense; it is easy to find.

**Food:** Coconuts and Modaka (Indian pastry)—really all kinds of sweets and candy. Other fruit he likes: bananas, sugarcane, pomegranates, mangos, apples, oranges, and so on. He also likes ghee (clarified butter). I offer him peanuts which he likes as well! For liquid offerings, I often offer coconut water, coconut milk, or various juices, and he is pleased by these. I also offer *Panchamrita,* a traditional mixture of ghee, milk (or cream), milk curds (or yoghurt), sugar and honey. (All deities like this; it is very traditional.)

**Flowers:** Hibiscus is a flower Ganesh loves; also, marigolds. He generally likes red, yellow or orange flowers, but any appropriate flowers are fine. I often choose what is in my garden.

## Mantras

Ganesh's seed Bija syllable is GAANG.

Om GAANG Ganapataye Namah
Om Shri Ganeshaya Namah
Om GAANG GAANG GAANG GAANG GAANG Ganapataye Namah

## Yantras

There are several Yantras for every deity. The two below are the most common ones I know, so I recommend that you use one of them. Colors and specifics vary. Sometimes the large triangle is missing from his traditional Yantra, but most display the 6-pointed star.

*Two Yantras of Ganesh (Ganpati)*

## Festivals

In the fantastical 'Twilight World' of Tantra, sources, special celebrations and traditions differ from area to area and sect to sect. Here are the most common special weekdays and festivals. Keep in mind that most festivals shift year to year so it is best to look them up.

**Weekday:** Ganesh is traditionally worshiped before dawn on Tuesdays or Wednesdays (depending on the source).

**Special Festivals:** The fourth day after the new moon and the fourth day after the full moon is called *Chaturthi,* and is dedicated to Lord Ganesha. Fasting is traditionally done on the latter date.

**Ganesh Chaturthi Festival (Ganesh's Birthday):** The date of this special festival varies year by year, so check. You should *not* look at the moon on this night: it is bad luck because of a long-ago fight Ganesh had with the moon god, Chandra!

## Ganesh Nath Tantra Puja

On the Zonule altar:

A candle, incense in a burner, a cup of appropriate liquid, a Yoni-Lingam, appropriate flowers, a pipeful of cannabis (if legal), the Arti bowl or tray full of offerings (food, a small cup of liquid, a small candle, and a stick of incense), and an image of the deity. (See the **Offerings** section above.) The appropriate Yantra should be laid flat before the Murti of the deity with the Arti tray placed on the Yantra. If desired, candles of the appropriate color can be placed on either side of the deity image, and another side plate of food and drink may be placed before or near the altar.

### *Honoring Ganesh*

The priest/ess bows to Ganesh:

OM GAANG GANAPATAYE NAMAH [3x]

The bell is rung. Others join in if this is a group Puja. The altar candle is lit.

### *Banishing*

PHAT! [5x]

This is done to the four directions and to the center by all present. Lightning bolts are visualized, banishing all negative energy.

### *Creating the Sacred Sphere*

The priest/ess casts a circle with the trident, *or* all hold hands in a circle. All chant:

OM MANI PADME HUM [3x]

while envisioning the circle/sphere of light about all. All pause for a moment and visualize 4 tridents at the 4 directions glowing with light and protective energy. All chant OM. The Zonule-Temple is set.

### *Honoring the Powers*

All bow and intone:

*OM Namaste! Honor to the Gods, the Spirits, the Ancestors, the Gurus and to All Wild Things That Play! OM to Shri Gurudev Dadaji Mahendranath and the Crystal Line of Tantric Gurus Whose Amrita and Power Helps Us Manifest True Knowledge, True Will, and True Action Through Our Guardian Spirits with Love! Guru OM! Svecchacharya!*

### *"Mea Culpa"*

All say:

*May any Errors We Make in this Ritual, any Slights, or any Negativity Generated be as Rain Striking the Ocean, Dispersed, Forgiven and Forgotten. By Our Efforts May All Beings Attain Liberation and Joy! OM!*

### *Purification (Devi)*

Purify and bless the self with the power of Shakti Devi: Each adept blesses the three Body Centers/Gunas by placing a hand over each area in turn and visualizing light pouring into *Head, Heart and Loins/Base* as they invoke Devi with this Mantra:

HREENG SHREENG KREENG PARAMESHVARI SVAHA
[1x at each body center]

### *Centering & Kusa/Sacrament (Deva)*

A pipeful of Kusa (cannabis) is held on top of the Yoni-Lingam as all sit in a circle and vibrate OM. Then all chant:

OM NAMAH SHIVAYA! [108x]

The Kusa is lit and passed around clockwise. All partake if they wish, or hold up the pipe and make offerings to Shiva if they don't. When done, offerings of pipe ashes are placed on the Yoni-Lingam, and each person dabs some on their forehead (third eye).

### *Preliminary Prayer/Invocation of the Deity*

Incense is lit before the image of the deity. All bow to the god. The bell is rung loudly 3x, and then all intone this prayer together:

O Lord Ganesha, We Invite You to Come into Our Temple.
By Your Sacred Names! NAMASTE SHRI GANAPATI DEVA!
Welcome You Who Remove Obstacles and Bring Prosperity!

All together chant the following 3x:

OM:
First, you are the ONE WITH THE TWISTED TRUNK; Vakratundam
Second, you are the ONE WITH THE SINGLE TUSK; Ekadantam
Third, you are the ONE WITH THE FAWN-COLORED EYES; Krsnapingaksam
Fourth, you are the ONE WITH THE ELEPHANT'S MOUTH; Gajavaktram
Fifth, you are the POT-BELLIED ONE; Lambodaram
Sixth, you are the MONSTROUS ONE; Vikatam
Seventh, you are the KING OF OBSTACLES; Vighnarajam
Eighth, you are the SMOKE-COLORED ONE; Dhumravarnam
Ninth, you are the MOON-CRESTED ONE; Bhalacandram
Tenth, you are the REMOVER OF HINDRANCES; Vinayakam
Eleventh, you are the LORD OF HORDES; Ganapatim
Twelfth, you are the ONE WITH THE ELEPHANT'S FACE; Gajananam
OM SHRI GANESHAYA NAMAH! [3x]

— adapted from the *Narada-Purana,* Narada

### Visualization Meditation

The priest/ess reads, and all silently meditate and visualize, eyes closed. (If you are alone, you may record this and listen to it, or read it silently, and then visualize it afterwards.)

OM GAANG GAANG GAANG GAANG GAANG GANESHAYA NAMAH!

The earth appears caught in the web
of many stars
and a handful of jewel-planets
in the pattern of a 6-rayed star

And this hexagram
Cast in celestial star stuff
coalesces upon the Earth
And it becomes, at the MOMENT of synergy,
A Pantacle
Formed of four dimensions
Height, length, depth and Time
And it is a Yantra
And it is the Yantra of Ganesh
And the moon and Sun mate
And $2 = 0$ and the dragon eats his tail
And there is an orange-tinged eclipse darkness
A circular shadow and halo of New Aeonic fires
And it is the orange-gray skin of the awakening Ganesha
Four dimensions, four arms
OM GAANG! Manifest upon the Throne of Earth!
OM GAANG! Weaving planet-gems about you
OM GAANG! You preside over the removing of obstacles
Old aeons and patterns
Old thinking and living
OM GAANG! You break through Restrictions
As you have for aeons and aeons
Since before humans, and when humanity was formed
And our bond was sealed
When the first Neanderthal spear
Pierced the first mastodon
And the thundering filled the valleys
And the mountains trembled
And with the last gasp HE whispers
"I am the maker and remover of obstacles
You are of me
Become anything you wish
There are no obstacles…"
The names of Ganapati are offered as sparkling gemstones
The chants, the offerings, the orgasmic Union with Ganapati
And the offering of the sun and moon and fire
And in the darkness Ganesh reveals his glory before you!
Right hand held aloft in the Mudra of the sword

Which cut the slave-chains off us!
In his left hand upraised is a lotus
The image of all humans in unity
Of all beings as one—the flowering of groupmind and harmony
Free of fear and full of healing
The lower right hand forms the Mudra of Giving
That our visions of healing and unity are granted
The lower left hand points up in the Mudra of Dispelling Fear
So that the cataclysmic shaking of the earth—
As age changes to age
Is the laughter of the mighty god
This booming laughter now merges with the sound of an elephant's trumpet
And all obstacles and sorrows are blown away like leaves in the wind
and your whole being and the world becomes clean and fresh and free
And the gentle breeze of love and prosperity come
Showering as flowers and gold upon us all, by the love of Ganesh!
And all is ever as it was— And all beings are Free
And all will be—Open!

Sit, be still, meditate on this. After 5–10 minutes, the bell is rung. Then:

### *Empowerment of the Deity*

All stand and stomp on the floor (or sit and pound hands on the floor lightly). Once the rhythm is going, all intensely chant the following 3 times while visualizing Ganesha dancing with you.

*'Dancing Ganesh'*

Dancing Dancing Dancing!
OM GAANG GANAPATAYE NAMAH!
    Pound Pound Pound the drums!
        Slap Slap the thundering feet—
On the Earth
On the Earth

On the Earth!
Hands rise up
   Flames rise up
      Shakti rise up!
Trumpet the Bliss
   Wave the Tusks
      Nod & Shake big pachyderm head!
O Great Elephant!
   Dance and lumber!
      O Elephant God, rear up and up!
         Dance and trumpet
            Swing—and sway—and spin away!
Dancing Dancing Dancing!
GAANG GAANG GAANG!
Swinging your Axe and Noose
   From massive arms and hands
      Swing-Swirling, double spiral spinning!
   Motion within Motion
Cosmos dancing with and as YOU
Bring it In!
   Swirling, expanding
      Embracing
         Arms of Galaxy open wide!
            Spinning in space!
         Float and slide!
Dancing Dancing Dancing!
Amidst the clouds of incense high
   Amidst the showers of bliss and rain
Begone all sorrows and all pain!
Swirls of Petals & pollens, seeds and fruit!
Until—finally!
   Stomp Stomp Stomp!
You come again!
Sparks & Flames
Creation
   Destruction
      Manifestation
Coming together now!

Forming
The Glowing
        Brilliant
     Glorious
Elephant LORD!
O Great Grey One
  Bound by a Serpent belt
     One Tusked god
        World encompassing
       Form of OM!
YA! Ganesh Embrace us!
  We advance with YOU
     Ride with YOU
        ARE YOU!
Filled with Love—OM GAANG
With Eternal Will—OM GAANG
Free of Troubles—OM GAANG!
All Obstacles are eliminated NOW!
JOY and PEACE and SUCCESS
     Pour down
As a shower of GOLD, of JOY, of BLISS!
OM SHRI GANESHAYA NAMAH!!!

Take time to move about, dance, laugh and howl. Then settle down, sit in meditation, and do some Pranayama as the energy of Ganesh fills and settles in you. Then, the bell is rung.

### *Magick Work (Optional)*

A small fireproof vessel with one small chunk of camphor in it is set upon another fireproof plate and is placed in the center of the circle.

The bell is rung three times and all focus. The camphor is lit. All meditate on the offering to the sacred fire. These represent the blockages and restrictions those doing the Puja want removed from their life through the power of Ganesh.

All chant:

OM GAANG SVAHA! [3x]

If the camphor flame dies down, add another small chunk. As all intensely meditate on the blue flame burning up obstacles, all chant the following Sanskrit and then English:

OM GAANG! VAKRATUNDAM MAHA KAYA KOTI
   SURYA—SAMAPRABHA
AVIGHNAM KURU ME DEVA SARVAKAYYESHU
   SARVADA

O Lord Ganesh! You with a big belly who is monstrous size and who has great power—come!
O light of a hundred thousand suns—fill us with your energy!
Always remove all our obstacles so we may do our True Will!!

Then all slowly chant the following as they 'see' their obstacles burn away to nothingness:

OM NAMAH GANESHAYA! [3x]

As the flame burns out, all pound the floor with hands and yell:

SVAHA! [So Be It!]

The magick is done.

### *Offering to & Feeding the Deity*

Silence. The bell is rung. The prepared Arti tray is placed before the deity. The Arti candle and incense are lit, and All bless the offerings with palms out and chant while visualizing brilliant 'orange energy' of love flowing into the offerings:

OM GAANG SVAHA! [11x]

Thus, the food is charged and blessed and offered to Ganesh.

The priest/ess raises the Arti tray and makes five circles clockwise in the air before the deity. During this, intensely visualize the deity partaking of the essence, energy and offerings while chanting:

OM SHRI GANESHAYA NAMAH [5x]

Then the Arti tray is passed clockwise around the circle, and each person holds it with eyes closed and communes directly with Ganesh with great love and a clear visualization of the deity, silently requesting needed boons and favors.

While this happens, all in the circle not communing with the deity softly (Japa) chant:

OM GAANG SVAHA

over and over. Each person is given the time needed to directly commune with the deity; there is no rush. When all have finished, the Arti is returned to the altar by the priest/ess and the bell is rung 3x.

This is a time for a short, silent meditation on the experience.

Pranayama is done as all absorb the blessings of Ganesh. After a time, the bell is softly rung by the priest/ess. Ganesh is now fully present, and is a powerful, energetic, happy presence in the room!

### Communing with the Deity

The Arti tray is passed around again, but this time all eat and drink some of the now blessed food and drink (Prasad) as well as other food that has been on a plate next to the altar. All may relax and laugh and chat, telling of their visions and experiences with Ganesh as they eat and have fun.

Following this is a time for playing drums, banging rhythm sticks, shaking rattles, clapping, singing, laughing, chanting, dancing, telling stories, doing divination and whatever else people want to do! All are intoxicated with the divine power of the deity who is very much present, and all may have fun as they please. More Kusa may be smoked, more food and drink consumed, and so on. This is the time to 'party with the god,' and it should be as wild, free and fun as possible.

This is also a good time to discuss the Puja and possible changes for the next time, agreeing on the next Puja dates, deciding who will be the priest/ess, and so on. As all are equal in a Kula circle, anyone may bring up topics or speak.

Once the merriment and ritual business is done and the energy ebbs, the priest/ess checks in with all to see if it is time to end. Everything is put away, hands are cleaned, and so on. Then all return to meditative pose and the bell is rung 3x.

### Farewell to the Deity

The priest/ess intones the following and all repeat line by line:

Oh Ganesh, Ganapati, great Vinayaka!
You remove obstacles and sorrows and bring clarity and prosperity!
You are the center of the universe and open all doors!
Thank you for your presence, your joy, your power and love.
May your divine grace follow us as we depart
That we may always do our True Will with Love! SVAHA!

All Chant the following as they visualize the deity depart to the celestial realm:

OM SHRI GANESHAYA NAMAH! [11x]

The bell is rung by the priest/ess.

### Ending & Dedications

With hands raised, all chant together the four Purusarthas (universal blessings), while sending blessings from the Puja to all beings:

*Balance, Wealth, Pleasure and Liberation to All Beings!*

Final ringing of the bell 3x:

The Will to Love is the Law to Live! SVECCHACHARYA!
OM SHANTI SHIVA SHAKTI [3x]

All bow to deity and all candles are blown out. Banish as at the beginning. All stand and do:

PHAT! [at each of the 4 directions and the center]

All touch the Earth and offer any leftover energies to the Earth Mother:

BHU DEVI—To You from You All Things! OM!

Puja is done! All help clean up the temple and maybe a group hug. Partying may continue elsewhere.

# Shiva:
# The Kind and Auspicious One

*Lord Shiva*
*(Photo by the Author)*

*"You are speech. You are consciousness. You are bliss. You are Brahma. You are being-consciousness-bliss. You are the non-dual. You are plainly Brahma. You are knowledge. You are intelligence."*
— Ganapati Upanishad, shivashakti.com/kular

## On the Deity

Lord Shiva is named Adi-Deva (oldest or primal one), and Maha Deva (the greatest god). It is said that he has always existed as the cosmos, for he is indeed the whole universe. He existed when there was nothing, and he will remain after the destruction of all. He is the infinite made manifest in all things, so philosophically Shiva is all things and no-thing, beyond conception or contemplation, the vibration that is All. He embodies and leads all to Liberation through

Samadhi, the becoming of pure consciousness beyond all understanding.

Shiva is the founder of all Tantra—the Adi Nath or 'First Lord'. All our wisdom flows with and through this mighty, all-pervasive vibration we refer to as 'Shiva'. Though Shiva is often shown as male, it is not completely correct to call Shiva 'he' in the sense that 'he' is beyond all conceptions of duality or identification. In his highest form, Shiva is worshipped as **All** that exists. As such, Shiva and Shakti are indistinguishable, for they are in complete Union (Yoga)—the cosmos as one.

Shiva is *Omkara,* the personification of OM, the universal vibration that created the cosmos, and within which it vibrates as the central point of light often called 'God.' Shiva is embedded within each of us as Atman, Guardian Spirit, or supreme Guru as well. Yes, these are varied descriptions, but such is our Twilight World.

Everywhere I went in Nepal and India, Shiva was simply called 'God' by Hindus and Tantrics alike. Shiva is everywhere venerated as the great Guru, Teacher, Liberator and transcendent inner and outer experience of spiritual bliss. All of these seeming contradictions are true because the attainment of true liberation (Samadhi) is beyond all form or substance, beyond all division or dichotomy, beyond all words or conceptions; it, like Shiva, simply *is.*

Shiva is mostly known as a 'Hindu god,' though his worship was old long before the migrations to the subcontinent that brought the Vedic practices and Aryan religious traditions that formed Hinduism. His pervasive worship could not be suppressed by the new invaders, so he was subsumed into Sanatana Dharma. In Hinduism, he became one of the Tri-Murti (three primal gods): Brahma (the creator), Vishnu (the preserver), and Shiva (the destroyer). Many different gods seem to have been merged with Shiva. The ancient, bull-horned Pashupati Shiva from Mohenjo-Daro became syncretized with the Lord of Destruction who obliterates the cosmos at the end of every age. Many other god-forms joined with Shiva over the ages to become aspects of this god.

The ancient Tantric Shiva is a more primal, feral deity. This is epitomized by the horned Pashupati images of Harappan prehistoric culture, as well the ancient indigenous Dravidian culture which still exists. This more primal Shiva is—as you might realize—the deepest Tantric Shiva, a survival from such ancient times.

Dadaji Mahendranath, when referring to Tantrics, uses the term 'Avedic'—meaning 'not Vedic'—which means predating the traditions expounded in the Vedas and the invasive traditions brought into India much later. As such, Brahma is not seen by most Tantrics as the creator of the cosmos, Shiva is—that is, Shiva-Shakti-as-One.

To see why we always see Shiva and Shakti as One, we must contemplate Shakti, the primal energy of the universe—the whirling energy-fire which manifests all things, including Samsara. Prakriti centers, coalesces about, and is anchored by the Bindu, the Center-Point of all that is Shiva. Thus, Shiva materialized and stabilized the Universe. Together they are One: OM. This centering of primal energy (Shakti) swirling about the 'non-existent' centerpoint or nexus (Shiva), renews the archetypal creation of every age. This cosmic union is venerated as the mating of Shiva and Shakti, celebrated yearly during one of the largest festivals in the world, Shivaratri. This eternal union of Shiva and Shakti embodies the Universe which is continually manifested, destroyed and renewed. In Tantra this is seen as the dance and union of Shiva and Shakti, which are reflected both spiritually and literally in the fertilization of every seed and the birth of every child. All of birth/life/death/rebirth recapitulates this eternal union between Shakti and Shiva who can never be separate, both being one—OM, that which is beyond all conception. It is said by some that this infinite consciousness manifesting as Shiva and Shakti does so to dance or *play*; and this play is called Lila, the dance of Creation and Destruction, Energy and Matter: *the whole world we live in and experience.*

However, when we honor and work with Shiva, we are focusing on the center point (Bindu) you see in every Yantra. You *become* this Bindu as you sit on your Dragon Seat in the center point of your Zonule. In this way, you become the point of light that is Shiva, god of meditation. The circle-sphere of the Zonule can then be seen as Shakti, the energy swirling about you. Shiva brings calm, centeredness, bliss and the attainment of deep, meditative discovery and personal liberation which he personifies. This is why he is called the supreme teacher (Adi Guru), and the origin of all Union as Adi Yogi, as well as the lord of magick as Adi Siddhi; and it goes on and on.

He has hundreds of names! Ultimately, he is OM, the union with the infinite, beyond words. Shiva contains hundreds of aspects and epithets, and this chapter can only scratch the surface of one of the longest-worshipped deities in the world. Go find the aspects of Shiva that light your fire!

## History

Thanks to recent archeology, we have a glimpse of the prehistoric Shiva, the Lord of the Beasts. Several ceramic Harappan seals are generally accepted as the earliest images of primal Shiva. Mohenjo-Daro and other Harappan archeological digs are notable because they existed around 2500 BCE, and were some of the largest settlements of the ancient Indus Valley Civilization—and some of the world's earliest urban settlements, contemporaneous with the civilizations of ancient Egypt, Mesopotamia and Minoan Crete. These images depict a horned, male deity, often seated upon a platform or throne in the classic meditation Asana, surrounded by wild and domesticated animals, including bulls, tigers, elephants and snakes. His long, curled bull-horns extend from his head, and with a topknot upon his head, forms a trident shape. He often has an erect phallus. Here we see the beginnings of some iconography of the present-day Shiva. The horns of a bull and the bull-image evolved into Shiva's Vahana (vehicle), the bull Nandi. The trident becomes his symbol or weapon, and he sits upon a tiger pelt in full-lotus Asana as he still does in images today. The tiger is the Vahana for his mate, Kali or Durga. The serpent image in these ancient seals is identified as the serpent demigod that is often shown about Shiva's neck. This Naga sidekick whispers secret wisdom into his ear as he meditates; some say it represents Kundalini. The primordial Shiva on these ancient seals is identified as 'Pashupati,' today a name of Shiva that means 'Lord of Beasts.' Dadaji Mahendranath has revealed in his teachings that the oldest name of this ancient, horned Shiva was AN, and so AN is the most ancient primordial Shiva who sits at the center of Nath Tantrika, the lineage informing this work.

Shiva is the Adi Nath, or First Lord of nature, of wild animals, of fertility, free sexuality, ecstasy and 'the natural Pagan way of life,' as Dadaji Mahendranath says. In this way, he is like many other naturalistic, horned gods like Pan and Cernunnos. Some have postulated that the bull horns of An/Shiva morphed over time into the crescent moon, points up, that Shiva wears on his head.

Though Shiva's aspects and symbols vary from town to town and region to region, he is often shown nowadays in human form with a trident, wearing his hair long with a crescent moon in it, naked or with a tiger skin loincloth. He holds a small Damaru drum, a water vessel, and a begging bowl, and wears a Rudraksha bead Mala and a serpent about his neck. Yet, there are so many forms of Shiva it is impossible to describe all of them! Sometimes he is dancing and destroying the universe as Nataraja; sometimes he is a small child; other times he rides Nandi, the bull; or he's sitting with his family (Parvati, Ganesh and Skanda) on top of Mount Kailash like a typical happy family. At other times he is lying between life and death in the cremation ground, with Kali dancing upon him! As Bhairav he is wild and intense with fangs; as Rudra he is red-skinned and has a moustache, a bow and is a great hunter who howls at windstorms! He has two arms, or four, or six, or more! He can be utterly peaceful and in Nirvana; at other times he can be warlike, destroying demons or even the universe! He is a god of nature, a god of the dead and the universe. He has one head, or three, or five… He can be meditating, having wild sex, dead, a point of light, a raging river, a phallus of fire—is there anything that is not an image of Shiva? In India and Nepal, people say "No, **he is all.**" He *is* all, including Shakti, for they, like all things, are One. Yes, it may be confusing, but it is also real. Meditate on all these things, and you will come to grasp the deepest gnosis of Tantra.

## *Myths*

There are countless Shiva myths, and most are easy to find. Here are a few seminal ones I feel are worth knowing:

### *Shiva as a Pillar of Fire*

Long ago, Brahma and Vishnu got into a fight over who was the supreme deity, and of course, each claimed that title. Shiva, being (among other things) an ancient god of fire, told Vishnu and Brahma he'd settle it, and suddenly became a huge Lingam, a column of fire stretching into the sky and down into the earth. His voice challenged them to find the top or bottom to prove who was more powerful.

Brahma and Vishnu set off to find the beginning and end of the mighty column, but were unable to find the ends of the fire Lingam and had to admit defeat. Both then bowed to Shiva as the greatest god of all.

### Shiva Swallows Poison and Saves the World

Long ago the Asuras (demons) and the Devas (gods)—though they weren't so dissimilar—had been fighting. The Asura got the upper hand and the Devas lost a lot of their mojo and wanted it back. Shiva, as usual, was too busy meditating, and ignored them all. The great milky sea was the target of interest of both tribes, and as the arguing continued they agreed to stir up the sea and see what emerged, each side hoping for treasures. The great Naga serpent Vasuki offered to help in this, and so, by using Mount Kailash as the churning rod, he became the churning rope. The Asura pulled the head of the snake, while the gods pulled its tail, thus churning the milky ocean (the Milky Way). However, during this, Vasuki exhaled a poison called Halahala. This terrified both the gods and demons because the poison could destroy all creation. They panicked and called on Shiva for help! Hearing their pleas, he sighed, quit his meditation, and calmly swallowed all the poison, thus saving the world. He didn't die because he was so very cool—he just absorbed and transmuted the poison, leaving his throat stained permanently blue. And so, he was named Nilakantha, the 'one with blue throat.' Then, no doubt he went back to meditating.

### Catching the River Goddess Ganga

The ascetic sage Bhagiratha, through intense yogic practices and devotions, compelled Shiva to grant him the boon of calling the celestial goddess Ganga (the river Ganges) down from the heavens to Earth. Bhagiratha wanted to do this to consecrate the ashes of his ancestors, and to stop a drought. When mighty Ganga fell to earth and threatened to destroy the world, the gods woke up Shiva who was meditating. He rushed to avert the disaster and broke the river's fall by catching it in his massive, matted hair. While the crisis was averted, the drought was not stopped. So, he worked things out with

Ganga and released her and her river from his hair in seven different streams which fell to earth. They were named Bhagirathi, Jahve, Bhilainagar, Mandakini, Rishiganga, Sarasvati and Alaknanda. Thus, super-Shiva saved the earth once again and more rivers were born.

There are many other myths about Shiva—many involving various goddesses—but some common themes are worth noting. Shiva usually doesn't play favorites, helping both Asuras and Devas (or not) depending on their piety or helpfulness. He often 'stays out of politics' as it were, loves all the nature spirits and other Ganas, and cares more about meditating and staying in a state of bliss (Nirvana). He prefers solitude and living in nature, often shown with his odd family atop Mount Kailash, away from everyone. He so loves his meditation, yoga, cannabis intoxication, and ecstasy that once he burned the god of love, Kama, to ashes with his open third eye because Parvati was lonely and pushed Kama to wake Shiva up! This is why there are no physical images of Kama anymore, and why no one bothers Shiva when he is meditating!

## Iconography

Like many popular deities in the ancient world, hundreds of lesser gods likely became absorbed into Shiva. Many of these gods, while worshipped separately in their own temples and rituals, are often identified as 'aspects' of Shiva. For example, there is Rudra, who was a potent storm deity, and was brought to India by the Aryan migration via the holy book called the *Rigveda*. Another is Bhairava (or Bhairav), meaning fearsome, an ancient god associated with protection and fierceness, especially in Nepal. Both of these, and many more brought different powers, symbols and attributes into the archetypal god Shiva, and so became some of his aspects. Often myths are added that explained such merging. In the case of Bhairav, it is said that Shiva 'created' him from himself to fight a fierce battle. This aspect of Shiva is also known as Maha Kala, as mentioned earlier. This flow and morphing of mythic deities and legends has always been common in Pagan cultures, not just in Tantra. Zeus, for example, absorbed hundreds of other gods, and Isis did the same with a multitude of goddesses. It is confusing in monotheism, but not in ever-shifting Pantheism; and it works for me.

## Some Epithets for Shiva

The variety of intersecting and ever-expanding forms of Shiva makes it impossible to describe him in a logical and straight-forward manner as Westerners may prefer. He has many forms and powers, so one way to understand the variety ascribed to this god is to look at some of his many epithets:

- He is the God of Creation.
- He is the God of Destruction.
- He is the Lord of Pleasure and Asceticism.
- He is the mate and lover of Parvati and of Kali.
- He is the hermit god who sits for aeons in solitary meditation.
- He is the Lord who teaches meditation, yoga and magick.
- He is the feral Lord of Beasts.
- He is the God of Trance, Wildness and Ecstasy.
- He is the God of Fire.
- He is the Lord of Sexuality and Power!
- He is the God of Peace and Tranquility.
- He is the Destroyer of Demons and Three Worlds!
- He is the wandering mendicant, Sadhu or Sannyasin who owns nothing.
- He is Omkara, the embodiment of OM, the vibration that is all.
- He is the Lord of Ghouls, Ghosts, Vampires, Demons, Demi-gods and Monsters!
- He is both God and Goddess in one body. This aspect is called Ardhanarishvara, what we might today call 'gender fluid'—half Shiva and half Parvati (Shakti).

Shiva has many aspects, but Tantrics take contradictions in stride, accepting the reality that apparently incongruous aspects of a deity may be honored at the same time. This points again to a flexible mindset that embraces many facets. Thus, we refer to this reality as the Twilight World, much like a dream, which is what reality is to a Tantric! The only constant is change; nothing stays the same, and we create and weave our own lives within the flow of Samsara. Shiva points to the eternal truth in the Tantric term *Svecchacharya*: you must do your True Will and find your own happiness, balance and liberation. The only 'savior' in Tantra is OM, *the unity of Shiva and Shakti that, in fact, **is you**.* To the best of your abilities, you grow, evolve or expand as *you* will, guided by love, will and your Guardian Spirit. Shiva reminds us to do our spiritual work and evolve *here,* in this world, so we don't waste or disrespect this incarnation. This is why we are here.

There are hundreds of aspects of Shiva. Read some of the texts in the **Bibliography** and do some research as your True Will guides you. Meditate on Shiva, chant his Mantras, do his Puja in your Zonule, and see how he reveals himself to you; then work with the forms he offers. Here are some common, archetypal forms of this god.

### *Shiva (The Blessed One): Mate, Creator and Destroyer*

Shiva is an ascetic god who cares more about meditation and liberation than most, but despite this, he is still a god and can be entranced by goddesses. There are many stories about his 'beautiful sacred marriage' (Kalyanasundar) to the Goddess Maha Shakti in all of her many forms. Shiva's female consort has many manifestations, too. Sati, Parvati, Uma, Gauri, Kali and many more—all aspects of Maha Shakti, the supreme power. Her influences sometimes tamed this wild, roaming god, and softened some of his intense impulses. At other times the goddess took a form, like Kali, who joined him in the wildest practices imaginable!

It is with Parvati that Shiva finds a kind of unusual domestic bliss on top of Mount Kailash where the divine couple lived in happiness (for the most part) with their kids, Ganesha and the warrior god. Many of the Tantras are written in the form of Shiva and Parvati (or a similar form of her) having conversations, as their feral kids played about them. Because she married such a blissed-out god, Parvati spends a lot of time trying to get his attention. As such the 'family' is often shown in images as exemplifying the sacredness of family—though they are more Bohemian than most couples, for sure.

### *Shiva as OM (Omkara)*

While Indus Valley language symbols have not been completely deciphered, there is one glyph—thousands of years old—that scholars say is the earliest representation of the symbol for OM. Like many of the other prehistoric symbols and images referenced, OM (or AUM) was incorporated into the later-introduced Sanskrit.

As the god Omkara (the form of Om), Shiva is the Godhead, source of All, the universe. He is the first and most important vibration. This is why most all of Shiva's Mantras begin with OM, and why his sacred syllable is his Bija Mantra.

### *Lord of the Linga*

Shivalinga, the god as Phallus, are among the earliest images of Shiva, found along with simple depictions of the Yoni. Conjoined, the Yoni-Lingam is likely the earliest representation of the 'Hieros Gamos' (sacred marriage) of the god and goddess in the world. Even today, Yoni-Lingams are seen *everywhere* in India and Nepal, from small street shrines to huge ancient temples. Many who worship Shiva, especially Tantrics, ritually honor a Shiva Lingam or Yoni in their Pujas. The overtly sexual nature of the image is just a shadow of the deep symbolism in this sublime image. Across India, the most holy primordial Linga (Jyotirlinga) are said to have 'emerged from the earth at the time of creation,' and are worshipped in twelve temples across India. These Jyotirlinga also represent 'the first mound of creation' arising from the chaos at the dawn of time, and can be seen as an image of the holy mountain, Kailash, which rises at the center of all things. What is more spiritual than honoring the origin and the manifestation of all life, of all creation? Sexuality and sex magick are completely acceptable and natural in Tantra, for Tantra is based on nature. Sadly, the puritanizing of India has caused a lot of sexual suppression—the results are evident today—with some Hindus arguing that the Lingam is not a phallus at all but is an egg! In Tantra, all aspects of orgasmic joy are honored as magickal, sacred techniques, and powerful tools for gaining liberation.

### *Prehistoric Horned Shiva*

The oldest Harappan images of Pashupati Shiva (AN) epitomize the most primal and natural 'horned god' of nature and animals. Wearing bull horns and surrounded by other animals, he is even today honored as the Lord and protector of animals, and a god of nature and fauna of all kinds. I was lucky enough to see original clay seals of this god in a New Delhi museum, and was told that the earliest clay images of Shiva show him to be the Lord of the Beasts, and the oldest of gods—in fact, Maha Deva, the 'Great God!'

### Ishvara & Adi-Guru

Manifesting as the cosmos, Shiva is *Ishvara,* both as the universe and as the divine spark or Guardian Spirit within each person. As *Adi-Guru,* the supreme first Guru, he is the greatest spiritual teacher who brings us gnosis in meditation. *Guru* is often translated as 'light emerging from dark,' but it actually means *'removing darkness from the ever-present light.'* Thus, the light is eternal, and darkness or ignorance is fleeting, like a cloud. In the *Guru Gita* it is said that the ultimate Guru is *your inner Guardian Spirit or Atman,* of which a human spiritual teacher is just a reflection. Ultimately, the inner Guru or Atman or Guardian Spirit *is identical with Shiva.* This is a deep mystery to contemplate.

### Yogaraja (King of Yoga) & Adi Siddhar (Great Magician)

Shiva is also called *Yogaraja* (King of Yoga), or sometimes *Adi Yogi* (First Yogi). He embodies the origin of all Yoga and all forms of spiritual, mental and physical practices of an esoteric nature. As *Adi Siddhar* (First Magick Maker), he is the Lord of Magick and all occult practices. This suggests that magical ritual techniques and practices were already well-developed and being taught during prehistoric times, before the Vedic incursions. Many of these things were later absorbed into Hinduism—though most Hindus refer to all such magick as 'Tantric'!

### Mahesha (Great Lord), Mahadeva (Greatest God), Adi Nath (First Lord)

Like the later-introduced, creator-god Brahma, the ultimate aspect of Shiva is beyond our knowledge—it is God. As such, he is the transcendental reality, the highest spiritual power of all. He is The Cosmic Lord who is all aspects of creation, preservation and destruction. The Great Lord Shiva (the Adi Nath) was the founder of the Tantric lineage I belong to. While likely a myth, it indicates that Shiva, as the Adi Guru, founded this Tantric lineage (Sampradaya). This is a way of saying that the lineage is exceedingly ancient.

## Shambhu (Kind One), Shan Shankar (Beneficent One), Bhola Nath (Easy to Please)

These all slightly different forms of Shiva as a young, blissed-out Ascetic, Solitary Wanderer, and Holy Man, filled with ecstasy and emanating positive vibes and blessings—all very popular forms of Shiva to invoke! They all reveal Shiva as a handsome, naked or almost naked holy man who often has bluish white skin covered in ashes from the cremation ground. He is usually shown sitting in blissed-out, deep meditation with his eyes half closed, often intoxicated with cannabis, chilling out on his tiger skin with a trident and a few other items. He is in a state of trance and ecstasy, and is smiling like a young, chill, kind, smiling, long-haired hippie! He owns nothing, but collects natural or abandoned things like his Mala, a begging bowl, a Trishul, and a few other items. He spends his days stoned, meditating and blessing people. This classic image of chill Shiva is seen everywhere—the young, kindly lord of bliss and blessings, living wild and free, often in the wilderness. He exemplifies meditative peace, kindness and liberation. As such, he exists in a constant state of Samadhi, and doesn't care for anything besides withdrawing in peace from Samsara, and granting blessings to all who spend time honoring him—whether they are humans, gods or demons! As Bhola Nath, (easy to please), even the briefest prayer or chant will be honored with his mellow blessings. Tantric Pujas often include cannabis offerings because it is his sacrament, and thus should be offered to him. Two common chants used for ritual cannabis smoking are *Bom Shankar* (Yea Shankar, god of bliss!), and *Esha Vijaya Shivaya Namah* (Victory to Shiva!)

## Ardhanarishvara 'Lord Who is Half Woman': Androgynous Shiva

Ardhanarishvara is different from the hundreds of other forms of Shiva. His body is half God and half Goddess, united as One. Thus, he is utterly free from divisions in the world and is the world itself, the divine god-goddess united in the form of Ardhanarishvara. The myth behind this form is that Shiva and Parvati were so intensely united in love for each other that they merged so they would always be one. As a divine being, 'They' represent the cosmic energies of the universe that are always interweaving, and yet always unified—like Energy and Matter. Different Tantric sects assign supremacy to Shiva or Shakti—my lineages tend to side with Shakti—but in the end we all acknowledge that Ardhanarishvara reveals the reality that Shiva and Shakti are always Woven as One.

### *Nataraja, the Cosmic Dancer*

There are other more intense and dangerous aspects of Shiva—like Bhairav and Rudra—but one of the most powerful is Nataraja, the 'King of the Dance,' whose dance creates the universe, but also destroys it at the end of each age. Nataraja is always shown dancing, balancing on one foot; his many arms are shown in various dance positions, all surrounded by a circle of obliterating fire! How is that for a very different aspect of Shiva? He is shown dancing in a classic posture, engulfed in apocalyptic flames, one foot raised and the other stomping upon a fallen demon! As such he is a dynamic, powerful and terrifying god-form, but he wears a serene expression because creation and destruction are both illusions. Some historians say that this harkens back to a primal form of Shiva as the God of Fire. As the wild, dancing, fiery God, he is also shown dancing on burning corpses in the cremation grounds. Sometimes he dances with Kali, and sometimes with monsters, ghosts, goblins and all kinds of disreputable Ganas! This form of Nataraja is a spooky god, the outsider, the dangerously wild one, the punk rocker! Tantra devotees of the wild, ecstatic Shiva often dance in ecstasy as their egos are crushed and burned like the demon being stomped under Nataraja's feet, releasing all illusion through spiritual, fiery transformation and release. It is therefore no wonder that a statue of Shiva Nataraja was erected before the massive, atom-smashing *CERN* Nuclear Collider in Switzerland. The plaque reads:

> *"Belief is that Lord Shiva danced the Universe into existence, motivates it, and will eventually extinguish it. Carl Sagan drew the metaphor between the cosmic dance of the Nataraja and the modern study of the 'cosmic dance' of subatomic particles."*
>
> — *cds.cern.ch/record/745737?ln=en*

## Bhairava, the Wrathful One

I have encountered several intense forms of Shiva in my travels. One of the most popular, but off-putting forms of Shiva deserves mention: Bhairava. Bhairav and Rudra were independent gods before being seen as aspects of Shiva. When I arrived in Kathmandu, Nepal, I wandered in Durbar Square right into a three-story carved and painted image of Bhairava Shiva. This huge, black, terrifying, primal god is depicted dancing with a tiger-skin loincloth, and carrying a Dandi (a staff topped with a skull). He is wearing a necklace of skulls, and has a massive, fang-filled, horrific grin! I was instantly in love. One of the goals of Tantra is to utterly let go of attachments, and Bhairava brings it! The name Bhairava comes from the word Bhiru, meaning fearful or terrifying. Indeed! Meat is offered at his temple.

Why work with and worship such a scary god? *To fight fire with fire.* Bhairav destroys fear *and is beyond fear,* and so can remove all your fears and set you free! Bhairav helps you overcome all the horrors and attachments of Maya, is a mighty guardian, and is a great bad-ass god to have on your side. Looking at him, you see a truly free deity, one who 'doesn't give a fuck,' who dances almost naked, laughing, covered in bones and ashes, and is wholly liberated, fearless and powerful!

Bhairav Shiva protects his devotees from all horrors. You can find many Bhairava meditations and charms to remove insomnia, stress, paranoia, and especially, fear of death. Bhairav is said to appear beautiful to those who find release from the bondage of fear. His animal vehicle is a black dog! Dogs are loyal, dutiful, loving and playful, and attack anyone or anything that messes with you, right? As a dog owner, I attest that any god with a dog must be awesome.

## Rudra, the Howling One

Rudra was a Vedic deity, but soon after being introduced into what is now India, was merged with Shiva. Rudra is a wild-man, a crazed aspect of Shiva for sure. His name means 'howler' or 'one who roars,' but may have originally come from an Indo-European root word meaning 'wild,' implying a wild or untamed nature. He is also invoked with terms meaning archer and hunter. He is a tempestuous god, and is described as being 'like a big wild storm,' which is likely one origin of his 'howling' epithet—though he is associated with wolves, too! He is often shown with red skin, holding arrows in one hand, and in the other a deer; and he always has a stylish moustache! Like other forms of Shiva, he wears a tiger skin and a Mala made of his namesake *Rudra*ksha (eye of Rudra) beads, always worn by Shaivites. Like Bhairav, he can protect his devotees, destroy evil, and cure and chase away diseases with his mighty powers and kick-ass attitude. Once again, we see that in Tantra 'negative' or 'scary' aspects of the god can be very useful for a devotee. Rudra is a popular kid's superhero in India by the way. The more you know…

There are many, many more aspects of Shiva, of course, but now that you know many of the most popular ones, go forth and find other aspects of this amazing, ancient god.

## SYMBOLS

Shiva is so all-encompassing, and so many symbols are ascribed to him, that I will focus on the most common ones.

### *The Third Eye Open*

This image has become hugely popular in occult and New Age symbolism, and it very likely came from him. Yet, his third eye (Ajna Chakra) is usually depicted as being a *sideways* open eye on his forehead, sometimes 'breaking through' three vertical lines, often marked in ashes. Those three lines represent the many triplicities you have already read about. When the third eye of Shiva opens, the world is destroyed! To a Shaivite, this means the destruction of separateness, the end of Samsara, and thus an awakening from illusion. The third eye is opened through ecstasy and esoteric exercises of focus, trance and meditation, and is literally 'mind blowing' as many psychedelic pioneers have discovered. When the eyes are shut and the mind is open and expanded, then the third eye opens, and the Great Work of magick and liberation can begin; so say the Gurus.

### *Tantric Sexual Positions*

In various forms, Shiva is often depicted in ecstatic sexual union with several goddesses, sometimes chanting, dancing, laughing, dead or lying prone on a pyre with his mate on top of him! All this shows that Shiva is an ancient, primal god of ecstasy. Wild worship, while deeply centered in meditation and bliss-states of Samadhi, is like many other shamanic practices aimed at opening the mind. This is why Tantrics love and imitate him! *The goal is not to worship Shiva, but to **become** Shiva.*

### *The Bull, His Sacred Animal Symbol*

Shiva's vehicle (Vahana) is Nandi, the White Bull. Nandi is likely connected with the image of ancient, bull-horned Pashupati or An. The worship of Shiva with Nandi can likely be traced back to the Harappan Civilization as evidenced by the distinctive 'humped' bulls appearing on many different clay seals. In Tantra, the bull represents fertility, strength, peacefulness and prosperity, and bovine herds still denote wealth in India where they are a source of everything from dairy for sustenance to fuel for fires. They wander everywhere with honor! In Sanskrit, Nandi means *happiness, joy and satisfaction,* indicating an appropriate helper and animal aspect for Shiva to ride upon. Nandi is the guardian deity of Mt. Kailash, the mountain home of Lord Shiva and family. This is why most Shiva temples display stone images of Nandi, lying down in a worshipful manner, facing Shiva or the Shiva Lingam. Nandi is a star with his own holy books, texts, Pujas and more. Sometimes the divine Nandi is shown with a human body, like a Tantric minotaur! He is a helper and sidekick for Shiva. In India you can't help but hang out with the lovely, mellow cows and bulls that wander about without a care, even into stores! In fact, I gave up beef because of my experiences with the bulls of Shiva!

### *The Shivalingam or Yoni-Lingam*

Much has already been said about this, but it should be noted that when the masculine Shiva is accentuated—especially in Shaivite temples—it is called a Shivalingam, even though it includes both male and female sexual images. In other temples and shrines, the term Yoni-Lingam, accentuating the feminine vulva first, is often common. In essence, they are the same image.

### The Trishul (Trident)

The trident (Trishul) is one of his most common symbols and one of the oldest; it is found on ancient artifacts from Mohenjo-Daro. If you see a trident in India or Nepal, the place is sacred to and protected by Shiva. Shiva's Trishul has been used to destroy more than a few demons as well as the 'three big cities' of all the Asuras! The three prongs of Shiva's Trishul have many symbolic meanings. They represent various trinities, some already mentioned: creation, maintenance and destruction; past, present and future; body, mind and Atman (soul); Dharma, bliss and emanation; compassion, joy and love; clarity, knowledge and wisdom; heaven, mind and earth; practice, understanding and wisdom; death, ascension and rebirth; creation, order and destruction; and so on. In Tantra, the three tines of the Trishul represent the triplicities already mentioned, including the three Gunas, the three Shaktis (Knowledge, Will and Action) and the three great forces (Fire, Sun and Moon). The Trishul is a tool of magick, a powerful emblem, and a mark of power and respect. As a weapon of Shiva, the Trishul is said to bring about the destruction of the *illusion of past, present and future*—Shiva being the Lord of Time. It can also represent the three Nadis—the body's energy channels (Ida, Pingala and Sushumna)—that rise up the body, meeting at the brow or third eye. Sushumna, the central conduit, continues upward to the Crown, so the central tine of the trident is longer than the other two. The Trishul often has a serpent wrapped about it, representing Kundalini.

It is said that placing a blessed Trishul in a place of ill omen will instantly remove all negativity and bless it, because wherever the Trishul is set, there is Shiva!

### Nagaraja: The Serpent King, Vasuki

A serpent is often shown about Shiva's neck. This serpent is actually a demi-god named Nagaraja—king (Raja) of the Nagas, a race of serpentine demigods. Also called Vasuki, this serpent is Shiva's guide, helper and sidekick. Vasuki is a powerful demigod, and his importance in 'churning the great milky ocean' has already been mentioned; remember, it was Shiva who drank his poison. I'm guessing this was a kind of bonding moment for them because since then, they have always been together. Near-death experiences do that.

Shiva honors this great Naga king by wearing him about his neck forever. It is said that Nagaraja whispers wisdom and secrets into Shiva's ear, thus aiding him in his magick and meditations. Naga are a powerful and sacred race of demigods who know many secrets. As such they are great allies and Shiva, as well as Ganesh, have always been their friend and protector, unlike some other gods. For more on Vasuki and the Naga, I refer you to my book *Naga Magick: The Wisdom of the Serpent Lords* (Falcon Press).

### *Three Lines of Shiva*

As has been mentioned, three parallel lines, drawn horizontally, often in ash, are depicted on devotees and on items sacred to Shiva. You can spot a Shaivite by the three lines on their forehead. The lines are often painted or drawn in colors, usually red, as well as ashes. They can be seen on other sacred items—Shivalingam, drums, charms, and so on—and before shrines or over doorways. Sometimes the central line has a dot or an actual vertical eye in the center, the third eye of Shiva. This three-line image is called the Tripundra. Most powerfully, ashes from a cremation ground are used for this, and are often rubbed all over the body of a Tantric to show dedication to Shiva. Some say these lines symbolize that Shiva can create, maintain and destroy the universe. Finally, there is the explanation that the Tripundra represents *the waking state, the dreaming state, and the 'deep sleep' state,* while Shiva, who has transcended all such states, exists in *true reality* (Turiya), beyond all thought or sleeping or waking.

### *Rudraksha Beads (Malas, Pendants and Ornaments)*

Rudraksha beads—seeds from trees of the same name—hold a lot of significance for followers of Shiva, and being holy to the god, are often worn for protection and power. They are sacred to Rudra, as noted, and thus are a primary emblem of Shiva. Most every Tantric and Shaivite has at least one Rudraksha Mala, and many wear special empowered Rudraksha beads on threads about their neck. It is said that when one wears Rudraksha with a lot of devotion and sincerity, all sins are washed away, you are protected from evil, and are purified and blessed by Shiva! Not bad for seeds you can pick up off the ground; the trees are common in India. The five-Mukhi (section) Rudraksha beads are holy and are used for Malas, and some very rare ones—like the 2-sided beads—are considered powerful talismans. The fact that they are seeds says much about the mysteries of Shiva.

### *The Damaru (2-Sided Drum)*

The Damaru is a distinctive, small, two-sided drum that looks like an hourglass; i.e., it consists of two small concave drums joined together, back-to-back. There are small thongs or threads with knots or beads attached that hang over each of the two drum heads so when it is twisted side to side, the drum heads are struck, Bom Bom Bom... Damaru drums seem very much like the small, shamanic drums used for trance work, and some Tantrics enter trances with it. This is done by holding it in one hand, and rotating it quickly back and forth to get a steady 'Bom Bom Bom' as the two knotted cords hit each side, while the other hand counts Mantras on their Mala. Damaru are used by Tantrics, Hindus and Tibetan Tantric Buddhists, as well as Bon Po sorcerers. The drum is used to 'call Shiva' for both Pujas and magical rites. It is an ancient, sacred tool, most always associated with Tantra. It is said to have been created by Shiva to produce powerful spiritual sound-vibrations used by him to create and maintain the whole universe. The two small drum heads, glued back-to-back represent Shiva (the Lingam) and Shakti (the Yoni), respectively. The most potent Damaru I've seen are made from two human skull-tops, one from a man, the other from a woman, joined crown to crown, with human skin as the drum head. Talk about powerful! (Mine is made of wood and I'm fine with that, at least for now.)

### *Crescent Moon Symbol*

Most pictures of Shiva show him with a small crescent moon, often with points up, in his long, matted hair. One theory is that this is what is left of his mighty bull-horns as depicted on the ancient seals.

Another is that Shiva is the Lord of Time (Maha Kala) and is thus himself timeless. The moon represents the constant changing of time, but he wears it as a charm because he controls it and is beyond it. Another hidden piece of lore states that, unlike in Western magick where man is seen as the sun and women as the moon, in Tantra it is reversed. The male Tantric embodies the moon, the female Tantric the sun, and their union generates the holy fire of Kundalini. Why? Because in Tantra, at least in the lineages I hold, the Goddess is supreme. Devi or Maha Shakti contains all power and embodies all of creation, just as all things on Earth are really solar energy. The moon, like Shiva, reflects the solar light of Shakti and softens and focuses it. This is why the lunar colors of silver and white (also representing ashes and sperm) are ascribed to Shiva, and the color red (fire, the sun, and menses blood) are ascribed to the solar Shakti. Shiva centers, focuses and reflects the fiery energy of Shakti, the cosmos, into the Bindu, the center point of every Yantra.

### *The Tiger Skin*

Many popular images of Lord Shiva show him sitting on a tiger skin, or wearing a tiger-skin loincloth, or walking with the skin wrapped around him. According to folklore, the tiger skin signifies Shiva as the controller of all the powers in the world. There is a myth that Shiva killed a tiger with his bare hands when it was sent to kill him by some snarky Rishis (holy men) who were jealous of him, thus proving his power. That is a bit much for me. A deeper explanation is found if we ask: whose Vahana (vehicle) is a tiger? There are two main goddesses who ride upon a tiger—Kali and Durga—and both are considered in various texts as mates of Shiva. Both are fierce, potent and intense. Durga represents the power of all the gods united to defeat an evil, and Kali is very much Shiva's Tantric partner who is often shown dancing upon 'dead' Shiva or mating with him while he is lying on a tiger skin *or a burning corpse*. Often the two are shown wildly dancing with demons and crazy spirits, both *wearing tiger skins*. Keep in mind that Kali is called Maha Kali and Shiva is called Maha Kala. *Both names mean the same thing*: Kala and Kali mean both *Time* and *Black*. If nothing else, the tiger has a history in India of representing power, fierceness and intensity. It is an ancient symbol of the deepest, primal jungle and the mysteries hidden therein.

## Offerings

**Colors:** In general, white (the color of the Milky Way, sperm and light) is Shiva's color. Lord Shiva is described as 'White as camphor,' or 'a snow-clad mountain.' There are many forms of Shiva though, so other colors may be used depending on the aspect being venerated. Rudra or fiery Shiva is red; Maha Kala and Bhairav are black; and so on. The term 'Shivam' means darkness, by the way. This whole universe originated from Shivam or dark energy that was present before the 'big bang' of OM. Could this be Dark Matter?

**Incense:**
  Sandalwood
  Aloe
  Camphor
  Other special 'Shiva' incense blends

**Flowers:** Traditional flowers to offer Shiva are: all white flowers, jasmine, red hibiscus, marigold, lotus, purple orchid, and white datura. The important thing is that they are fresh and, if possible, picked by you. Any flower offered to Shiva devoutly is fine; as a Tantric I simply ask Shiva what he'd like or I find appropriate flowers from the garden.

## Mantras

  Om Namah Shivaya
  Shiva Hum
  Esha Balih Shivaya Namah
  Esha Vijaya Shivaya Namah
  Bom Shiva

## Yantras

Shiva is the Bindu (CenterPoint) of every Yantra, the Yantra image being the Goddess. This is why there isn't a general Yantra for Shiva, because he is the CenterPoint of all of them. The Shivalingam is, in many ways, his Yantra; however, there *are* Yantras for specific aspects of Shiva:

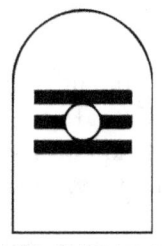  

*Shiva Lingam Murti*    *Yantra of Parama Shiva*    *Shiva as 'All' (Trika Shaivism Yantra)*

## Festivals

Shiva has hundreds of local festivals everywhere he is honored, so ubiquitous is his worship. Here are two large ones:

**Shiva Ratri:** The most popular—and worldwide—festival of Shiva is Shiva Ratri, the Divine Marriage of Shiva and Parvati (Shakti). I was fortunate to be in Varanasi (Kashi) in India on that date, and on top of the millions of people already there, over 10 million pilgrims came. It was wild! Every Hindu and Tantric celebrates this festival all over the world.

**Deepavali, the Festival of Light:** Karthik Poornima or Diwali, the Festival of Light, celebrates the day in which Lord Shiva destroyed the Asuras (demons) and their three cities, and then danced the great Tandava dance as Nataraja during this destruction. On this day, people celebrate Shiva's victory over evil and burn many lamps. Karthik Poornima usually falls near the end of November.

## Shiva Nath Tantra Puja

Place the following on the Zonule altar:

A candle, incense in a burner, a cup of appropriate liquid, a Yoni-Lingam, appropriate flowers, a pipeful of cannabis (if legal), the Arti bowl or tray full of offerings (food, a small cup of liquid, a small candle, and a stick of incense), and an image of the deity. (See the **Offerings** section above.) The appropriate Yantra should be laid flat before the image of the deity with the Arti tray placed on the Yantra. If desired, two candles of the appropriate color can be placed on either side of the deity image, and another side plate of food and drink may be placed before or near the altar.

You will also need a plate to put under the Yoni-Lingam, a hand-drawn OM symbol or a simple Shiva Yantra, some Kumkum (red sandalwood) powder or ashes, and a little solid camphor in a small ceramic plate.

### *Honoring Ganesh*

The priest/ess rings the bell 3x. All bow to Ganesh and chant:

OM GAANG GANAPATAYE NAMAH [3x]

The altar candle is lit.

### *Banishing*

PHAT! [5x]

This is done to the four directions and to the center by all present. Lightning bolts are visualized, banishing all negative energy.

### *Creating the Sacred Sphere*

The priest/ess casts a circle with the trident *or* all hold hands in a circle. All chant:

OM MANI PADME HUM [3x]

while envisioning the circle/sphere of light about all. All pause for a moment and visualize 4 tridents at the four directions glowing with light and protective energy. All chant OM. The Zonule-Temple is set.

### Honoring the Powers

All bow and intone:

*OM Namaste! Honor to the Gods, the Spirits, the Ancestors, the Gurus and to All Wild Things That Play! OM to Shri Gurudev Dadaji Mahendranath and the Crystal Line of Tantric Gurus Whose Amrita and Power Helps Us Manifest True Knowledge, True Will, and True Action Through Our Guardian Spirit with Love. Guru OM! Svecchacharya!*

### "Mea Culpa"

All say:

*May any Errors We Make in this Ritual, any Slights, or any Negativity Generated be as Rain Striking the Ocean, Dispersed, Forgiven and Forgotten. By Our Efforts May All Beings Attain Liberation and Joy! OM!*

### Purification (Devi)

Purify and bless the self with the power of Shakti Devi: Each adept blesses the three Body Centers/Gunas by placing a hand over each area in turn and visualizing light pouring into *Head, Heart and Loins/Base* as they invoke Devi with this Mantra:

HREENG SHREENG KREENG PARAMESHVARI SVAHA
[1x at each body center]

### Centering & Kusa/Sacrament (Deva)

A pipeful of Kusa (cannabis) is held on top of the Yoni-Lingam as all sit in a circle and vibrate OM. Then all chant:

OM NAMAH SHIVAYA! [108x]

as the Kusa is lit and passed around clockwise. All partake as they will or hold up the pipe and make offerings to Shiva if they don't. When done, offerings of pipe ashes are placed on the Yoni-Lingam and each person dabs some on their forehead (third eye).

### Preliminary Invocation of Deity

Incense and one or more candles are lit before the image of Shiva. All bow to the god, the bell is rung loudly 3x and then all say:

OM!
O Lord Shiva, we honor you by all your sacred names! You are beyond all names, attributes and forms being all things!
NAMASTE—Welcome to our temple. MAHA DEVA SHIVA!
OM! [3x]

All visualize the light of Shiva filling the temple.

The priest/ess holds the trident while another Tantric plays a drum (preferably a Damaru). Both lead the others in gently dancing clockwise about the Zonule, building up energy while ecstatically chanting:

ESHA VIJAYA SHIVAYA NAMAH

over and over until the priest/ess feels the energy is rocking and raises the trident. At this, all stop chanting and sit down, energized and probably laughing.

The trident is stood upright by the Shivalingam on the altar or leaned against the front of the altar.

All briefly meditate upon a point of light glowing within their heart like a brilliant star. This is the Atman/Guru/Guardian Spirit. When all have this clear image, they join together in a long OM… Then the priest/ess rings the bell and all invoke Shiva together:

OM NAMAH SHIVAYA!
HARA HARA MAHADEVA
SHIVA-SHAMBU
Hail, Lord of the World
KASHI VISHWANATHA
Lord of the Universe!
OM THE CREATION
OM THE PRESERVATION
OM THE DISSOLUTION!!!
MAHESHWARA: GURUS
Guru is the Infinite!!!
TAT TVAM ASI!!!
"I am That" Star!!!
OM NAMAH SHIVAYA!
SHAKSHAT PARAMBRAHMAN
TASMAI SHRI GURUVE NAMAH!

Honor to the Guru within and without. All is Guru, all is light!
Shiva is Point, Axis, Mountain Peak, Star.
The Center of All Creation and Cosmos which is SHAKTI MA!
OM NAMAH SHIVAYA!

Offerings are made to the Shivalingam by the priest/ess. If there is a group, offerings can be placed on the Shivalingam by different people in turn. Incense is offered and waved. This is the expansive Mind of Shiva. Then all say:

ESHA BALIH SHIVAYA NAMAH! [3x]

A dab of Ghee (purified butter) is offered. This is the intense Will and Energy of Shiva.

ESHA BALIH SHIVAYA NAMAH! [3x]

A dab of honey & yoghurt is offered. This is the Grace, Love and Compassion of Shiva.

ESHA BALIH SHIVAYA NAMAH! [3x]

The red flower is offered (placed on the top). This is the manifesting of the Blessing of Shiva.

ESHA BALIH SHIVAYA NAMAH! [3x]

All hold out their hands and chant OM as Spirit is offered. Each sees Shiva as the star within.

ESHA BALIH SHIVAYA NAMAH! [3x]

All sit and meditate in silence while doing Pranayama, focusing on the star-self glowing and growing within as the center of all things, expanding from the heart and filling the whole body. In this way each person focuses on *becoming Shiva* by assuming the posture and aspect of Shiva. As all meditate in this way, they should raise their right hands, open and palm facing outward, and hold their left hand open, pointing down, palm facing outward. These are the Mudras of banishing fear and granting boons. Each should visualize themselves intensely as Shiva.

After all is calm and centered, the priest/ess rings the bell, lights the small lump of camphor and the visualization begins.

### *Visualization Meditation*

The priest/ess reads and all silently meditate on the burning camphor, and visualize the flame as Shiva, eyes half closed:

SHIVA HUM!
There is nothingness, all is void.
Then there is the swirl of fire-energy-power. It is Prakriti, the whirlwind of Shakti who is All.
A center of glowing light appears.
A Bindu-spark about which the swirling energy circles, collects, orders itself.
This is the One-pointed fire, The One God: Shiva.
So manifests the One world, and the One people.
But soon ignorance transforms the truth of One into the illusion of many.
Thus, we give greetings and worship to this Naked Fire!
As this holy fire burns, it destroys all our delusion and bondage.
See now, only the shining ash of Liberation and freedom is left!
So, we give praise and worship to this Naked Fire!
Now, let the fire destroy the drag of the senses which pulls our consciousness here and there in bondage.
So, we give praise and worship to this Naked Fire!
In the Naked Fire we see our True Selves, our minds regenerated and renewed.
We open to attain the true vision of Reality.
Thus, we give praise and worship to this Naked Fire!
As the burning of Shiva OM releases the fire from wood
May mankind be released from bondage and illusion.
So, we give praise and worship to this Naked Fire!
Watch now as this sacred fire burns away all Karmas and all restrictions.
See the fire of Shiva freeing us to attain equipoise and freedom!
So, we give praise and worship to this Naked Fire!
The center flame in the fire is Shiva: the symbol of Wisdom.
The Naked Fire fills us and frees us so our inner consciousness glows!
So, we give Greetings and Worship to this Naked Fire!
Feel now the realization of our True Self! It is immortality!

See now the supreme attainment, it is spontaneous!
We give praise and worship to this Naked Fire!
The cosmic fire burns without thought or intention;
So, we attain that free state of Bliss, Samadhi.
Thus, we give praise and worship to this Naked Fire!
See now the round firepit before you, the symbol of Shakti ablaze.
See the flame rising up as one large fire!
This is the Lingam of Lord Shiva!
Praise and worship to this Naked Fire!
We are reflections of the infinite cosmos: As above, so below.
All that burns becomes ash and all the worlds of the universe turn to dust.
This we give praise and worship to the eternal Naked Fire!
This Naked Fire exists in all wood before it burns.
As our Star-Selves already exists in our body before birth!
So, we give praise and worship to this Naked Fire!
We exist in the fires of painful burning Samsara, immersed in sorrow.
So, we call upon Shiva, the grace of the absolute, to descend on us and reveal to us the way of liberation
Thus, we escape from the illusions of Samsara!
Thus, we give praise and worship to this Naked Fire!
As fire takes the form of everything it consumes, our immortal Spirits take the form of the bodies we wear!
Thus, we give praise and worship to this Naked Fire!
In the firepit, flame passes from log to log
Just as your Star-Self passes from one body to another.
Thus, we give praise and worship to this Naked Fire!
This knowledge awakens us to Immortality;
For we are the true Naked Fire for all Eternity!
So, we give praise and worship to *this* Naked Fire!
In the fire of unhappiness Wisdom grows
And from this Eternal Fire of Wisdom, release from attachment is born.
From letting go of all things, your liberation is born!
This is the blessing of Shiva, the Naked Fire
All you do is everything that needs to be done!

As eternal Naked Fire you will shine forever!
With every breath we give praise and worship to the Naked Fire!
OM! OM! OM!

All meditate in silence on the truth of Shiva and the Naked Fire within and without, and do Pranayama for a short time until the camphor flame dies. Then the priest/ess signals the end of the meditation by gently ringing the bell once. All chant OM.

### *Empowerment of the Deity*

All chant together with Malas, and invite and empower Shiva who is now manifesting as waves of power from the Shivalingam and his Murti upon the altar.

The priest/ess uses the Kumkum powder (or ashes) to mark three lines upon the Shivalingam, and places a bit on the top. All chant:

OM NAMAH SHIVAYA [108x]

The priest/ess places a red flower on the top of the Lingam. Then all Invoke the Primal Shiva known as AN:

Om Namah An-ya!
Om Namah An-ya!
Om Namah An-ya!
Horned Lord of the Beginning
Wild Bull—Earth Shaker
Beast of Lightning and Thunder
Lord of Wildness
God of All Plenty
Link with All Life
Mate of Earth Mother and Shakti Fire
One with the Animal Spirits
Form of the Trident
Open Eye Dissolving the Universe
Gate of Ecstasy and Laughter
Wild One Dancing Free
Lord of Meditation and Stillness
He who Howls like the Storm wind
Secret Force of Evolution

Lord of Utter Liberation
Power of Sex and Birth and Death
Fountain of Prosperity
God of Wanderers and Blissed-out Tantrics
Path Keeper
Holy Madman
Terrifying Fiery God
All Devouring One
Pure Child of Stellar Light
Serpent emerging from the Womb of Earth
Lord of Life with Waterfall Hair
Beast God
Lingam of Singing Flame
Tree of Life
Chintamani Wish-Giving Stone
Flashing Body of the Full Moon
Lord of All Creatures
Adi Yogi of the Mysteries
Greatest Guru
Flower of the Heart of Nature
Remover of all that hinders Liberation
Greatest OM, Teacher and Star
Earth-born primal Linga
Lord of the Open Mind
Green-Blue of Twilight Sky
Blue-throated devourer of all poison
One Who Plays
Bom Shankar, Bom Shiva, Bom Bhairav, Bom Rudra, Bom AN!
OM NAMAH AN-YA!

### *Magick Work (Optional)*

This is a simple 'spell' or work of magick that can be used to take upon yourself the power and 'magickal gifts' of one specific aspect of Shiva. Here are a few examples of potent aspects of Shiva:

SARVACHARYA (All-Begetter)—This form would be useful for aiding fertility or birth.

PRIYABHAKTA (Loved by All)—This could be used for attracting love.

SHANKARA (Joyful One)—This form would be useful to bring happiness!

There are many aspects of Shiva, 108 at least! Do a bit of digging, meditate on that form, create a simple invocation and off you go.

This rite uses the DHYANADHARA DEVA (the Focus of Meditating) aspect of Shiva—used here to increase skill with meditation, for Shiva is the Lord of Meditating.

*Shiva Magick Rite*

A simple drawing of a Shiva Yantra, or just the symbol for OM is placed upon a plate on the floor before the altar for a solo working, or on the altar for a group working. The Shivalingam is placed upon the Yantra, and a small piece of camphor is placed on the Shivalingam.

All sit and meditate quietly on the aspect of Shiva being assumed, and do Pranayama for 10 minutes or more. Then the priest/ess rings the bell, and all chant OM.

The camphor is lit by the priest/ess and all say:

OM DHYANADHARA DEVA!
O Focus of Meditating.
Help us to not Think but Just BE
So we may become the ONE thing
Uniting ALL things as No-Thing
As Maha Maya (great Illusion) becomes Silence.
Becoming is beyond ONE
Thus none!
OM SVAHA

The priest/ess rings the bell again, and all meditate on their Lower Body Chakra and visualize a bonfire at the base of the body, growing in intensity and height. All chant:

SHIVA HUM [3x, with eyes closed; intensify the visualization]

After a short time, the priest/ess rings the bell once again.

All meditate on their heart center, and visualize a growing sun shining forth. The flame from the lower center rises and empowers the sun which grows and glows with increased intensity. All chant:

SHIVA HUM [3x, with eyes closed; intensify the visualization]

After a short time, the priest/ess rings the bell once more.

All then meditate on their upper body energy center, and visualize a shining moon-disc on their 3rd eye, growing in intensity. The center of this lunar nimbus is the glowing, opening third eye. All chant:

SHIVA HUM [3x, with eyes closed; intensify the visualization]

As everyone's third eye is opening, all are focusing silently on the goal: *gaining increased proficiency in meditation.*

Then the priest/ess places a small piece of camphor on the top of the Lingam and lights it on fire. All open their eyes, and silently focus on the flame while doing Pranayama, letting the spell dissolve into the flame until it dies out.

After 5 or ten minutes of meditation, the priest/ess rings the bell. All visualize their third eye closing, breathe deeply, and place a finger to the lips in the 'sign of silence.' As the cosmic vision begins to fade and the head-centered moon-energy sinks into the heart-centered sun, the 'heart-centered sun' merges with the lower fire center in your body.

All then visualize and feel the blazing bonfire at the base body-center as it slowly dies into glowing coals, and finally, to ashes.

There is calm and peace. All remain open to any final visions or teachings that come after for a minute or two until the priest/ess rings the bell. Then all chant:

OM SHANTI SHIVA SHAKTI [3x]

All bow to the Shivalingam. Let all the conjured forces unite and be absorbed by it as the priest/ess places a flower upon it. OM, the rite is done. Now is a time to chat and share what each experienced!

### *Offering to & Feeding the Deity*

The bell is rung. The Arti bowl or tray which has been prepared with offerings, candle, incense, and so on is now placed before the Lingam of Shiva. The Arti candle and incense are lit, and All bless the offerings—with palms out—by chanting while visualizing brilliant 'naked fire' of love flowing into it. All chant:

ESHA BALIH SHIVAYA NAMAH [11x]

Thus, the food is charged, blessed and offered to Shiva. The priest/ess then raises the Arti tray and makes five circles in the air before the enthroned Shiva as the Lingam. During this, the deity is intensely visualized partaking of the essence and energy and offerings. All chant:

OM [5x]

The Arti Tray is passed clockwise around the circle. Each person holds it up with eyes closed, and communes with Shiva. Visualizing Shiva intensely, he or she silently requests boons they need as long as they are focused on positive goals or practices such as healing or spiritual blessings for oneself or others.

While this happens, all in the circle not communing with the deity quietly chant:

BOM SHIVA [Yea! Shiva!]

over and over. Each person is given time to directly commune with the deity. There is no rush. When the Arti tray is returned to the altar by the last person, the bell is rung.

This is a time for a short, silent meditation on the experience. Shiva is now with all present, and is a powerful and energetic presence in the room. All take a few minutes to absorb this energy! Then the bell is rung again.

### *Communing with the Deity*

The Arti tray is passed around and all eat and drink some of the now blessed food and drink (Prasad), and other food that has been around the altar. All relax and laugh and chat, telling of their visions and experiences with Shiva as they like.

Shiva is a god of ecstasy, trance, cavorting and wildness! This is a time for all such things, including playing drums, banging rhythm sticks, shaking rattles, clapping, singing, laughing, chanting loudly, dancing, telling stories, doing divination, and whatever else people want to do! It is a great time to try out new Shiva Mantras or chants, or read invocations or poems to Shiva! All are infused with the divine power of the deity and may act as they please. More Kusa may be smoked in his honor with chants of BOM SHANKAR or BOM SHIVA! This is time to 'party with the god' and it should be as wild, free and fun as possible.

This is also a good time to chat about what could be added to or changed with the Puja for next time, setting the next Puja dates, assigning the priest/ess for the next time, and so on. All are equal in the Kula circle!

Once the merriment is done and the party ebbs, the priest/ess checks in with all to see if it is time to end. Things are cleaned, and all return to a meditative pose. The bell is rung.

### *Farewell to the Deity*

The priest/ess intones the following and all repeat line by line this healing chant (Gayatri):

OM! TRYAMBAKAM YAJAMAHE SUGANDHIM PUSHTIVARDHANAM;
URVAARUKAMIVA BANDHANAAN- MRITYOR MUKSHEEYA MAAMRITAAT.

The priest/ess intones the translation (below) and all repeat 3x:

OM.
We worship the Three-Eyed One—Lord Shiva—who smells of flowers,
Who is immensely merciful and who is the Protector of devotees.
May we be liberated from illness and death and become divine, just as the ripe fruit easily falls from the vine.
Shiva! Let me be in the state of liberation and be protected from fear, sickness and death.
May I attain Liberation!
OM.

All chant the following as they visualize the deity departing to the celestial realm:

OM NAMAH SHIVAYA! [11x]

The bell is rung by the priest/ess.

### *Ending & Dedications*

With hands raised, all chant together the four Purusarthas (universal blessings) while sending blessings from the Puja to all beings:

Balance, Wealth, Pleasure and Liberation to All Beings!

The bell is rung 3x:

The Will to Love is the Law to Live!
OM SHANTI SHIVA SHAKTI [3x]

All bow to the deity and all candles are blown out.
All stand and banish as at the beginning:

PHAT! [at each of the 4 directions and the center]

All touch the Earth and offer any leftover energies to the Earth Mother:

BHU DEVI—To You From You All Things! OM!

Puja is done! All help clean up the temple and maybe a group hug. Partying may continue elsewhere.

# Shri Lalita—Tripurasundari: The Red Goddess, The Beautiful One, She Who Plays

*Goddess Lalita TripuraSundari*
*(Image by the Author)*

*"...Tripura is the ultimate, primordial Shakti, the light of manifestation. She, the pile of letters of the alphabet, gave birth to the three worlds."*

— Vamakeshvaratantra

Shri Vidya is the gnosis of the human body
Symbolized by the Shri Yantra
It is both a sacred diagram, the key Yantra, and a map of the
    cosmos
Every corner, every triangle, every level contains a Goddess
All of them are aspects of One Goddess: Maha Devi
The Great Red Goddess
We call her Lalita Tripurasundari or just Shakti

She is Shri: The Sacred Divine
These are the 9 openings in the human body spoken of in Tantras:
The Portals of our body:

The two eyes
The two ears
The two nostrils
The mouth
The Lingam/Yoni
The anus

These are the 9 gates to the Temple of The Goddess
—there is only one real temple: the human body
OM

— Hermeticusnath

## On the Deity

Much is written about the Red Goddess, but little is explained. She is a beautiful, ancient, erotic goddess who goes by many names. She is commonly called *Tripurasundari* or *Lalita* or both together. Tripurasundari means 'Beauty of Three Worlds'; Lalita means 'She Who Plays'. As with other deities, she has other epithets; sometimes she is called *Rajarajeshwari* ('Queen of Queens'), or *Shodashi* ('the Vermilion-Colored One'). It is rare to find her images or shrines because she is a Tantric goddess who is often worshipped in secret; she is not generally part of Hinduism because of her esoteric and erotic nature. Her worship originated in prehistoric times, and some of her Mantras are so ancient that they have no connection with Sanskrit. Her most important sect is known as Shri Vidya (Sacred Knowledge of The Honored One). Shri Vidya is generally secret, and is wholly Tantric.

Lalita Tripurasundari is seen as the embodiment of Maha Shakti or Para Shakti (primal power), and she is always depicted as a beautiful, young woman, often naked, with glowing red skin. He lovely, sexy playfulness epitomizes the powers of sacred sexuality and the play of Nature. If you want to dig deeper, she is also noted as one of the Mahavidyas, the ten 'great wisdom goddesses.'

Importantly, Lalita Tripurasundari is identified as the Goddess Kundalini, which is activated with her Tantric practices. Such Shri

Vidya teachings and practices of Lalita Tripurasundari are generally secret because such work is exotic and erotic, and is nowadays considered sinful in much of India—though such devotion is more accepted in Nepal.

Lalita is also identified as Tripurasundari or 'The Transcendent Beautiful One of the Three Cities'—which really means 'The One who is very beautiful and manifests the three forms of existence.' 'The Three Cities' can be seen as the three states of consciousness, and can also reference the three Gunas and other triplicities. As Great Shakti, she is the very essence of all things representing her 'three jewels,' the aforementioned Fire, Sun and Moon powers. The 'Three Cities of Lalita Tripurasundari' are said to be made of silver, gold and iron, representing the moon, sun and fire. If this sounds like alchemy, you are right! Working with her is esoteric alchemy of the highest order.

All these attributes are found in her sacred texts. As Para Shakti (or Adi Shakti), she is also a combination of the 'three Shaktis'—*Will* (Iccha), *Knowledge* (Jnana), and *Action* (Kriya)—and in Tantric practice manifests as *Thinking, Feeling* and *Body Sensations* which are manifested in the three 'Body Chakras' as powers of your *Mind, Heart* and *Body* respectively.

The worship of Lalita Tripurasundari is often secret—like many occult practices—and involves the ritual magick of sexual gnosis and body energies. Such erotic rituals, be they symbolic or literal, are held in small, secret temples in private 'in-groups' (Kula) of initiated Tantrics. This lovely Red Goddess is symbolized as the Yoni in art, Yantras and sacred items like the Yoni-Lingam. Most importantly, she manifests as her Shri Yantra. Clearly there are many layers to this most esoteric and secret goddess in our Twilight World!

In the Tantric lineages I am part of, she is the *true* manifestation of the whole universe, being identified as Great Shakti, but also as Prakriti who creates all with her storm of energy. OM is the seed vibration of the cosmos, the CenterPoint, while Lalita is the energetic whirling manifestation of all things. This is represented in the expanding Shri Yantra which opens from the centerpoint into a full cosmic flower. Lalita Tripurasundari, creatrix of all, is thus also Samsara, the illusory realm of appearances. Therefore, she is the totality of the human body as well *as all its senses and experiences,* and so is the secret goddess who grants liberation! Clearly, she is many things, but of all the gods and goddesses of Tantra, she is the one who gives the true wisdom or gnosis of the divine temple of your body and its magical aspects.

Tripurasundari is depicted as a gorgeous, seductive, commanding young woman who emanates rays of light and power. When not naked, she is often shown dressed in lovely, red clothing, her neck and arms covered in rich jewelry. Her hair is long, black and flowing over her shoulders. She often has an open third eye; those three eyes represent the Moon, Sun and Fire. She is birth, life, death and the ever-changing whirlwind of our crazy life. Lalita manifests in our world as Lila, the play of all we experience. Tantrics see her as the capricious swirling unfolding of the cosmos, and through her we may perceive this as cosmic play rather than chaos. If we focus through her gnosis, we can master our senses, our mind, our perceptions, and our emotions; then we *dance with Lalita* as our life unfolds as mostly play, not just suffering.

Lalita Tripurasundari is said to produce different magical emanations (Kalas) on each of the 15 days of the waxing lunar cycle, from new moon to full moon (the 16th Kala). These specific days and the emanations of the moon are said to provide the 'Lalita Nityas'—Nitya meaning eternal powers. These Nitya emanations are the spiritual essence of her ever-changing energy, and they flow through the body of a female Tantric who channels Lalita Tripurasundari in ritual work. Each of these waxing moon emanations manifest a different aspect of this goddess, and bestow a different Siddhi (magickal power), a different divine aspect of Her. This is why she is often shown with a crescent moon in her hair. It is also why Tantric Priestesses are the source of power and magick.

Tripurasundari is most commonly depicted with four arms; her four hands hold her symbolic tools. In one is a bundle of five 'flower arrows' representing the five senses. In another is a 'sugarcane bow' representing mastery of the mind, perception and thoughts. The other two hands hold a noose, representing attraction, and a goad, representing repulsion, of which she is the mistress. Tripurasundari is called 'She Who Plays,' her play being Maya (the illusionary reality surrounding us). Tripurasundari is, in fact, Shakti at play (Lila); she is the world we perceive around us. This is why her blessings offer us the way to gain detachment and liberation from our chaotic world.

Working with Lalita Tripurasundari grants the ability to *weave* our feelings, emotions and sensations into a path of joy and peace. We can more fully embrace, understand and manifest peak experiences and 'aha' moments full of love and pleasure, and accept and move past difficulties and sorrows.

Lalita Tripurasundari is a goddess of pragmatic magick, not faith, and is the embodiment of the unlocking of the mysteries of the human nervous system through meditation, magick and energetic ritual work. Unlike Kali and Lakshmi, who represent aspects of our abundant life and liberated death respectively, Lalita Devi offers inner gnosis of the body, heart and mind *here and now*.

Through her wisdom and our focused and channeled bioelectric energy, we can manifest, control and channel her essence to achieve miracles. Her work is done through meditation, physical and energetic rituals, magick, all the practices you have learned, and of course, erotic play with the aim of attainment. You have already been practicing many of the techniques used in her magick, and this is represented in the items she holds. 'She Who Plays' is the goddess who helps us understand how to live in happiness amidst the whirlwind, and utilize our knowledge, will and action using our senses and sexuality to achieve real happiness and liberation. She also holds up a mirror, showing us that everything we need to liberate ourselves is here now in our body, mind and spirit.

## History

Unlike the other Gods and Goddesses in this book, Tripurasundari is hard to pin down, and no one really knows for sure her origins. One of her key Mantras (see the Mantra section below) is not even Sanskrit, and no one knows its origin. Much of this is because she and her mysteries are ancient, clearly pre-Aryan, and have always been about very secret Magick. The Tantric wisdom of Lalita's mysteries and rituals are somewhat daunting to work with; I have only scratched the surface over the last forty years. Shri Vidya, the secret wisdom teachings of Lalita Devi, is completely apart from Vedic Hinduism and has ancient roots. Shri Vidya and Tantric Kaula work is not just about asking the gods for boons or good luck; it was and is more like primal body-centered rites, initiations and pragmatic sorcery. My work with her has been deeply personal, sexual and transformational. Working with Lalita Tripurasundari does several things for you once you get 'in sync' with your body as the cosmic body of the goddess through the Shri Yantra.

It is a complex system, and to know it all takes many years of memorizing, understanding and working with the 111 deity forms, Mantras, ascribed stones, incenses and ritual items that are assigned to each corner of the Shri Yantra matrix! If you are drawn to the Red Goddess, then follow her with determination and devotion, and she will reveal her wisdom to you.

This book offers only a small taste of her loveliness and power. You can experience her electric beauty and gnosis in your Zonule by doing her rituals. I urge you to form your own relationship with Lalita Tripurasundari, and thus form a deep esoteric relationship with the mysteries of your own infinitely powerful body. If you invoke her, listen to her! Honor her! *She is, in fact, the universe itself* manifesting as the most beautiful goddess of bliss and power! Remember, her 'flower arrows'—your senses—have points. All hail the Red Goddess, Maha Shakti, Kundalini Devi, Shri Lalita Tripurasundari! Om Hreeng!!!

### *The Power of Lalita Tripurasundari*
### *The Lalita Sahasranama*

Unlike many other deities, Lalita Tripurasundari is pervasive, yet not solidified into clearly defined aspects or forms like other deities, such as Lakshmi. As the great, fiery, cosmic goddess, Adi Shakti, the ultimate power of the cosmos, she pervades many Tantric lineages. The text that is most often used in her worship is the *Lalita Sahasranama* from the *Brahmanda Purana*—though her veneration and rituals are much older. The *Lalita Sahasranama* is written in the form of offering the thousand names or epithets of goddess Lalita Devi because she is seen as the ultimate pervasive power of the cosmos by those who see Shakti as the supreme power of the universe. The text really contains homages and invocations *of most all of the goddesses*. This may seem confusing because Lalita Tripurasundari is Adi Shakti, the ultimate pervasive power of the cosmos, the supreme power who contains all goddesses. As such, the *Lalita Sahasranama* is used in rituals and Pujas dedicated to other goddesses like Kali, Parvati, Durga and Lakshmi, among many others. In my opinion, few other goddesses in Tantra are seen as literally *all* goddesses. This gives some sense of the all-encompassing nature of Lalita Tripurasundari Devi! In many ways she is seen *as all women,* much as another red goddess, Babalon, is seen in Western occultism. The reason is clear: the gnosis of Lalita Tripurasundari implies that every woman is a manifestation of her, and that Lalita Tripurasundari is only present through women.

## *Lalita's Island of Jewels*

Lalita's Island of Jewels is referred to as *Nagara,* and is a mythic abode of all-embracing delight. Her devotees, through ritual ecstasy and rites, may reside with her in this secret 'nine-jeweled Island'— her secret temple and place of bliss. This mysterious, hidden island is sometimes represented as a jeweled lotus; it is also described as a glowing Shri Yantra. This astral, archetypal, nine-jeweled island is a place of bliss and sensual joys, but also a place of erotic magick. As the esoteric version of the Shri Yantra, the form of the island reveals a cosmic map of your energetic body, your spiritual centers, and more. This is pretty esoteric stuff! By focusing on her 'tools' and her 'Island,' you are actually contemplating the process of energizing your power-centers and the potential flow of Kundalini energy.

The Jeweled Island is said to have twenty-five walls, each representing a Tattva or aspect of reality. Twenty-five streets encircle it, crafted of precious metals and gems. Along these streets are holy forests, guardian deities, and goddesses like Varaki (one of the 'Mother Goddesses' who was Lalita's 'commander' in her battle with the demon Bhandasura; see below). Many demi-goddesses (Yoginis) and a bunch of other gods and goddesses live there as well. There is also 'the forest of love' which sounds fantastic and I'm sure is beloved of Lalita! Much of this flowery language seems to describe ritualistic visionary language describing the 'astral' form of the Shri Yantra or of a hidden Tantric temple as a separate world where the Great Adi Shakti Lalita resides. Keep in mind that the cult of Lalita Tripurasundari was secret, esoteric and erotically focused, and like other initiatory sects, it had few members.

## Lalita Devi Fights the Demon Bhandasura and Recreates the Universe

This lengthy story is told in the *Lalitopakhyanam,* but here is a short version.

The demon Bhandasura was created from the ashes of Kama Deva, the god of love, who was destroyed by the laser-like glance of angry Shiva. (It's a long story, which I briefly related earlier in this book. It's why Kama is now invisible.) Anyway, the demon got on Shiva's good side with a lot of sycophantic devotion, and Shiva gave him a great deal of power which, of course, he abused. Basically, he took over the world from all the gods. So, the gods went into exile, and began intense worship and thousands of years of magick to empower the Goddess Para Shakti. The demon found out, and descended on them; they were so scared they jumped into the firepit and were all destroyed. When Bhandasura left triumphantly, Para Shakti—incarnated as Goddess Tripurasundari—resurrected all the gods of the multiverse, and recreated the universe! Then Tripurasundari went after Bhandasura with her army of angry gods and a ton of weapons, and destroyed him with her bow and arrows. She set things right and all was well.

This wild myth shows that her worshippers see Lalita Devi as *the* supreme deity, Adi Shakti.

### ICONOGRAPHY

While many Tantric gods and goddesses have multiple aspects and forms, Lalita Tripurasundari is remarkably singular. The ecstasy and power of Lalita Tripurasundari can trigger utter transcendence, and lead to a blissful state akin to Samadhi. This is reflected in her manifestation as Kundalini Devi. In images, she is often shown naked and in sexual union atop Shiva who lies beneath her in a trance. In union with Shiva, she is the supreme Shakti and thus also Kundalini. Lalita and Tripurasundari are really two aspects of the same goddess and so are often referred to with one title, Lalita Tripurasundari. No matter what aspect she takes, she is young and beautiful, with glowing red skin, and wearing many jewels. Her aspect as Lalita is shown holding her four 'weapons'—flower-arrows, a bow, a goad and a noose. Her aspect as Tripurasundari is similar, but is shown holding a stalk of sugarcane, a sexual symbol of virility, fecundity and sweetness. Images of Lalita and Tripurasundari often show the Shri Yantra at their feet, as shown above.

Although Lalita and Tripurasundari are technically different aspects and have slightly different images, they are almost always seen as *one goddess*. Her ultimate aspect or form is that of Para Shakti, Adi Shakti, or Maha Shakti, all terms for the ultimate power of the universe, the primal power that pervades and manifests all things. As the ultimate goddess, she is also said to manifest as the Mahavidyas, the great Wisdom Goddesses. In myth, Lalita Tripurasundari is often identified as Maha Devi—the Greatest Goddess who lives in Nagara, the Island of Jewels. She is said to abide on Mt. Kailash with Shiva as well. To devotees of Lalita Tripurasundari, she is essentially *all goddesses* because she is *the goddess*. In images used to worship her, two very important goddesses are often shown on either side of her—Lakshmi and Sarasvati—implying that these two goddesses are actually 'aspects' of Lalita Tripurasundari. To many Tantrics, all goddesses are aspects of the ultimate form of the creatrix of the universe who is seen as Para Shakti, the great primal energy of the cosmos worshipped as Lalita Tripurasundari.

### Symbols

Lalita Tripurasundari holds the following 'tools' with these attributes:

Noose—Attraction.
Goad—Repulsion.
Flower arrows—The Five Senses.
Sugarcane bow—Concentration, Will, Power.
Sprouting sugar cane staff—Vitality, Sexuality, Power.
She sometimes wears a serpent or has one nearby—Kundalini.
Sometimes she is shown riding on a lion—The power of Para Shakti.
The Shri Yantra image is often shown displayed at her feet—this indicates that the Shri Yantra is literally part of her or

can be seen as a manifestation of her, especially when it is shown in its 3-dimensional (3D) form.

Her Vahana (vehicle) may be a serpent, but there are hints that her vehicle might, in fact, be human beings.

Her throne (or bed) is held up by Brahma, Vishnu, Rudra, Isana and Sada Shiva. These mostly later gods are synonymous with enlightenment, liberation, Yoga, Samadhi and Nirvana.

Lalita Tripurasundari "is superior to all the male gods and dominates them all," so it is said in Shri Vidya.

She sometimes sits upon a large Lotus.

She sometimes wears a Moon crescent, referencing her lunar Kala emanations of bio-magick.

## Offerings

**Colors:** The altar cloth and your clothing should be red, crimson, scarlet or other shades of red or pink. She also prizes yellow or gold accents; she is sometimes shown wearing green in her images as well.

**Incense:**
Red or yellow sandalwood.
Any sensuous or erotic and intoxicating scent like Ylang Ylang, sandalwood, jasmine or rose.
Red Kumkum sandalwood paste or powder is sacred to her and can be used to bless images or ritualists. When anointing a ritualist, it is often put on the third eye.

**Food & Flowers:** All things lovely, sensuous and beautiful!
Red fruits and flowers.
She also prizes all yellow offerings.
Erotically charged Amrita.
Sugarcane, sugarcane juice, all sweet drinks, and other sweet things pleasing to her, like honey.

## Mantras

Lalita Tripurasundari's Bija Mantra is HREENG.

HREENG LALITA MAHASHAKTI SVAHA
HREENG: Lalita Goddess, you are the Great Shakti so be it!
HREENG SHREENG KLEEM AIM LALITA TRIPURA SAUH [Vibrate intensely]
HREENG SHREENG KLEEM AIM Great Goddess of Three Forms
KA E I LA HREENG, HA SA KA HA LA HREENG, SA KA LA HREENG HA—SVAHA You may note that this Mantra is not Sanskrit—it is likely pre-Sanskrit in origin and there is no translation I know of, except 'Svaha', meaning 'So Be It.'

## Yantras

*Lalita's Shri Yantra (2-Dimensional)*        *Lalita's Shri Yantra as the Human Body (3D)*

*"The Yantra of Devi Lalita is Shri Yantra. The divinity of the Yantra always occupies the center or apex. The different parts or petals and lines of the Yantra are usually arranged in concentric circles (mandalas) and contain rays or sub-limbs of Devi. The Shri Yantra has nine of these mandalas, each filled with various aspects of the Devi. The Shri Yantra is said to be a geometric form of the human body, which*

*implies that the goddess as Macrocosm is one with human being as Microcosm."*

— shivashakti.com/tripura.htm, Mike Magee

Lalita Tripurasundari's Yantra is the Shri Yantra. This may seem a bit confusing because this Yantra is also ascribed to Lakshmi, but there are differences.

First, I address the 'flat' two-dimensional (2D) Shri Yantra. It is one of the oldest and most potent Yantras, and no one knows its origin. If you look carefully, you will see it is an amalgam of most other Yantras. The innermost central triangle is identical to the Kali Yantra, representing the dark moon and contraction of the force of the goddess. As the moon expands from new to full, the energy and the diagram can be seen as opening like a flower into the full Shri Yantra until it withdraws back into the middle triangle of the Yantra as the moon goes from full to new moon.

In Tantra, potent lunar energy flows through the body, changing in aspect depending on the moon's phase. Most Tantras ascribe this powerful magick to women, who are often referred to as Shaktis. These energies are called Kalas (emanations or time) and are primarily associated with Lalita Tripurasundari. The Kalas change as the moon changes, from new moon to full which takes 15 days. The Kalas of each of these 15 days each have different powers and aspects, and all flow through the Tantric priestess empowering her magick. You may wish to research much more of this complex system, especially in shivashakti.com.

An important difference between the ritual use of the Shri Yantra with Lakshmi, and for the worship of Lalita Tripurasundari, is the way it is seen and understood. Often a Shri Yantra used for Lakshmi is used just like any Yantra: it is laid flat on the altar, items are placed on it, and so on. Lakshmi's Shri Yantras often are simple and use basic colors.

Shri Yantras that *specifically represent Lalita Tripurasundari* often have differently-colored, expanding 'rings' within the diagram. These rings are made up of lotuses, circles and interlocking triangles. When invoking Lalita Tripurasundari as embodied in the Shri

Yantra, keep in mind that you will be visualizing your seated body and the 3D Shri Yantra as one.

The 2D (flat) Yantra is a stylized, simple image as are most Yantras. However, the 3D Yantra is unique to Tripurasundari work. It is seen as her very being, and when you visualize your seated self as the Shri Yantra, you and Lalita Tripurasundari become united in this meditation. Look at the image of the 3D Shri Yantra below. Visualize it *as yourself seated on the floor medita*ting. As such, the top point is centered on the crown of your head and it becomes wider until the base, the widest part where you are sitting on the floor. This 'base' is shown as the outer square representing the Earth. As you visualize yourself as this mountain-like 3D Yantra, also visualize each level as a ring of energy. These rings of energy, from crown point to wide base, are shown as levels in the 3D Yantra above.

This 3D Shri Yantra model of the cosmos represents the seated body of Lalita Tripurasundari. By doing this visualization, you become one with her body seated in meditation. See yourself as this mountain-like 3D Yantra; visualize each level overlaying and energizing the nine different parts of your body, from crown to base.

*Another 3D Representation of*
*Lalita's Shri Yantra*

The use of the 3D form of the Shri Yantra is something of a secret, for it is a magick map for activating the esoteric aspects of the goddess within your body. If you sit comfortably on the floor with crossed legs, you can visualize your body as this 3D form. It also represents your body as a mountain. As such, it is analogous to Mount Kailash, the mountain which is the center of the universe and upon which Shiva and Shakti reside. The tip of the 3D Shri Yantra represents the crown of your (or Lalita's) head, the top of Mount Kailash, and the center of the Yantra, all at once!

As you visualize moving down the mountain-like 3D Shri Yantra, visualize the energy of Lalita Tripurasundari filling you with light at each level, from your crown to your base.

This is a simple description of the hidden, esoteric wisdom surrounding Tripurasundari's Shri Yantra. It is expounded on in a vast array of occult wisdom teachings, Tantras and practices under the term 'Shri Vidya', roughly meaning 'Wisdom of the Supreme Goddess.' These symbols hide a pragmatic and useful occult formula for directly accessing a goddess who represents your energetic and erotic nature. The description of the different levels follows, but there is much more to be found if you are drawn to her; this is simply an introduction to this mysterious goddess and her immense power. Research the term 'Shri Vidya' to lead you deeper into her Gnosis.

The following information seeks to explain this gnosis of Lalita Tripurasundari Devi and her magick Shri Yantra. Simply meditating on your body as the 3D form of this Yantra will yield important visions through this unique goddess.

To understand 'the form' of Lalita Tripurasundari as embodied in the 3D Shri Yantra *as* your human body, it will help to describe the levels or Chakras of the 3D Shri Yantra as they are superimposed on your body. Sit cross-legged in your Zonule. Look at the 3D version of the Shri Yantra (above). See the wide base (Root) as where your butt meets the floor, and see the different steps as sections of your own body until it reached the tip—the Crown on your head. In short, see your body as the 3D Shri Yantra. As your energy flows from your Root Chakra to the Crown, it denotes the energy of your body arising.

These 9 levels of the 3D Shri Yantra correspond with the nine Chakras, from Root to Crown. In a sense, they 'stack' upward from the widest earth level to the narrow top. The point at the top corresponds with the Bindu point in the center of the 2D image. If you look at the flat and 3D forms above, this will become clearer.

Sit on a cushion in your Zonule or somewhere else that is quiet. *Close your eyes and visualize yourself as the 3D Shri Yantra.* The Bindu (center point) of the 3D Shri Yantra glows at your Crown. The wide base of the Yantra is the wide Root of your body and crossed legs sitting on the ground. In other words, the Crown is the peak of the mountain, and the Root is the base of the mountain. The mountain *is* the 3D Shri Yantra; you will visualize *becoming* that mountain, becoming the 3D Shri Yantra, from the Root to the Crown.

### The Shri Yantra
### *(The Body of Lalita as Your Body in Meditation)*

Here is a step-by-step meditation for visualizing the levels of the 3D Shri Yantra as your body. Meditating intensely in this sequence will sync your mental, emotional, energetic and physical bodies with the whole 3D Shri Yantra. In this way you will attune yourself to Lalita Tripurasundari as well as your physical and energetic bodies. Working with this system can also prepare you for Kundalini work, for Lalita Tripurasundari *is* the Goddess Kundalini.

Review the following as you prepare to do the meditation. Keep a copy nearby the first few times; it is somewhat complex but you'll get the hang of it. Close your eyes when visualizing, then open them, and silently read each section, one at a time as you need, until you have finished all of the levels. Take your time; you are seeking to understand and feel this process, and the Gnosis of Tripurasundari's form. (Note: the term 'Trikona' is used often, and simply means a triangle-form of which there are many in the Shri Yantra.)

First, go to your Zonule and PHUT! banish; then sit cross-legged on a pillow on the floor and:

Breathe deeply and relax.
Visualize a circle of white light about you.
Do Pranayama as you like, visualizing your body as the 3D Shri Yantra form. Take your time.

#### *Visualizing Yourself Within the 3D Shri Yantra*

Sit on the floor and visualize your body as a mountain, the 3D Shri Yantra. Now visualize yourself being *within and part of the 3D Shri Yantra;* it is your astral or energy body. You will begin empowering your body with the 3D Shri Yantra by visualizing your Root Chakra as the bottom of this 'mountain,' and the peak as your crown. As you visualize each layer, from Root to Crown, you will see the Shri Yantra as rings of light filling your body. As you move up your body, you will visualize each 'layer' as a glowing ring that permeates your body with light and power, from the widest base to the point of light at your crown. Here is a quick review of this experience to prepare you for visualizing each power center from the Root (base) to the crown:

- Chakra Ring 1: Your legs and butt form the base of the Shri Yantra Mountain, the Bhupura, the Root Chakra where you sit.
- Chakra Ring 2: The next level up is a wide Chakra ring of 16 petals, visualized as a ball of light pervading you at your Genitals.
- Chakra Ring 3: Moving up, the next slightly smaller Chakra ring of 8 petals encircles your Solar Plexus, filling it with a ball of light.
- Chakra Ring 4: The next Chakra ring, formed of 14 Trikonas, hovers at your Belly/Navel, filling you with a ball of light.
- Chakra Ring 5: The next Chakra ring has a circle of 10 Trikonas, and is visualized glowing and pervading your Heart with a ball of light.
- Chakra Ring 6: The next Chakra ring also has a circle of 10 Trikonas, though smaller than the previous Chakra ring, and is visualized glowing and filling your Throat with a ball of light.
- Chakra Ring 7: The next Chakra ring is visualized as energy filling your whole Head and Mind with light.

Note: Between Chakra 7 and 8 you visualize a 'sacred space' that is important, but is not a Chakra. It is where you visualize the four sacred weapons of Tripurasundari: the flower-bow, flower arrows, noose and goad.

- Chakra Ring 8: The Third Eye (the point at the center of your Brow) is visualized as the cosmic energy that opens your Third Eye, opening your spiritual mind to a new, higher consciousness.

- Chakra Bindu 9: The final Chakra is visualized as a glowing point of light at the top (Crown) of your head. It is brilliant with light, and the fountain of your body-energy moves upwards into the heavens. This is where all the forms of the goddess and Shiva unite and converge into one: OM.

Go over this sequence while looking at the 3D Shri Yantra. Then visualize yourself *as* the 3D Shri Yantra, Base to Crown. Then visualize where each Chakra ring connects to you as you move from your Base to your Crown as you 'become' the Shri Yantra.

Begin by visualizing the wide Root Chakra or layer, the 'base' of the 'mountain' as it were. Read the 'Root' section (below), close your eyes and visualize this part of you as the Root Chakra of the 3D Shri Yantra. Breathe deeply until you can see and feel the light from the Root Chakra filling you, then move up to the second Chakra ring of light, and so on. Keep visualizing each Chakra/ring/level as you work your way up your body. You are merging with this 3D 'mountain' of the Shri Yantra. Step by step, read each Chakra-Level, and visualize the energy of each Chakra within your body as you move up. When you reach the Crown, you will be a mountain of light; you will embody the 3D Shri Yantra, the body of Lalita Tripurasundari.

*Chakra-Ring 1—The Bhupura or Walled Square (Base or Root)*

The first level is the base of the Yantra, called the Bhupura—the 'earth square' that surrounds the base of the Yantra. It has four gates open to the four directions. This represents your Zonule, protecting and earthing your work. Traditionally it is guarded by eight Siddhi Shaktis (magick aspects of the goddess). You can visualize these as you like.

*Chakra-Ring 2—The Fulfiller of Desires (Genitals)*

The next level is visualized as an open lotus of 16 petals around you (see the 2D Yantra). Sitting upon each petal is a goddess of magick; these are called The Hidden Ones. You can visualize them as protecting and filling you with erotic energy. They embody the 16 Kalas—lunar emanations of the Goddess manifesting as Desire.

### Chakra-Ring 3—The Agitator of All (Solar Plexus)

The next Chakra level is the 8-petal lotus which is visualized as glowing with magickal Yogini (demi-goddesses) sitting on each of the petals. These Yoginis offer secret wisdom, it is said.

### Chakra-Ring 4—Giver of Auspiciousness (Belly/Navel)

The next Chakra level is visualized as a circle of 14 triangles that sits within you as a glowing ring. Each triangle has a goddess form; they are called 'intoxicating goddesses' in that they open your senses and body to enjoyment.

### Chakra-Ring 5—Accomplisher of Purpose (Heart)

The next Chakra is visualized as a circle of 10 triangles that sits about and within you as a glowing ring. Visualize each triangle as a lovely goddess which dispels fears and give boons.

### Chakra-Ring 6—The Giver of Protection (Throat)

The next level up, at your throat, is a Chakra forming a circle of 10 triangles, visualized within you as a glowing ring. Each can be visualized as forms of Lalita that glow with protective and helping Powers.

### Chakra-Ring 7—Remover of All Ills (Head)

The next level up is a small Chakra-circle formed of 8 triangles. These triangles contain goddess forms of Lalita that dispel sickness and ills.

### 'Space Between'—Tools of Lalita and Their Guardians (No Chakra)

The next level is a space between Chakra 7 and 8 where the four weapons of Lalita Tripurasundari are visualized to empower you. These are her flower-bow, the flower arrows, her noose, and her goad. Each represents an erotic and empowering state of being. The bow is will-desire; the 5 arrows are the inflamed five senses; the noose is the power of attraction; and the goad is the power of repulsion. All are wisdom-powers of Lalita, and *are visualized both as powers within you and as protective items at this time as you move up the layers in your mind and on your body.*

### Chakra-Ring 8—The Trikona of All Success (Third Eye)

Having the form of the inverted triangle (Kali Yantra), this is the most secret and hidden shrine of Lalita. This can be visualized as three different Shaktis or goddesses, one at each of the three points. One is called Lady of Lust who is white in color; another is Adamantine Lady who is red; and the third is Flowery Vagina who is gold. They are glowing as white, red and gold goddesses respectively. Note: They also represent Moon (white), Sun (gold), and Fire (red).

### Chakra-Point 9—The Bindu Chakra; Purely Blissful (Crown)

Visualize your Crown Chakra as a Bindu (center point) where resides Shri Lalita Maheshvari (Lalita Greatest Goddess) or Maha Tripurasundari (Greatest Tripurasundari). This is the traditional 'Crown Chakra,' and it is from there that Kundalini fountains forth when invoked correctly, causing Samadhi (true liberation). Thus, the correct invocation of Tripurasundari and her many powers—from Base to Crown using these visualizations—helps the arising of Kundalini.

When you are done with this meditation, breathe deeply, and from the Crown, begin to work your way down through each of the 9 levels. Visualize each level empowering your physical and emotional body as you move down. When you reach the Base Chakra, do Pranayama and relax with your eyes closed. How has this energized you? What visions or feelings did you have? This is just a practice, but hopefully gives you a taste of Lalita's nectar!

## FESTIVALS

### Lalitha Jayanti—Jayanthi Puja

The most important festival for Lalita is the Lalitha Jayanti, the Puja observed on the full moon day of Magh (January–February; as a lunar calendar, it changes yearly). Lalitha Jayanthi is the day dedicated to Lalita Devi, a form of Great Shakti who symbolizes the totality of the five elements: Earth, Water, Fire, Air and Spirit.

It is quite popular in Northern India where the Tantric worship of Lalita Devi is strong and intense. Ornate Pujas are celebrated on this day in temples and in the homes of devotees.

### *Lalita Panchami*

Another important festival sacred to the Goddess Lalita is held during the nine-day Navaratri festival on the fifth day of Saran Navratri in Ashwin month (often in October, but changes year to year). It celebrates the battle between her and the Demon Bhandasura, and is a big deal in Northern India. People often fast and do special Pujas to her in temples or in their homes.

## LALITA-TRIPURASUNDARI NATH TANTRIKA PUJA
### Some Notes on Worshipping Lalita Devi Tripurasundari

It is best to do Pujas or other rituals to her on the full moon, or on the fifth day of the waning moon. It is traditional to wear green and to face northeast when honoring her. It is best to use a Ghee (purified butter) lamp. It can be simple and homemade—just a wick and some Ghee. It is best to offer her yellow flowers, yellow sandalwood paste and incense, and yellow candy or other sweets.

On the Zonule altar:
A red candle, incense in a burner, a cup of appropriate liquid, a Yoni-Lingam, appropriate flowers, a pipeful of cannabis (if legal), the Arti tray or bowl full of offerings (food, a small cup of liquid, a small candle, and a stick of incense), and an image of the deity. (See the **Offerings** section above.) A large Shri Yantra, large enough for all to see clearly, should be laid before the altar; it will be used in the center of the circle. A smaller image of the Shri Yantra is placed flat before the image of the deity with the Arti tray placed upon it. Both Shri Yantras should be blessed and protected in some way. In this Puja, two red candles should be placed on either side of the deity image, and another side plate of food and drink may be placed before or near the altar.

### Honoring Ganesh

The priest/ess rings the bell 3x. All bow to Ganesh and chant:

OM GAANG GANAPATAYE NAMAH [3x]

The altar candle is lit.

### Banishing

PHAT! [5x]

This is done to the four directions and to the center by all present. Lightning bolts are visualized, banishing all negative energy.

### Creating the Sacred Sphere

The priest/ess casts a circle with the trident, *or* all hold hands in a circle. All chant:

OM MANI PADME HUM [3x]

while envisioning the circle/sphere of light about all. All pause for a moment and visualize 4 tridents at the four directions glowing with light and protective energy. All chant OM. The Temple is set.

### *Honoring the Powers*

All bow and intone:

*OM Namaste! Honor to the Gods, the Spirits, the Ancestors, the Gurus and to All Wild Things That Play! OM to Shri Gurudev Dadaji Mahendranath and the Crystal Line of Tantric Gurus Whose Amrita and Power Helps Us Manifest True Knowledge, True Will, and True Action Through Our Guardian Spirits with Love! Guru OM! Svecchacharya!*

### *"Mea Culpa"*

All say:

*May any Errors We Make in this Ritual, any Slights, or any Negativity Generated be as Rain Striking the Ocean, Dispersed, Forgiven and Forgotten. By Our Efforts May All Beings Attain Liberation and Joy! OM!*

### *Purification (Devi)*

Purify and bless the self with the power of Shakti Devi: Each adept blesses theree Body Centers/Gunas by placing a hand over each area in turn and visualizing light pouring into *Head, Heart and Loins/Base* as they invoke Devi with this Mantra:

HREENG SHREENG KREENG PARAMESHVARI SVAHA
[1x at each body center]

### *Centering & Kusa/Sacrament (Deva)*

A pipeful of Kusa (cannabis) is held on top of the Yoni-Lingam as all sit in a circle and vibrate OM. Then all chant:

OM NAMAH SHIVAYA! [108x]

as the Kusa is lit and passed clockwise around. All partake as they will, or hold up the smoking pipe and make offerings to Shiva if they don't wish to partake.

When done, offerings of pipe ashes are placed on the Yoni-Lingam, and each person dabs some on their forehead (third eye).

### *Preliminary Prayer/Invocation of the Deity*

The bell is rung 3x. All say:

> Oh, Shri Lalita Devi, Great Tripurasundari, Holy Red Goddess!
> We call you now by your sacred names!
> NAMASTE SHRI DEVI. WELCOME TO OUR TEMPLE!

> Let us now invoke the Beautiful Goddess
> The youthful Devi, the Red Goddess
> Shri Lalita Tripurasundari!

The red fire-candle and incense are lit as well as the two red candles on either side of the image of Lalita Tripurasundari Devi.

All bow to the goddess, the bell is rung 3x, and all invoke:

> HREENG SHREENG KLING AIM LALITA TRIPURA SAUH [3x]

> OM Shri Lalita!
> Primal Goddess!
> Primal Shakti Light of All
> We call you as
> TRIPURASUNDARI
> Three-fold Beautiful One!
> Rays of energy come from your being
> Manifesting as SUN, MOON and FIRE!
> Thus, you O Shakti Ma encompass Shiva and
> For you are the center of ALL
> Here now eternal
> Pure consciousness
> Manifesting three-fold; Tripura
> As Sattvas Shakti
> Rajas Shakti & Tamas Shakti
> Knowledge Devi!
> Will Devi!
> Action Devi!
> Maha Devi!
> We understand all through you,

We feel all through you,
We experience all through you!
OM! Svaha!
By you the universe is created and destroyed
So, we call you the Dance, the Play, the Swirl; LILA!
Awake you are all
Asleep you are all
In Emptiness you are all!
Manifesting as Air Shakti and Fire Shakti,
Water Shakti and Earth Shakti
United as Prakriti, you are Pure Spirit
O luminous energy that pervades and IS ALL
Thus, you PLAY as One
Manifesting as THREE
Vibrating as 15 Nityas
O Shri Vidya! True Knowledge!
Grant our True Will desires!
HREENG!
O Shri Devi!
Manifest our True Will desires!
O Shri Yantra!
Embody our True Will desires!
O divine mirror of the universe; Adya Shakti
HREENG SVAHA!

## *Visualization Meditation*

The larger Shri Yantra is now placed in the center of the Zonule, either on a smaller table or on the floor.

The priest/ess reads the following and points to relevant parts of the Shri Yantra as the reading progresses, and as all meditate on the Shri Yantra. This 'pointing' can be done with the trident.

As this is done, all visualize the slowly unfolding image of the Shri Yantra being described as a three-dimensional form of the Yantra superimposed on their body.

Each person's body is thus visualized as a 3D Shri Yantra mountain (Mount Kailash), with the peak at their crown where Shiva-Shakti reside. Each person's body is this mountain/Yantra.

The Concentric rings of the Yantra are 'Chakras' that encircle and infuse the body at specific points. There are 9 such Chakras in this system.

The Crown Chakra is the top of the mountain, the CenterPoint (Bindu) of the Shri Yantra.

The Bhupura (square) surrounding the Yantra is the Base or bottom Chakra. This surrounds and supports where you are sitting.

As the visualization/invocation ascends from a wide Bhupura base to the point of the mountain-top crown, the energy is raised and each circle, decreasing in size, is visualized within the body.

All should enter a deep meditative state, focus on the Shri Yantra before them, and track which 'ring' is being invoked. The job of the priest/ess is to point to each 'ring' so all can focus on it and manifest it in their body.

All should be aware that every petal and triangle has a deity form—a particular goddess—in it, yet all need not know their names and functions.

This system comes from the occult teaching of Shri Vidya (Great Goddess Knowledge), and is a very complex system within Tantra. *This is a simple beginner meditation to align the Tantric's body as the Shri Yantra/Sacred Mountain to become one with Lalita.*

All should keep in mind that the energies flowing through the Ida and Pingala meridians (channels) and Sushumna (central channel) all weave and flow up through the spine and come together at the crown, the top of the Mountain—the heavenly abode—where Shiva-Shakti are fully embracing.

The priest/ess prepares for this intense meditation. A small, red flower is present. All sit, relax and enter meditation, focusing on the Shri Yantra before them, and doing Pranayama for a few minutes.

When all is calm, the priest/ess rings the bell 3x and all focus on the Shri Yantra as she begins:

HREENG!
Let us Meditate upon the Shri Yantra!
The Jewel Island Palace of The Supreme Goddess
    Tripurasundari
Her blessed seat which is in fact Mount Kailash

This is the Body Temple of our Beings Within which she lives
   as a Red Serpent
Life and Energy and Magick awakening within Matter!

The Priest/ess points to the square base of the Yantra:

We manifest Bhupura—the earth square
May the Dikpala protectors guard us
May the 8 Siddhi Shaktis empower our work
May the 8 Prakata Yoginis be sublimated and empower us
HREENG SHAKTI SVAHA!

The Priest/ess points to the outer, 16-petal-circle Chakra:

We invoke the 16 Nitya Kalas
The Petals of Desire Fulfilled:
May we attain our desires by using our willpower to focus and
   control our mind, ego, sound, touch, sight, taste, smell,
   intellect, steadiness, memory, name, growth, etheric body,
   revivification and physical body.
HREENG SHAKTI SVAHA!

The Priest/ess points to the next 8-petal-circle Chakra:

As the 8 Hidden Shaktis/Petals unfold
May we be filled with bliss
HREENG SHAKTI SVAHA!

The Priest/ess points to the outer circle, the Chakra of 14 triangles:

May we be renewed and intoxicated by the glowing ring of 14
   Triangles
O Chakra of Good fortune, Empower and bless us!
HREENG SHAKTI SVAHA!

The Priest/ess points to the next circle, the Chakra of 10 triangles:

May we activate and be empowered by
The Chakra of the inner 10 triangles
The Kuka Kaula Shaktis who grant All Things
HREENG SHAKTI SVAHA!

The Priest/ess points to the next circle, the Chakra of 10 triangles:

> May we be protected by
> The Chakra of the inner 10 triangles
> The Ring of diamond—protection and banishing of evil
> HREENG SHAKTI SVAHA!

The Priest/ess points to the next circle, the Chakra of 8 triangles:

> May the Disease-banishing inner 8 triangle Chakra cleanse us
> Empower and heal us by the energies of Tripura Siddha!
> HREENG SHAKTI SVAHA!

The Priest/ess points to and prompts the listeners to visualize Lalita's 4 sacred weapons glowing at the four quarters of the base:

> May the 4 weapons of Tripurasundari protect and empower us!
> The flowery bow of WILL,
> The flowery arrows of our FIVE SENSES,
> The noose of delicious ATTRACTION
> and the goad of REPELLING all that is not Her
> O guard, protect, empower and bestow blessings!
> HREENG SHAKTI SVAHA!

The Priest/ess points to the Inner-Yoni/triangle:

> May the great Goddess Tripura Amba;
> Lady of Lust, Diamond Lady, Red Yoni of Bliss
> Innermost Triangle of Red, Portal of all Power
> Grant us all success in what we here now will/desire
> So opens our Third Eye to her Gnosis!
> HREENG SHAKTI SVAHA!

The Priest/ess points to the Bindu/point in the center, prompting each to now focus on their 'crown':

> OM!
> Point of ruby light!
> Goddess of all Goddesses
> You who are Both Shiva & Shakti As One
> Center of all creation, destruction and Eternity
> May we center
> May we glow
> May we transcend through you.
> Lalita Maheshvari Maha Tripurasundari!

We are you
We adore you
We dissolve into your bliss!!
HREENG SHAKTI SVAHA!

The priest/ess intones the syllables of her Mantra and each repeat it *syllable by syllable.* This is done 3 times. As this is being done, each person visualizes becoming Tripurasundari, the supreme Maha Shakti, the Red Goddess who is all desiring and who all desire.

Now all do this arcane Lalita Mantra 108x:

KA E I LA HREENG
HA SA KA HA LA HREENG
SA KA LA HREENG
HA!

When done, the priest/ess rings the bell 3x.

All meditate in silence, becoming the Red Goddess as well as the infused Shri Yantra. After a time, the priest/ess rings the bell 3x.

All keep their eyes closed and meditate as the priest/ess says the following stanzas. They repeat (call and response) HREENG! and OM SHANTI SHIVA SHAKTI! each time it is said by the priest/ess. Each person should also intensely envision the descent of the Shakti power from crown to base, as well as visualizing this as a descent from the top of the Holy Mountain where Shiva-Shakti dwell, down to earth. This should be done slowly and take some time, with the priest/ess pausing for a time between each stanza. The priest/ess begins to slowly and clearly speak:

Now we descend from the state of bliss!

HREENG!
We descend from the top of Mt. Meru
Union with OM and the Bindu supreme: Shiva-Shakti as One
The Red Jewel of Lalita!
OM SHANTI SHIVA SHAKTI!

HREENG!
Union with and Earthing of The Red Inner Yoni Shakti!
OM SHANTI SHIVA SHAKTI!

HREENG!
Honor to and Installing of the 4 Blessed Weapons of Shakti!
OM SHANTI SHIVA SHAKTI!

HREENG!
Union with and Earthing of Disease-Banishing Chakra Shakti!
OM SHANTI SHIVA SHAKTI!

HREENG!
Union with and Earthing of Diamond Protection Chakra Shakti!
OM SHANTI SHIVA SHAKTI!

HREENG!
Union with and Earthing of The Wish-Granting Chakra Shakti!
OM SHANTI SHIVA SHAKTI!

HREENG!
Union with and Earthing of Good Fortune Chakra Shakti!
OM SHANTI SHIVA SHAKTI!

HREENG!
Union with and Earthing of The Hidden Bliss Lotus Shakti!
OM SHANTI SHIVA SHAKTI!

HREENG!
Union with and Earthing with the Shakti who embodies 16 Lotus Petals!
OM SHANTI SHIVA SHAKTI!

HREENG!
Union with and Earthing of The Fortress of Earth Shakti!
OM SHANTI SHIVA SHAKTI!

The priest/ess then places the red flower in the center of the Shri Yantra as all the powerful energies are earthed. The priest/ess directs all to bow low and touch the edge of the Yantra, and then says:

HREENG!
We are forever Shri Yantra
We are the body of the Goddess
We are the Flame of Power
May we always be balanced, blessed and beautiful!
OM SHANTI SHIVA SHAKTI SVAHA!
ADYA LALITA DEVATA SVAHA

## Empowerment of the Deity

The priest/ess rings the bell 3x. All now focus on the red flower in the center of the Shri Yantra and visualize the actual presence of the beautiful red goddess originating from this flower.

Led by the priest/ess, all chant together using their Malas, and empower the Goddess Lalita Tripurasundari now manifesting within the Shri Yantra, chanting:

HREENG LALITA MAHASHAKTI SVAHA! [108x]

## Magick Work (Optional)

This is a spell-ritual to gain love, sex or to attract a person you desire. It can be used to ask for a Tantric partner, or to inflame your love life.

A Shri Yantra should be handmade or printed out, and laid flat upon a red cloth. It's best if it is printed or drawn in red. Have 16 red flowers in a small bowl nearby, and one red tealight candle. You'll also need some red wine, 16 additional red flowers, another small, red candle, and some sandalwood oil.

When you are ready to do Magick:

Light the small, red candle. Then anoint yourself (or yourselves if in a group) with the oil on your third eye, heart and above your genitals, chanting HREENG each time.

Take a few minutes to meditate on Lalita Tripurasundari, and let her power fill you with red desire. Clearly hold her image in your mind, and yearn for her presence. When ready, the priest/ess rings the bell, and all open their eyes and chant:

HREENG LALITA MAHASHAKTI SVAHA [16x]

Then place the red tealight in the center of the Shri Yantra, light it, and invoke her, saying:

HREENG SHAKTI SHAKTI SHAKTI!
Tongue of fire
Electron burn of ruby light
Perfect, Crystalline—alive!
Pure energy dancing!
Swirling Vortex—Spin embrace
Spiral helix hurricane!

Centered—Illuminated spark
I sing of you here and now with my whole body!
For My body is your divine being!
Enfold us with rapture!
Energize and revitalize us!
Inspire us O Yoni of Fire!
Fill; Thrill; Distill Within us
The rose-red jewel of your glowing heart
Thank you for being with us, loving us
Filling us with your glowing Knowledge, Will and Action
Blessing to you, O Great Mother and the Love and Will you bring!
HREENG LALITA TRIPURASUNDARI SVAHA!

The priest/ess rings the bell 3x. Now, invoke each of her 16 DESIRE petals on the Shri Yantra. As you invoke each Shakti, place a red flower upon each of the 16 petals on the Shri Yantra, *and visualize that goddess-aspect of Lalita sitting there.* All may chant as each flower is placed on a petal, beginning at the top and proceeding clockwise.

Adya Kamakarsini Devata Svaha!
 Brilliant Scarlet Flame of Desire
 Bursting honey taste
 Of One ripe fruit
 KA!

Adya Buddhykarsini Devata Svaha!
 Sword-Dancing Red One
 Three-eyed and sharp of tongue
 Leaping gazelle—
 E!

Adya Ahankarakarsini Devata Svaha!
 Slowly Opening Lotus of Dawn
 Woman-child of daybreak
 Softly walking in rose robes—Ruby woman.
 I!

Adya Shabdakarsini Devata Svaha!
 First Vibration

Rising from the darkness
Vibrant cascade of Music—Pure as Mountain Water
LA!

Adya Sparshakarsini Devata Svaha!
   Caress of Breeze
   Rain and Sunlight
   Upon the naked body—You are laughing with pleasure
   HREENG!

Adya Ruipakarsini Devata Svaha!
   I see you Sliding between
   A glimpse of something—Intangible
   As One thing becomes Another
   HA!

Adya Rasakarsini Devata Svaha!
   Bittersweet and Textured Loveliness
   Liquid gold form of woman
   Joy feasting lady!
   SA!

Adya Ghandakarsini Devata Svaha!
   An elusive cloud
   You gather the alchemical dew
   Bathing the swimmers and the trees in shining clarity
   KA!

Adya Cittakarsini Devata Svaha!
   Awareness echoes outward
   Embracing and creating
   All things, experiences, ideals—The beautiful dance of being
   HA!

Adya Dhairyakarsini Devata Svaha!
   Great Red Warrior Woman!
   Come striding forth
   In golden armor—Whirling the deadly sword of truth
   LA!

Adya Smrtyakarsini Devata Svaha!
   Ocean wave sparkling light

Every tide carrying memories, Stealing feelings
Red one! Reveal the universe that is locked within.
HREENG!

Adya Namakarsini Devata Svaha!
Weaver of Absolute into Adamantine Form
Sigil maker, synthesis flow—I am That
As you reveal true self and Nature
SA!

Adya Bijakarsini Devata Svaha!
Great Invisible Seed Center
Point of Light—Flowing-Wavelike; The jewel
KA!

Adya Atmakarsini Devata Svaha!
Beautiful one of the Stars
Infinite Bliss Diamond
There is awakening to Nothingness in your embrace
LA!

Adya Amrtakarsini Devata Svaha!
Slowly...Your Rose Opens...
The jewel—Glowing softly within; Blood Red
I smell the scent, become and remember—O gate of dreams
HREENG!

Adya Sarirakarsini Devata Svaha!
OM: The Body Temple Explodes in Brilliance
As flames of Shakti awaken
From deep in the Earth—Erupting with the red desire
OM!
SVAHA.

If you are with others, close your eyes and visualize making love and reaching orgasm as you silently chant HREENG SVAHA! If you are alone, focus intently on Lalita, and bring yourself to orgasm. If you're with your partner, make love as you breathe together, and whisper HREENG over and over, and SVAHA at orgasm. Place the resulting sacred elixir on the 16 petals of the Shri Yantra with 16 chants of HREENG.

Sit and meditate on the experience. Let the red tide of desire within you flow from head to heart to genitals and base. As you focus your will and desire upon the Yantra, visualize Lalita Devi seated there, smiling, glowing with energy, and granting your desire. When done bow three times and chant:

OM SHANTI SHIVA SHAKTI [3x]

You may keep the now-charged Shri Yantra for future Lalita work, or you may burn it.

### Offering To & Feeding the Deity

Silence. The bell is rung 3x. The Arti is placed gently upon the large Shri Yantra in the center of the circle. The Arti candle and incense are lit, and with palms out, all bless the offerings by chanting while visualizing brilliant 'crimson energy' of love flowing into it. All chant the following 11x:

OM AIM HREENG SHREENG SRI LALITA
   TRIPURASUNDARI
PADUKAM POOJAYAMI NAMAH

We call you Great Lalita Tripurasundari
We bow to your Holy Feet and offer Love and Devotion!

Thus, the food is charged, blessed and offered to Lalita Tripurasundari Devi.

The priest/ess then raises the Arti tray, stands, and makes five circles in the air before the image of the deity on the altar. *During this, the deity is intensely visualized partaking of the essence and energy and offerings with joy.* All together chant:

OM HREENG [5x]

Then the Arti tray is passed clockwise around the circle. Each person holds it with eyes closed, and communes with the Red Goddess with great love and clear visualization, requesting the help and desires that they need.

While this happens, all in the circle not communing with the deity, quietly (Japa) chant HREENG over and over. Each person is given time to directly commune with the deity; there is no rush.

When all are finished, the Arti tray is returned to the center of the large Shri Yantra in the center, and the bell is rung 3x.

This is a time for a short, silent meditation on the experience. Pranayama is done as all absorb the blessings and power of Shri Lalita Tripurasundari. After a few minutes, the bell is rung 3x again.

Lalita Tripurasundari is a powerful and energetic presence in the room! Time to party!

### Communing with the Deity

The Arti tray is passed around, and all enjoy some of the now-blessed food and drink (Prasad) and the other food that has been on or around the altar. All may relax, laugh and chat, sharing their visions and experiences with Lalita Tripurasundari as they like.

Following this is a time for playing drums, banging rhythm sticks, shaking rattles, clapping, singing, laughing, chanting, dancing, telling stories, doing divination, and whatever else people want to do! All are infused with the divine power of the deity, and may act as they please. More Kusa may be smoked, more food eaten, and so on. This is the time to 'party with the goddess' and it should be as wild, free and fun as possible.

This is also a good time to chat about what could be added or changed with the Puja for next time, setting the next Puja dates, assigning others to be the priest/ess, and so on. All Tantrics are equal in the Kula circle!

Once the merriment is done and the party ebbs, the priest/ess checks in with all to see if it is time to end. Everything is put away, hands are cleaned, and so on. Then all return to meditative pose.

### Farewell to the Deity

When the partying is done, all have eaten and had fun, the Puja ends with a final invocation by all of Shri Lalita Tripurasundari. The bell is rung 3x. All chant:

HREENG SHAKTI SHAKTI SHAKTI!
Tongue of fire
Electron spark of ruby light
Perfect, Crystalline—alive!
Pure energy dancing!

Swirling Vortex—Spin embrace
Spiral helix hurricane!
Centered—Illuminated spark
I sing of you here and now with my whole body!
For My body is your divine being!
Enfold us with rapture!
Energize and revitalize us!
Inspire us O Yoni of Fire!
Fill; Thrill; Distill Within us
The rose-red jewel of your glowing heart
Thank you for being with us, loving us:
Filling us with your glowing Knowledge, Will and Action
Blessing to you, O Great Mother and the Love and Will you bring!
HREENG SHAKTI SVAHA!

The bell is rung slowly 3x as all visualize the departure of the lovely Red Goddess, and chant and clap their hands:

HREENG LALITA MAHASHAKTI SVAHA [3x]

### *Ending & Dedications*

With hands raised, all chant together the four Purusarthas (universal blessings) while sending blessings from the Puja to all beings:

Balance, Wealth, Pleasure and Liberation to All Beings!

The bell is rung 3x, then all shout:

The Will to Love is the Law to Live!
OM SHANTI SHIVA SHAKTI [3x]

All bow to the deity, and all candles are blown out. Banish as at the beginning. All stand and do:

PHAT! [towards each of the 4 directions and the center]

All touch the Earth and offer any leftover energies to the Earth Mother:

BHU DEVI—To You From You All Things! OM!

Puja is done! All help clean up the temple and maybe a group hug. Partying may continue elsewhere.

# The Goddess Lakshmi

*Goddess Lakshmi
(Photo by the Author)*

## On the Deity

Lakshmi is one of the sweetest and most popular Goddesses in the world, with a huge heart and millions upon millions of fervent devotees who pour prayers and love into her every day. That is quite a lot of energy to have access to, and once you take a swim in her blessings, you'll be better for it.

Lakshmi is one of the oldest deities in South Asia, and her image can be found everywhere. Very old, crude, carven images have been found and identified as her. The most primal image identified as an aspect of her, Padma (lotus) Goddess, is as a lotus-headed, reclining, naked goddess displaying her Yoni for veneration. Note that Padma Devi is one of her aspects even today. Many think she was likely a primal earth-mother long before inhabiting the set Hindu Pantheon as a wife of Vishnu.

The name 'Lakshmi' is derived from the Sanskrit word *Laksya* ('aim' or 'goal'). She evolved from an Earth Mother who granted prayers for bountiful harvests, into a goddess who offers all kinds of prosperity. Lakshmi has always offered a way to gain your desires, especially in terms of material things, and she is thus the most popular goddess in India and wherever Hinduism thrives. She is the goddess of wealth and prosperity, but that can be karmic or spiritual as well. Her temples are often lavish and beautiful. I went to one in New Delhi that was like a palace, all crafted of white marble! Her temples (often included in Vishnu temples) and her Pujas are very well attended. Travel around India or Nepal and you will see her image and countless small personal shrines to her everywhere.

Lakshmi is very much a maternal looking goddess. In her images and statues, she is depicted as a beautiful woman of rosy or golden complexion, sometimes with two, but often with four hands. She is often sitting or standing, often on a full lotus, holding a lotus bud or one or two open lotuses in her upper hands. The lotus has many meanings, and here stands for beauty, prosperity and fertility. It is possibly her oldest symbol as the Earth Mother.

Her four hands represent the four ends of human life: Dharma, Kama, Artha and Moksha—what we call balance, wealth, pleasure and liberation. She is often depicted with pots or cascades of gold coins flowing from one or two hands, showing that those who worship her can gain wealth in many different forms. Her other lower hand is most often in the Mudra of dispelling fear. What a lovely combination: don't be worried, be prosperous!

She often wears a gold embroidered Sari; sometimes she is dressed in green or white or a combination. It is said that red symbolizes activity, and gold decorations indicate prosperity. However, in the *Mahalakshmi Ashtakam Stotram* (hymn), she is in her most sublime form, and is described as being dressed all in white. It is likely that she represents Adi Shakti in this form, for she is in and of herself a supreme form of the primal goddess. In that hymn she is called the wife of Rudra, a form of Shiva. She is not connected with Vishnu, her later husband ascribed to her in Hinduism. This reveals that Lakshmi is much older and more primal than the Aryan or Vedic gods that came later. In fact, Lakshmi is firmly rooted in prehistory, with many simple images of her as an erotic Earth Mother being found. She is also referenced as a manifestation of the primal, ancient Goddess called Para Shakti. We who practice Householder Tantra love Lakshmi as do Hindus and others. We realize the attractiveness of some stability, prosperity and wealth in our lives as we maintain a home, a job, and often a family. Thus, we invoke the more prosaic, nurturing mother Lakshmi, but to us she is mostly known as the more primal Maha Lakshmi, and as such is recognized as Adi Shakti. Thus, to us, like all goddesses, she is one with Shiva (Rudra) who is all gods.

## History

*"Salutations to thee, Maha Maya, abode of fortune, worshipped by gods, wielder of conch and mace, Maha Lakshmi, I bow to thee!"*
— *Mahalakshmi Ashtakam Stotram*

Lakshmi is, in many ways, the supreme mother of prosperity and nurturing. Revered in Tantra and Hinduism as the Goddess of blessings and wealth, she is also the primary Goddess of security and material comfort, who showers gold and material needs upon her worshippers. She is connected with, and is often shown with, the god Ganesh, the elephant-headed god of removing obstacles and bringing prosperity. In the Tantric trinity of the triple Goddess, Lakshmi has the earthiest role.

Yet today, she is usually shown in the role of the dutiful wife of the later-introduced god Vishnu, the preserver of the world. However, her earlier husband was the god Rudra, the red-skinned archetypal wild man, god of storms and wild animals. She had a more primal past, for sure.

Lakshmi is often called Mata (Mother), not just Devi or goddess. This reveals her pervasive nurturing powers, indicating that she is one of the great Mother Goddesses.

For ages she has been one of the most popular Goddesses in India—especially those in need of material prosperity or good crops. She is seen as an ancient Earth Goddess like Bhu Devi, usually in her aspects as Padma Devi (Resembling a Lotus) or Kamala Devi (Lotus Goddess).

She is present in every Indian or Nepalese business, and is prayed to by millions of businessmen, workers and householders for economic prosperity.

She has been honored by Tantrics as *Maha Lakshmi,* who is seen as a form of Adi Shakti. She is also seen as a form of the great primal Shakti, for they all are different and yet all are one. Maha Lakshmi is called 'the primordial energy, Mother of the Universe' in her hymns, and she is often called 'Shri' or 'Maha Devi', just as Lalita is.

As wisdom-mother, Lakshmi is represented by her rarely shown owl symbol. She is called 'the knower of all' in her hymns, and is praised as 'without beginning or end, primordial energy, Goddess of all and *the great power of Shakti!*' Often invoked as the Goddess seated on a lotus, she is also seen as the creatrix of all and Universal Mother.

It's easy to see the universal appeal of this powerful Goddess. She is worshipped by millions, not just because she is an ancient cosmic deity, but also because she is a nurturing Goddess who brings prosperity and wealth to her devotees. Your petitions to Lakshmi need not be only for money, however. Her owl and primal origins remind us that she grants knowledge and wisdom of the Earth as well.

## *Myths*

In Tantra, *Maha Lakshmi* (Great Lakshmi) is one of the important aspects of the Mother Goddess, and as a manifestation of Adi Shakti, Maha Maya, and Maha Devi, the great Goddess, and thus the mate of Maha Deva or Shiva.

Some of the earliest myths of Lakshmi name her as Bhu Devi, the primal Earth Mother. It is said that she lay beneath the primal waters at the beginning of time. However, the waters had no life, and she urged the great Sky Father to help her bring life to the earth. He lifted her up, and she unleashed the powers of Nature which awoke and covered the planet with life. As the great Earth Mother (who we might call Gaia), she was venerated before the Aryan Vedic culture swept into India. Ancient images of her as a primal Earth Mother show her as a naked, reclining, lotus-headed goddess called Padma (like a lotus) Devi, one of her names even now. Today in India, she is mostly seen as the goddess of wealth and prosperity, and the dutiful wife of Vishnu, the preserver of all—including the *status quo.* Yet she is also called the Shakti of Rudra, the wild god who is an aspect of Shiva. In short, her origins and status are complex.

After the creation of the Earth, Lakshmi (and the Earth) fell into cycles of decline and rebirth. The Asuras (demons) held sway over the Earth, and Lakshmi became the mate of their greatest king, Bali. But Bali abused Nature, so she "withdrew and dissolved herself into the primal milk-white ocean." Without her, the Asuras and the big boss Bali, were conquered by the gods; and without Lakshmi, the world fell apart, crops did not grow, and Nature was barren. Humans, animals and even the gods, were perishing. Both the Devas and Asuras panicked, joined together, and asked Vasuki, the Naga King, for help. At their urging, he looped his huge serpent-body around Mount Kailash; the Asuras grabbed one end and the Devas the other, and they took turns pulling Vasuki's head and tail as soon as he had set the mountain in the center of the milky-white sea. In myth, this divine white ocean is the Milky Way. From this churning and foaming, many things arose from the depths and emerged—including the goddess, Lakshmi!

After this rebirth of the Great Mother, she was assigned as Vishnu's wife, a common occurrence when conflicting pantheons merge. Shiva longed for Lakshmi, but was married to the Mountain Mother Parvati—who, like Lakshmi, is another aspect of the Earth Mother. They are considered to be aspects of each other in some texts. I guess it was decided that Shiva had enough wives!

## ICONOGRAPHY

These are the key aspects of Lakshmi as set out in her various scriptures and invocations. She, like every Goddess, has many titles and faces, but here are some of the most important aspects:

**Dhanya Lakshmi** means 'Grain Lakshmi', an aspect of the goddess as agricultural plenty. She has eight-arms, dresses in green, and holds two lotuses, a bundle of green grain, a living sugarcane, and bananas.

**Gaja Lakshmi** means 'Elephant Lakshmi'. She bestows animal wealth like goats and cattle, and is associated with royal power. Gaja Lakshmi found the treasure lost by Indra in the ocean. Narayanan interpreted the name as "one who is worshipped by elephants." Even today she is often shown with elephants, and in images is often paired with Ganesh. She has four-arms, wears red garments, and holds two lotuses. Her other two arms are in Abhaya Mudra and Varada Mudra which banish fear and give blessings respectively. She is flanked by two elephants, sometimes bathing her with water pots.

**Santana Lakshmi** is the 'Fertility Lakshmi' who helps bring children into the house. She has six arms, and carries two Kalashas (water pots) with mango leaves and a coconut on top. This is one of her most ancient symbols. She also holds a child on her lap, of course.

**Veera Lakshmi** means 'Courageous Lakshmi'. She bestows courage during fighting, and gives strength to overcome difficulties. She has eight arms, and is dressed in red. She carries a Chakra or disc; a small, conch-like shell; a bow; an arrow; a trident (or sword); and a bound, palm-leaf, holy book. As with many of these aspects, two of her hands are in Abhaya Mudra and Varada Mudra.

**Vijaya Lakshmi** means 'Victorious Lakshmi', and she is thus the goddess of success in both battles and the daily fight to achieve success in life. She has eight-arms, wears red garments, carries a Chakra (circular weapon), a shell, a sword, a shield, a lotus, and a noose, clearly ready for victory.

**Vidya Lakshmi** means 'Knowledge Lakshmi', and is the goddess of mastering arts and sciences.

Clearly Lakshmi was and is an astoundingly popular and talented goddess who manifests as several aspects, and is beloved for a variety of powers. As with many gods and goddesses, many of these aspects were originally minor goddesses who became one with Lakshmi over millennia.

Some of the many other aspects of Lakshmi are:

Aishwarya Lakshmi—Prosperity Lakshmi
Saubhagya Lakshmi—Giver of good Fortune
Rajya Lakshmi—Royal Lakshmi
Vara Lakshmi—Boon (wish-granting) Lakshmi
Padma—Lotus-dweller
Kamala—Lotus-dweller
Padmapriya—One who likes lotuses
Padmamaladhara Devi—One who wears a garland of lotuses
Padmamukhi—One whose face is as beautiful as a lotus

Padmasundari—One who is as beautiful as a lotus
Shri—Greatest Goddess
Jagadishwari—Peaceful Mother
Ulkavahini—One who rides an owl

Lakshmi is so popular and has so many divine aspects that, as is usual in Tantra, many of her 'names' that are chanted are also the names of other Goddesses she is identified with, including Shakti.

## Symbols

The Owl: Her animal vehicle (Vahana) is the Owl. She is often displayed with elephants, however.

The Lotus: She often holds a lotus or sits upon one, and is known as Padma (lotus) Devi. As such she represents love, bountiful nature, fulfillment and nurturing, as well as the Earth itself.

Gold coins: Her images often show gold coins showering down from the heavens or from her downward-pointing hand open in the Mudra of giving boons. The symbolism is clear and means prosperity, wealth and wishes granted.

A sacred pot or jar: Often in her Murti, Lakshmi has an elegant water pot with mango leaves and a coconut atop it. Sometimes it is full of gold or gems; at other times, it is a pot of Amrita, the nectar of immortality.

Mudras: Various forms of Lakshmi have other symbols as per her aspects, but she is commonly shown with two hands in the Abhaya Mudra (which dispels Fear) and Varada Mudra (which gives Boons and Blessings). Many other gods and goddesses are often shown displaying the same Mudras.

## Offerings

**Colors:** Primarily red and gold, but also white and green.

**Incense:**
Lakshmi Dhoop is a popular Lakshmi incense that is malleable. You roll some into a small stick and light it. It is earthy and deep, and is very useful for her rites.

Red or yellow Sandalwood.

Nag Champa, or any earthy or 'prosperity' incense you feel is right, like Patchouli.

**Food, Flowers and Others:**
Lakshmi loves most anything offered with love. Think 'Mother Goddess,' and you really can't go wrong with your love offerings. She loves luscious fruit like mangos, bananas and young coconut, as well as sweets, candy, and so on.

All beautiful, sweet-smelling flowers are great for her: red, white and green work best.

A special offering for her is Panchamrita (milk, ghee, sugar, yogurt and honey mixed together).

Offer her coins and red Kumkum (sandalwood) paste or powder.

## Mantras

Lakshmi's Bija is SHREENG.

Om Hreeng Shreeng Lakshmi Namah Svaha!
Om Shreeng Hreeng Klem Mahalakshmi Namah Om
Om Sri Maha Lakshmi Namah

## Yantras

*Shri Yantra of Lakshmi*

**Note:** It may be confusing to see the Shri Yantra ascribed to both Lalita Tripurasundari *and* Lakshmi, but this is a part of the ancient, multi-layered, and sometimes contradictory myths and beliefs which have combined and shifted over thousands of years. The Shri Yantra of Lalita Tripurasundari is a more ancient, esoteric and magical tool of spiritual liberation, whereas the Shri Yantra of Lakshmi is a simple tool for bringing wealth and prosperity. In this way they are really two different forms of the Yantra—which is so ancient that no one really knows its origins. The simpler Shri Yantra shown in this section is widely used for the more mundane but important goals of generating prosperity and success via the goddess Lakshmi. (It is very effective in this regard, I might add.) Lakshmi's Shri Yantra is used as other Yantras are: laid flat as a sacred nexus from which Lakshmi manifests, and as a 'tool' for blessing and charging items dedicated to her. Remember, Hinduism and the 'Twilight Worlds' of Tantra overlap, and thus produce variants and contradictions among a widely diverse population of sects, traditions and lineages. Even Tantrics in the same lineages often disagree! Yet no one in India or Nepal is bothered by this. They simply say 'all is God!' and smile. This relaxed, flexible thinking is why I love Tantra.

*Kalasha Sacred Goddess Lakshmi Pot  
(With Mango Leaves & Coconut)*

## Festivals

### Weekday

Friday is Lakshmi's day.

### Diwali, the Festival of Lights

Lakshmi has several key holy days, but the biggest is Diwali, the Festival of Lights. It is celebrated on the last day of the last month of the lunar calendar (usually in October or November of the solar calendar). It is one of the most popular religious festivals in the world, with over a billion people celebrating on these days. This is a powerful explosion of magickal energy to be a part of! In one tradition, this festival celebrates her union with Shiva, though Vishnu as her husband is mentioned more often. This night, all wives dance for their husbands, invoking Lakshmi and the fortune, prosperity and success she brings to family and home.

Lights of all kinds are key symbols in Diwali, and in Tantra light signifies many things—both Shiva and Shakti are honored as 'Fire'. Light dispels darkness as Vidya (knowledge; really, gnosis) dispels ignorance. Light also imitates the gold that falls from Lakshmi's hands as rays of light. So, during the Festival of Lights, 'Deeps' (oil lamps), are burned throughout the day and into the night to banish darkness and evil, and bring blessings and prosperity. Homes are filled with oil lamps, candles and colored lights.

### Mahalakshmi Virat (Fasting)

Mahalakshmi Virat begins on Shukla Ashtami during the month of Bhadrapada which comes after four days of Ganesha Chaturthi (often in August). Mahalaxmi Virat is less a festival and more of a 16-day magickal ritual observance, usually in the home, but many go to a Lakshmi temple. Lakshmi rituals are generally centered around the women of the home, and are done to appease and seek the blessing of Maha Lakshmi for spiritual blessings, and of course, for wealth and prosperity. Those honoring her fast during the day then do Puja to Maha Lakshmi, and use the energy from the fasting and praying to benefit their home, family and others.

## Maha Lakshmi Nath Tantra Puja

On the Zonule altar:

A candle, incense in a burner, a cup of appropriate liquid, Yoni-Lingam, appropriate flowers, a pipeful of cannabis (if legal), the Arti bowl or tray full of offerings (food, a small cup of liquid, a small candle, and a stick of incense), and an image of the deity. (See the **Offerings** section above.) The appropriate Yantra should be flat before the image of the deity, with the Arti tray placed on the Yantra. If desired, two candles of the appropriate color can be placed on either side of the deity image, and another side plate of food and drink may be placed before or near the altar.

### *Honoring Ganesh*

The priest/ess rings the bell 3x. All bow to Ganesh and chant:

OM GAANG GANAPATAYE NAMAH [3x]

The altar candle is lit.

### *Banishing*

PHAT! [5x]

This is done to the four directions and to the center by all present. Lightning bolts are visualized, banishing all negative energy.

### *Creating the Sacred Sphere*

The priest/ess casts a circle with the trident, *or* all hold hands in a circle. All chant:

OM MANI PADME HUM [3x]

while envisioning the circle/sphere of light about all. All pause for a moment, and visualize 4 tridents at the four directions glowing with light and protective energy. All chant OM. The Zonule-Temple is set.

### *Honoring the Powers*

All bow and intone:

*OM Namaste! Honor to the Gods, the Spirits, the Ancestors, the Gurus and to All Wild Things That Play! OM to Shri*

*Gurudev Dadaji Mahendranath and the Crystal Line of Tantric Gurus Whose Amrita and Power Helps Us Manifest True Knowledge, True Will, and True Action Through Our Guardian Spirits with Love! Guru OM! Svecchacharya!*

### *"Mea Culpa"*

All say:

*May any Errors We Make in this Ritual, any Slights, or any Negativity Generated be as Rain Striking the Ocean, Dispersed, Forgiven and Forgotten. By Our Efforts May All Beings Attain Liberation and Joy! OM!*

### *Purification (Devi)*

Purify and bless the self with the power of Shakti Devi: Each adept blesses the three Body Centers/Gunas by placing a hand over each area in turn and visualizing light pouring into *Head, Heart and Loins/Base* as they invoke Devi with this Mantra:

HREENG SHREENG KREENG PARAMESHVARI SVAHA
[1x at each body center]

### *Centering & Kusa/Sacrament (Deva)*

A pipeful of Kusa (cannabis) is held on top of the Yoni-Lingam as all sit in a circle and vibrate OM. Then all chant:

OM NAMAH SHIVAYA! [108x]

as the Kusa is lit and passed clockwise around. All partake as they will, or hold up the smoking pipe and make offerings to Shiva if they don't wish to partake.

When done, offerings of pipe ashes are placed on the Yoni-Lingam, and each person dabs some on their forehead (third eye).

### *Preliminary Prayer/Invocation of the Deity*

Incense and candles are lit before the image of Lakshmi. All bow to the goddess, the bell is rung loudly 3x, and then all intone the prayer together:

Oh Shri Lakshmi, we call you now by your sacred names!
NAMASTE—Welcome to our Temple!

# Tantra for All

All stand and call the lovely Goddess Lakshmi from the EAST, with arms raised. All visualize her dressed in a white and gold Sari, covered in jewels and say:

SHREENG SHREENG SHREENG!
Lakshmi, Bless us with the winds of prosperity. SVAHA!

All call her from the SOUTH, with arms raised. All visualize her dressed in a red and gold Sari, covered in jewels, and say:

SHREENG SHREENG SHREENG!
Lakshmi, Bless us with the materialization of wealth. SVAHA!

All call her from the WEST, with arms raised. All visualize her dressed in a blue and gold Sari, covered in jewels, and say:

SHREENG SHREENG SHREENG!
Lakshmi, Bless us with the gentle rains of nurturing. SVAHA!

All call her from the NORTH, with arms raised. All visualize her dressed in a green and gold Sari, covered in jewels, and say:

SHREENG SHREENG SHREENG!
Lakshmi, Bless us with the peace and fulfillment of satiety!

All call her in the CENTER, facing each other, with arms raised. All visualize Maha Lakshmi (Great Lakshmi) as a goddess of flaming, golden brilliance with many arms, wearing a brilliant white Sari, and covered with all kinds of precious gems and gold jewelry. All chant:

OM SHREENG HREENG KLEEM MAHA LAKSHMI NAMAH! [3x]
Center us! Fill us! Bless us!

The priest/ess rings the bell 3x, and all sit and together read the invocation called *Mahalakshmi Ashtakam Stotram*:

> Greetings and Honor to You, Mahamaya, Abode of Fortune, Worshipped by All Gods, You Who Wield a Conch and Mace, Mahalakshmi, We Honor You With Love! Namaste!

> Hail to You Who Rides the Demi-God Garuda, O Terror to the Demon Kola, Remover of All Negative Karma, O Beloved Goddess, Mahalakshmi, We Honor You With Love! Namaste!!

O Lakshmi, You Know All and Give Us All Blessings, You Frighten the Wicked, and Remove All Sorrows, O Beloved Goddess, Mahalakshmi, We Honor You With Love! Namaste!!

You Grant Us Intelligence, Success, Enjoyment of Life, and O Goddess of All. You Are in Truth Great Shakti, One Born of Cosmic Union! O Mahalakshmi, We Honor You With Love! Namaste!!

You Take All Mundane and Subtle Forms, You Are Rudra's Shakti, and the Source of All, O Remover of Errors and Negative Karmas, O Beloved Goddess, Mahalakshmi We Honor You With Love! Namaste!!

O Goddess Who Is Seated on A Brilliant Lotus, You Are the Truest Essence of the Supreme Creator, O Supreme Adi Shakti, Universal Mother, Mahalakshmi, We Honor You With Love! Namaste!!

O Goddess Clothed in a Shining White Sari of Light and Wearing Every Multi Colored Jewel! You Support the Whole Cosmos, O Greatest Universal Mother, Mahalakshmi, We Honor You With Love! Hail The Greatest Source of Wisdom, the Queen of All! Namaste! Svaha!

### *Visualization Meditation*

The priest/ess reads as all silently meditate and visualize, eyes closed:

Breathe deeply
Feel yourself unwind
Relax each part of your body
Become aware of the earth as one living being
You can feel and hear her heartbeat
It echoes your heartbeat
Breathe deeply, feel the connection.

Now…

A vast milky sea is before you
Endless and translucent

The stuff of glowing stars and galaxies
Gently undulating
Rippled by a warm and sultry breeze
The sky is light blue
Sparkling with gold-tinted clouds
Sunshine is everywhere

Suddenly there is turbulence
In the center of this glowing sea
A shaking and swirling
Churning and spinning
Until a whirlpool forms
Growing larger and larger
More and more intense
And suddenly
A beautiful Goddess, Lakshmi emerges
Parting the milky sea
Eyes closed
Beautiful white robes
Covered in gold and jewels
Holding a lotus in her left hand
And gold coins in her right
At her feet is a pot of gold
And fountains of gold pieces erupt
And shower the sea about her

She opens her eyes
They are burning emeralds
The scent of honey fills the air
And sandalwood
She smiles
And the sky is filled with a bright light
All is gold
And she opens her arms
And the ocean changes
Into a golden field

She is suddenly standing
Amidst waves of grain
The sun shining above her

She smiles again and points with her hand
To the jar at her feet
It is golden
With a lid
Shaped into the image of an elephant
And red threads
Wrapped about it

She bends down and picks it up
Nodding her head
She hands it to you
And gestures behind you

You open the jar
There are jewels and pieces of gold
All are for you
And for those you love

The world is filled
With joyous happy people
Spinning about Lakshmi

Lakshmi gently hugs you
And whispers

"You have given well
Now
Look into the bottom of the jar
For there is a special gift for you"

You look into the jar
It is there for you
It is what you NEED
You take it
And kiss Lakshmi on the cheek
Uttering your thanks

Suddenly all the dancers
Flow into whirling liquid
Like milk filled with stars
Lakshmi dissolves
Leaving the smell of perfume behind

And the milky sea is suddenly still again
And a warm breeze blows
Over the darkening sky

Now you are done and must return...

Now you come back to your body
You feel the joy and peace of Lakshmi fill all your limbs
Your torso
Your heart and mind
You feel the earth's heartbeat, and it begin to fade
You feel this within you
As you breathe deeply, relaxed and refreshed and earthed

Now: Come out of the meditation energized and ready to receive prosperity!

The priest/ess rings the bell 3x.

### *Empowerment of the Deity*

All take up their Malas and chant together, inviting and empowering the descent of the Goddess Lakshmi as now manifesting within the image upon the altar. All visualize the Murti of Lakshmi glowing with her power. All chant:

OM HREENG SHREENG LAKSHMI NAMAH SVAHA
[108x]

In silence all welcome and feel her presence as she fully manifests in her image and the circle. The bell is rung 3x.

### *Magick Work (Optional)*

*Lakshmi Prosperity Spell*

This spell is to give prosperity and the blessings of bounty that all doing the Puja need.

**Needed:**
- Some Lakshmi Dhoop or yellow sandalwood incense.
- A small gold candle.
- Beautiful yellow or red flowers, one for each person and one for Lakshmi.
- Lakshmi's Shri Yantra, red- or gold-colored if possible.

- Some freshly cleaned coins; silver is best.
- A small bell.

The Yantra is placed in the center of the altar, but without the Arti tray on it.

All the flowers are on the Yantra. The coins are laid out around the edge of the lotus circle rimming the Yantra. Place the small gold candle in a holder to the right of the Yantra, and the incense to the left. The priest/ess rings the bell 3x.

All bow and silently ask Ganesh to remove all obstacles to wealth.

Then all intently focus on the Lakshmi image, and mentally focus on the money or other things you need.

The priest/ess lights the candle and incense; all bow and honor Lakshmi, saying together:

OM SHREENG LAKSHMI SVAHA! [3x]

Now, each person takes up a flower, and then together hold up the flowers and offer them with intense love and will to each of the directions and to the center as directed. Each time, all visualize a cascade of golden coins and light falling upon you!

The bell is rung and the priest/ess says:

> Blessing Goddess, open the gate of the East.
> For Wealth & Prosperity to come to us!
> By your Blessings of Gold, let it be so!
> SHREENG SVAHA!

The bell is rung and the priest/ess says:

> Blessing Goddess, open the gate of the South.
> For Wealth & Prosperity to come to us!
> By your Blessings of Gold, let it be so!
> SHREENG SVAHA!

The bell is rung and the priest/ess says:

> Blessing Goddess, open the gate of the West.
> For Wealth & Prosperity to come to us!
> By your Blessings of Gold, let it be so!
> SHREENG SVAHA!

The bell is rung and the priest/ess says:

> Blessing Goddess, open the gate of the North.
> For Wealth & Prosperity to come to us!
> By your Blessings of Gold, let it be so!
> SHREENG SVAHA!

All face the center, holding flowers in the middle. The bell is rung and the priest/ess says:

> Blessing Goddess, open All the gates and be here now!
> You are Here-Now, the Center of All!
> That Wealth & Prosperity may come to us!
> By your Blessings of Gold, let it be so!
> SHREENG SVAHA!

All intensely silently visualize the things they need, focus on the center of the Yantra, and bow to Lakshmi *who is now visualized standing and emanating light from the center of the Yantra.* Then all chant together:

> Golden Mother Bring Us Money! SHREENG!
> Shining Mother Bring Us Wealth! SHREENG!
> Cosmic Mother Bring Us Plenty! SHREENG!
> Loving Mother Bring Us Luck! SHREENG!
> Life to the Mother of Prosperity!
> You Are a Golden Loving Sun.
> By Your Love, Wealth Now Come!

Now, let all the flowers fall onto the Yantra, and visualize the room and your life filled with a shower of golden coins from her hands as the spell releases!

All hold both hands, palms facing out over the Yantra and flowers and say:

> We Call Forth Treasures of the Earth.
> Come and Fill, Come and Fill.
> We Ask You Now for Wealth and Mirth.
> Come and Stay, Come and Stay.
> Be Here Prosperity, Never Go Away!
> OM SHREENG SVAHA!

Ring the bell 3x. Then all say:

SHANTI SHANTI SHANTI
O LAKSHMI MA
Grant Blessing and Prosperity
To All Those in Need! SVAHA!

When done, all touch the earth and 'earth' the spell by chanting MA. Then the flowers are gathered and placed on the Arti tray which is then placed on the Yantra. The coins are left there, but after the Puja is done, the coins are shared with all present. Each takes one coin home to place on their personal altar, but must donate any others so the blessings of prosperity Karma will come back again.

### *Offering to & Feeding the Deity*

Silence. The prepared Arti bowl or tray is placed before the deity. The Arti candle and incense are lit, the bell is rung 3x, and all chant 3x:

SHREENG SHREENG SHREENG—Joyful Mother Come
SHREENG SHREENG SHREENG—Shining as the Sun
SHREENG SHREENG SHREENG—Plenty to Us All
SHREENG SHREENG SHRI—Let the Blessings Fall!
JAI MAHA LAKSHMI! [shouted!]

The bell is rung 3x. All gather about the Arti tray and bless the offerings with palms out while visualizing brilliant 'golden energy' of nurturing and prosperity flowing into the offerings, while slowly and intensely chanting:

OM SHREENG HREENG KLEEM MAHA LAKSHMI NAMAH [3x]

The priest/ess then raises the Arti tray and makes five circles in the air before the deity. During this, the deity is intensely visualized partaking of the essence and energy of the offerings. All chant:

OM [5x]

The Arti tray is then passed clockwise around the circle; each in turn holds it with eyes closed and communes with the Goddess. Each person holds the Arti tray out towards the image of Lakshmi with great love, and silently or aloud requests boons or gifts for themselves or others. The Arti tray should be moved a few times in a clockwise circle as this is done. If in a group, each person may silently commune with Lakshmi and receive her blessings with closed eyes before handing the tray to the person on their right.

While this is happening, all in the circle not communing with the deity quietly (Japa) chant SHREENG over and over. Each person is given time to directly commune with the deity. There is no rush.

When the Arti tray is returned to the Yantra, the bell is rung. This is a time for a short, silent meditation on the experience. Pranayama may be done as all absorb the blessings of Lakshmi.

After a time, the bell is rung again. Lakshmi will now manifest as a powerful and energetic presence.

### *Communing with the Deity*

All sit and relax. The Arti tray is passed around again. All eat and drink some of the now-blessed food and drink (Prasad) as well as any other food that has been set near the altar. All may relax, laugh and chat, relating their visions and experiences as they like.

Following this is a time for playing drums, banging rhythm sticks, shaking rattles, clapping, singing, laughing, more chanting, dancing, telling stories, doing divination, and whatever else people want to do! All are infused with the divine power of the deity, and may act as they please. More Kusa may be smoked, more food eaten, and so on. This is the time to 'party with the goddess,' and it should be as wild, free and fun as possible.

If there is a Kula, this is also a good time to chat about what could be added or changed with the Puja for next time, setting the next Puja dates, assigning others to be the priest/ess, and any other such business. All are equal Tantrics in the Kula circle!

Once the merriment is done and the party ebbs, the priest/ess checks in with all to see if it is time to end. All the food is put away, hands are cleaned, and so on. Then all return to a meditative pose and the bell is rung.

### *Farewell to the Deity*

All absorb the light, joy and prosperity that Lakshmi has brought to the Puja by chanting 3x:

OM SHREENG HREENG SHREENG KAMALE
KAMALALAYE PRASEEDA PRASEEDA SHREENG
HREENG SHREENG OM MAHA LAKSHMIYAI
NAMAH!

OM Purity and Power of the Divine Lotus Flower!
Bring Blessings To You Who are All Blessings!
We Deeply Honor You O Greatest Lakshmi!

All bow to Lakshmi and the priest/ess rings the bell. All chant:

SHREENG SHREENG SHREENG—Joyful Mother Sow!
SHREENG SHREENG SHREENG—May Prosperity Grow!
SHREENG SHREENG SHREENG—Plenty to Us Flow!
SHREENG SHREENG SHREENG—Wealth to All Now—Go!
OM HREENG SHREENG LAKSHMI NAMAH SVAHA!
[11x]

Thank You Mother LAKSHMI MA!
Live Within Our Hearts and Within Our Daily Lives
Help Us to Think—Speak—Live and Give Prosperity
Always in Gratitude!
JAI MAHA LAKSHMI! SVAHA!

### *Ending & Dedications*

With hands raised, all chant together the four Purusarthas (universal blessings) while sending blessings from the Puja to all beings:

Balance, Wealth, Pleasure and Liberation to All Beings!

The bell is rung 3x:

The Will to Love is the Law to Live!
OM SHANTI SHIVA SHAKTI [3x]

All bow to the deity, and all candles are blown out. Banish as at the beginning. All stand and do:

PHAT! [toward each of the 4 directions and the center]

All touch the Earth and offer any leftover energies to the Earth Mother:

BHU DEVI—To You From You All Things! OM!

Puja is done! All help clean up the temple and maybe a group hug. Partying may continue elsewhere.

# The Goddess Kali:
## Kali Ma—Black Goddess of Time

*Goddess Kali*
*(Photo by the Author)*

*"Just as all colors disappear in black, so all names and forms disappear in her."*

— *Mahanirvana Tantra*

### On the Deity

The lovely, maternal and fierce goddess Kali has been accused of being a dark and scary deity, and her image in the West has become a kind of horror-movie trope. Yet, she is one of the more honored, beloved and ancient goddesses in Asia. So, who is Kali? Devotees call her the most powerful form of the female force in the Universe, and that is a good place to start. Kali Ma, as she is often known, describes herself in the *Kulachudamani* as she 'speaks' to Shiva:

> *"I am Great Nature, consciousness, bliss, the quintessence, devotedly praised. Where I am, there are no Brahma, Hara, Shambhu or other devas, nor is there creation, maintenance*

> *or dissolution. Where I am, there is no attachment, happiness, sadness, liberation, goodness, faith, atheism, guru or disciple.*
>
> *"When I, desiring creation, cover myself with my Maya and become triple and ecstatic in my wanton love play, I am Vikarini, giving rise to the various things.*
>
> *"O All-Knowing One, if I am known, what need is there for revealed scriptures and Sadhana? If I am unknown, what use for Puja and revealed text? I am the essence of creation, manifested as woman, intoxicated with sexual desire, in order to know you as guru, you with whom I am one. Even given this, Mahadeva, my true nature still remains secret."*
>
> — **shivashakti.com/kali.htm**

She is infamous in the West and on Indian TV where she often appears as a dark goddess whose followers are dangerous cultists, bent on mayhem, and practicing evil magick! Some Hindus see her this way, but many Hindus and Tantrics revere her. Admittedly, the many images of her with fangs and blood, swinging a sword and wearing a necklace of skulls can be a bit off-putting to some who prefer sweet and lovely goddesses like Parvati or Lakshmi; yet she is also shown as a beautiful, dark-skinned woman who is loving and protects children. She is ancient and mysterious. She often holds a severed human head dripping blood. She also often holds a Kapala (a ritual cup made from the top of a human skull) filled with blood from the severed head. She has lots of skulls! She is often shown wearing a necklace of skulls, and a skirt of severed limbs! She is often dancing, standing or squatting on an entranced or unconscious Shiva, sometimes in sexual union. Such scenes are commonly set in a cremation ground full of burning corpses. Pretty spooky stuff, but there is a deeper symbolism.

This can be a bit difficult for Westerners to understand, but I am reminded of an Indian student of mine who was horrified at seeing a bloody, crucified Jesus! Symbolism is cultural, and the often-intense images of Kali Ma encode ancient symbols of liberation, wisdom, acceptance and transcendence. This is why she is one of the most worshipped goddesses in the world.

Sometimes she is depicted without the long tongue and severed head or Kapala, but as a lovely young woman whose black skin is the star-filled night sky. She is often paired with Shiva, especially in his wilder forms because, like him, *she represents the radical wild path of intense dedication to liberation, release and Samadhi.* Often her images show her holding her palm pointed down in the Varada Mudra for granting boons. What blessing is she offering? Release from all attachments and repulsions; release from all illusions; and, if you wish, the cessation of rebirth. As some Tantric devotees pray to her, *"O Mother, by your grace may I never be reborn!"*

## History

Kali is one of the oldest and most widely worshipped goddesses of Tantra and Hinduism, and as you might guess, her origins lie in ancient, prehistoric cults in places like Mohenjo.

> *"...It is widely assumed by scholars that she represents a survival of a Dravidian (pre-Aryan) goddess and is thought of as the great creatrix of the ancient Indian pantheon as she is well over 2000 years old. Kali is thought to be a pre-Aryan goddess, belonging to the civilization of the Indus Valley ...Her dark skin evidences the fact that she predated the lighter-skinned Aryan invasion of the darker-skinned inhabitants of the Indian sub-continent."*
>
> — *dollsofindia.com/library/kali*

For eons she has been associated with Tantra, and is even now the divine protector of initiates in the two Tantric lineages I belong to. As such, she is our patron and protector, in line with her fierce powers. She protects her devotees, especially children and women. For centuries Kali has been a perfect goddess for Sadhus and Tantrics fervently focused on spiritual work and liberation. She is rarely seen in her images as a wife or mother, but rather as the wild goddess who is free of all restrictions. Usually, when she is shown with Shiva, she is clearly in charge; or they are dancing together in feral, ecstatic excitement, often amidst a crowd of ghosts and, demons. As the most intense Tantric couple, they are also often shown fighting

Asuras and other demonic entities together, or dancing with them. She is always seen as the epitome of sheer wildness, the raw power of the dark jungle, the ferocity of Nature, and the transformational experiences of life and death.

Mother Kali offers spiritual illumination, initiatory experiences and release from the attachments of this world of Samsara by facing and accepting the challenges and horrors of life. She is very popular in Nepal and Northern India, especially in Calcutta which was originally 'Kali Ghat,' referring to her huge, famous temple that is still the center of the city. Unlike most temples in India, animal sacrifice is common there, and the resulting meat is cooked and eaten by her worshippers. I have witnessed such sacrifices to Kali, and have seen the river run red with goat blood while the many cooking fires filled the air with roasting goat. This is a bit of a surprise to many since most people in India are vegetarian, and let cows wander freely.

Her more extreme devotees, like those of Tantra sects such as the Aghori, can be found meditating and performing rites in cremation grounds, sometimes seated upon corpses. They do this to let go of all attachments, revulsion, and especially, fear of dying—Kleshas that most Tantrics work on banishing. This is seriously intense, magickal psychotherapy. I see Kali as the ultimate hardcore, independent, punk-rock, don't-mess-with-me goddess. She is one of the few goddesses that all the gods and spirits fear. This is why I call on her for protection.

Tantrics have honored Kali as a potent goddess for ages, long before the infusion of Aryan/Vedic culture. Kali and Shiva have always been venerated, and in these places where the old ways continue, her Tantric practices remain deeply rooted and still survive. Even the flood of Aryan customs, gods and Brahminic culture could not suppress the primal worship of Shiva and Kali. In Nepal and Tibet, Shiva and Kali have also been worshipped for centuries by Tantric Buddhists as Maha Kala (Great Shiva) and Maha Kali (Great Kali). They are often depicted dancing together, or in a face-to-face sexual 'yab yum' posture. Both Kala and Kali mean 'black' as well as 'time', which says a lot about their unity.

Kali, like the similar Durga, is well known as a primal Nature goddess, and is venerated in the deepest jungles as the wild—and at times dangerous—face of Mother Nature.

It has always been said in Tantric teachings that when you embrace her, her form changes from horrific to beautiful and loving. This happens as you work through your deep fears of darkness, pain, life and death. Nature is MA, your mother. It is easy to embrace the nurturing, 'nice' aspects of MA, but the dangerous, frightening, violent aspects of nature and life offer the greatest opportunity for personal growth and power in our work. Kali has been worshipped in cremation grounds from ancient times, for it is in these liminal, challenging places where one can embrace *and pass through* the horrors of Samsara—pain and death—with Her acceptance and gifts of equipoise and calm.

Devotees can, through Her, avoid reincarnation, and thus dissolve into her infinite, cosmic bliss, never to incarnate again.

Sir John Woodruff (aka Arthur Avalon), a Victorian-era British Tantric initiate, wrote many important works and translated several Tantras, including the famous *Hymns to the Goddess and Hymn to Kali*. He often names Kali "the Goddess of the cremation ground and one who also embodies it." The 'cremation ground' is a multi-level symbol for Tantrics. 'The cremation ground of Kali' is Tantric 'twilight language' for two important Tantric truths: the Yoni of the goddess (and thus female Tantrics), and the world of Samsara, illusion and suffering. This poetically signifies the embrace of divine sexuality and Tantric sex magick, and the acceptance and ritual use of Samsara for gnosis and liberation. Such things are looked down upon or seen as 'sinful' by many Hindus today.

No matter how old you are or where you live, death and the challenges of life are all around you in very concrete ways. Kali embodies our calm acceptance of death, and through that, transcendence of the fear of death. In this way she is often considered the greatest goddess of all. Meditation on Kali offers a healthy view of death as spiritual transformation, not as a frightening ending. It is only your flesh you leave, because your soul (Atman) is eternal. Kali reveals that our reality is just 'smoke and mirrors,' and reminds us that we are beyond all these things—we are eternal, so there is nothing to fear. Thus, it is said that devotees of the bloody, fanged goddess—who wears severed limbs and skulls and swings a sword—can be visualized transforming into a lovely, young goddess full of infinite stars and infinite space. In this way, Tantrics perceive the truth of Kali's true beauty and embrace eternity.

Such experiences with Kali reveal that Samsara, our chaotic world, can be accepted, spiritually illuminating, and enjoyable when we embrace this wonderful, horrible and crazy life without attachment, repulsion or fear, but as a source of joy and wisdom. The goal of Tantra is to transcend *time* (Kali) in this way, with her help. Kali worship is an ongoing *memento mori*!

Kali offers you direct and intense emotional, psychological and spiritual work on all of the core 'knots' of the Kleshas—especially Ego, which is often cited as the most intractable 'knot' to cut. Doing Kali Sadhana, you will evolve and become tough, sharp and pointed, just like Kali's sword. Such Tantric ritual work helps you find and reside within the calm center of the Wheel of Life *where time stops*. In this way, you escape the *circumference of the Wheel to reside, even for a short time,* in the center, the timeless place of peace. Amidst the wild, bloody, chaotic dance of Kali, you become the still, silent point, Shiva, upon whom she dances! From this still Bindi (CenterPoint), you can truly observe 'reality.' *This is your first taste of real liberation.* Learning to hold this state of ego-less freedom is *true liberation.*

Tantra acknowledges that every human being is important to this world. We are each a divine part of Lila, the dance of life. Yet society restricts our True Will with layers of programming we must break through to discover our spiritual path. *You are responsible for your own liberation; no one else is.* Thus, Tantrics say Svecchacharya! Do your True Will! Get to work on your own liberation now! *Wake up!* says Kali, shaking her bones and her sword at us! As a Tantric, you are not a religious follower or observer, but are actively in charge of your own path and life choices guided by your own Knowledge, Will and Action. As you do this, keep in mind that these three Shaktis *are also the three points of Kali's Yantra.*

### *Myths*

In India I found that myths about Kali vary widely from area to area, but here are a few that are most consistent.

## The Birth of Kali

The great goddess Durga was formed of all the powers of all the gods when they faced a demonic attack that none of them could stand. After multiple losses, they combined all their powers and Durga was born. With her ten arms she wielded all the divine weapons of the gods, and went forth to slay Mahishasura, the big boss buffalo-demon who threatened all the gods. During the battle, she became so furious that the goddess Kali emerged from her (some say her third eye), slew all the demons, and just kept killing and devouring as she went until she was pacified, some say by Shiva. In a sense, this connection between Durga and Kali makes sense; both are ancient Goddesses, and are considered aspects of one another by many.

## The Pacification of Kali

Kali is a goddess of death and darkness, but she is also a powerful maternal goddess, and is often called simply MA—Mother. Jai MA! (Hail Mother!) is one of her chants. She is famous for protecting women and children, and this myth shows how strong her motherly feeling is.

It is well known that Kali can be a deity of destruction as can her mate, Shiva. One day she was really furious. She went on a violent rampage, and began destroying everything and everyone. She was death running amok! She devoured people, livestock and whole cities, and threatened to destroy the whole world! Most of the gods quailed in fear of her, though some tried to stop her and failed. All of them retreated, injured, crying and fearing the destruction of the world! Shiva, who had stayed silent in the face of his violent mate, watched things unfold. He knew her well, and had a plan. He sneaked up close to her huge, bloody, terrifying form, and using his magick, turned himself into a small helpless baby lying in the path of her rampage! As she hovered over the baby—bloody arms and weapons raised—her heart melted. She suddenly lost all her fury, gently picked up the baby Shiva in her massive, motherly arms, and cuddled him with love; she forgot her anger, and thus ended the violence! All the gods were thankful to Shiva, and he was known from then on as 'the one who could cool the fires of Kali Ma.'

## Kali and Parvati

One story of Kali's birth is mentioned in the *Matsya Purana*. Keep in mind that all the goddesses in Tantra are ultimately one goddess as this story tells how Kali 'emerged' from Parvati, the wife of Shiva and the mother of Ganesh and Skanda. Parvati, sometimes called Gauri (light golden one), is the nice, beneficent, loving wife of Shiva, but this shows how she and Kali are really different aspects of one Goddess.

In this myth, the gods were being terrorized by Daruka—a bad-ass demon—and the gods called on Parvati to help them. Not being much of a warrior, she reached deep into her mate Shiva (one trusts with his permission), and *magickly merged with the dark poison Halahala he had swallowed when saving the world,* and thus transformed into the black goddess, Kali! Leaping from Shiva's body as Kali Ma, she raced to the fight and quickly slew Daruka, using a sword to behead him. I am sure Shiva and their kids cheered her on!

§ § §

There are many more such myths, but it is important to remember that Kali is primarily an intense goddess who uses her sword to cut through the delusions of Samsara, and confront the evils and horrors of the universe head on, devoid of illusions. Most of us prefer things to be sweet, kind, positive and beautiful, but Tantrics honor Kali because we seek to cut through the extremely difficult 'demons' of Ego, Ignorance, Attachment, Repulsion and Fear of Death. In many ways Kali is seen as the goddess of death and darkness—as the Goddess of Time—which, from one point of view, destroys all things. Yet Kali is our benefactor, our mother, our protector, and our teacher who helps us work through the challenges of life and death, to see that the world is transitory illusion, and is what we choose to weave of it. She gives us independence and strength. Keeping this in mind, Shiva and Kali destroy the universe at the end of every Yuga (age), said to be thousands of years long. According to Hinduism and Tantra, we are currently in the middle of the Kali Yuga! Contemplating the crazy, surreal world we live in now is an indication to many that indeed we are in the Aeon of Kali!

## Iconography

Kali is the radical, loving goddess who will remind you that your physical body, worldly success, pride, and egotism—like all else in life—are transitory and will fade with time. Kali offers you the loving but difficult truth that clinging to all the illusions of life causes the pain and sorrows of Samsara. I sometimes suspect she is the patron goddess of existentialists! Kali is the most liberating, loving and kind goddess as well as the most terrifying, pitiless and brutally honest Devi. If you are serious about making rapid spiritual and magical advancement, and overcoming blockages and limitations, or if you simply need protection and strength, then Kali is the goddess to call on. Don't let her scare you. She is really very sweet, and is called Great Mother for a reason. So much more can be said about this ancient and important goddess, and she has many aspects and epithets. Those that follow are paraphrased from the *Mahanirvana Tantra*, by Sir Arthur Avalon.

As **Kali** she is Time, the Destroyer of Time, and One Who Is Black. As **Kareli** she is wonderful, lovely and sweet. As **Kalavati** she possesses and knows all the arts. And as **Kamala** she is as a lotus, like Lakshmi. She is the destroyer of this Age (the Kali Yuga) as **Kalidarpaghni,** and is the Mother of Time as **Kalamata**. She is described as the mate and beloved of Shiva with many titles.

As **Kapardini** she is 'Spouse of Him of the matted hair.' As **Krsnanandavivardhini** she is 'One who increases the joy of the Lord of creation,' that is, Shiva who is also called Kashi Vishvanatha (Lord of the Cosmos). As **Kripamayi** she is 'the Merciful One,' and as such she is described as one who gives mercy in such epithets as 'the Vessel of Mercy' and 'Limitless Mercy.' As **Krsanu** (fire) she is worshipped with ritual fires. She is the very 'essence of desire' as **Kamarupa,** and the 'liberator from the bonds of desire' as **Kamapasavimcini**. In her virgin aspect as **Kumarirupadharini,** she manifests as and protects all women. She protects powerful women as the embodiment of a spiritually, sexually-active **Kulakamini**. As **Kamaniyagunaradhya** she is 'Adorable, the image of all tenderness.' She is named 'the beloved helper, protector and Goddess of the Tantrics (Kaulas), and of the Kula (Tantra group).' She is 'Adored by Kaulikas' (Tantrics), 'Benefactress of the Kaulikas,' and 'the Revealer of the path of the Kaulikas.' Kali is called the ancient Goddess who is our 'protector, helper, and wisdom-teacher.' And so she is named **Kulakamini,** or 'Lady of the Kaulas.'

This paraphrased section of the *Mahanirvana Tantra* ends with a final short hymn to Kali that is important in understanding Tantra:

*"You [Kali] are Kreeng, Hreeng, Shreeng Mantravarnena kalakantakaghatini, One Who by the three Bijas, KREENG HREENG SHREENG Destroys the fear of death."*

This quote is important for two reasons: First, Kali both destroys your fear of death and offers you a chance to *get off the wheel of incarnations so you are never reborn.* Second, and most important for this book, Kali manifests as three goddesses with three different Bija Mantras: **Hreeng,** *the Bija of Lalita Tripurasundari;* **Shreeng,** *the Bija of Maha Lakshmi; and* **Kreeng,** *the Bija of Kali.* These are *the* three key goddesses in this book, and they are revered in the Pujas as well. They are also the three key goddesses noted in the 'Chart of Triplicities' in the **Tantric Triplicities** chapter. In Nath Tantrika, these three great Tantric goddesses are the core forms of Great Primal Shakti! It is Kali who reveals this to us because she is the Protector Goddess of the Kaulas (Tantrics). Jai Ma!

Kali has many other aspects, of course; the *Hymn to Kali* (translated by Sir Arthur Avalon) offers over a hundred epithets for her. Some are commonly used to invoke and honor her in rituals. Here are some of the most popular epithets of Kali found in Pujas:

Adya Kali (primal ancient Kali), Chintamani Kali (wish-fulfilling Kali), Sparshamani Kali, Santati Kali, Siddhi Kali (magick Kali), Dakshina Kali (naked Kali), Bhadra Kali, Smashana Kali (cremation ground Kali), Adharvana Bhadra Kali (Ceaseless Power), Kamakala Kali (Essence of Desire), Guhya Kali (Secret Kali), Hamsa Kali (Union of Sun and Moon Kali), and Kalasankarshini Kali (Formless Kali.)

## Symbols

Kali's four arms represent the complete circle of creation and destruction which is contained within her. She has many esoteric symbols as well:

Her sword (or cleaver) and the severed head, both held by Kali, symbolize *the destruction of ignorance and the awakening to real knowledge.* The sword is the sword of knowledge that cuts Kleshas and frees the head or consciousness of the devotee from the delusions of Samsara.

Kali is often naked except for a skirt of severed arms or bones *because it is said that 'she is infinite and pure.'* Most deities are not shown naked, and as such she is called *Digambara,* meaning 'clad in space' (naked) because nothing can hide her infinite form.

The necklace of skulls or heads Kali that wears *symbolize the letters of the Sanskrit alphabet.* This indicates that Kali is the Ultimate Reality as the primal vibration **OM**.

The skull-top cup (Kapala) full of blood she often holds symbolizes the release of gnosis or true knowledge from human ignorance.

Her many skull-symbols or ornaments represent the illusion and transcendence of death which Kali embodies. Death and life are one continuum.

Her fangs and large lolling tongue are wild aspects of Kali and are unique to her. In her temples the extended tongue of her image is often daubed with the blood from animal sacrifices, the only goddess I know who has this done. This means she is like a wild tiger of the deep jungle: primal, unstoppable and without limits. In one famous myth, she unrolls her tongue to cover warring demons and swallows them all in one gulp!

Her long, flying, wild, black hair: She is the wildest Goddess, free of all limitations and subject to none, including her mate Shiva. Along with her nakedness, her fangs, tongue, wild unkept hair, and red hands and feet indicate she is utterly free from all restriction. In many ways this makes her the most powerful goddess of all.

Her Third Eye is open because she and Shiva are one; they are creator and destroyer. In fact, her blazing, open third eye and countenance reveal her to be primeval Nature, untamed. Under her third eye is often shown the three key symbols of sun, moon, and fire. She thus contains the Three Shaktis, and is a form of Adi Shakti, containing all things and all divine aspects.

The ferocious tiger is Kali's vehicle (Vahana). She is often shown with a tiger skin as a skirt or upon which she treads. Keep in mind that her mate Shiva is often shown wearing or sitting upon a tiger's skin, so close are the two deities.

### Offerings

**Colors:** Her colors are black or dark blue and deep red.

**Incense/Scent:**
Camphor
Red sandalwood
Jasmine, Rose

**Common Offerings:**
All Red flowers (hibiscus is often used)
Many fruits: apples, coconuts, papaya, etc.
Sweets
Rice
Lentils
Red Wine
Fiery Liquor
Fresh Meat

### Mantras

Kali's Bija Mantra is **Kreeng**

Kreeng Kreeng Kreeng Hum Hum Hreeng Hreeng Dakshine Kaliki, Kreeng Kreeng Kreeng, Hum Hum Hreeng Hreeng Svaha
Adya Kali Devata Svaha
Kreeng Hum Hum Svaha
Jai Kali Ma! [Yea Kali!]

## Yantras

*The Kali Yantra*

Kali's Yantra is likely the most ancient Yantra, a simple inverted triangle representing the vulva of the Great Mother. Primitive Kali Yantra carvings are found in prehistoric sites along with Yoni-Lingams. Kali is indeed ancient. The symbolism is obvious, but the three points of the Yoni (vulva) represent all the triplicities previously mentioned: the three Shaktis; Knowledge, Will and Action; the Sun, Moon and Fire; and so on. In the lineages I was initiated into, Kali Ma (Mother Kali) is the most powerful deity and the protector of all Tantrics and the lineages. She and Durga are the earliest goddess images found in the Harappan culture, often shown as a simple inverted triangle with a Bindu-point in the center. In fact, this simple image is found across cultures, and I have seen them in many countries. Often, she is just called MA, and the chant JAI MA is common at her festivals. The five lines framing the Yoni represent the five spiritual attributes of each human: the physical, life energy, the emotional condition, deep inner wisdom (gnosis), and a natural state of bliss.

## Festivals

**Kali Puja** is a famous festival that takes place in West Bengal in October or November. It goes on for about twenty days.

**Shyama Puja** originates from India and coincides with the big, global festival of lights, Diwali. Most honor Lakshmi at Diwali, but in some areas, it is Kali (Shyama) who is ritually honored.

**Dipanwita Kali Puja** is celebrated on the new moon in the Indian lunar month of Kartika (around October).

Since many Tantrics (including you dear reader), are likely not Indian, you may want to work with Kali on dark or new moons. This is traditional, and many Tantrics celebrate Kali festivals or Pujas on Dark Moon or New Moons.

In general, to keep things simple, I'd advise you to do Puja and honor Kali at dark or new moons, worship Lakshmi on full moons, and honor Lalita Tripurasundari as the crescent moon is waxing.

## Kali Nath Tantrika Puja

On the Zonule altar:

A candle, an incense burner for stick or powder incense, a cup of red wine or a red juice (such as pomegranate), a Yoni-Lingam, appropriate red flowers, a pipeful of cannabis (if legal), a sword or dagger, some camphor, and a few dark sticks of incense of your choice (myrrh is good). Also, have slips of paper and red pens or pencils to use in the rite.

Also on the altar is the Arti tray with offerings: some appropriate food such as sweets or fruit, like grapes; a small cup of the same liquid that is on the altar (wine or juice); a very small red candle; a red flower; and a separate stick of incense. (See the **Offerings** section above.) A small image or symbol of Kali should be added as well. The Kali Yantra should be laid flat before the image of the deity with the Arti tray placed on the Yantra. If desired, two candles of the appropriate color can be placed on either side of the deity image, and another side plate of food and drink may be placed before or near the altar.

### *Honoring Ganesh*

The priest/ess rings the bell 3x. All bow to Ganesh and chant:

OM GAANG GANAPATAYE NAMAH 3x

The altar candle is lit.

### *Banishing*

PHAT! [5x]

This is done to the four directions and to the center by all present. Lightning bolts are visualized, banishing all negative energy. The priest/ess rings the bell three times and raises *the sword of Kali* as all stand about it. All touch the sword hilt as it is raised, and together carefully and slowly rotate the sword, point out, counterclockwise about the circle, all chanting:

KALI MA!
Put to flight, put to flight
All demons and spirits
Who would hinder this rite!

SVAHA!

At the center everyone grasps or touches the sword handle as the sword is pointed down, and then touched to the ground in the center of the circle as all intone:

SHIVA HUM
So be it here
Let our vision
Become clear
OM. SVAHA!

The sword is then placed back on the altar before the image of Kali.

### Creating the Sacred Sphere

The priest/ess casts a circle with the trident, *or* all hold hands in a circle. All chant:

OM MANI PADME HUM [3x]

while envisioning the circle/sphere of light about all. All pause for a moment and visualize 4 tridents at the four directions and one in the center glowing with light and protective energy. All chant OM. The Temple is set.

### Honoring the Powers

All bow and all intone:

*OM Namaste! Honor to the Gods, the Spirits, the Ancestors, the Gurus and to All Wild Things That Play! OM to Shri Gurudev Dadaji Mahendranath and the Crystal Line of Tantric Gurus Whose Amrita and Power Helps Us Manifest True Knowledge, True Will, and True Action Through Our Guardian Spirits with Love! Guru OM! Svecchacharya!*

### "Mea Culpa"

All say:

*May any Errors We Make in this Ritual, any Slights, or any Negativity Generated be as Rain Striking the Ocean,*

*Dispersed, Forgiven and Forgotten. By Our Efforts May All Beings Attain Liberation and Joy! OM!*

### Purification (Devi)

Purify and bless the self with the power of Shakti Devi: Each adept blesses the three Body Centers/Gunas by placing a hand over each area in turn and visualizing light pouring into *Head, Heart and Loins/Base* as they invoke Devi with this Mantra:

HREENG SHREENG KREENG PARAMESHVARI SVAHA
[1x at each body center]

### Centering & Kusa/Sacrament (Deva)

A pipeful of Kusa (cannabis) is held on top of the Yoni-Lingam as all sit in a circle and vibrate OM. Then all chant:

OM NAMAH SHIVAYA! [108x]

as the Kusa is lit and passed clockwise around. All partake as they will, or hold up the smoking pipe and make offerings to Shiva if they don't wish to partake.

When done, offerings of pipe ashes are placed on the Yoni-Lingam, and each person dabs some on their forehead (third eye.)

### Preliminary Invocation of Deity

Incense and other candles are lit before the image of Kali Ma. All bow to the goddess. The bell is rung loudly 3x, and then all throw their hands in the air and yell:

JAI KALI MA! [3x]

Then all bow to Kali Ma and chant 3x:

HREENG SRIM KREENG
Let the circle ring
HREENG SRIM KREENG
Let the circle sing
HREENG SRIM KREENG
Let the circle bring
ADYA KALI DEVATA SVAHA!

## TANTRA FOR ALL

The priest/ess brings the empty offering bowl and the vessel of wine and hands it to one of the Kula (or, if solo, places it on the altar). Then a small amount of wine is poured into the bowl and the priest/ess raises it to the South and all say:

> In darkness we honor the ancestors and honored dead
> Bring blessings and understanding Kali Ma for they are of you!
> TARPAYAMI [giving offerings] NAMAH! SVAHA!

The priest/ess turns to the center with the offering vessel, and another person (if there are others) is given the vessel of wine and pours out a small amount into the offering bowl. The priest/ess then raises it to the North and all say:

> In darkness we honor the primal Earth Mother
> Bring blessings and understanding Kali Ma for you are all nature
> TARPAYAMI NAMAH! SVAHA!

The priest/ess turns to the center with the offering vessel, and another person (if there are others) is given the vessel of wine and pours out a small amount into the offering bowl. The priest/ess then raises it to the East and all say:

> In darkness we honor the starry Sky Spirits
> Bring blessings and understanding Kali Ma for you are the cosmos!
> TARPAYAMI NAMAH! SVAHA!

The priest/ess turns to the center with the offering vessel, and another person (if there are others) is given the vessel of wine and pours out a small amount into the offering bowl. The priest/ess then raises it to the West and all say:

> In darkness we honor the deep, dark spirits of the Primal Ocean
> Bring blessings and understanding Kali Ma for you are the endless sea
> TARPAYAMI NAMAH! SVAHA!

The priest/ess then takes the offering bowl with wine and places it before the image of Kali. All bow and say:

> We honor you, most ancient mother of all things
> Kalika Ma! By your many names we call you with our hearts

Shri Maha Kali, secret self, great teacher come!
Digambara, Maha Devi, Maha Shakti, Adya Kali, and by all your names—
Be here now! bring blessings and understanding
TARPAYAMI NAMAH! SVAHA!

All bow to Kali and all chant while clapping or stomping their feet:

KALI KALI KALI Some day we will die.
KALI KALI KALI We will let our ashes fly
KALI KALI KALI We will to be free
KALI KALI KALI We dance and become thee
KALI KALI KALI We own our death so clear
KALI KALI KALI Release us from all fear
KALI KALI KALI Dispel sorrow and pain
KALI KALI KALI Banish ills, bring gain
KALI KALI KALI From Samsara set us free
KALI KALI KALI By your love so may it be!
ADYA KALI DEVATA SVAHA! [3x]

### *Visualization Meditation*

All sit, get comfortable and slip into a meditation. When ready, all begin to do simple Pranayama as they visualize the Goddess Kali.

The priest/ess rings the bell and vibrates KREENG once.

As all enter deeper contemplation of Kali, the priest/ess quietly narrates the visualization script as all follow silently. (If you are doing this alone, record this script and listen to it as you meditate.)

You are in a dark forest at night
You hear all the jungle noises about you
You are robed in black and the path is lit by faint starlight
You are walking to the primal jungle shrine of Kali
You hear a deep low growling whisper… MA… MA… and the noises of many animals in the darkness
The smells are rich, earthy and exotic
Following a narrow path through the moist and dense jungle
You soon come to a rocky clearing…

Before you is a cave entrance, a cleft in black rock surrounded with hibiscus vines bearing red, fragrant flowers
You pick one flower and squeeze through the opening
The cave suddenly opens up to a womb-like cavern
There is a roughhewn stone circle surrounded by five torches
In the center is a small bonfire made of human bones
Behind it is an ancient, primitive image of the naked goddess Kali
It is decorated with strings of bones and anointed with blood
There is a bowl before the altar filled with ashes and blood
You take off your robes and toss them aside
You go to bonfire and the bowl and bow to the Kali statue
Silently honor her and ask permission to be blessed
You will feel acceptance, take a bit of blood from the bowl
Now anoint your forehead, heart and sex and as you silently vibrate KREENG! KREENG! KREENG!
Now, you and others begin to dance about the fire and the image in a counterclockwise circle... You hear drums and a rhythmic... MA... MA... MA...!
When you feel it is right, approach the image of Kali
And offer the flower you picked for her; place it on her head
You stare at her black, onyx eyes inset in the rough stone
Her third eye is a red ruby and emits a red ray which pierces your third eye and...everything dissolves
You hear a whisper... Maha Kali... the great darkness, the end of all
Time conquers all... death conquers all... she is all...
Suddenly you are in a vast cremation ground, surrounded by bones and burning bodies, smoking pyres and ashes
You are surrounded by terrifying ghosts and skeletons
Monsters and ghouls...and they all begin to dance about you
Howling and pounding skulls as drums!
Before you is Kali Ma in the flesh, naked, leading the dance!
Her skin glistens black as night, her skirt of bones is rattling, she wears a necklace of severed heads! Her long black hair is flying as she laughs as her long, red tongue extends through fangs!
She is smeared with ashes and blood, horrifying but beautiful

All fear dissolves from you and you howl and leap into the party
You dance with her and you embrace her *and accept all she is...*
Suddenly...darkness—then...
You are in outer space, surrounded by infinite stars!
The stars take shape... It is Kali—the darkness of space and the infinite stars are her body; she is beautiful and she embraces you.
Then Kali silently speaks to you:
Now you know... I am life and death and rebirth, all and nothing for I am eternity...your true being manifests all these things
You are eternal, a star beyond the dance of time, beyond the illusion of life, death or any part of Samsara
Remember...
And your third eye opens
And you know that the world
And all things
And all people
And all experiences
And all of life's temptations, horrors and pleasures
Are generated by you to teach yourself and liberate yourself
If you will it so with love
The decision is always yours, by the grace of Kali Ma
The infinite star goddess Kali embraces you with love
Now you descend from infinite stars and space...back into your body
You are in the Zonule, at peace, for you are loved by MA
You feel your third eye close as the visions disperse like smoke
Now you breathe deeply as you readjust to your body
But the Gnosis of Kali remains within you as truth.

The bell is rung 3x slowly as all breathe deeply and 'come back.' Together all softly chant:

JAI MA [3x]

# TANTRA FOR ALL

## *Empowerment of the Deity*

All chant together with Malas, and invite and empower the GODDESS KALI who is now glowing and manifesting within the image upon the altar, filling the Zonule with her love:

ADYA KALI DEVATA SVAHA! [108x]

Once chanting is done all begin clapping, banging rhythm sticks, or pounding drums while all chant. It is powerful as a 'call and response' with the priest/ess leading it:

KALI MA KALI MA
O great mother
Dance with us!
Black hair flying
KREENG KREENG KREENG
Bells on ankles ringing
KREENG KREENG KREENG
Bloody sword is flailing
KREENG KREENG KREENG
Wide mouth is laughing
KREENG KREENG KREENG
Severed head smiling
KREENG KREENG KREENG
Hand held up, dispelling fear
KREENG KREENG KREENG
Hand held out, offering bliss
KREENG KREENG KREENG
Eyes of burning fire
KREENG KREENG KREENG
Body naked filled with stars
KREENG KREENG KREENG
White skull necklace glowing
KREENG KREENG KREENG
Drums of Puja beating
KREENG KREENG KREENG
Dancing thunder lightning
KREENG KREENG KREENG
Piles of bodies burning

KREENG KREENG KREENG
Imps and corpses dancing
KREENG KREENG KREENG
Bloody mouth is howling
KREENG KREENG KREENG
Great Kalika mother
Lady of endings and release
Goddess of death
Mother of peace
Banish our ills
And what hinders our will!

The drumming stops and all shout:

JAI MA JAI MA JAI KALI MA!

All chant once:

KREENG KREENG KREENG HUM HUM HREENG HREENG DAKSHINEE KALIKI
KREENG KREENG KREENG, HUM HUM, HREENG HREENG SVAHA!

All then quietly say together:

Mother Kali we are your children
Hold us and protect us
Teach us and show us
Reveal to us the secrets
Great mother, grant us wisdom
So that we fear nothing
In the warm protection
Of your loving arms
ADYA KALI DEVATA SVAHA!

The bell is rung 3x and all bow to MA.

### *Magick Work (Optional)*

Note: the following spell is for addressing issues with the help of Kali. It may be done as a group with all focusing on one thing, or individually. For example, all could wish for protection from crime, poverty or illness; or for an endangered species like tigers, Kali's special animal. Another possibility is that each person can think of something they *personally* need protection from or something they want eliminated from their life, but without sharing this. This should be agreed upon ahead of the rite.

All sit in a circle, and the Kali Yantra is placed in the center with the offering bowl, partly filled with dark wine, set upon it. The camphor in the small bowl is brought out, and all contemplate the infinite power of Kali for a moment. The priest/ess rings the bell, takes up the camphor, and says:

> *Now we contemplate the illusions, troubles, problems, blockages, fears and sorrows we choose to banish, confront and remove. Kali Ma help us banish all our troubles, and release or destroy what needs to go! Help us accept what we must so we may learn and grow. She reveals that our perceived reality is Samsara—illusion—and so she helps us come to terms with the joys and horrors of life. She is our Great Mother who fiercely loves and protects us, her children. She helps us come to terms with the joys and pains of life in this material world, and shows us that there is a cosmic truth beyond this illusionary world. Jai Ma!*

The priest/ess begins the chant and all pick it up. He or she sprinkles a bit of camphor into the bowl of wine whispering:

JAI MA!

It is then passed around clockwise to all the participants in turn, and each person does the same: visualizing his or her magickal goal, sprinkling a bit of camphor in the wine, and whispering:

JAI MA!

When done, the bowl of camphor-wine is placed back on the Yantra and all hold their hands over the bowl, palms out, and visualize red energy projecting from the palms. All chant 3x together:

KREENG KREENG KREENG, HUM HUM, HREENG
   HREENG DAKSHINEE KALIKI
KREENG KREENG KREENG, HUM HUM HREENG
   HREENG SVAHA!

Then all hold up their hands and say together:

May ghosts clinging to life be released
May that which is clinging to pain be released
May all suffering and terror be released
May those seeking calm be given peace
May we live fully and die beautifully in the embrace of MA
Becoming the mirror of true understanding and liberation
TAT TVAM ASI! ['I am That'] JAI MA!

*Other Magick Work*

Following is a simple Kali magick rite for protection or pushback against those who would harm you. Kali Ma protects! You will need:

- A large Kali Yantra (about 2 feet or 60cm square) that can be hand-drawn or painted while continuously chanting her Bija Mantra KREENG. It is best to do so in the Zonule.
- A small metal or ceramic bowl atop a plate
- A small piece of camphor and a lighter
- Small pieces of natural paper upon which to write
- A red Mala (for Kali, a bone-bead Mala is great, but any will do)
- A red shirt, blouse or scarf to wear
- On the altar: Appropriate incense (see the **Offerings** section above), a cup of red wine, a red flower, fruit, and an image of Kali Ma, arranged as you wish.

Do the Zonule ritual as usual.

When ready, ring the bell, focus on Kali, and visualize her clearly. Offer her what you have brought. Center yourself and say:

KALI MA! Greatest Mother, Fierce Protector, Be Here With Me!
I Who Love You, Call On You At This Time Of Peril.
You Help Your Children, Please Help Me Now, OH MA!
KREENG KREENG KREENG HUM HUM HREENG
   HREENG DAKSHINE KALIKE
HUM HUM HREENG HREENG SVAHA!
Hear My Prayer.

Now, either out loud or silently, say a short, adlibbed prayer from your heart about the problem you face, and the solution you wish. Then bow, thank her, and say:

KREENG HUM HUM SVAHA! [3x]

In meditation, focus on what is troubling you—that is, what you need protection from or what you need to repel. If this is being done for another, meditate on their problem. Place the Kali Yantra before you, place the plate on the Yantra, then the bowl atop the plate, and the camphor in the bowl.

When you are deeply focused on the issue, write in red on the small slips of paper exactly what your goal is. Then murmur:

KREENG HUM HUM SVAHA [3x]

As you do so, feel the energy of Kali infuse the papers with power. Dip your finger in the wine, and sprinkle it on the altar, the papers, the three points of the Yantra, and about the circle as well. Say:

OM HREENG KREENG SVAHA [3x]

Visualize a circle of glowing red light about you.

Now, place your hand upon parts of your body while chanting KREENG each time and visualizing bright light flowing there. You are creating a simple Kavacha (magical 'armor') to protect and empower yourself. Touch, chant and empower the following: each foot, the genitals, each breast, the back, each hand, and the third eye/head. Visualize your body protected and glowing with this armor. End with:

KREENG HUM HUM SVAHA! [3x]

Now, take up your Mala in one hand, and the lighter in the other. Light the camphor as you begin chanting using the Mala:

OM HREENG KREENG SVAHA [108x]

As you do so, intensely visualize Kali dancing in the cremation ground where you both sit before a fire. Call to her, honor her, and ask for her help as you chant. When you feel her power fill you, take up the slips of paper and drop them into the small camphor fire, chanting louder. In your mind see Kali taking care of the problem!

Finish chanting, sit in meditation on Kali and let go. Continue sitting in meditation until the camphor fire burns out. When it is cool, take the ashes and put a bit on your head/third eye, hands, breasts, back, genitals and feet, visualizing her protection and love filling you.

Offer the last of the ashes to her on the Yoni-Lingam that sits before her image.

End by ringing the bell and chanting:

KREENG KREENG KREENG HUM HUM HREENG
HREENG DAKSHINE KALIKE
HUM HUM HREENG HREENG SVAHA!
KALI MA! Greatest Mother, Fierce Protector,
I Honor And Thank You For Your Help,
SHANTI SHANTI SHANTI!

Bow to her and see her depart after blessing you. Close the circle as you would any Zonule Ritual.

### *Offering to & Feeding the Deity*

The Kali Yantra is left in the center on the floor (or on a small table), and the Arti tray is placed upon it. The offering bowl of wine is placed before the image of Kali.

The Arti candle and incense are lit, and all bless the offerings with palms out by chanting while visualizing brilliant 'red energy' of love flowing into it.

HREENG SHREENG KREENG PARAMESHVARI SVAHA
[11x]

Thus, the food is charged and blessed and offered to Kali.

The priest/ess then raises the Arti tray and makes five circles in the air before the deity. During this, the deity is intensely visualized partaking of the essence and energy and offerings. All chant:

KREENG KREENG KREENG JAI KALI MA [5x]

Then the Arti tray is passed clockwise around the circle. Each person holds it up with eyes closed, presents the offerings, and communes with Kali Ma with great love and clear visualization, silently requesting the help they need.

While this happens, all in the circle not communing with the deity quietly chant KREENG over and over. Each person is given time to directly commune with the deity; there is no rush.

When the Arti tray returns to the altar, the bell is rung.

This is a time for a short, silent meditation on the experience. Pranayama may be done as all absorb the blessings of Kali After a time, the bell is rung! Kali is now with all present, and is a powerful and energetic presence in the room!

The bell is rung again.

### Communing with the Deity

The Arti tray is passed around, and all eat and drink some of the now-blessed food and drink (Prasad) and other food that has been around the altar. All may relax, laugh and chat, telling of their visions and experiences with Kali as they like.

Following this is a time for playing drums, banging rhythm sticks, shaking rattles, clapping, singing, laughing, chanting, dancing, telling stories, doing divination, and whatever else people want to do! All are infused with the divine power of the deity and may act as they please. More Kusa may be smoked, more food eaten, and so on. This is the time to 'party with the god' and it should be as wild, free and fun as possible.

This is also a good time to chat about what could be added or changed with the Puja for next time, setting the next Puja dates, assigning others to be the priest/ess, and so on. All are equal in the Kula circle!

When the merriment is done and the party ebbs, the priest/ess checks in with all to see if it is time to end. Everything is put away, hands are cleaned, and so on. Then all return to a meditative pose and the bell is rung.

### Farewell to the Deity

The priest/ess intones the following and all repeat line by line:

Honor to the Mother
Honor to the Teacher
Honor to the Initiator
BHADRA KALI, DIGAMBARA, SMASHAN KALI,

ADYA KALI, GREAT MAHA KALI!
We gratefully receive your teachings and blessings with joy
JAI KALI MA!

All chant the following as they visualize the deity depart to her celestial realm:

ADYA KALI DEVATA SVAHA [11x]

The bell is rung by the priest/ess 3x.

### *Ending & Dedications*

With hands raised, all chant together the four Purusarthas (universal blessings), while sending blessings from the Puja to all beings:

Balance, Wealth, Pleasure and Liberation to All Beings!

The bell is rung 3x, then all shout:

The Will To Love Is The Law To Live!
OM SHANTI SHIVA SHAKTI [3x]

All bow to the deity and all candles are blown out. Banish as at the beginning. All stand and do:

PHAT! [toward each of the 4 directions and the center]

All touch the Earth and offer any leftover energies to the Earth Mother:

BHU DEVI—To You From You All Things! OM!

Puja is done! The offering bowl with wine and camphor in it is carefully taken outside and poured out by a tree or on the earth with a silent prayer to MA. All help clean up the temple and maybe a group hug.

# APPENDICES

# GLOSSARY

This Glossary explains many of the Sanskrit terms used in this book. The definitions are derived from several sources, many of which are part of the Nath Tantric Lineage.

This Glossary is much indebted to my brother, the late Shambalanath, and to the work of many other brother and sister Tantrics. I am especially thankful for the many works of Nath Guru Shri Lokanath. For those interested, a more complete Tantric Glossary can be found at *shivashakti.com*.

## A

**Adi.** Supreme. Primordial.

**Adi-Nath.** Sub-sect of the Nath line. Consciousness; awareness itself. A title of Shiva.

**Adi Shakti.** Primordial Power, the supreme form of the Goddess.

**Agama (Agamic).** The tradition of the Tantrics and Kaula, as opposed to that of the orthodox or Aryans known as *Veda*.

**Agamas.** Tantric scriptures dealing with rites, Dharma and cosmology.

**Aksamala.** A Mala of 108 Rudraksha beads.

**Aloka.** 'Invisible.' The spiritual world; the 'astral plane.'

**Amrita.** That which is immortal. Nectar of the Gods that gives immortality; charged sexual fluids.

**Ananda.** Bliss. Joy.

**Aryan invasion.** The migration of Indo-European tribes into what is now India, bringing what became known as Vedic traditions, scriptures and religions that overlay the indigenous Agamic or 'Dravidian' cultures known as Tantric.

**Asana.** Symbolic and/or magickal body postures, often seen in Hatha Yoga.

**Asuras.** Anti-gods, 'demons' or other sets of gods, often earlier gods. Naga are sometimes classified as such, but are usually seen as a separate species of demigod.

**Atman.** The highest or true self as distinct from consciousness or ego. Shiva embodied. Some connect it with the Spirit, Soul or Guardian Spirit.

**Avatar(a).** Incarnation of a God or Goddess into a human or animal form.

# B

**Bhang.** A drink made with cannabis, imbibed ritually and during festivals like Shivaratri.

**Bhogavati.** This is the great 'land of pleasure' where the Naga dwell.

**Bindu.** The point without a center from which proceeds Cosmic Sound (Nada). Drop. Dot. Semen.

**Bija.** A 'root' or 'seed' sound or syllable of a Mantra. It can also mean sperm, or point of light (Atman). The male Bija Mantras in this book and their related gods are as follows:

OM: Shiva (Atman, the origin of all things).
HREENG: The Goddess Shakti, Lalita or Tripura, the youthful Goddess.
SRIM: The Goddess Lakshmi, Maha Devi, The Mother.
KREENG: The Goddess Kali, the crone.
PUUH: Naga Bija.
AIM: The Goddess Sarasvati.
DUM: The Goddess Durga.
There are others, of course.

**Bon Po.** Pre-Buddhist Tibetan shamanic religion and practices.

**Brahma.** In Hinduism, Brahma is the creator of the Cosmos.

**Brahmin.** In Hinduism, one who knows Brahma as the Absolute.

## C

**Chakra.** Circle or wheel, often applied to the diagrams or Yantras used in ritual worship, or to centers of spirituality within or without the body Lotus. A center of energy. A place of worship.

**Chandra.** The Moon and Mood God.

**Chela.** Pupil of a Guru.

## D

**Dakke.** A slim, hand-held drum with two drumheads, one on either end. Similar to the more famous Damaru.

**Damaru.** An hourglass-shaped, hand-held drum with two drum heads, one on either end. It is played by rotating it side to side as knotted cords hit the skins. It is a symbol of Shiva.

**Darshan.** Vision. Direct experience of spiritual energies and forces.

**Deva(s) (or Dev).** God(s). Shining ones. Maha (great) Deva is Shiva.

**Devanagari.** Spoken Sanskrit. Sanskrit is an ancient written language used in several spoken languages in India. This relates to the 'English' sacred names in this book; what you see is a way that approximates how the Sanskrit is spoken. Many phonemes or sounds are found in India that are not in English; thus, the different (English) spellings of some names are words. Pooja, Puja, Pujah is an example.

**Devi.** Goddess or Shakti. There are said to be 33,000,000 Devis, but all are aspects of one primordial Goddess.

**Dhanvantari.** God of healing.

**Dhuni.** Sacred 'fire'. It only smolders. Made of wood or cow dung. Of non-Vedic origin. Usually circular (Yoni image) used in Tantric rituals.

**Dhyana.** Meditation. Bliss Consciousness.

**Diksha.** Empowerment. Initiation-blessing.

**Dragon Seat.** The center of a Zonule or power-zone. The Dragon Seat is the place a Sadhaka sits to do magick.

# E

**The Eight Naga Kings.** There are said to be Eight (sometimes Nine) Great Naga Kings. This concept is found in India, Southeast Asia, and China where Naga are called Dragons and the eight Naga Lords are called Dragon Lords. They are often connected with the eight trigrams. One of the three Naga Kings is Vasuki Naga who hangs around Shiva's neck and gives him wisdom.

# F

**Flower Arrows.** The five senses.

# G

**Gam.** The Bija Mantra of Ganesh. Pronounced 'Gaang.'

**Gana.** A wild spirit, akin to a satyr or bacchante, roaming the wilderness, having revels; a kind of wild tribe of entities that cavort at the base of Mt. Kailash where Shiva & Shakti preside. Their leader is the Lord of Ganas, Ganapati (Ganesh).

**Ganesh (or Ganesha or Ganapati or Vinayaka).** The marvelous elephant-headed God of giving and removing 'obstacles,' Lord of Categories and the beginning of all things, he was at the creation and he is invoked before any and all Tantric or Hindu rituals.

**Garuda.** Garuda is the giant, golden bird-demi-god and is the mount (and Vahana) of Vishnu.

**Gayatri.** Gayatri is the name for a Sanskrit poetical meter that contains three lines of eight syllables each. There are, therefore, many Gayatri Mantras, but *the* Gayatri (named after the Goddess of the same name) is the oldest.

**Goad.** Represents repulsion or driving away.

**Guna.** Quality or trait. There are three: Rajas—active; Tamas—passive; and Sattvas—the balance of Rajas and Tamas. They are often represented by fire, sun and moon, respectively.

**Guru.** 'The Dispeller of Ignorance.' A guide; spiritual mentor. One who brings Light from Darkness. Also, can refer to one's Guardian Spirit or Higher Self.

## H

**Halahala.** The cosmic poison created when the gods and demons churned the primal ocean of milk (stars) using the Great Naga Nila (Vasuki) as a spindle. Shiva saved the world by drinking the poison, turning his neck (and body) blue (Nila).

**Harappan Civilization.** An ancient civilization existing in what is now India and Pakistan and the source for the roots of Tantra. It existed ca. 3300–1300 BCE in the Indus Valley. The Indus Valley Civilization is also known as the Harappan Civilization, named after Harappa, the first of the sites to be excavated in the 1920s. This discovery was soon followed by the famous Mohenjo-Daro where cylinder seals depicting Naga and horned Shiva were found.

**Hatha Yoga.** (See Yoga.) 'Sun-Moon Yoga'. Exercises for better physical health.

**HRIM.** A Mantra of Maya Shakti, Lalita Devi. Pronounced 'Hreeng.'

## I

**Iccha Shakti.** The Shakti or Energy of Will. (See Shaktis.)

**Ida.** The feminine, lunar Nadi (pathway) moving up the left side of the body opposite the Pingala Nadi. Together they entwine and rise up and through the central Sushumna Nadi (spinal path), uniting as Kundalini.

**Indus Valley Civilization.** (See Harappan Civilization.)

## J

**Japa(m).** Repetition of a Mantra. Often Japa indicates that it is done very quietly.

**Ji.** Honorable. Often tagged at the end, for example, Nagaji.

**Jnana.** Knowledge.

**Jnana Shakti.** The Shakti or Energy of Knowledge. (See Shaktis.)

# K

**Kali (or Kala).** Time, star, a ray, essence or emanation.

**Kali.** (Devi) Goddess of Time; also, black. Greatest Mother Goddess of ancient India. Presiding Goddess of the Naths.

**Kailash (or Kailasa).** The holy mountain (also called Meru) upon which Shiva and Shakti reside. It is the World Mountain, the Axis Mundi of the cosmos. It is also the Shri Yantra in full (three-dimensional) form. It is a great mystery of Tantra.

**Kalpa.** (See also Yuga.) An age in Hindu mythology, often lasting thousands of years. After each age, Shive destroys the universe and a new Eon begins. We are currently in the Kali Yuga.

**Kama.** God of erotic love, lust, sexuality.

**Kamandalu.** A metal open pot used for water; a sign of a Sadhu; also, an important symbol of Shiva.

**Kartikkeya (or Skanda or Murugan or Subrahmana).** A son of Shiva. His Vahana is a cockerel, and he is a God of war.

**Kashi.** (See Varanasi.)

**Kaula.** A Tantric. Also, a knower of Kali/Kala. The perfect assimilation within oneself of the three Shaktis represented by the powers of Sun and Moon and Fire. Symbol: an eclipse.

**Kavacha.** A protective amulet. Armor. A practice of armoring oneself or another magickly.

**Kleshas.** The five Knots that cause pain: Ignorance, Ego, Repulsion, Attachment and Clinging to Life (Fear of Death). Tantrics seek to 'pierce' the Kleshas to attain liberation.

**Krim.** Bija Mantra of Kali. Pronounced 'Kreeng.'

**Krishna.** In Hinduism he is 'The Black One'; the eighth incarnation of Vishnu. A playful and popular fertility God.

**Kriya.** 'Action.' In this book, it roughly means Active Magick, that is, the manifesting of Will through Love in the sense of working with powers and energies of a spiritual nature to accomplish goals (such as illumination), or practical work (such as increasing fertility, causing rain, and so on).

**Kriya Shakti.** The Energy or Shakti of Action or Power.

**Kula.** 'Clan,' Shakti or Energy. A family or cluster of Kali's Shaktis: some build, some maintain, and some withdraw.

**Kumkum.** Red sandalwood powder.

**Kundalini (or Kundulini).** The 'fire snake' supposedly at the base of the spine (Kunda). Really, a term for the balanced, bioelectric energy of the whole person, focused and manifested through love and will via the nervous system, the 'snakelike' bundling of which runs through the spinal column. Kundulini is the supreme 'serpent goddess' energy that is the sum total of our spiritual energy. For millennia it has been seen as a fiery serpent that resides in the base Chakra of our body, and through spiritual energetic exercises, rises to the crown. When successful, one attains Nirvana. Tripura Devi (Maha Shakti) is the deity form of Kundalini.

**Kundalini Devi.** (See also Tripurasundari and Lalita.) The supreme Red Goddess, Lalita Tripurasundari, sometimes seen as The Great Naga deity form.

**Kusa.** A sacred grass native to India. It is recommended for use in certain ceremonies. In some rites it is a code for cannabis, an herb sacred to Shiva.

# L

**Lalita.** (See also Tripurasundari.) Youthful, beautiful, sexual aspect of Shakti. Collective form of the three Shaktis of Shiva: Will, Knowledge, Action. She is often described as Lila, or the Play of the cosmos. She is Mahamaya, the goddess of the illusion that is the world.

**Linga(m).** Phallus; image of the male genital organ. The special symbol of Shiva. The stone (etc.) Lingam set within the Yoni (vulva) of Shakti is present in most Tantric and Hindu rituals and can be found at almost every Shiva shrine.

# M

**Maha.** 'Great.'

**Mahadeva.** 'Great God'; that is, Shiva.

**Mahadevi.** 'The Great Goddess'; that is, Shakti (all aspects of the Goddess as One).

**Maithuna.** Ritual sexual intercourse.

**Mala.** Prayer beads used in Sadhana and Mantra work. It is a string of beads (rosary), usually 108 beads (representing the stars about us), counted as one does Mantra.

**Mani.** Sacred magick 'stone,' symbol of the Atman or Spirit. It is both a magickal and spiritual symbol, and at times material. The Wish Fulfilling gem is a common mythic theme in sacred texts.

**Mandala.** A magick circle or symbol, used more in Buddhism as a focus of meditation, often put upright.

**Mantra (or Mantram).** Words with inherent power. A sacred power, vibration; a God or Goddess in sound form. The ultimate Mantra is OM, source of all.

**Maya.** The world which is illusion; the power by which the universe becomes manifest; the illusion we manifest as the world.

**Meru.** (See Kailash.) Mt. Meru, home to Shiva and Shakti.

**Mohenjo-Daro.** (See Harappan Civilization.)

**Moksha.** Ultimate spiritual liberation from material bondage. One of the four duties of a human. The others are Dharma, Artha and Kama.

**Mudra.** Symbolic and/or magickal gestures, usually with the hand.

**Mukti.** (See also Moksha.) Liberation.

**Murti.** Sacred Image, usually of a God or Goddess.

# N

**Nada(m).** Vibrational energy which pervades all things. It manifests as sound. Described as 'a sound beyond sound.'

**Nadi.** 'River.' Current or channel of bio-electric energy. Flows or 'streams' of Prana/energy that travel via passages up the body.

**Naga.** 'One who slithers on the ground'; 'one without legs.' Naga also means 'serpent,' but usually refers to the demigods which may appear as a snake, a human or a combination of the two. Naga are part divine, and this makes them unique in the spiritual universe of Tantra and Hinduism. Many royal lineages in Asia trace themselves to ancient, human-Naga matings.

**Nagi (or Nagini).** A female Naga spirit ('Naga' may generically refer to one or many serpent spirits of different sexes). Often mentioned in reference to Shiva (Naga) and Shakti (Nagi).

**Namah.** 'Salutations!'

**Narada.** A Hindu saint who authored many beautiful hymns.

**Nataraja.** Dancing form of Shiva, Creating and Destroying the Universe, surrounded by a nimbus of fire.

**Nath(a).** Nath: Lord, Master; Natha: Mistress. One who follows his/her True Will, an initiate of a Nath Tantric lineage. One who gives equal importance to the three energies within: Lunar (intellect), Solar (emotions), and Fire (bodily sensations). The Naths are an ancient Indian and Nepalese cult of Tantra Magick; there are many branches. This book is based on one branch, Nath Tantrika.

**Nilakantha.** Name of blue-throated Shiva.

**Nitya.** A 'digit' or period of time, essentially one day in a lunar cycle. A Nitya is also a Goddess of that digit. All of this is associated with the Kalas (emanations of the 15 digits) of Lalita Tripurasundari, and these are the 15 Nityas or emanations from her during the 15 days from new moon to full moon.

**Noose.** Represents attachment or attracting/attraction.

**Nyasa.** 'Applying' drawn energy for a purpose—such as transferring power to a candidate during initiation, or to someone in need of healing.

# O

# P

**Pada.** 'Feet.'

**Padma.** 'Lotus.' Symbol of Yoni.

**Padukam.** Sandals, symbolizing the feet of the Guru or Guardian Spirit. Blessing or honoring these is in fact an offering to the 'feet' of a Guru or deity, a way of honoring or offering devotion.

**Pancha.** 'Five.'

**Panchamrita.** A traditional mixture of ghee, milk (or cream), milk curds (or yoghurt), sugar and honey offered in Puja to several gods and goddesses.

**Panchatattva.** The five elements: Earth, Air, Fire, Water and Spirit. Also, other sacred '5s', like the Tantric five sacred items: fish, meat, grain, sexual union, wine.

**Pashu.** Animal or animal nature. Literally 'a beast'—in Tantra, not all bad!

**Pashupati.** Lord of the Wild Beasts; an ancient title of Shiva from Harappan sites. He is shown with bull horns.

**Phat!.** 'Crack!' The Thunderbolt Mantra. Used to drive off negative energy or spirits. The index and middle fingers should be extended. Then the palm of the other hand is struck hard: *Crack!* while the Mantra is yelled. (It sounds like PADT!)

**Pingala.** The male, solar Nadi (pathway) moving up the right side of the body opposite the Ida Nadi. Together they entwine and rise up and through the central Sushumna Nadi (spinal path), uniting as Kundalini.

**Prakriti.** Universal Life Force, materialized nature. It is the basis of the three Gunas or states of matter.

**Prana.** The body's energy or spirit. It is moved and focused via breath.

**Pranayama.** Rhythmic breathing in a prescribed fashion, used in meditation and other Sadhana practices to direct body energies, still the emotions, center the mind, and so on.

**Prasad.** A blessed offering, often of food from a Puja, that is eaten by worshippers to gain divine blessing. Also 'peace.'

**Puja.** 'Magick ritual.' Worship. A ritual of honoring a deity.

**Purana.** 'Ancient.' A Hindu class of Sanskrit scriptures concerning Brahma, Vishnu and Shiva. There are 18 Puranas.

**Purnima.** Full Moon, often indicating a special festival. For example, Guru Purnima (usually in July) is a big festival where Gurus or sacred teachers are honored. In Tantra, this is often a day for initiating new Tantrics and honoring the Gurus of the Lineage.

# Q

# R

**Rajas.** Guna of activity. Indicates power-in-action. Associated with red and energy; it also is connected with menstrual blood.

**Raksha.** 'Protection.'

**Rasa.** The elixir in Alchemy. 'Liquid.' 'Mercury.' 'Sperm.' Rasa Yoga can refer to Tantric Alchemy.

**Ravana.** The mighty Demon of the Ramayana who was conquered by Rama and Hanuman.

**Rishi.** A Seer. Sage. Maharishi means Great Sage.

**Ropna.** 'Healing.'

**Rudraksha.** Named for Rudra, an ancient form of what later became Shiva, meaning red, howling. Rudraksh is a tree and the seeds are beads sacred to Shiva, often used in a Mala.

# S

**Sadhaka.** A practitioner of Sadhana. An adept of Magick. A serious Tantric who practices.

**Sadhana.** 'Direct way.' The regular practice of Magick or other spiritual work. A spiritual practice within the Tantric or Hindu tradition. Sadhana is often a regular spiritual practice leading to enlightenment, or for a specific goal.

**Sadhu.** 'Holy man.'

**Sahaja.** 'Spontaneous.' 'Naturally born together.' Letting illumination arise naturally without restrictions.

**Samadhi.** Complete contemplation where the mind and soul attain one. Bliss.

**Samagri.** Tools or items used in Sadhana or Puja.

**Sampradaya.** Lineage. Tradition. Sect history of important Gurus.

**Samsara.** The world of illusion (reality) where we repeat cycles of birth, suffering, death and rebirth, all involving karma.

**Sannyasin.** An ascetic Tantric or Hindu who has renounced the world, abandoning society and all mundane things.

**Shakti.** Power. Energy. Primordial essence. The Goddess. Life Energy. Great Mother of All. Shiva is Shakti as Shakti is Shiva.

**Shaktis (three).** Three primal energies which create diversity in the cosmos: Knowledge, Will and Action.

**Shanti.** Peace. Tranquility. Often repeated three times after a prayer.

**Shastra.** Compendium or collection of knowledge.

**Shav(a).** Corpse. "Shiva is Shava without Shakti."

**Shiva.** Blessed One, Lord of the center, pure consciousness. Shiva possesses three Shaktis or Powers: Iccha (Will), Jnana (Knowledge), and Kriya (Action).

**Shivalingam.** (See Yoni-Lingam.)

**Shloka.** Short, sacred verse.

**Shri.** Auspicious. Holy. Beauty. Awesome.

**Shri Yantra.** The 'great' Yantra, two-dimensional form of the Supreme Goddess which, when depicted in three dimensions, is the body, the Chakras and Mt. Meru.

**Srim.** A Bija Mantra of Maha Devi (Lakshmi), also known as Shri. Pronounced 'Shreeng.'

**Siddha.** An adept or enlightened being. One who possesses Siddhis.

**Siddhi.** Magickal or spiritual powers.

**Smashan.** Cremation ground, which is often associated with Kali.

**Soma.** Nectar of Ecstasy, possibly derived from psychoactive plants. Also, a lunar God. Mentioned in the Vedas.

**Stele.** A stone or wooden slab, generally taller than it is wide, erected as a monument. Ornamentation may be inscribed, carved in relief, or painted onto the slab.

**Stotram.** A prayer or hymn to a God or Goddess or other divine being.

**Surya.** The Sun God.

**Sushumna (or Shushuma).** Main Nadi (pathway of energy). It runs vertically through the spine. This is the 'path' of the Kundalini. (See Ida and Pingala.)

**Sutra.** 'Thread.' An aphorism. One of many books of aphorism, collected wisdom, commentaries, and so on.

**Svaha.** 'Hail!' or 'So be it!'; used in Mantras as greeting or honoring.

**Sveccharchara (or Svecchacharya).** The path of doing one's own Will with Love; a powerful term that connotes the Tantric path, similar to 'Thelema' in Western magickal concept.

# T

**Tamas.** Guna of rest, passivity.

**Tankas.** Banners, often Tibetan or Nepalese, often showing Gods or Buddhas.

**Tantra.** A system of spiritual beliefs and practices said to be derived from Sanskrit roots signifying: 'Body' (because of its emphasis on bodily activities); 'Stretch' (because it extends the faculties of humans); 'Rope' (because it secures the devotee to deity); 'Harp' (for the music and beauty of its philosophy); 'Interior-ness' (for the secrecy of its doctrine); 'To Weave' or 'Loom' suggesting the two cosmic principles, male and female, that make up the warp and woof of the woven fabric of the universe. Also, a Tantra is a book of wisdom and magick offering instructions on the system of Tantra, or the art of doing these things in a magickal context; i.e., Tantric Sadhana.

**Tantrika.** The practice, art or lifestyle of being and doing Tantra. It can also mean a practitioner of Tantra, but in this book, it is used to indicate the esoteric initiatory tradition as a whole.

**Tarpayami.** Oblations. The pouring of sacred water (or divine energy) as an offering.

**Tika.** A mark placed on the third eye (forehead) as a blessing. It imitates the open third eye of Shiva.

**Tripura.** 'Three Cities.' A Form of Lalita. Her three cities are her Shaktis or Powers.

**Tripurasundari.** (See also Lalita.) The Triple Goddess, composed of Bala (the young virgin), Sundari (the mother of the universe), and Bhairavi (the crone). Shri Lalita Tripurasundari is also a personification of Kundalini, and in the Tantric system, can often be seen as the pervasive Power inherent in all things (Shakti).

**Trishul (or Trishula).** 'Trident.' This is the key weapon and holy symbol of the God Shiva, and is said to have been used to sever the original head of Ganesha. Durga also holds Trishula, along with many other weapons as do many deities. The three points have various meanings and have many stories behind them. They are commonly said to represent various trinities: creation, maintenance and destruction; past, present and future; the three Gunas; and so on. The Trishula is said to destroy the three worlds, a mythos that encompasses many different concepts. The three cities or worlds are said to be 'destroyed' by Shiva into a single non-dual plane of existence that is bliss alone. In the human body, the

Trishul can represent the three main Nadis, or energy channels (Ida, Pingala and Shushuma) running up the body and meeting at the brow. Shushuma, the central channel, continues upward through the spine and channels Kundalini.

**Turmeric.** A yellow spice originating in India. It has many medicinal uses, and is used in offerings—especially for Naga—often along with milk.

## U

**Urvara.** 'Fertility.'

## V

**Vajra.** Adamantine. A lightning bolt. In the Nath tradition it means 'that which survives all.' The Alpha Ovule. Shiva. A double trident. It signifies the human body. As a tool, it is a wand that has three prongs at either end.

**Vahana.** Animal 'vehicle' or aspect of a deity. The Vahana of Shiva is the bull, Nandi.

**Varanasi.** (Ancient name: Kashi.) The most sacred holy city in India, site of many ancient, prehistoric temples and holy places. It is holy to Shiva especially, and contains the most venerated Shiva Temple in India and so much more.

**Vedas.** The core religious texts of Hinduism. They also influenced Buddhism, Jainism and Sikhism. There are four Vedas: *Rig Veda, Sama Veda, Yajur Veda,* and *Atharva Veda.* The *Rig Veda,* the oldest, was created circa 1500 BCE., and codified circa 600 BCE. Often connected with the Indo-European invasion and the injection of this culture into India, they are coexistent with other scriptures and practices, such as Tantras.

**Vedic.** The two main streams that inform 'Hinduism' can be seen as Vedic (originating with the *Vedas)* and Agamic (originating outside of the Vedic flow, from the *Agamas*—non-Vedic sources). Agamic informs Tantra and 'folk religious' traditions like Naga Sadhana.

**Vidya.** 'Knowledge.' One could compare it to Gnosis, or direct knowledge of the divine. Also 'Female Mantra' or Goddess in the form of sound, as in the Shri Vidya (Magick of Lalita).

**Vira.** 'Hero.' An initiate or aspirant for higher, spiritual life. One who strives on the path of Tantra.

**Vitta.** 'Wealth.'

## W

## X

## Y

**Yakshis (or Yaksha).** A Tree spirit or demigod.

**Yantra.** An energized glyph or symbol. It looks like a Mandala and is said to have a life of its own. Devi in geometrical or patterned form. It is referred to at times as a kind of 'magick machine' or 'generator' of magick. Every God or Goddess has a Yantra. Yantras, unlike Mandalas, are used flat on the ground. The centerpoint (Bindu) of every Yantra is Shiva, and the circular or flower-like image about it is a form of Shakti. During Puja, the deity manifests in the center of the Yantra.

**Yoga.** 'Union,' 'Yoke.' The transformation of the mind/body through spiritual activity leading to higher levels of divinity. There are many kinds of Sadhana that help the Sadhaka (Yogi) attain illumination. Shiva is the Mahayogi, the creator of Yoga.

**Yogi.** One who has mastered himself and controls his senses.

**Yoni.** Female sexual organ or a representation thereof. Every Lingam has as its base a Yoni.

**Yoni-Lingam.** One of the most ancient religious symbols in the world. Yoni-Lingams were found in Harappan sites and are thousands of years old. A Yoni-Lingam is often carved in stone and forms an image of a Yoni (vulva) and a Lingam (phallus) joined together, the phallus standing atop the vulva-base. As such they are venerated as the creation of the universe as well as the creation of life. While it is obviously a fertility symbol, its meaning goes far deeper. It represents the primal god Shiva uniting with the primal Goddess Shakti.

**Yuga.** (See Kalpa.)

# Z

**Zonule.** A small zone of magick. A Tantric power area or private Tantric temple. Also, a circle of Tantrics (Kula) who generate such a zone.

# BIBLIOGRAPHY

## Publications

AMOOKOS. *Tantra Magick*. Mandrake of Oxford, 1990.

Arguelles, Jose & Arguelles, Miriam. *Mandala*. Shambhala Publications, 1974.

Bae, James H. *Ganesh*. Jaico Publishing House, 2013.

Bandyopadhyay, Pranab. *Tantra, Occultism and Spirituality*. Firma KLM private Limited, 1994.

Camphausen, Rufus C. *The Yoni*. Inner Traditions, 1996.

Carroll, Cain & Carroll, Revital. *Mudras of India*. Singing Dragon, 2012.

Chawdhri, L.R. *Secrets of Yantra, Mantra and Tantra*. Sterling Publishers Pvt. Ltd, 1992.

Colaabavala, Capt. F.D. *Tantra, the Erotic Cult*. Vision Books, 1983.

Dallapiccola, Anna L. *Dictionary of Hindu Lore and Legend*. Thames & Hudson, 2002.

Daniélou, Alain. *Shiva and Dionysus*. Inner Traditions, 1984.

— *Shiva and the Primordial Tradition*. Simon and Schuster, 2006.

— *The Myths and Gods of India*. Motilal Banarsidass, 2017.

— *While the Gods Play*. Inner Traditions/Bear & Co, 1987.

Dwivedi, Bhojraj. *Yantra Mantra Tantra and Occult Sciences*. Diamond Pocket Books Pvt. Ltd., 2016.

Dye, Joseph. *Ways to Shiva*. Philadelphia Museum of Art, 1980.

Fouce, Paula & Denise Tomecko. *Shiva*. White Orchid Books, 1996.

Fries, Jan. *Kali Kaula*. Avalonia, 2010.

Grimes, John A. *Ganapati*. SUNY Press, 1995.

Gupta, Shakti M. *Shiva*. Nataraj Publishing, 1993.

Harding, Elizabeth U. *Kali*. Nicolas-Hays, Inc., 1993.

Jansen, Eva Rudy. *The Book of Hindu Imagery*. Binkey Kok, 1993.

Johari, Harish. *Tools for Tantra*. Simon and Schuster, 1988.

Karcher, Steven & Ritsems, Rudolf. *I Ching: The Classic Chinese Oracle of Change*. Element Books, 1994.

Khanna, Madhu. *Yantra*. Inner Traditions, 2003.

Kinsley, David R. *Tantric Visions of the Divine Feminine*. Motilal Banarsidass Publ., 1998.

Magee, Mike. *Kali Magic*. Twisted Trunk Publishers, 2022.

— *Yaksini Magic*. Twisted Trunk Publishers, 2020.

Mahendranath, Shri Gurudev Dadaji. *The Amoral Way of Wizardry*. Tryckt I Sverige Publishing, 1985.

Misra, Munindra. *Lalita Sahasranama*. Osmora Incorporated, 2018.

Mookerjee, Ajit. *Kali*. Brill Archive, 1988.

— *Kundalini*. Destiny Books, 1981.

Mookerjee, Ajit, & Madhu Khanna. *The Tantric Way*. Thames & Hudson, 1977.

Morgan, Mogg. *Tantra Sadhana*. Mandrake of Oxford, 2008.

Muktananda, Swami. *The Nectar of Chanting*. SYDA Foundation, 1978.

— *Shree Guru Gita*. SYDA Foundation, 1981.

Namboodiri, N.M. (Author), Dev, K.V. (Editor), T.V. Narayana Menon. *The Thousand Names of the Divine Mother: Shri Lalita Sahasranama*. MA Center, 2015.

Odier, Daniel. *Yoga Spandakarika*. Simon and Schuster, 2005.

O'Flaherty, Wendy Doniger. *Siva*. Oxford University Press, 1981.

Pattanaik, Devdutt. *99 Thoughts on Ganesha*. Jaico Publishing House, 2015.

— *Devi, the Mother-Goddess*. Vakils Feffer & Simons Limited, 2000.

— *The Goddess in India*. Inner Traditions/Bear & Co, 2000.

Peters, Gregory. *Yogini Magic*. The Original Falcon Press, 2022.

Power, John. *Rainbow Bridge: Shakta Tantra of the Uttarakaulas*. Mandrake of Oxford, 2020.

— *The Nu Tantras of the Uttarakaulas*. Phoenix Publications Chelmsford, 2011.

— *Uttarakuru*. Phoenix Publications Chelmsford, 2015.

— *Uttarakuru and the Return of the Goddess*. Phoenix Publications Chelmsford, 2016.

— *Uttarakuru and the Return of the Goddess*. Phoenix of Chelmsford, 2016.

— *The Nu Tantras of the Uttarakaulas*. Phoenix Publications, 2011.

Rawson, Philip. *Tantra*. Bounty Books, 1973.

— *The Art of Tantra*. Thames & Hudson, 1978.

Saraswati, Swami Satyananda. *Kali Puja*. Sunstar Publishing, 2004.

Sargent, Denny. *Clean Sweep*, Red Wheel/Weiser Publishing, 2007.

— *Global Ritualism,* Llewellyn Worldwide, 1994.

— *Naga Magick*. The Original Falcon Press, 2014.

— *The Tao of Birth Days*. Tuttle Pub, 2000.

— *Werewolf Magick,* Llewellyn Worldwide, 2020.

— *Werewolf Pack Magick,* Llewellyn Worldwide, 2022.

Satguru, Sri. *A Glossary of Tantra, Mantra and Yantra*. Shri Garib Das Series. Sri Satguru Publications, 1995.

Storl, Wolf-Dieter. *Shiva*. Simon and Schuster, 2004.

Sinha, Indra. *The Great Book of Tantra*. Destiny Books, 1993.

Vanamali. *Shakti*. Simon and Schuster, 2008.

Woodroffe, Sir John. *Hymns to the Goddess and Hymn to Kali*. DK Printworld (P) Ltd, 2019.

— *Kularnava Tantra*. Motilal Banarsidass, 2010.

— *Mahanirvana Tantra*. Nuvision Publications, 2007.

— *Principles of Tantra*. Motilal Banarsidass, 2014.

— *Sakti and Sakta*. CreateSpace, 2017.

— *Tantrarāja Tantra*. Ganesh and Company, 1964.

Woodroffe, Sir John & Avalon, Arthur. *The Serpent Power*. Courier Corporation, 1974.

— *The Garland of Letters*. Classic Wisdom Reprint, 2019.

— *Tantra of the Great Liberation* [Mahanirvana Tantra]. Martino Fine Books, 2012.

## Important Tantric Websites

*Shiva Shakti Mandalam shivashakti.com*

*The International Nath Order internationalnathorder.org*

## Important Tantric Groups

*Uttarakaula 2=[+1]+[-1]*
 *facebook.com/groups/1846498742296989*

*AMOOKOS (Arcane and Magical Order of the Knights of Shambhala) facebook.com/groups/214753100471*

*NathTantrika facebook.com/Hermeticusnath*

# ABOUT THE AUTHOR

Denny Sargent is the holder of the Nath Tantrika branch manifesting as the Emerald Shambala Zonule in Seattle, WA. He is a prolific writer and University Instructor. He has a BA in Education, and was awarded an MA in Ancient History/Cross Cultural Communications from Western Washington University where he also taught.

He was initiated into the Nath Lineage of Tantra in 1980 as taught by Shri Gurudev Dadaji Mahendranath, and received initiation in the Uttara Kaula (Western) lineage as well. He has practiced and written about Tantra for over 40 years, often under his initiated name of Hermeticus Nath. From the 1980s, he has helped found, write and edit journals of contemporary mythology and magick: *Mandragore Aeon Magazine, Kalika Magazine,* and *Silverstar Journal.*

Denny taught, lived and wrote for four years in Japan where he studied Shinto and taught at Sundai University. He has done extensive traveling and on-site esoteric research around the world, including in India, Nepal, Thailand, Cambodia, Korea and many other areas of Asia. His previously published books include: *Global Ritualism*; *Myth & Magick Around the World*; *The Tao of Birth Days*; *Your Guardian Angel and You*; *Clean Sweep*; *Dancing with Spirits: Festivals & Folklore of Japan*; *The Book of the Horned One (as Aion131)*; *Naga Magick: The Wisdom of the Serpent Lords*; and more recently, *Werewolf Magick* and *Werewolf Pack Magick.*

He likes snakes. And wolves. Really, all wild animals. He has a dog, of course.

He can be reached at *feralmagick.com*

# MORE TANTRA TITLES FROM FALCON

## NAGA MAGICK
*The Wisdom of the Serpent Lords*
**by Denny Sargent**

What are the Naga? They are the Serpent Lords of Hindu, Tantric and Buddhist traditions. Whether you wish to learn the history and mythos of the Serpent Spirits, or if you wish to work directly with these luminous beings, *Naga Magick* provides unique access to the power and wisdom of the Naga Lords.

## YOGINI MAGIC
*The Sorcery, Enchantment & Witchcraft of the Divine Feminine*
**by Gregory Peters**
*Foreword by Phil Hine*

What are the Yoginis? Some say they are witch-like Tantrik goddesses that reign over magic, sorcery, enchantments and yoga. Are they human? Supernatural? Divine? For the sincere practitioner, they can provide great boons of wealth and pleasure… But it will not go well for the fool — the Yoginis will tear off his head and drink his blood.

# MORE TANTRA TITLES FROM FALCON

## SEX MAGICK, TANTRA & TAROT
*The Way of the Secret Lover*
**by Christopher S. Hyatt, Ph.D.**

With Lon Milo DuQuette
Illustrated by David P. Wilson

A wealth of practical and passionate Tantric techniques utilizing the Archetypal images of the Tarot. Nothing is held back. All methods are explicit and clearly described.

## TANTRA WITHOUT TEARS
**by Christopher S. Hyatt, Ph.D.**

With S. Jason Black

For the Westerner, this is the only book on Tantra you will ever need. A bold statement? Perhaps. However, the idea behind this book is simple. It is power. It is Kundalini, dressed in Western clothes. It describes experiences and techniques which allow you to glimpse beyond ordinary day-to-day reality, into the world of marvels — and horrors — of the Hindu and Tibetan Tantric traditions.

# MORE TANTRA TITLES FROM FALCON

## SECRETS OF WESTERN TANTRA
*The Sexuality of the Middle Path*
**by Christopher S. Hyatt, Ph.D.**
*Preface by Robert Anton Wilson*

Dr. Hyatt reveals secret methods of enlightenment through transmutation of the *orgastic reflex*. Filled with explicit, practical techniques.

"The world's first scientific experimental yoga that does not expurgate the sensory-sensual-sexual aspects of the Great Work."
— Robert Anton Wilson

## THE ENOCHIAN WORLD OF ALEISTER CROWLEY
*Enochian Sex Magick*
**by Christopher S. Hyatt, Ph.D.**
*With Aleister Crowley & Lon DuQuette*

Many consider Enochiana the most powerful and least understood system of Western Occult practice. For the first time this esoteric subject is made truly accessible and easy to understand. Includes an Enochian dictionary, extensive illustrations and detailed instructions for the integration of Enochiana with Sex Magick.

# THE *Original* FALCON PRESS

## Invites You to Visit Our Website:
### originalfalcon.com

At our website you can:

- Browse the online catalog of all of our great titles
- Find out what's available and what's out of stock
- Get special discounts
- Order our titles through our secure online server
- Find products not available anywhere else including:
  – One of a kind and limited availability products
  – Special packages
  – Special pricing
- Get free gifts
- Join our email list for advance notice of New Releases and Special Offers
- Find out about book signings and author events
- Send email to our authors
- Read excerpts of many of our titles
- Find links to our authors' websites
- Discover links to other weird and wonderful sites
- And much, much more

**Visit us today at** *originalfalcon.com*

www.ingramcontent.com/pod-product-compliance
Lightning Source LLC
Chambersburg PA
CBHW070044080526
44586CB00013B/910